Fishing Ohio

Help Us Keep This Guide Up to Date

Every effort has been made by the author and editors to make this guide as accurate and use-ful as possible. However, many things can change after a guide is published—trails are rerouted, regulations change, techniques evolve, facilities come under new management, and so on.

We welcome your comments concerning your experiences with this guide and how you feel it could be improved and kept up to date. While we may not be able to respond to all com-ments and suggestions, we'll take them to heart, and we'll also make certain to share them with the author. Please send your comments and suggestions to the following address:

The Globe Pequot Press
Reader Response/Editorial Department
P.O. Box 480
Guilford, CT 06437

Or you may e-mail us at:

editorial@GlobePequot.com

Thanks for your input, and happy angling!

Fishing
Ohio

**An Angler's Guide to over 200 Fishing Spots
in the Buckeye State**

TOM CROSS

THE LYONS PRESS
GUILFORD, CONNECTICUT
AN IMPRINT OF THE GLOBE PEQUOT PRESS

The Lyons Press is an imprint of The Globe Pequot Press.

All interior photos by Tom Cross unless otherwise credited
Text design by Casey Shain
Maps created by Tim Kissel © Morris Book Publishing, LLC

Library of Congress Cataloging-in-Publication Data

Cross, Tom.
  Fishing Ohio : an angler's guide to over 200 fishing spots in the Buckeye State / Tom Cross.
    p. cm.
  ISBN 978-0-7627-4326-1
  1. Fishing--Ohio--Guidebooks. 2. Ohio--Guidebooks. I. Title.
  SH535.C76 2008
  799.1209771--dc22
                                        2008000168

Printed in the United States of America

10 9 8 7 6 5

To Benjamin, Patrick, and Elizabeth.
Perhaps no greater memory can a father have than to
share time on the water with his children.

Contents

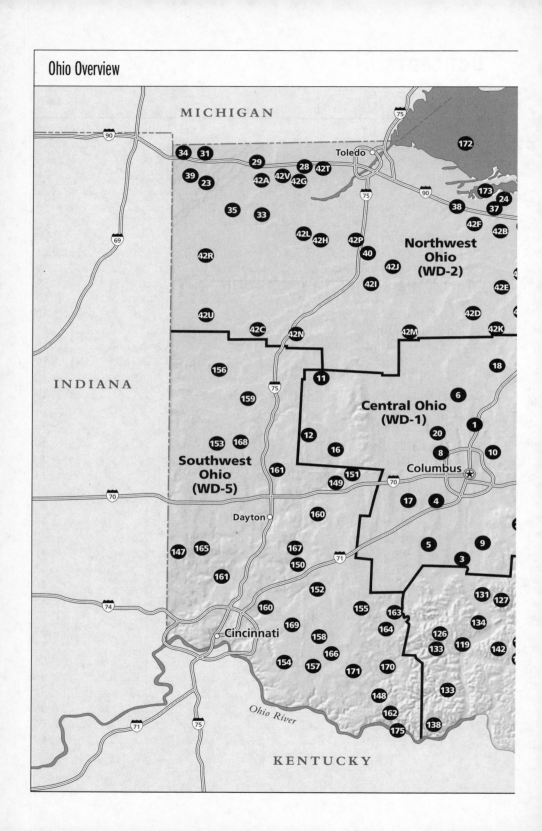

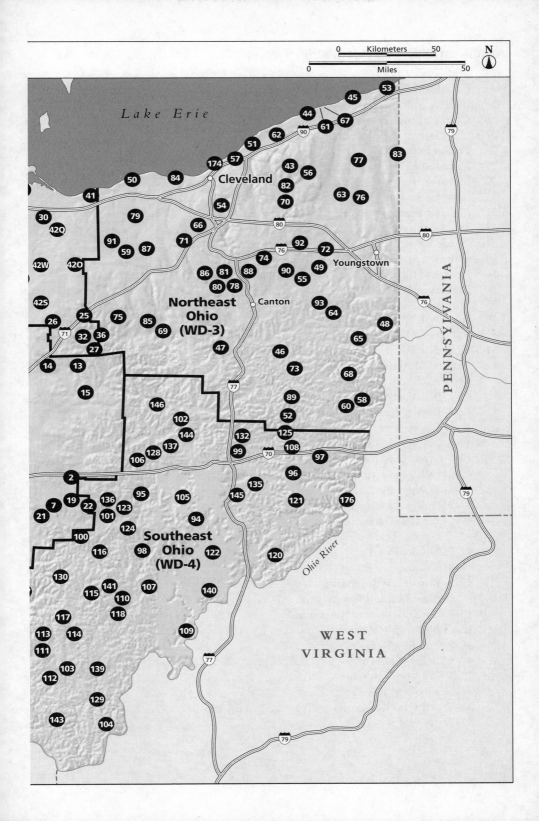

Preface

I have been on the most incredible journey, having personally visited nearly every public lake, river, stream, and pond in Ohio. This book was not written upon some finely crafted oak desk in an office. This book was written on a laptop computer off the tailgate of my pickup while parked next to the rivers, lakes, and streams throughout this great state. I knew of no other way to write it. During the summer of 2006, when this book was written, I lived on bologna sandwiches, beans, soup, and coffee. I stayed overnight at state parks, wildlife areas, at pulloffs, and next to streams, and was away from home two and three weeks at a time. I slept more in the back of my truck than I did my own bed that summer.

I started this book in earnest in May 2006, visiting every lake and stream in my home district in southwest Ohio. After that I visited every lake in central Ohio. Next I was off to the waters in the southeast side of the state, and then to northwest Ohio and Lake Erie. By October I finally made it to the lakes and streams in the northeast corner of the state. After I finished there, I did a six-day trip up the Ohio River, then headed to Conneaut Creek to do some steelhead fishing, where I caught 5 inches of snow from a lake-effect snowstorm that had me snowbound in a motel for two days. After the snow passed, I went on to the Grand River, the Chagrin River, and finally the Cuyahoga River, which was my last stop on November 4.

In all, I spent 13 weeks on the road. In my truck I carried a cardboard box full of food, a cooler, a sleeping bag, a camp stove, a lantern, clothes, a digital camera, a briefcase, and my laptop. In addition, I kept close a couple of fishing rods, a tackle bag, and my waders. I slept in the back of my pickup at various state park campgrounds. Twice I stayed in a cabin, twice I stayed in a motel room, and twice I spent the night with a couple of outdoor writer friends. I occasionally had to wash my own clothes. Most of the time I fixed my own breakfast, lunch, and dinner. While I camped at Piedmont Lake, an elderly couple graciously shared with me an exquisite dinner of fried catfish and saugeye they had just caught. I also had homemade pumpkin pie and on several occasions was given a bag of fresh garden tomatoes. I guess at times I must have looked like a homeless fishing bum. I even had a few meals paid for.

I vividly recall a night spent at Clouse Lake with hordes of mosquitoes and the night I slept in the Delaware Lake Wildlife Area, which was the only place in the state I thought I needed a gun. There were some very special times, too, including the time I spent on the historic Muskingum River and that special invite to a cookout with the charter captains at Vermilion Harbor. Memorable too were those few autumn days I passed at Pymatuning Lake and the hot meal at the local diner with members of the Norton Bass Club after a cold, rainy tournament on Portage Lakes. All and all these turned out to be some of the best moments amid all the work that was piling up and yet to be put to paper.

I did a lot of writing over that summer, too. I spent countless hours researching and hammering out page after page about these Ohio lakes, rivers, and streams. I talked, interviewed, and wrote from literally daylight to dark. This work is the cumulative knowledge of all those I listed in the acknowledgements and it is the result of a lifetime of fishing that has become a passion for me. And when you turn the page and start reading, you will find that every lake has a story, and within that story is a kernel of knowledge that may help you catch a fish. There are, after all, few pursuits more enjoyable on which to spend a lifetime than catching fish.

Acknowledgments

I would like to gratefully acknowledge the following people who freely provided information used in this book and a more important commodity, their time. Without these individuals help this book would not have been possible.

Zac Williams, John Gillespie, Paul Creech, The Antler Shop, South Shore Marina, The Boars Head, Matthew Palmer, Tim Carr, Mike Richards, Louise Williams, Jim Wray, Cece and Wiley Tabor, Charlie Huddleston, Mort Pugh, Craig Morton, Dave Sheets, Doug Maloney, Mark Bertholomey, Charlie Cambell, Charles Kaiser, Fred Nickol, Joe Sharp, Lenaia Finkler, S. Hemingway, Bob Romage, Judy Holtzapfel, Jack McKirgan, Jerry Boone, Jack Guyton, Ryan Peterson, Kevin Good, Chuck Wadley, Pat Howard, Ben Bierbaugh, Jim White, Susan Maynard, Roger Deem, Jim Henery, Jeff Hatley, Sean and Cassedy Stephens, Jim Fugitt, Jeff Riley, Tony Sexton, Wes Roffe, Kyle Grupenhof, Paul Osborne, Denise Shivers, Dick Warrer, Dale Francis, Jason Carpenter, Ralph Adkins, Richard Warner, Frank Dailey, Geoff Roche, Mike Timmons, Tim Moore, Albert Delancy, Cody Downs, Clifton Kilpatrick, Ethel Eblin, Erin Hillman, Kurt Partee, Brian Gregory, Mike Zaborowski, Tom Cassity, Gloria Chrismer, Jerry Book, Rich Carter, Chris Smith, Jane Shipman, Bill Hughes, Linda Scowden, Dustin Mefford, Joe Cook, John Janosko, Dave Zacharias, Nick Cole, Eric Frost, Bernie P. Barlock, Dick Ford, Marty Webb, Vick Ricks, John Wargo, Randy Zeisler, Dwight Miller, Dave Ayers, Jeff Ayers, Scott McDonald, Joe Grega, Andy Seib, Lamar Ware, Eddie Fields, Steve Baker, Bob Orewiler, Richard Bires, Harry Collins, Mike Collins, Terry Flint, Karie Amstutz, Ed Lewis, Jerry VanZile, Austin Imm, Brock and Phil Thorp, Clare Varwig, Dan Mesker, Ron DeLong, Gerry Combs, Ron Singer, Brian Martin, Jeffrey Tyson, Bob Bowman, Capt. Ken Burris, Capt. Dave Farmer, Dan Burnside, Lyle Brown, Chris Martin, Charles Timbs, Doug Dobson, Craig Howell, Kevin Higgins, Sherman Jones, Capt. Ron Johnson, Andy Skodnik, Don Svab, Bruce Carpenter, Bob Kotch, Ron Kotch, Matt Amedeo, Will Spitzer, Scott Moles, Barbara Neill, Mike Westfall, Steve Moss, Andy Zagotti, Howard Wiff, Don Wiff, Jim Worley, Gary Camron, Dan Wright, Mike Stvdeny, Andy Peters, Kaylee Governor, Gregg Cappitte, Joe Sofchek, Ron Ferenchak, Patty Curtis, Ed Koren, Leonard Boley, Lowell Owens, Jerry Herman, Travis Hobart, James Fellows, Joe McGlothlin, Matthew Backhaus, Andra Keister, Josh Marshall, Bruce Weisburn, Mike Cunningham, John Grantham, Doug Henley, Scott Morrison, Carey Knight, Tim Bader, John Deller, Michael Blakeman, Leon Cole, Joe and Bob Pocki, Melissa Hathaway, Jim Marshal, Phil Hillman, Larry Goedde, Mike Greenlee, and Cathy Behr.

I would also like to extend a very special thank you to Dan West and the staff of the Ohio Division of Parks and Recreation for providing information and much needed resting and camping locations during the summer of 2006. A special thank you goes to the fishery biologists, hatchery personnel, and wildlife officers with the Ohio Division of Wildlife who provided valuable information, and at times a good story and a lighter moment.

Thanks also go to my good friends with whom I share a passion of outdoor writing: Jeff Frischkorn, Paul Liikala, Chip Gross, and George Laycock. They lent not only their expertise, time, and information, but also provided much needed encouragement. And a special thank you to Melissa Roe for taking the time to edit my entire book. And finally special appreciation goes to my wife Judy for her encouragement and patience.

Introduction

The Fishing

Every year Ohio licenses approximately 800,000 anglers. About one-third of those licensed anglers fish Lake Erie. The eight counties that border Lake Erie account for more than one-fourth of all fishing-license sales. Ottawa County, which includes Port Clinton and the Bass Islands, leads the state by a wide margin in one-day, three-day, and nonresident fishing-license sales. Each year Fish Ohio, one of the largest angler-recognition programs of its kind in the country, awards more than 12,000 certificates to anglers with outstanding catches; of those, half are for fish caught from Lake Erie.

Lake Erie draws so much gravity that it has a tendency to steal the spotlight from the state's other fisheries. Ohio inland fishery consists of a number of small, older impoundments that are typically stained with water visibility not much beyond a foot. Only five public lakes have been built since 1970. The latest, completed in 1978, is East Fork in the southwest corner of the state.

Outside the impoundments Ohio's other great lake, the Ohio River, is a chain of 10 pools with 9 locks and dams stretching some 450 miles along the state's south and east borders. The river offers an immense fishery for sauger, hybrid stripers, channel and flathead catfish, and both largemouth and smallmouth bass. Other Ohio rivers that provide high-quality fishing include the Muskingum, the Great Miami, and the Maumee. Each possesses a unique and special fishery.

The steelhead fishery in the northeast streams during late winter is hands down the best inland fishery in the state. Although there is an abundance of public access on many of the steelhead steams, landowner complaints have skyrocketed, thus casting potential shadows over the highly successful program.

There is no denying that the state's greatest smallmouth fishery south of Lake Erie is the Ohio River. The habitat in the upper river pools above Racine Dam is much more conducive to smallmouth than largemouth, and the overall improvements in water quality have resulted in a smallmouth fishery second only to that of Lake Erie.

Perhaps the most overlooked and underrated fishery in Ohio is its inland stream fishery. The state is blessed with a handful of absolutely stunningly beautiful and highly productive smallmouth streams. The Kokosing River, Little Beaver Creek, Ohio Brush, the upper Sandusky, Hocking, and Darby Creek are among Ohio's best smallmouth streams. Nearly every stream in the state is home to a resident population of smallmouth. In southwest Ohio the streams located in the till plains of the Great Miami and Little Miami watersheds, and the limestone streams in the bluegrass region of the Ohio Valley as a whole, contain arguably the state's best inland stream fishery for smallmouth.

Trout fishing, in a state that contains only one natural trout stream, has some surprisingly fine candidates when the call to don a pair of waders and uncase a fly

Derek Maxey used a crankbait to take this big hybrid striper from the tailwaters below Robert C. Byrd Locks and Dam. Photo by Jeremy Stevenson

rod becomes too great to resist. The Mad River is Ohio's premier trout stream and yields brown trout in excess of 20 inches. Clear Creek in Hocking County is a nice getaway that doesn't produce big trout but does offers quiet fishing on a scenic stretch of small stream. Perhaps the state's most well-known stream is the Clearfork of the Mohican and that beautiful stretch of water below Pleasant Hill Dam to the state park campground. If surreal trout fishing is what you desire, then by all means throw your name in the hat for a chance to fish Cold Creek, located on the Castalia Hatchery grounds. It is an experience no trout fisher will ever forget.

The put-and-take trout fishery that is known as "Catchable Trout" is among the most popular fishing programs ever devised in Ohio. To kick off the fishing season each spring, many of the smaller lakes in the state are stocked with approximately 1,000 to 3,000 trout. These trout releases are immensely popular with anglers just waiting for the hatchery truck to arrive. Although the fishing is short-lived, it is intense, and usually it's only a matter of weeks before most of the trout are caught.

Muskie anglers have a good selection of notable reservoirs from which to fish for the king of game fish. Clear Fork, Alum Creek, Piedmont, Caesar Creek, Salt Fork, Leesville, West Branch, and Pymatuning are all top waters from which 30-pound fish are a real possibility. Although muskie fishing is primarily a trolling sport as practiced in Ohio, casting is productive at Caesar Creek, Piedmont, West Branch, and Leesville. There are also some streams that contain natural and stocked muskie populations.

Perhaps the biggest boost and the savior to inland fisheries is the saugeye stocking program. A saugeye is a hybrid of a walleye and a sauger, and the result has introduced a walleye-style fishery to Ohio lakes. Saugeye also bring to the table another fine eating fish, growing larger in inland reservoirs than do walleyes. However, the saugeyes' greatest contribution to the state's sport fishery is the tailwater fishery below dams during periods of high-water releases. With the introduction of saugeye in the early 1980s, a whole new fishery came alive in the tailwaters. The tailraces below Paint Creek and Deer Creek dams have developed into some of the state's best saugeye fishing.

Walleyes are stocked only in lakes within the Lake Erie watershed. While there is a walleye fishery in C. J. Brown Reservoir in southwest Ohio, this is primarily maintained as a brood stock lake for saugeye production. The best inland walleye lake in Ohio is Mosquito Creek Reservoir, followed by Pymatuning, and then perhaps Grand Lake St. Marys would round out the top three. Lake Erie is considered the walleye capital of the world, and the spawning run up the Maumee and Sandusky Rivers in April is the kind of fishing every buckeye fisher should experience at least once.

Channel catfish probably inhabit every body of water in the state. Fishing for cats is widespread and for the most part an easy and tasty catch. Rivaling the walleye and yellow perch for the best-tasting fish in Ohio waters, the channel cat should be named the Ohio state fish. Fishing for channels is done during the summer nights, but they are just as readily caught on artificials during the day. Many are taken while fishing for walleyes and saugeyes off the bottom. Some lakes are revered for their cat fishing; however, most lakes in Ohio, regardless of size, offer quality cat fishing.

Flathead catfish are the largest game fish that swim in Ohio waters. They are not found in every impoundment or river, but they are well distributed throughout the state and offer a true trophy potential for those with the tackle strong enough to handle a fish this powerful. Catches of 40- to 50-pound flatheads are fairly common; most are caught at night with live bait. It is a select breed of fishers who targets flatheads. Fishing for flatheads takes place at the dams on the Maumee River; at Grand Lake St. Marys, the Ohio River, the Muskingum River, and Mosquito Lake; and of course at all the Muskingum River watershed lakes, which have a reputation for producing some of the best flathead fishing in the state.

Crappies have a cult-like following in the spring. Either black or white crappies are found in nearly every reservoir in the state and can reach lengths of 14 to 16 inches. A simple minnow and a slip bobber is the universal crappie rig throughout

A fish-attracting crib is anchored to the bottom of Lake Vesuvius during winter drawdown. By spring the crib will be submerged under 8 feet of water. Photo courtesy of Ohio Division of Wildlife

Ohio. Crappies are found under docks, pontoon boats, brush, timber, and stickups on nearly any lake during April and May. Some lakes have a reputation for producing big crappies—some produce numbers, not sizes. Other lakes simply cycle between good years and bad years. Every angler can be assured that there is at least one good crappie lake within a couple hours' drive from anywhere in the state.

Bluegills and sunfish are common throughout the lakes and streams of the Buckeye State. A number of lakes produce nice hand-size bluegills during the spring, and other lakes rarely give up bluegills longer than 5 inches. Some of the best bluegill water in the state is at the Lake La Su An Wildlife Area. Other top places are Indian Lake and the AEP ReCreation Lands. Nearly all Ohio streams have longears, pumpkinseed, and warmouth. Redear sunfish are not as widespread, but a few impoundments and ponds do have this outsize sunfish. Among the best of the best are Mogadore Reservoir and Lake La Su An.

Hybrid striped bass are produced by crossing a male striped bass and a female white bass, resulting in a game fish that has transformed the fishery on the Ohio River. Few inland lakes are stocked with these fish; they are almost exclusively stocked into the Ohio River. A schooling fish, hybrid stripers are often observed surface feeding on schooling shad in the river and its tributaries. They are the favorite tailwater sport fish below the locks and dams on the Ohio River and are taken year-round. The only fishery for pure striped bass is at Seneca Lake, and perhaps Kiser Lake in the future. At one time several lakes in Ohio received regular stocking of striped bass. Today, in addition to providing a viable striped bass fishery, the stocking of striped bass is done primarily to supply brood stock for the hybrid striped bass program.

A fair number of lakes in Ohio are managed as trophy bass fisheries. These lakes are small to medium impoundments with 10-hp limits or are restricted to electric motors only. A few lakes in Ohio have the potential to produce bass over 10 pounds; there is a select handful that regularly gives up 7- to 8-pound bass every spring. Most large unlimited horsepower lakes seldom produce bass over 6 pounds, although several of these lakes have high-quality bass fishing with good numbers of largemouth. These larger impoundments are favorite haunts within bass tournament circles. However, if an angler is looking for that 8-pound-plus bass, then the smaller reservoirs and a handful of select strip-mine ponds in southeast Ohio are the place. Tycoon Lake, Knox Lake, Oakthorp, Mogadore, perhaps LaDue Reservoir, and some of the more remote strip-mine ponds in the Conesville Coal Lands are among the most likely candidates. If a new Ohio state record bass weighing over 13 pounds is ever caught from a public body of water, I predict it will be a prespawn female that will be caught in April from either Barnesville Reservoir 3 or Hammertown Lake.

Public and Private Access

A variety of government agencies and private concerns provide access to Ohio lakes, rivers, and streams. The Kokosing River is a good example how various agencies can work together to provide access to a river or stream. On the Kokosing, six different agencies—the Ohio Department of Natural Resources, the Knox County Park District, College Township, the City of Mount Vernon, the Knox County Engineer, and the Muskingum Watershed Conservancy District—have contributed access points and canoe launches along the river.

This cohesion of government and private agencies working together to provide recreational opportunities on various waterways is reflected throughout Ohio. On the Ohio River, for example, township, county, municipal, state, and federal agencies all have a hand in providing launching facilities and shoreline access. The Ohio State Park system provides the bulk of access on public lakes. On typical Ohio lakes, the Division of Parks and Recreation provides the infrastructure by which shoreline access, wheelchair access, and launch ramps are part of the state park. The Corps of Engineers provides access and facilities to the tailwaters area, and if a wildlife area exists, then the Division of Wildlife usually offers access roads to the water and possibly boat ramps or a canoe launch.

On wildlife area (WLA) lakes and ponds, the Division of Wildlife does a good job of providing shoreline fishing, boat ramps, and wheelchair-accessible piers. The Corps of Engineers, the US Department of the Interior, Division of Watercraft,

The Mad River offers some of the best trout fishing in the state.

Natural Areas and Preserves, Division of Forestry, and Department of Highways all contribute resources to provide boating and angling opportunities on various bodies of water across the state.

Metro parks managed by various cities and counties provide the bulk of stream access in Ohio. The Lake Erie tributaries of the Maumee, Sandusky, Vermilion, Black, Rocky, Euclid, Chagrin, Grand, and Ashtabula Rivers all benefit from extensive metro park systems that seek to preserve green space and stream corridors and provide recreational benefits to residents. Other streams that benefit from metro parks are the Mad, Little Miami, the Great Miami, Darby, Clear Creek, the upper Cuyahoga, and Stillwater.

Other access is gained by way of small community parks or private parks and preserves, by the graces of various industries, and through easements or leases. In Adams County the tourism bureau worked with the Department of Highways to secure public canoe launches at four bridges that cross Ohio Brush Creek.

A majority of streams in Ohio still flow through private property, and friction usually arises when crowds of anglers start appearing and the privacy of the landowner is threatened. The popularity of northeast steelhead streams has resulted in a surge of landowner complaints that could negatively impact this tremendous fishery. This phenomenon is normally not a problem on most streams, and access at bridges and pulloffs is still largely tolerated. According to Ohio law, while an angler may float a stream legally, wading in a stream could result in a trespassing violation, as private property extends under a stream to the streambed. The easiest way to gain permission is to ask. Simple courtesy goes a long way.

There are anglers out there who leave trash, old fishing line, bait containers, and pop cans lying around, which reflects badly on all of us. As responsible anglers, we are asked only to show respect, leave no sign of having been there, act responsibly, and not abuse the privilege. Seek permission where needed, or if questions or doubt arise seek clarification. Above all, be discrete and leave as little impact as possible. Nobody wants to see a no trespassing sign on his or her favorite stream.

Camping

Ohio State Parks has camping facilities on 42 lakes, the Muskingum and Maumee Rivers, Beaver Creek, Clearfork of the Mohican River, the Little Miami River, Lake Erie, and the Ohio River. There are more than 56 state park campgrounds that offer everything from primitive camping to thoroughly modern, updated campgrounds. Most state parks have electric and nonelectric sites; some offer cabins, cottages, tepees, and rent-a-camp sites that are complete with everything.

State park lodges are located at nine locations throughout Ohio. In addition, some state parks offer golfing and tennis, nearly all have swimming beaches, and most offer naturalist programs and hiking, biking, and bridle trails. Several state parks are open year-round and offer ice-fishing opportunities and winter sport activities. Nearly all state parks accept reservations, and there are always a limited number of open or walk-in sites available.

The Muskingum Watershed Conservancy District (MWCD) has campgrounds on nine MWCD lakes and a lodge at Attwood Lake.

The U.S. Corps of Engineers provides camping at some lakes. Wayne National Forest has camping facilities throughout the national forest in southeast Ohio. The Division of Wildlife has primitive camping only at a few select wildlife areas, although overnight stays for anglers are permitted at most wildlife area lakes. On some lakes and streams, private campgrounds are conveniently located.

Camping facilities are noted at the end of every description. Although I made no mention of the number of electric or nonelectric sites, that information is easily obtained from the state park Web site or by calling Ohio State Parks. Reservations for campsites and cabins also can be made by phone.

Bugs and Snakes

Because I live near the unglaciated plateau of southeast Ohio, I'm always hearing good snake stories. I happen to live in a county that has one of the last viable populations of timber rattlesnakes in the state, and copperheads are fairly common too. A turkey hunter is more apt to run into a rattlesnake than a fisher is. The only legitimate chance that a fisher would run into a timber rattler is if he or she were fishing the lakes and ponds in the Shawnee State Forest and perhaps along Scioto Brush Creek. Outside of that, the chances for an encounter are slim to none. Timber rattlesnakes are on the state's endangered species list and killing one is a crime in more ways than one. They are shy, reclusive reptiles and if given the chance will quickly retreat. A bite by a timber rattler is a serious matter, and getting out of the woods and into an emergency room is vital. However, venomous snake bites are rare and much more likely to be inflected upon folks tending gardens or cleaning up around old buildings than fishing.

On the other hand, copperheads possess a nasty disposition and will often stand and fight. It is possible to come across a copperhead anywhere in southeast Ohio, along the banks of a stream or lake, but you're much more apt to fall off a cliff looking for a strip-mine pond than to find a copperhead or get bit by one. Copperhead bites are seldom fatal, but you could lose a finger or some feeling in your bitten appendage if you don't seek immediate medical attention.

Another poisonous snake in Ohio is the eastern massasauga rattlesnake. While it is very rare, small remnant populations have been noted in Killdeer Plains WLA, Mosquito Creek, Spring Valley WLA, and Cedar Bog near the Mad River. Like the timber rattlesnake, this rattler is also on the state endangered species list. It typically inhabits more northern climates. I once encountered a healthy population of massasauga rattlesnakes on Bois Blanc Island in Michigan. Only nine counties in Ohio may have any populations at all. They are so low in numbers that the chances for an encounter are virtually nonexistent.

The snake that fishers regularly encounter is the common northern brown water snake. These snakes can be found under every rock ledge, tangle of roots, bridge, boat ramp, and debris pile on every lake, river, pond, and stream in the state, and they are often observed sunning themselves atop rocks or logs. I have a natural tendency to avoid snakes, and water snakes are the reason why, as they are short-tempered and can deliver a quick, nasty bite that bleeds profusely.

Buckeye anglers are also likely to encounter snapping turtles and soft-shelled turtles. Neither like fishers and will beat a hasty retreat upon approach. Let them go; both can deliver the kind of bite that can ruin your day. In the case of a snapper, it may take a piece of your finger with it.

During the hot summer the woods are full of every kind of spider, tick, and mosquito you can imagine. If you are bushwhacking along stream banks or weedy pond edges, check regularly for ticks. You will also encounter spider webs, and some spiders can deliver a bite that will cause swelling. Yellow jackets and hornets are another source of agony, should you somehow disturb a ground or hanging nest.

Mosquitoes are every angler's bane, but compared to other places, such as northern Michigan or the Everglades, they are mild in Ohio. Still, with the chance for West Nile virus and possibly bird flu, strong bug spray with deet will repel most bites. In the far north I came across a mixture of Vicks rub and fuel oil that seemed to ward off the mosquitoes better than anything else.

Weather

Weather in Ohio changes every two or three days. In the Ohio Valley during summer, it is hot and humid and the fishing is slow. May and June offer the best fishing weather in southern Ohio, and then again in October when it starts to cool down. In northeast Ohio, Lake Erie creates weather patterns and winter usually comes early and stays late. Lake-effect snowstorms can pop up anytime, and while steelhead fishing in March, it's not unusual to find 3 or 4 inches of snow and icebergs piled up along stream banks.

During a typical summer anglers always encounter a few heavy downpours and an occasional severe thunderstorm that sends everybody and everything to shelter. Tornadoes are most likely to occur in the southwest part of the state during April and May, but they do occasionally pop up with thunderstorms during the summer. Wind is always a problem on Lake Erie and on some of the larger reservoirs such as Grand Lake St. Marys, Buckeye Lake, Pymatuning, and Mosquito. The Ohio River can also be a dangerous place when the wind kicks up. Any seasoned boater knows weather, and it doesn't take a scientist to know it's time to head for shore when the horizon turns dark gray.

Wildlife

Raccoon and deer are the most common wildlife you will see along any stream or lake in Ohio. Turkeys are becoming a familiar sight, too. Great blue herons, green herons, bitterns, egrets, and cormorants are all regular sights, as are waterfowl of every description, including gulls, sandpipers, eagles, and ospreys. Beavers, too, are common, but mink tend to stick to streams and riverbanks and are shy and seldom seen except by the stealthiest fishers. Otters are becoming more common, but they are extremely wary and few fishers get a chance to observe them in the wild. However, if you have a chance encounter with one, you will find the animal beautiful to behold. Occasionally a fox or coyote can be observed patrolling the shoreline, and squirrels and groundhogs are everywhere. Once in a while a bear is spotted along the rivers in northeast Ohio.

There is no wildlife in Ohio that is dangerous to humans, but I wouldn't want to accidentally corner a boar raccoon or stick my hand in a bank den and encounter a mink. Wildlife will leave you alone if you leave them alone.

Trophy Recognition

There is not a fisher in Ohio who doesn't want to hook a whopper and land it. Every angler wants a photo of him- or herself holding up a fish that will wow another fisher. It is the nature of us anglers to compete and seek admiration for our outstanding catches.

There are basically two programs in Ohio that award recognition for trophy catches. One is the Fish Ohio Awards administered by the Ohio Division of Wildlife. The other is the State Record Fish program administered by the Outdoor Writers of Ohio.

Fish Ohio has length requirements for all game fish in Ohio waters, which are printed on the fishing regulations along with a simple application that must be mailed in or e-mailed. Those meeting the requirements are awarded a very nice Fish Ohio pin that depicts a selected sport fish for that year. A collection of the pins is quite an achievement and a valued treasure. There is also a Master Angler pin awarded to anglers who catch four fish that meet the Fish Ohio requirements and a Grand Slam award for catching three species from Lake Erie, the Ohio River, or the inland fisheries.

While the Fish Ohio Award is given to any angler who catches a fish meeting the length requirements, the State Record Fish program is limited to an exclusive group of anglers who actually catch the largest of that particular species in the state. The Outdoor Writers of Ohio is the official record keeper of Ohio state record fish and is the only writers' group in all 50 states to keep, maintain, and certify record fish. It is done in cooperation with the Ohio Division of Wildlife, whose fisheries biologists examine every potential state record fish to determine the correct species. Only then will the application be circulated among the five members of the State Record Fish Committee for possible certification into the record books. Anyone catching a potential state record fish should contact the Ohio Division of Wildlife or the Outdoor Writers of Ohio. All fish must be weighed on certified scales and examined by a fisheries biologist. An application is filled out and submitted to the chairman of the Ohio Writers of Ohio Record Fish Committee.

The Freshwater Fishing Hall of Fame, located in Wisconsin, keeps line-class records. Although individual lake records are not kept, state park headquarters at various public lakes have a good idea of the largest species to come from their particular body of water.

Maps

Lake, stream, and wildlife area maps are available online at www.ohiodnr .com/wildlife. For state park maps refer to www.ohiodnr.com/parks. For maps of metro parks see listings of park Web sites on the information page. Other stream and river maps are available online too; please refer to the "For More Information" section at the end of the book.

Ohio's Game Fish

Blue Catfish

Ohio's largest and newest game fish is primarily found in the Ohio River. Blue cats can weigh more than 100 pounds. For years the blue catfish was listed on the Ohio endangered species list, but it was down-listed in 2007 to a "species of special concern," thereby making it legal to catch and possess. The best location to catch blue catfish is the Ohio River between Cincinnati and Portsmouth.

Bluegill

Probably every fisherman's first fish, the bluegill is a fine eater and fine fighter, and as much fun to catch on a fly rod as anything that swims. Big male bluegills are usually caught in the spring from mid-May through June when they are spawning. They are prolific at spawning and can easily overrun a pond and become stunted. Harvesting bluegills is highly recommended. In a well-balanced lake, hand-size bluegills are common; on a great lake, 8- to 10-inch bluegills should be available.

Channel Catfish

Found throughout Ohio in every lake, river, and stream, the channel catfish is perhaps the most common game fish in the state. The best cat fishing is usually at night during June, July, and August. Common baits are chicken livers, night crawlers, and cut shad. Most channels will average 1 to 4 pounds.

Crappie

Both white and black crappies inhabit the state's waters. They are normally found in spring around timber, brush, and boat docks, but fishing picks up again in fall. Good crappie lakes can produce a live well full of fish from 12 to 15 inches long. Best fishing is in late April through May. Black crappies are predominant in the Ohio River tributaries.

Flathead Catfish

One of Ohio's largest game fish, flathead catfish can reach in excess of 60 pounds and are frequently taken with live bait at night during the summer. The Ohio River, the Muskingum River, and the Muskingum watershed lakes are the top locations in the state for flathead catfish.

Hybrid Striped Bass

This aggressive game fish is right at home in the Ohio River and is the king of game fish in the tailraces below the locks and dams. Hybrid striped bass often achieve a weight of over 10 pounds. They are caught on a variety of baits, from chicken liver to crank baits. The hybrid is a cross between a pure striper and a white bass. Identification between the two is sometimes hard to tell, but a hybrid has broken and irregular stripes along its top side.

Largemouth Bass

Largemouth bass are found in lakes, ponds, the Ohio River, and every tributary harbor of Lake Erie. They are widespread and the primary target of bass tournaments throughout the state. They are caught in a variety of ways and by several different techniques. Usually found near riprap, rocks, stumps, brush, log, and timber, bass in Ohio are, for the most part, shoreline orientated. Largemouth in Ohio generally average 1 to 3 pounds.

Muskie

The Division of Wildlife has been stocking muskies into Ohio waterways since the mid-1950s. Muskies are pursued by a select group of hard-core individuals, including myself, who spend long fruitless hours trolling or casting. Only found in a handful of lakes and streams, muskies can reach over 40 pounds if the conditions are right. Trolling over points, humps, and creek channels during the summer is the most productive way to catch muskies in Ohio. Some streams and tailwaters also have muskies. Few lakes in Ohio will support a natural spawning population; that's why stocking is necessary to continue the fishery.

Northern Pike

Not a numerous fish compared to other game fish species, northern pike are found primarily in northeast Ohio rivers and lakes. Seldom do they achieve any real size, averaging 20 to 28 inches, but occasionally a 40-plus-inch fish is pulled from some of the larger reservoirs. The upper Cuyahoga River and Killbuck Creek have natural populations. Pike are taken in early spring after ice-out.

Rock Bass

Primarily a stream fish found throughout Ohio, rock bass is an aggressive biter and a fair fighter. Most rock bass will measure 6 to 7 inches, and occasionally something 10 inches will show up. They usually bite when nothing else will.

Sauger

Primarily a fish of the Ohio River, sauger also inhabit the Great Miami, the Maumee, and the Muskingum Rivers. Sauger do not get large—an 18-inch fish is a whopper—and are found on the rock banks, the sediment, and sandbars on the Ohio River. Some of the best places to catch sauger are in the tailraces below the locks and dams. A fine eating fish, they are similar to walleye but are much slimmer in profile.

Saugeye

The saugeye is a fine eating catch and are easy to reproduce, making them a favorite of the Division of Wildlife to stock into inland lakes and reservoirs. The saugeye is a hybrid of a male sauger and a female walleye, often achieving a weight of 8 to 10 pounds. They are found on flats, gravel bars, long points in lakes, and also below dams after periods of water releases. A jig and fluorescent grub is the top bait.

Smallmouth Bass

The sportiest game fish in Ohio waters, smallmouth bass are widespread from Lake Erie to the Ohio River and in every stream in between. The smallmouth fishing in Lake Erie is phenomenal, and it's nearly that good on the upper Ohio River.

Primarily a stream fish, smallmouth are found in varying degrees in every creek in the state. Smallmouth in Lake Erie get huge, often weighing 3 to 5 pounds, while stream smallmouth are lucky to average 14 inches. Crank baits, tubes, and crayfish are the top producers. Several years ago an effort was made to establish the small-mouth as the state fish. That effort failed, but few will disagree that the smallmouth is the greatest sport fish in the state.

Spotted Bass
Also known as Kentucky bass, spotted bass are found only in the most southern lakes in Ohio and in the Ohio River. Lake White has a tremendous population of spotted bass. They are feisty fighters, although they are the smallest of the black bass family in Ohio, averaging 12 inches. Seldom does a spotted bass grow beyond 16 inches.

Steelhead
The type of steelhead found in Ohio is of the Little Manistee strain from Michigan, which originally came from the McCloud River basin in California. Ohio has some of the best steelhead fishing in the United States.

Steelhead spend the summer in the cool depths of Lake Erie and return to the tributaries starting in the fall in order to spawn in early spring. The tributary streams will not support steelhead fingerlings during the summer; regular stockings have to be maintained in order to support the fishery.

Striped Bass
This fish is currently stocked in Seneca and Kiser Lakes, while the state of Kentucky stocks the fish in the three Ohio River pools that sit along its border with Ohio. Stripers are caught below the tailraces at Greenup and Meldahl Dams on the Ohio River and can exceed 20 pounds.

Sunfish
Longear, pumpkinseed, warmouth, and green sunfish are primarily stream species, although the larger specimens have come from lakes and ponds. Vicious little fighters, they are usually eager to snatch up a fly or red worm drifted down a stream channel. When they are big enough, sunfish make fine eating. The best fishing is usually May through June, but sunfish can be caught all summer long in deeper pools under logs and roots.

Trout
There are three species of trout in Ohio: brook trout, rainbow trout, and brown trout. The golden trout is a rainbow hybrid. Brook trout, which is actually a char, is listed on the state endangered species list. Fishing for them is not encouraged. Rainbow trout are stocked in various small lakes in the spring and fall and provide a popular fast catch-and-keep fishery. Brown trout are stocked into three streams in the state and provide a year-round fishery, with many trout surviving several summers in the deep, spring-fed pools of these streams. Taken with flies, small spinners, and live bait, the brown trout in these streams can reach 20 to 24 inches.

Walleye

Walleye may be the most sought-after fish in Ohio. Stocked in most northern lakes and reservoirs, they seldom achieve their true potential in inland waters, where they average only 1 to 3 pounds. In Lake Erie, however, 6- to 8-pound walleyes are common catches. In fact, walleye in Lake Erie support an entire fishing industry.

Walleye spawn in early spring in the rivers and reefs on the western basin and then come summer typically move eastward to cooler waters in the central basin. Walleye are fairly easy to catch and are one of the finest eating fish on the planet. It's no wonder they are a favorite of anglers from across the state.

White Bass

These schooling fish provide fast action in the spring, when spawning runs occur up rivers and streams in late April. Found in many Ohio lakes during the summer, white bass can be seen in a surface feeding frenzy as they gorge themselves on shad.

Most white bass average 10 to 12 inches; big females can range from 15 to 18 inches. The state's largest populations of white bass occur in Lake Erie and on the Ohio River. They can be caught year-round at warm-water discharges.

Yellow Perch

Some would argue that yellow perch are the best eating fish in Ohio waters. Regardless, the best perch fishing on inland lakes pales in comparison to perch fishing on Lake Erie. Perch gather in large schools offshore in 20 to 40 feet of water and feed primarily on emerald shiners. Fishing for them can be fast and furious at times. Early fall is the best time to catch perch that average 10 to 15 inches. On average, perch in the central basin are larger than perch in the western basin. Perch are caught near the bottom using spreaders, fishing two shiners at a time.

Ohio's Other Fish

Carp

Found in every body of water in the state, carp are popular with bow fishermen and can grow up to 50 pounds. The backwaters of Lake Erie's western basin are loaded with carp, as are the backwaters of most impoundments.

Longnose Gar

Common in the Ohio River and another favorite with bow fishermen, gar are frequently seen on the riffles in the Ohio River tributaries in May as they spawn and resting on the surface during the summer. Longnose gar can reach a weight of 20 pounds and a length of over 4 feet.

Freshwater Drum

Found mostly in the Ohio River drainage and in Lake Erie, this fish has gained little respect with fishers. Drum can get large, achieving a weight of 20 pounds or more. Any drum over 10 pounds is a handful to handle on a rod and reel.

White Amur

Known as grass carp, white amur are originally from China and stocked into various lake and ponds by the Division of Wildlife to control aquatic vegetation. Fishing for them is not recommended, nor is the species recognized by the State Record Fish Committee. They will not reproduce in ponds or lakes. White amur can live up to 15 years and attain a weight up to 50 pounds.

State Fish Hatcheries

The Division of Wildlife operates six hatcheries; each, to a varying degree, is tailored to a particular species. Naturally occurring populations of trout, steelhead, muskellunge, and striped bass (a saltwater species) are nonexistent or occur in such low numbers that they cannot support a fishery. In the case of hybrid stripers and saugeye, natural spawning rarely occurs. Hatcheries are one of several means that the Division of Wildlife uses to provide a quality fishery on inland lake and rivers.

London State Hatchery

The oldest of Ohio's hatcheries, the London State Hatchery was originally built in 1896. The hatchery's primary production is rainbow trout, brown trout, and muskies. Wells and spring-fed ponds allow for the production of cold-water species.

Kincaid State Hatchery

Kincaid State Hatchery was constructed in 1935 on the banks of Sunfish Creek in Pike County. The hatchery is primarily used for rearing muskellunge. It was the birthplace of the state's muskie program in 1953, when native stream muskies were captured from Sunfish Creek, incubated, and released as fry into Rocky Fork Lake. The hatchery also raises rainbow trout and hybrid striped bass.

St. Mary's State Hatchery

Located next to Grand Lake St. Marys, this state hatchery was originally built in 1913 by a private game and fish club and was acquired by the state in 1936. Its primary production consists of saugeye, walleye, and yellow perch in the spring, and channel catfish and largemouth bass during summer.

Hebron State Hatchery

Hebron is Ohio's largest hatchery facility, covering more than 230 acres, and uses water from nearby Buckeye Lake transferred through the old Erie Canal system. The hatchery was originally a federal hatchery until 1982. The primary production at Hebron is saugeye, walleye, and channel cats.

Senecaville State Hatchery

Located just below the dam of Seneca Lake, Senecaville State Hatchery was once a federal hatchery acquired by the state in 1987. Senecaville is the primary facility for saugeye and hybrid striped bass production in Ohio. The hatchery also raises walleye and channel catfish. Water supply for the hatchery comes from Seneca Lake.

Castalia State Hatchery

Castalia is Ohio's newest hatchery, purchased from a private concern in 1997. It is also the state's most unique hatchery in that the water supplied for its production comes from a cold-water spring hole called a "blue hole" that is devoid of oxygen. The water is oxygenated and then used for rearing rainbow trout and steelhead. It is the only hatchery in Ohio used to raise steelhead. Through the hatchery grounds flows Clear Creek, where trout fishing is permitted by drawing only.

How to Use This Book

This book is divided into chapters according to the different regions of the state, using districts determined by the Ohio Division of Wildlife. I found this division helped avoid confusion about specific bodies of water whenever I spoke with the Division of Wildlife fisheries biologists. There are five districts/regions: Wildlife District One covers central Ohio, Wildlife District Two covers northwest Ohio, Wildlife District Three covers northeast Ohio, Wildlife District Four covers southeast Ohio, and Wildlife District Five covers southwest Ohio. There are also chapters that cover the Ohio River and Lake Erie. Lake Erie itself could warrant its own book, but much ink has already been written about the fisheries on Lake Erie and I had no desire to write yet another book on the subject. Instead I condensed the primary fisheries, how to catch fish, and where you are most likely to encounter the game fish that make Lake Erie the premier fishery of the state.

I start off each body of water with a **key species** index that lists the primary game fish available in that particular body of water. I left out the rough fish, the suckers, and the species that exist in small numbers or have little sport value.

Next I include a **general description** that could more aptly be called "a quick description," which gives a short one-sentence description of the body of water.

Next I give an **overview** that covers important details about the body of water, including some in-depth information regarding state parks, marinas, boat ramps, wheelchair access, shoreline fishing, and various facilities that may be of use to a fisher. I also include bits of interesting history.

In **the fishing** segment, I relate all the information about fishing for the various species of game fish in that body of water, including the best time, average sizes of fish an angler can expect, and methods and locations.

In the **special regulations** section, I list all the current laws and regulations that govern that stream or lake, including outboard motor restrictions, size limits, and closed seasons. If there are no special regulations, I mention that as well. Be sure to consult current regulations when visiting any lake.

Facilities/camping covers mostly overnight camping options, if available. I also touch briefly on the nearest town in the event that an angler needs gas or to get a sandwich. I also touch on any special facilities on that particular lake or stream.

In **additional information** I discuss any side trips or interesting sights that might be of interest to visiting fishers and their families.

Finally, in the **directions** section, I try to the best of my ability to not get you lost. Some locations are so far out that they defy any reasonable attempt to put the directions in writing. Please consult a detailed map and keep in mind that all mileage is approximate.

Ohio's All-Tackle State Record Fish (as of January 2008)

The Ohio Record Fish list is maintained by the Outdoor Writers of Ohio State Record Fish Committee.

Hook & Line Division

Bass, Hybrid Striped	17.68 pounds	Deer Creek Lake
Bass, Largemouth	13.13 pounds	Farm pond
Bass, Rock	1.97 pounds	Deer Creek stream
Bass, Smallmouth	9.5 pounds	Lake Erie
Bass, Spotted	5.25 pounds	Lake White
Bass, Striped	37.10 pounds	West Branch Reservoir
Bass, White	4 pounds	Gravel pit
Bluegill	3.28 pounds	Salt Fork area (possibly a strip-mine pond)
Bowfin	11.69 pounds	Nettle Lake
Bullhead	4.25 pounds	Farm pond
Burbot	17.33 pounds	Lake Erie
Carp	50 pounds	Paint Creek
Catfish, Blue	No record at time of publication	
Catfish, Channel	37.65 pounds	LaDue Reservoir
Catfish, Shovel/Flathead	76.5 pounds	Clendening Lake
Crappie, Black	4.5 pounds	Private lake
Crappie, White	3.90 pounds	Private pond
Drum, Freshwater (Sheepshead)	23.5 pounds	Sandusky River
Gar, Longnose	25 pounds	Ohio River
Muskellunge	55.13 pounds	Piedmont Lake
Muskellunge, Tiger	31.64 pounds	Turkeyfoot Lake
Perch, White	1.42 pounds	Green Creek
Perch, Yellow	2.75 pounds	Lake Erie
Pickerel, Chain	6.25 pounds	Long Lake
Pike, Northern	22.38 pounds	Lyre Lake
Salmon, Chinook	29.5 pounds	Lake Erie
Salmon, Coho	13.63 pounds	Huron River
Salmon, Pink	3.06 pounds	Conneaut Creek
Sauger	7.31 pounds	Maumee River
Saugeye	14.04 pounds	Antrim Lake

Sucker, Buffalo	46.01 pounds	Hoover Reservoir
Sucker (other than buffalo)	9.25 pounds	Leesville Lake
Sunfish, Green	0.99 pound	Farm pond
Sunfish, Hybrid	2.03 pounds	Farm pond
Sunfish, Longear	0.2 pound	Big Darby Creek
Sunfish, Pumpkinseed	0.75 pound	Farm pond
Sunfish, Redear	3.58 pounds	Farm pond
Sunfish, Warmouth	1.19 pound	LaDue Reservoir
Trout, Brown	14.65 pounds	Lake Erie
Trout, Lake	20.49 pounds	Lake Erie
Trout, Rainbow (Steelhead)	20.97 pounds	Lake Erie
Walleye	16.19 pounds	Lake Erie

Bowfishing Division

Bowfin	8.79 pounds	East Harbor
Carp	40.25 pounds	Lake Erie
Gar, Longnose	14.57 pounds	Ohio Brush Creek
Sucker, Buffalo	37 pounds	Hoover Reservoir
Sucker (other than buffalo)	11.21 pounds	Maumee River

Map Legend

Interstate Highway	64	Park	⛰
U.S. Highway	13	Campground	⛺
State Highway	316	Park Office	👥
County or Local Highway	CR 114	Lake/Reservoir River	
Trail/Trailhead	- - - 🚶 - - -	State Boundary	- - - - -
City/Town	○	Visitor Center	?
Fishing Site	2	Swimming Area	🏊
Boat Ramp	🚤	Point of Interest	▪
Fishing Access	🐟	Parking	P
Marina	⚙	Restrooms	🚻
Dam	—	Wheelchair Access	♿
Fish Attractors	•••		

Central Ohio—Wildlife District One

Central Ohio has some quality fishing waters, and most of them are within a couple hours' drive of Columbus. Two of Ohio's top streams, the Kokosing and Darby Creek, offer float fishing for smallmouth and have an abundance of public-access points. For trout fishers, it would be hard to beat the Mad River when it comes to big browns and quality trout fishing.

Deer Creek has one of the top tailwater fisheries for saugeye in Ohio. The tailwaters of Griggs Reservoir have been known to give up some big smallmouth. Alum Creek Lake is one of my favorite lakes in the state; it has great saugeye, muskie, crappie, and bass fishing and is probably the best bet in Ohio to hook a muskie from the tailwaters.

The central part of Ohio also boasts a couple of very good trophy bass lakes in Knox Lake and Oakthorpe Lake. While Buckeye Lake has some fairly good saugeye fishing, the best saugeye fishing in central Ohio would have to go to Indian Lake. Indian Lake also has some of the biggest bluegills in Ohio. Kiser Lake is not well-known, but it does give up some big hybrid stripers, and plans for a future striper fishery are a possibility.

As far as crappies go, Delaware Lake and Alum Creek Lake are the two best, and Buckeye Lake is not far behind.

If I were forced to pick a place in central Ohio I would want to spend most of my fishing time, it would be tough choice between Alum Creek Lake and Knox Lake.

1 Alum Creek Lake

Key species: Muskie, saugeye, crappie, largemouth and smallmouth bass, white bass, channel catfish, and bluegill.

General description: One of the top lakes in the state for crappie, saugeye, and muskie.

Overview: Alum Creek Lake is among the largest reservoirs in Ohio and one of the last impounded by the U.S. Army Corps of Engineers. Completed in 1974, the lake covers 3,387 acres, is nearly 12 miles long and a mile wide at the dam. Sitting in central Ohio, Alum Creek Lake is also one of the most heavily used lakes in the state by recreational boaters.

The Alum Creek State Park has a campground, four boat ramps, docks, a marina with boat rental and fuel, numerous picnic and parking areas, and the state's longest inland beach. The U.S. Army Corps of Engineers provides access to the dam, a picnic area, and fishing access at the tailwaters below the dam.

The lake lies in a north-south direction, with the shallow headwaters at the north end. There are three roads built on causeways that cross the lake, effectively dividing

Central Ohio Region Overview

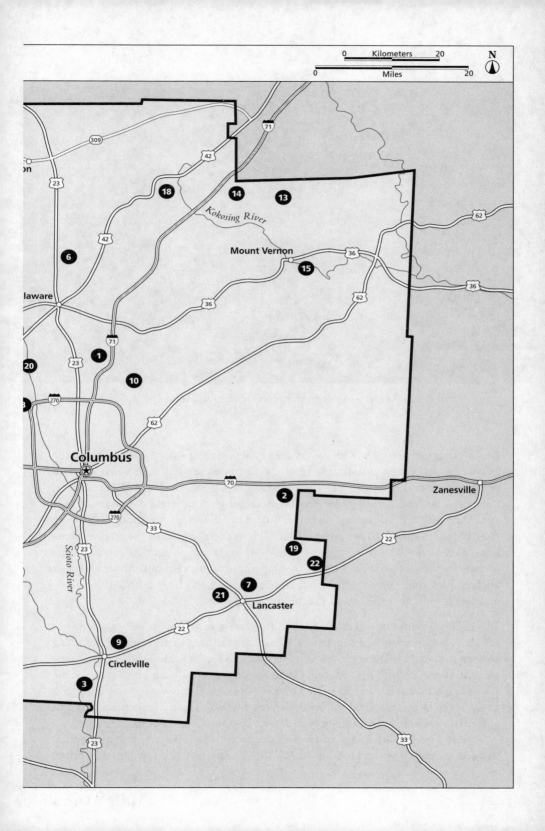

Greg Hastings caught this 42-inch muskie while trolling on Alum Creek Lake. Photo by Greg Hastings

the lake into four sections. With each causeway acting like a sedimentation barrier, the north end can become turbid from heavy rains, while the south end, where the dam is located, remains clear with 3 to 4 feet of visibility. County roads parallel the lake on both sides, with numerous parking areas offering anglers excellent shoreline access.

The north end of the lake averages a depth of 5 feet; at the south end, at the dam, depths can reach 60 feet, with a 30 to 40 foot average. One of the unusual characteristics of the lake is its approximately 145 bays and inlets that run along its length. These bays provide countless fishing opportunities for both shore and boat anglers, plus they offer shelter from the heavy weekend boat traffic. Park headquarters is located at the end of Peachblow Road.

The fishing: Alum Creek Lake is the kind of lake you wish you had in your area. It's clear, has a variety of game fish, has numerous fishing opportunities, and is big enough to spend a lifetime exploring its secrets. It is one of Ohio's top muskie, crappie, and saugeye lakes. It produced a state record saugeye, it can boast some of the state's biggest crappies, and 30-pound muskies are caught here every year. It also has a mixture of largemouth and smallmouth bass, white bass runs in the spring that will put 30 fish on a stringer, and plenty of 10- to 12-pound channel cats.

Alum Creek Lake is one of the top producers of muskies in the state and is stocked annually by the Division of Wildlife at one fish per acre. In the spring, muskies migrate to the shallow north end of the lake and into the longer coves such as Big Run Cove. In spring the west shoreline and coves south of Howard Road Bridge are top muskie spots. Anglers cast and work the shoreline there with deep runners, crank baits, and muskie-size spinner baits. Many of the coves have the remains of standing timber, stumps, and fallen trees, which should never be overlooked. As the water warms, trolling for muskies takes over, and trolling off both sides of the Cheshire Causeway is productive. Troll the edge where the causeway riprap meets the lakebed. That same pattern is repeated at the dam, where trolling along the edge of the dam is productive. Troll in front of the coves and off points on the east side from Cheshire Road, trolling south toward the dam and along the west shore on the outer edge of the shoreline drops.

At one of the nicer tailwater fisheries in the state, muskies are caught from the bank below the dam. Most muskies stay in the deep pool at the base of the dam, and fishing from the end of sidewalk into that pool can produce a follow or a strike. The water is crystal clear in the summer, and often you can spot muskies cruising the surface or shallows in the tailwaters. Snagging muskies has been a problem at the tailwaters, and wildlife officers are keenly aware of it.

Saugeyes grow big in Alum Creek Lake, producing a 12.84-pound state record in 2002. That fish was caught at night in January, fishing the riprap with crank baits. Saugeye anglers who target saugeyes have good success, but most anglers pick up fish haphazardly along shallow flats in bays, off long points and edges, and around the riprap on the causeways and rock piers in the lake's south half from the U.S. Highway 36 & Highway 37 Bridge. Saugeye are taken off the shoreline using jig and minnow, shad raps, and worm harness fished on the bottom and by jigging in the spring. Two of the better locations are the riprap on both sides of the Cheshire Road Causeway and at the dam. Don't overlook the rock jetty at the marina, either.

Anglers at the campground have access to some of the best saugeye fishing in the lake. Parking at the campground boat ramp, anglers can walk out along the riprap at the Cheshire Road Causeway and pick up saugeyes from the shoreline, casting small deep-diver crank baits. Saugeye fishing holds up good all year long. Fishing for trophy-size fish is always better in the evening and at night. The tailwaters are also good for saugeye in late winter and early spring.

Crappie fishing at Alum Creek Lake is something to brag about. In spring, the coves along the lake's east side from US 36 south are filled with big black and white crappies. Crappie fishing starts in early April and doesn't slow until Memorial Day weekend. There is good access all along Africa Road. A bobber and a minnow are all you need to catch a bucket of crappies 9 to 14 inches long. Fish the shoreline brush, any downed trees, or stickups.

White bass fishing in Alum Creek Lake is limited to the upper north half. From April through Memorial Day, white bass up to 16 inches long can be caught from the lake at the Kilbourne access off Highway 521. The best fishing is at that access and along the old fishermen's path that follows Alum Creek Lake upstream for as far as you want to walk. If the white bass are running, you can be in them from daylight to dark. Use white Mepps, Rooster Tails, and small jigs with grubs.

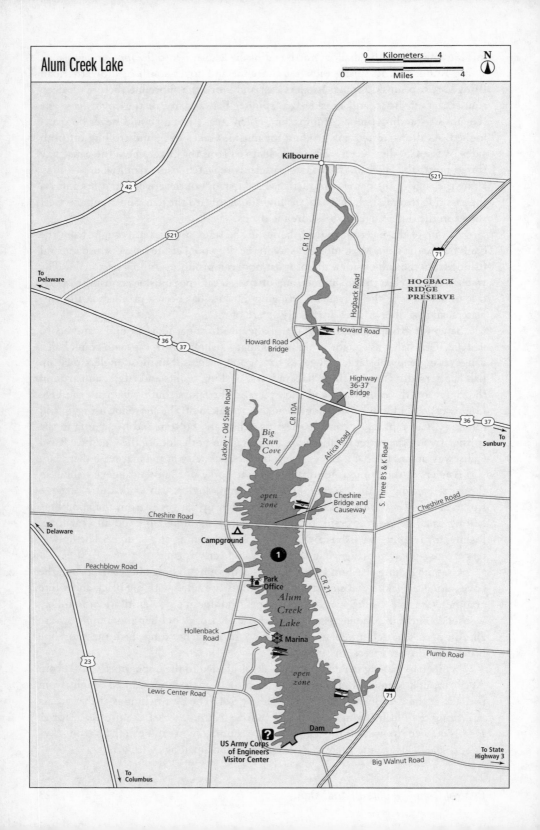

Channel cats have an ideal habitat from the Howard Bridge north, and that is where you will find the lake's best cat fishing. Pulloffs along Hogback Road and on North Old State Road provide access to this area. Boaters can launch from the Howard Road ramp and go north under the bridge. This is a no-wake zone, and most days you won't see another boat in the area. There are a couple of inlets with feeder streams, the old creek channel runs against the bank in several places, and shallow flats averaging 1 to 4 feet deep are common. Cut bait, chicken livers, and night crawlers are the favorite of channel cats everywhere.

Alum Creek Lake is more of a smallmouth lake than a largemouth lake. Some 5-pound smallmouth have been taken from the lake. Crank baits, tube baits, and jigs worked off any of the deep points on the lake's south end will get smallmouth. Soft crawls also work well around wood and rock shorelines. Look too for steep, rock-boulder-gravel shorelines, particularly for any woody structure that might be nearby. You should expect to catch a few saugeye while smallmouth fishing.

You can catch largemouth by throwing crank baits, spinner baits, plastics, or Carolina rigs at shoreline brush and structures in any of the deeper coves and woody structures from Howard Road south. Water is usually more stained in that area. During summer when boat traffic allows it, work the edge and points along the east side above Cheshire Bridge. In spring, the bass are in the back of shallow coves on the main lake; throw to shoreline cover during that time. Main lake points are always good during summer.

Special regulations: Crappies must be 9 inches, and there is a 12-inch minimum length limit on largemouth and smallmouth bass.

Facilities/camping: The state park has 289 campsites and a boat ramp. There is a marina, restaurant, boat ramp, and boat rental at the end of Hollenback Road. You can find amenities at Delaware and at the US 36 and Interstate 71 interchange.

Additional information: There is a spectacular view of osprey nests at the north end of the lake on Hogback Road. The nests occupy the various platforms set out in the lake. Ospreys raise their young from early May through mid-July. The Delaware County Hogback Ridge Preserve, located on that same road, is also worth a visit.

Directions: Take I-71 north out of Columbus, then west on US 36 and Highway 37.

2 Buckeye Lake

Key species: Saugeye, hybrid striper, crappie, largemouth bass, bluegill, channel and shovelhead catfish.

General description: Buckeye Lake is a resort lake heavily used by recreational boaters.

Overview: Buckeye Lake is another one of the early canal lakes impounded for the purpose of supplying water for the Erie Canal system. Work started on the lake in

Jim Henery caught this nice saugeye on Buckeye Lake.

1825 and was completed five years later. The lake covers nearly 3,000 acres and is 7.5 miles long and over a mile wide. The lake averages 6 to 8 feet deep.

Buckeye Lake State Park was created in 1949. It is unusual in the fact that it has no state campground. As a result of the previous development, the park is limited to only 175 acres, consisting of five boat ramps, picnic areas, swimming beaches, piers, and docks. Homes, cottages, and businesses surround the lake, and most of the islands are inhabited.

There have been fish die-offs in the past; nutrient loading from inadequate sewage systems were once a problem. New city sewage systems were installed, and the water quality has improved. The improvement was so dramatic that the Hebron Fish Hatchery, which receives its water from the old canal system, had to begin adding nutrients to the canal water to make it fertile enough to be used in fish rearing. The lake does have algae bloom, and the water is a semitransparent pea green. Visibility is 6 to 8 inches in most places.

Buckeye Lake is full of pleasure boats, Jet Skis, and houseboats most of the time. This is due in large part to the more than 20 islands on the lake, of which approximately a dozen are developed with summer and weekend cottages. The lake has an extensive canal system, and new ones are being built to accommodate the new development. There are two dams, or spillways, on the north side of the lake, but neither provides any tailwater fishing.

There are several communities on Buckeye Lake; the most noted are Miller-sport, the village of Buckeye Lake, and Fairfield Beach. State park public boat ramps are located at Liebs Island and Brooks Park on the west side, Fairfield Beach on the south side, and at Buckeye Lake in the north shore. There are also two other boat ramps—one small ramp at Thornport on the east side and another private ramp at Avondale Marina on the northeast shore.

Buckeye Lake can get very dangerous when severe weather hits. Locals know the signs of approaching weather; new boaters should head for shelter or a canal when storms approach.

The fishing: In talking to local anglers, most seem satisfied with the quality of fishing in Buckeye Lake. The lake is large enough to accommodate all lake users, but fishers point out that weekdays are best if you want to avoid the heavy weekend boat traffic.

The lake has good fishing for saugeyes. Saugeyes seem to be the savior in most lakes, providing excellent fishing wherever they are stocked. There are a variety of ways to catch saugeyes. Success comes in many forms, but throwing deep-diving crank baits around old main lake stumps and rocky and gravel areas produces well. Most anglers troll for saugeyes, looking for hard bottoms, off points, reefs, islands, and rock piers. In the fall saugeyes are found near the shoreline, and catches of saugeyes from bank anglers improves considerably. Saugeye fishing seems well placed throughout the lake, but the main lake is the best. Saugeyes are the year-round catch, even in late winter and through the ice.

Channel catfish are plentiful throughout the many channels and canals and near the shoreline. They are well distributed, but the lake points at Fairfield Beach stand out. Channels are the best catch for shoreline anglers, as they are numerous, even pesky. Some fishers have caught nice 10- to 11-pound channels.

Buckeye Lake has shovelheads—even some 50-pound ones—but they are not given much attention. Most fishers are not equipped to handle the size of the shovelheads in this lake. Hybrid stripers are popular, but the glory fish of the Ohio River is reduced to feeding on chicken livers fished on the bottom. Liebs Island and its sister islands produce well for hybrids, but they are well distributed throughout Buckeye Lake. The hybrid produced for Buckeye is the result of a female white bass crossed with a male striped bass. They are vigorous growers, reaching 20 inches in three years. The abundant gizzard shad population should strengthen and grow some incredible hybrid stripers. The bluegill population is good here, but expect average-size fish. They are numerous in the canals and around the islands off Fairfield Beach. Largemouth bass fishing is only so-so, but the lake does draw its share of bass tournaments. Most fish range from 12 to 14 inches; a good one is 3 pounds. The best largemouth fishing is in early spring and fall; look for fish in the canals, against the riprap, around docks and shoreline structure on the east side of the lake, and around Cranberry Bog. Serious bass anglers choose spinner baits, crank baits, and plastics; it is no different here. Crappie fishing is good in early spring, after ice-out, and do achieve a respectable 10 to 12 inches. Like crappies in all canal lakes, you

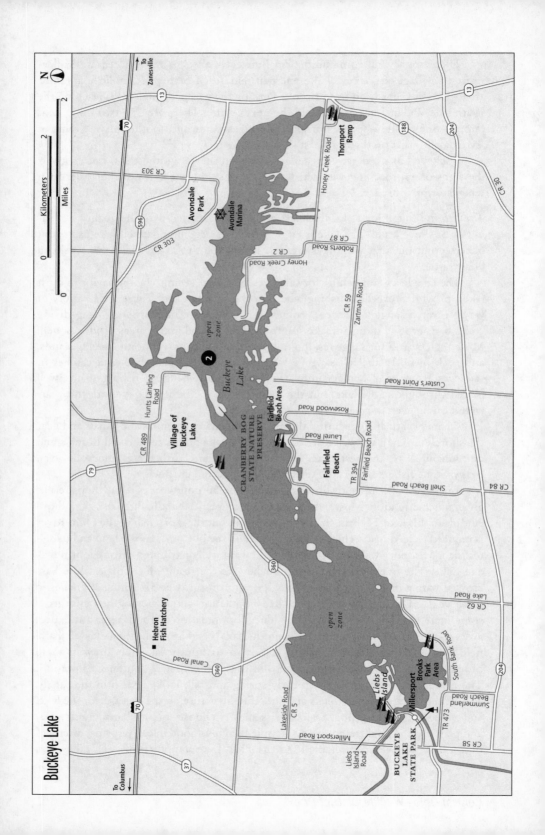

Buckeye Lake

N

Kilometers
0   2

Miles
0   2

To Zanesville

To Columbus

To Columbus

Hebron Fish Hatchery

Village of Buckeye Lake

Avondale Park

Avondale Marina

CRANBERRY BOG STATE NATURE PRESERVE

Buckeye Lake

open zone

2

Fairfield Beach Area

Fairfield Beach

Thornport Ramp

Liebs Island

Brooks Park Area

Millersport

BUCKEYE LAKE STATE PARK

open zone

Canal Road

Hunts Landing Road

CR 489

CR 303

CR 303

CR 596

Honey Creek Road   CR 2

Roberts Road   CR 87

Honey Creek Road

CR 59

Zartman Road

Custer's Point Road

Rosewood Road

Laurel Road

Fairfield Beach Road

TR 394

Shell Beach Road

CR 84

Lake Road

CR 62

South Bank Road

Summerland Beach Road

TR 473

CR 58

Liebs Island Road

Millersport Road

Lakeside Road

CR 5

Canal Road

37

70

70

79

596

303

489

360

360

360

5

13

188

204

30

13

204

can find them around boat docks and under moored houseboats in the canals. As a side note, there are some bruiser carp in the lake. Look to the shallows to find them. There is also public fishing for channels, bluegills, and crappies in the canal through Millersport, which is wheelchair accessible.

Special regulations: There is a 12-inch limit on bass.

Facilities/camping: There are no state campgrounds at Buckeye Lake. There is a mixture of private campgrounds, bed-and-breakfasts, motels, and hotels in the area. The towns of Millersport and Buckeye Lake have all the amenities. For information on lodging, contact the Buckeye Lake Chamber of Commerce at www. buckeyelakecc.com.

Additional information: There is much to see and do around Buckeye Lake. The lake boasts one of the largest blue heron rookies in the state on Hunts Landing Road. The Cranberry Bog State Nature Preserve is the only bog of its kind in the United States. You have to make arrangements to visit the floating bog through the Division of Natural Areas and Preserves. The Hebron Fish Hatchery is located on Canal Road and is open weekdays. The Dawes Arboretum, located northeast of Buckeye Lake on Highway 13, is open seven days a week and well worth a visit. Many small shops and quaint eateries are located in Millersport.

Directions: East of Columbus on I-70, south at the Highway 79 intersection.

3 Circleville Canal

Key species: Bullhead and channel catfish, bluegill, carp, bass.

General description: Some remaining sections of the Erie Canal are open for fishing at Canal Park.

Overview: Built in the 1830s, this section of the old Erie Canal still remains and offers a historical look back when the canal played a vital role in Ohio's industry and transportation. The old dam, the original canal, and several locks have been preserved through the efforts of the Pickaway County Historical and Genealogical Society at Canal Park.

The fishing: More for history buffs than for fishers, the old canal still offers fishing for catfish, bluegills, and bass. Approximately 2 miles of the historical canal is accessible along Canal Road west of Circleville. Parking areas and pulloffs are next to the canal. Big shady trees line the banks, and the area is well maintained. Some private land and a gravel mining operation are located along the canal. Buzz baits and spinner baits might bring up a few small bass, but the canal is loaded with bullhead (yellowbelly) catfish and bluegills. The canal is approximately 60 feet wide, 3 to 4 feet deep, and easy to walk. Using a small boat is also possible but not necessary.

Special regulations: None; state game and fish laws apply.

Facilities/camping: Nearby Circleville has all the amenities.

Additional information: Canal Park also offers carry-on watercraft access and fishing on the Scioto River.

Directions: West of Circleville on U.S. Highway 22, after crossing the Scioto River, turn south on Canal Road. Drive 1 mile, and Canal Park is on the left.

4 Darby Creek

Key species: Smallmouth bass, sunfish, rock bass, channel catfish.

General description: Darby Creek is one of the top float streams in Ohio for smallmouth bass.

Overview: Darby Creek is a highly regarded stream and designated State and National Scenic River for most of its 80-mile length from the Champaign-Union County line west of Marysville, to its confluence with the Scioto River at Circleville. Access to the Big Darby is gained by way of landowner permission, bridge crossings, roadside pulloffs, and at various township, village, and city Metro Parks. There is public access at the small town of Plain City, at a park north of town at the US 42 Bridge; another access site is east of town at the McKitrick Recreational Fishing Area on Highway 161. Downstream approximately 5 miles is the 1,438-acre Prairie Oaks Metro Park with fishing and canoe access off Amity Road, north of I-70. The 6,319-acre Battelle Darby Creek Metro Park is 6 miles downstream from Prairie Oaks. It has fishing and canoe drop-off locations at the junction of Alkire and Gardner Roads and also at the Opossum Run and Harrisburg-Georgesville junction.

Prairie Oaks and Battelle are Columbus Metro Park recreation areas that provide approximately 20 miles of public access on both Big and Little Darby Creeks. Little Darby Creek joins Big Darby Creek just north of the small town of Georgesville, at Battelle Darby Metro Park. One-day float and fishing trips on Big Darby Creek are possible from the McKitrick Fishing Area to Prairie Oaks, from Prairie Oaks to Alkire-Gardner Road, and from Alkire-Gardner to the Harrisburg-Georgesville canoe launch. The latter is a four- to six-hour float.

The fishing: Darby Creek is considered one of Ohio's showcase smallmouth streams, and any day spent here is rewarding. Because of its proximity to Columbus, Darby Creek does get a fair amount of fishing pressure. Popular with the canoe and kayak crowd, Darby Creek is less crowded on weekdays. Columbus Metro Parks has been purchasing tracts, preserving stream corridors, and expanding public areas on Darby Creek, while the Ohio Nature Conservancy has been quietly pursuing conservation easements and working with local governments to ensure future watershed protection.

Darby Creek is a good stream to wade or float. The smallmouth here get big by stream standards; 15- to 18-inch smallmouth are fairly common catches. I have always felt that smallmouth in special places like this should be fished only with a

Darby Creek is a premier smallmouth stream and a State Scenic River.

fly rod, preferably an 8.5- or 9-foot bamboo with Woolly Buggers and terrestrials. Rock bass and green and longear sunfish are in good numbers and at times pesky. Channel catfish are found in about any pool. Fish soft craws, hellgrammites, and night crawlers in the pools below riffles; you're liable to catch just about anything. Small crawdad-colored crank baits, fox squirrel tail Mepps spinners, and tubes catch the lion's share of smallies.

Good stretches of fishing water exist all over. There is ample parking at either Prairie Oaks or Battelle, but water closest to the parking area always gets the most pressure. Most stretches of water in the Metro Park require long walks to get to, but miles of park trails help. Sometimes, though, a canoe or kayak is the only practical way to fish the Darby.

Fishing is good all through the Darby. In the lower stretches you'll find more flathead, largemouth, and spotted bass, and the occasional muskie shows up. Smallmouth fishing begins in mid-April, depending on water conditions, and slows down after June. It picks up again in October. Stream conditions vary; slow-rising, cloudy water seems to trigger channel cat; clear stable conditions attract smallmouth and sunfish.

Special regulations: Smallmouth bass minimum size limit is 15 inches on Big Darby Creek between US 40 and downstream through Battelle Darby Metro Park to Highway 762 at Orient.

Facilities/camping: Camping is available at Plain City at the Pastime Park city campground on US 42.

Additional information: Several quarry ponds, stocked with bass, bluegill, and channel catfish, provide additional fishing opportunities at the Prairie Oaks Metro Park. All quarry ponds are bank fishing only, except the largest that allows electric motors. Contact Metro Parks at www.metroparks.net.

Directions: Both Prairie Oaks and Battelle Metro Parks are located west of Columbus off I-70. Take Highway 142 north off I-70 to Prairie Oaks Metro Park. Take Highway 142 south off I-70 to Battelle Darby Metro Park.

Little Darby Creek can be accessed at the Dyer Mill Ski Trail parking area off Gardner Road at Battelle Darby Metro Park.

5 Deer Creek Lake

Key species: Largemouth and smallmouth bass, saugeye, white bass, channel and flathead catfish, crappie, and bluegill.

General description: Good stream, tailwater, and lake fishing in one package.

Overview: Impounded by the U.S. Army Corps of Engineers in 1968 as a flood control project for the Ohio River Valley, Deer Creek Lake covers 1,227 surface acres, is nearly 6 miles long, and has an average depth of 15 feet. The lake is surrounded by the 2,337-acre Deer Creek State Park and the 4,085-acre Deer Creek

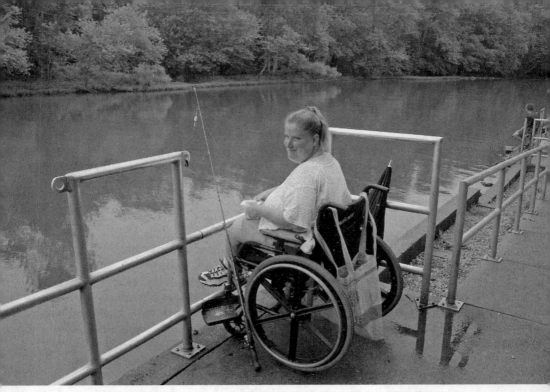

Linda Scowden fishes from one of the wheelchair-access sites provided at the Deer Creek Lake tailwaters.

Wildlife Area. The state park facilities include a campground; a lodge; cabins; hiking, biking, and bridle trails; picnic areas; a golf course; a beach; two boat ramps; and a marina. Park headquarters is located on Yankeetown Road, 1.5 miles east of Highway 207.

Shoreline access is good throughout most of the lake. At the dam the Corps of Engineers provides access to the tailwaters, with two parking areas, a shelter house, picnic tables, and concrete walkways along the bank that are wheelchair accessibile. As a flood control lake, Deer Creek Lake is prone to fluctuating water levels. Normal pool level is 810.5 feet above sea level; in January 2005 the water level rose to 839.61 feet, exceeding 29 feet above pool. Fluctuations of 8 to 10 feet are expected during spring; usually within a week, the lake has returned to normal levels. In the fall the lake is drawn down 14 feet. During the summer, lake visibility is good, averaging 12 to 18 inches.

Through the wildlife area, you can access more than 4 miles of Deer Creek stream before it enters the lake from the north. There are two access roads with parking areas off Highway 207 north of Yankeetown Road from which to access the stream. You can also access the stream at the Yankeetown Bridge. South of Yankeetown Road, you can gain access to the stream from roads D-57 and D-58. Boat ramps on the lake are located off Highway 207 at the marina on the lake's west side and off Deer Creek Road on the east side at the Harding Cabin. Small boat and canoe launching is possible at most wildlife area access points. The marina, located off Highway 207 on the lake's west side, offers boat rental and fuel.

Three different government agencies administer Deer Creek Lake and the area surrounding it: Division of Parks, Division of Wildlife, and the U.S. Army Corps of Engineers. Deer Creek Lake allows unlimited horsepower.

The fishing: Deer Creek Lake offers the angler a variety of fishing opportunities, from small stream fishing for smallmouth, lake fishing for channel cats and crappies, to some of the finest tailwater fishing in the state for saugeyes.

Smallmouth can be taken from Deer Creek stream before it enters the lake from the north. Parking areas north of Yankeetown Road provide access to the upstream portion. To access the stream near the Yankeetown Bridge, park at the west side of the bridge. Tubes, Woolly Buggers, and small crank baits get their attention. Rock bass, sunfish, saugeyes, and white bass will likely fill out a day's catch. North of the bridge you can wade; south of the bridge you need a boat when lake levels are normal.

From early April through mid-May, while the lake is still well below pool level, white bass from Deer Creek Lake make a run upstream. The northwest section of the lake is reduced to a channel during this drawdown time, and white bass follow this channel upstream. Catching 30 to 40 fish a day is common. This area can be accessed from road D-58. Fishing is good from Pancoastburg to as far upstream as you want to go.

A few hybrid striped bass are also in Deer Creek Lake. In fact, a state record hybrid striper of 17.68 pounds came from the lake. The Ohio Division of Wildlife has never stocked hybrid stripers in Deer Creek Lake. The nearest source for hybrids would have to be the private Choctaw Lake Resort, impounded on Deer Creek, 32 miles upstream. Choctaw Lake has been privately stocked with hybrid stripers, and two state record hybrid striped bass have come from tributary pools downstream of Lake Choctaw.

Channel cat fishing is also good at Deer Creek Lake. Fish the upper north end, where road D-58 runs along the shoreline. There are plenty of parking and fishing areas to choose from along this road. Use chicken livers, night crawlers, and cut shad. During the summer the tailwaters below the dam are full of channel cats in the 15- to 22-inch range. Flatheads are also in the lake; fish the main lake for them and use a big shad for bait.

Largemouth bass fishing is average at Deer Creek Lake, with most in the 12- to 14-inch range. A few hogs do show up from time to time. Like most Ohio lakes, the majority of bass are caught from shoreline cover, riprap, and rock points. Spinner baits and plastics take the lion's share. Lots of overhanging trees, brush, and downed timber are found along the shorelines. Fish the north arm and the bay that runs back toward the camping area, the bank across from the marina as well as the point, the steep shoreline in front of the lodge, the south bank, and the area along the old roadbed on the southwest corner. Check the riprap around the old Waters Road Causeway and at the Harding Cabin boat ramp on the lake's east side.

Good crappie fishing starts in early April; fish docks, bank structures, stick-ups, and downed trees all over the lake. Crappies up to 13 inches are taken, with most averaging 7 to 10 inches. Use minnows and bobbers or small jigs and minnow combos. Fish the shoreline brush and around boat docks from the bank. Deer Creek Lake has a 9-inch length minimum on crappies.

In 1978 Deer Creek Lake became one of the first lakes to be stocked with saugeyes. But the saugeye fishing here is a typical example and the paradox of stocking saugeyes in flood-control lakes. While over 300,000 fingerling saugeyes are stocked in the lake each May, the primary fishing for saugeyes at Deer Creek Lake is in the tailwaters below the dam. A former 9-pound state record saugeye came from the tailwaters, and another one is probably waiting there. Look for saugeyes around riprap, rock, and flats 6 to 10 feet deep around the beach. The best spot to pick up saugeyes in Deer Creek Lake, however, is off the tip of Adena Ridge—the long, narrow point across from the marina. Slow troll, drift, or cast night crawler harnesses and weight-forward spinners tipped with minnows. Fish the tailwater for saugeyes in late fall through early spring or after any discharge of lake water. The best months are January, February, and March. Use jigs tipped with bright grubs or minnows; let the size of the jig be determined by the strength of the current. Access and parking is on both sides of the tailwaters.

Six miles downstream of Deer Creek Lake there is access to Deer Creek stream at the U.S. Highway 22 bridge, west of Williamsport.

Special regulations: The minimum length on crappies is 9 inches.

Facilities/camping: Deer Creek State Park offers 25 cabins and 227 campsites. The State Park Lodge has 110 rooms. Facilities outside the park are scarce.

Additional information: An osprey nest is located at the end of the Waters Road causeway. To view the nest, take road D-58.

Directions: Deer Creek Lake is located approximately 15 miles west of Circleville. Take US 22 west to Highway 207 north. Follow the signs.

6 Delaware Lake

Key species: White and black crappie, largemouth bass, channel catfish, saugeye, white bass, and bluegill.

General description: This is a flood impoundment lake known for its crappie fishing, but don't overlook it for bass.

Overview: Impounded by the U.S. Army Corps Engineers in 1951 as a flood control project on the upper Olentangy River, Delaware Lake is subject to spring flooding and drawdown during the fall. The lake covers approximately 1,300 acres. Depths range from 6 feet at the shallow north end, to 15 and 20 feet from the marina south to the dam. Delaware State Park, on the lake's west side, has a campground, two boat launches, a beach, picnic areas, boat docks, and a marina where fuel is available. Park headquarters are also here.

The marina rents a variety of boats: pontoon boats, ski boats, aluminum V-hulls, canoes, and kayaks. Surrounding the lake on the north and east sides is the 4,670-acre Delaware Wildlife Area. From the rough and tumble roads in the wildlife area, you can access the lake's east shore at seven different locations. There is also one ramp in the wildlife area, but I would not want to tow a nice bass boat down the road that leads to it. As a result of being a small lake on a large watershed, Delaware Lake frequently floods in the early spring. On occasion, flooding in the park has been severe enough to put the marina underwater. While the lake has no restrictions on horsepower, the north end of the lake is a no-wake zone.

The fishing: This is one of the better crappie lakes of central Ohio. It has a mixture of black and white crappie. The Division of Wildlife is experimenting with a 9-inch minimum length limit on crappies on Delaware Lake, in the hopes it will improve or maintain the quality of the fishing. Crappie fishing holds up well all summer; it simply becomes a matter of relocating to the deeper lake edges and structures after the spring spawn. During the spring, crappies are found in the many coves and backwaters around shoreline stickups, brush, docks, and the usual crappie haunts. Stringers of black crappies from 9 to 15 inches are common catches.

Beginning in mid-June the crappies gradually make their way south into the deeper main lake body to relocate along channels and drops-offs. Frequent spring flooding generates a good supply of shoreline cover in the way of downed trees and shoreline slips. This flooding has been both a boom and a bust for the crappies. While it generates a great deal of cover, it also has affected crappie fishing in negative ways. Floods often occur during peak fishing and spawning periods. After the flood of 2005, which put half the park underwater, crappie fishing is said to have fallen off measurably.

There is always that speculation among fishers that crappie fishing will never rebound to pre-2005 quality. When flooding occurs, the Corps of Engineers usually is able to return the lake to normal levels within three to five days. Good crappie fishing begins right after ice-out at Delaware Lake, and with seasonal adjustments one can be in crappies all year long.

Delaware Lake is one of the more popular bass tournament lakes in the state, with upwards of 200 bass tournaments each year. Fishing begins in early spring at the headwaters of the Olentangy River and Whetstone Creek at the north end. The water there averages 4 to 6 feet deep, with lots of brushy shorelines, downed trees, and old snags. Anglers pitch spinner baits and plastics right against the shoreline structures in the many small bays, coves, and side channels on this north end. Later in the year the same shoreline pattern continues but moves toward the deeper south end. Again, the same shoreline cover is still there, but the water is a bit clearer and deeper. The old Olentangy creek channel is not to be overlooked, as bass relate to that channel, particularly as it sweeps against the shoreline in several places. There are some riprap structures around the boat docks that shouldn't be overlooked. Delaware Lake has an incredible amount of shoreline cover, and I suspect that cover is the reason for the continued good bass fishing. Bass range anywhere from 1 to 4 pounds, and they are not hard to find.

Channel cats are in good supply, and any spot on the bank will suffice. The usual lineups of catfish baits do well, as they do anywhere, which is chicken livers, shrimp, soft craws, and night crawlers. Some of the top spots are at the Highway 229 Bridge and the old bridge abutments at the end of Cole Road. There is plenty of shoreline access from the old roads in the wildlife area that place you right in catfish heaven. The channel cats in this lake reach a respectable 10 to 12 pounds. Of course the night bite is the best bite, so bring your lantern.

There are white bass in Delaware Lake, but they don't seem to get much attention. Most are caught by happenstance while largemouth or cat fishing. Some minor runs do occur up the Olentangy River and Whetstone Creek.

Saugeyes are stocked annually in Delaware Lake, but fishing for them is not popular or productive. Their locations seem to be here today, gone tomorrow. About the only place where saugeyes are caught with any regularity is around the island at the north end of the lake. If you can locate some hard, flat bottom or some rocky reefs, you might be in business. Saugeye fishers might take a cue from some other lakes and fish around deep, rocky piers or jetties at night. What is not unusual is the fact that saugeye fishing below the Delaware Lake dam is very productive. This pattern is repeated at many Ohio lakes, where the tailwater fishery for saugeyes is much better than the lake fishery.

The easiest way to access the tailwater is to park at the U.S. Army Corps of Engineers office located off U.S. Highway 23 and walk down from behind the main office. The water is shallow, and most fishers wade out and sit on the concrete break wall and fish both sides. Other fishers stand downstream of the break wall and cast to the center break cut in the wall, which channels the water into the stream. Brightly colored jigs and grubs are the standard tailwater lures for saugeyes.

Special regulations: Crappies must be 9 inches to keep; bass must be 12 inches.

Facilities/camping: The state park campground has 214 sites, a camp store, a nature center, and boat docks. The nearby town of Delaware has all the amenities.

Additional information: Great wildlife viewing can be found at the Delaware Wildlife Area. Of interest is the eagle's nest and wetlands found at the end of Leonardsburg Road.

Directions: Four miles north of the town of Delaware on US 23, watch for signs. To get to the wildlife area, take Main Road east off US 23, then go north on Horseshoe Road.

7 Greenfield Lake

Key species: Largemouth bass, crappie, bluegill, channel catfish.

General description: A small, but clear lake, with fair bass fishing and plenty of channel cats.

Overview: One of several lakes impounded as part of the Upper Hocking Watershed Project, this lake covers 12 acres and has some weed growth at the shallow north end, deep cover, and overhanging and fallen trees on the east and west banks. Foot access is good, a fishers' path circles the lake, but fishing from small watercraft is better. No boat ramp is available, but a small craft can be carried down from the parking area.

The fishing: Bass fishing is best in the morning and evenings. Some good bass are caught, but most run small. Spinner baits against the shoreline cover produce. Locals tell me some occasional 3-pound bass are caught. Crappies up to 12 inches are caught around the shoreline timber in the spring. Channel cats are good, averaging 12 to 20 inches, with some bigger. Fish for them near the dam during the summer nights. Bluegills are common, but run small.

Special regulations: Electric motors only.

Facilities/camping: No facilities; nearby Lancaster has everything.

Additional information: If you can locate them, there are some sunken brush piles along the dam that hold bass and bluegills.

Directions: Take Highway 158 north from Lancaster, turn east on Coonpath Road, and watch for Wildlife Area sign.

8 Griggs Reservoir

Key species: Largemouth and smallmouth bass, channel catfish, bluegill, green sunfish, crappie, saugeye, and white bass.

General description: A long, narrow body of water with good bass fishing and an excellent tailwater fishery.

Overview: In 1904 Griggs was the first of two water supply reservoirs impounded on the Scioto River by the city of Columbus. Named after Julian Griggs, the city's chief engineer at the time, Griggs Reservoir covers approximately 360 acres, is 6 miles long, but is only about 500 feet wide. Like its upstream twin, O'Shaughnessy, it is a long, narrow body of water, running in a north-to-south direction and resembling a river more than a lake. The lake is generally clear, with 12 inches or better visibility, and has an average depth of 15 to 20 feet. Like all city reservoirs, there are some water level fluctuations during dry periods. Nearly all shoreline access is on the east side by way of gravel lane pulloffs and at the recreation areas on the southeast bank off U.S. Highway 33. The only west-side public access is at the Hayden Falls Park Preserve at the Hayden Road Bridge.

Griggs has two public boat ramps, and both are located at the recreation area off US 33, south of the Fishinger Road Bridge. The reservoir is located within the suburbs of Dublin and Upper Arlington on the west side of Columbus and is administered by the City of Columbus Division of Watershed Management. Headquarters are located at the dam on the south end of the lake off US 33.

The fishing: Griggs is a quality bass lake with good populations of both largemouth and smallmouth bass. It is long and narrow with good shoreline cover but not much in the way of lake structures, other than the limestone breaks or bluffs that run along its length. The bass are shoreline oriented, and that is where you should concentrate your efforts. Look for the usual shoreline cover, overhanging trees, slips, and riprap and around old boat docks. Spinner baits, crank baits, Rapalas, tubes, and plastics are what the Griggs bass fishers pitch. Throw tight against the bank. The bass aren't real big, but 15- to 16-inch bass are fairly common. Like most state lakes, Griggs has regular weekly bass tournaments during the summer and is considered one of the top bass tournament lakes in the state. Fish the west shoreline across from the boat ramp from the Fishinger Bridge south and also 0.5 mile north of the bridge on the east bank.

For smallmouth, head north (upstream) to the islands north and south of the Highway 161 bridge. Fish around the island with olive or brown tubes and crawdad-colored crank baits. Approximately three-quarters of a mile north of that bridge, the lake becomes a stream again, and anglers can park their boats and wade the shallows for smallmouth that approach 18 to 20 inches.

White bass are also found in this upstream, northern part of Griggs Reservoir during the spring run that occurs in late April and into May. Use white Mepps, Rooster Tails, or white jigs with curly tail grubs.

Channel cat fishing is not what it used to be at Griggs. In the late 1990s, sewage overflows from the town of Dublin into the reservoir affected the channel cats with bacterial skin infections, killing off a substantial population. Even though the sewage problems have been long corrected, the channel catfish population has yet to fully recover, and fishing for them has been slow. There is also a nagging question of consuming the fish from the reservoir, and that too has placed a damper on the channel cat fishing. Most channel cat fishing is done from the various public access areas on the east shore at night.

Crappie fishing at Griggs is fairly good; again, fathead minnows and a bobber fished around brush, bank slips, and docks will get crappies of all sizes.

Some nice bluegills and green sunfish come from Griggs. Most are caught by shoreline anglers and kids fishing the east bank around brush with wax worms and a bobber.

Saugeye fishing is only fair at Griggs, even though it is stocked regularly. Most fishing for saugeyes is done below the dam. Saugeyes in this type of river impoundment relate to currents that move either upstream or downstream and sometimes out of the reservoir with high water levels and during storm events that cause water releases. In summer look for saugeyes in the south half of the reservoir off the underwater limestone bluffs and breaks, on both sides in 6 to 12 feet of water. Troll, cast, or drift orange-bladed night crawler harnesses, jigs with lime green grubs, or shad raps along the edge of these breaks. Some nice 24- to 26-inch saugeyes have come from Griggs.

The smallmouth and saugeye fishing at the dam at Griggs is excellent. The saugeye fishery is related to high-water discharges, especially in the late winter and early spring and again after heavy rainstorms cause a release of lake water. Small-mouth that top 20 inches are taken on tubes and small crawdad-colored crank baits; fish the pool just below the island where the streams come together. It is a beautiful place to fish, with pools and riffle water. The easiest way to get to the tailwaters is to walk down from the parking area next to park headquarters located at the south end of the lake off US 33.

Special regulations: None; state game and fish laws apply. Griggs Reservoir has no horsepower restrictions but does have speed, ski, and idle speed zones at the north and south ends. Fishers using pontoons or float tubes are required to stay within 25 feet of the shoreline.

Facilities/camping: There are numerous restaurants, gas stations, and convenience marts south of the dam on US 33. Camping is not permitted at the lake.

Additional information: You can view a nice waterfall at the Griggs Nature Preserve, Hayden Falls Park, located on the west side of the lake at the Hayden Bridge.

Directions: Located on the northwest side of Columbus, Riverside Drive/US 33 follows Griggs Reservoir's east shoreline. You can also access the dam and boat ramps from US 33.

9 Hargus Lake

Key species: Largemouth bass, bluegill, channel catfish, crappie.

General description: A small, weedy, deep lake with good bass and channel catfish fishing and motor restrictions.

Overview: Built in 1948, Hargus Lake covers 145 acres and averages 20 to 25 feet deep. It is a very clear lake with visibility up to 4 feet in some areas. Hargus is weedy and mossy around the edges, with lily pads in the shallows, riprap along the dam, and a couple of small islands. One boat ramp is located on the west side at A.W. Marion State Park; another primitive boat launch is located at the east side near the campground. There is a marina at the state park with a boat rental, picnic tables, shelters, and a 5-mile loop trail that encircles the lake.

The fishing: Hargus Lake boasts good fishing for bass, with a lot of smaller bass patrolling the weedy edges. Some nice bass are occasionally taken in the 3- to 4-pound range. Most bass fishing consists of fishing shoreline structures, rocky banks, deep-weed edges, and riprap. Plastics and spinner baits work well in the weeds. You will find bass anywhere on this lake; there are plenty of steep banks, deep cover, and rocky points.

Channel cat fishing is popular, with fish up to 24 inches taken regularly. Weekly catfish tournaments are held at the marina. Crappie fishing is fair, with most fish running small; the same is true for bluegills. Shoreline access is good at Hargus, with the Hargus Lake perimeter trail encircling the lake. The Ohio Division of Wildlife has stocked white amur to help control the weed growth in the lake. Zebra mussels were discovered in the lake in 1992.

Special regulations: Minimum length on bass is 15 inches. If caught, white amurs must be immediately released. Hargus Lake is limited to electric motors only.

Facilities/camping: There are few facilities at Hargus Lake. A bait and tackle shop is located at the entrance to the state park; bait is also available at the marina. The state park campground has 58 sites, 29 are electric.

Additional information: There is a well-maintained beaver dam at the campground boat launch, which has created a small wetlands pond on one of the lake's feeder streams.

Directions: East of Circleville, off US 22, take Bolender Road north to get to the boat launch and marina. Two miles farther take Ringgold-Southern Road to the camping area.

10 Hoover Reservoir

Key species: Largemouth bass, saugeye, channel catfish, white bass, bluegill, crappie.

General description: Hoover is a large reservoir with good bass and saugeye fishing; it is one of the primary water sources for the city of Columbus. It has a 10-hp limit.

Overview: Impounded in 1955 in the confluence of Big and Little Walnut Creeks, Hoover serves as a water supply reservoir for Columbus. Named after two brothers, Charles and Clarence Hoover, who both served on the city's waterworks, the lake covers 2,800 acres with approximately 48 miles of shoreline. It is over 8 miles long and a mile wide at its widest point. A deep lake by Ohio standards, Hoover's average depth is from 20 to 50 feet. Hoover is one of three water supply reservoirs administered by the City of Columbus Division of Watershed Management. Like all city reservoirs, there are some water level fluctuations during dry periods. Headquarters are located at the dam on Sunbury Road.

Boat ramps are located at Oxbow Road, Maxtown Road, at the west side of the Sunbury Road Bridge, near the dam off Walnut Street, and off Red Bank Road at the twin bridges. The water is generally clear, with 12 to 18 inches of visibility. Sailboats and small boats make up the bulk of the boat traffic; outboards are limited to 10 hp. Several small islands dot the north end. Main lake shoreline access is good on the lake's west side; access to several of the lake's larger inlets is on the east side. Hoover is an urban lake, lying in a north-south direction, with the dam at the south end. It is surrounded by residential neighborhoods and small villages.

The fishing: Despite having to put up with the occasional sailboat regatta and windsurfers, fishers in Hoover don't have to contend with Jet Skis and speedboats due to the 10-hp limit. However, it does make getting from point A to point B on such a large reservoir more time consuming, but good fishing shouldn't be hurried. And after a weekend at Alum Creek, you will appreciate Hoover's slower pace.

Bass fishing is relativity good at Hoover; it rates among the top five inland lakes in the tournament circuit. You'll find patterns here similar to other Ohio lakes, in that bass are shoreline oriented, utilizing overhanging trees, downed timber, and brush. In spring, bass are found at the lake's shallow north end between Oxbow and Galena, and as the weather warms, they gradually move toward the lake's deeper south end. Spring bass are caught on spinner and buzz baits, worked tight against the willows and shoreline cover and around the islands north of the Sunbury Road Bridge. This shoreline pattern still holds during summer, but points and ledges 6 to 8 feet deep on the lake's east shore between Sunbury Road Bridge and County Line Road start to pick up activity from anglers using plastics and tubes.

Look for big rock or boulder shorelines and points during the summer; work these areas with crank baits, lizards, and small plastic night crawlers. Jigs and tubes flipped to shoreline brush and wood in 3 or 4 feet of water is effective as well. The old creek channel that flows against the northeast bank in three places between the bridges is good during the summer and fall when worked deep with plastics.

Good catches of white bass are made in the headwaters at Big Walnut Creek near Galena during the spring run that occurs in late April and May. White bass continue to be picked up all summer long in the lake off the south causeway on County Line Bridge and near the popular public fishing area at the dam just off Walnut Street. Surface-feeding white bass can be observed periodically feeding on shad in the main lake. White Mepps, Rooster Tails, jigs, and crank baits fished 10 to 20 feet deep pick up most fish during the summer.

Saugeyes in Hoover are caught off the points between the County Line Bridge and the dam, on the lake's east bank in 6 to 8 feet of water by slow trolling or drifting brightly colored worm harnesses, weight-forward spinners, crank baits, and jig and worm combos. Look for shallow flats and shallow points in the lake's midsection on the west bank and along riprap. Saugeyes over 20 inches are common at Hoover, but fish are spread out and caught in every way imaginable. Shoreline anglers pick up saugeyes off the shallow banks using jigs and grubs, while other fishers trolling shad raps in 12 to 16 feet of water pick up their fair share, too. Look for fish along breaks and drops, humps, shallow flats, and points. Drifting night crawlers in 3 to 8 feet of water is popular. Hoover is stocked with saugeyes at 200 fingerlings per acre. Fishing is good for saugeyes throughout early spring, summer, and fall and at the tailwaters below Hoover Dam.

Crappies are plentiful at Hoover. Most are caught in the spring with minnows and bobbers in the backs of coves on the east and west banks. To find crappies, fish the brush, stickups, and any woody structure near shore and around boat docks in the spring. Come summer, crappies are found in 20 feet of water suspended over structure from Sunbury Road Bridge south. Hoover is abundant with small crappies, but a few 9- to 12-inch ones are usually in the mix.

Some nice channels come from Hoover; most of the fishing is done at the shallow north end around the Oxbow boat ramp and north into the headwaters. Fish Oxbow and the east side coves between the Sunbury Road Bridge and County Line Bridge after dark. Chicken liver, cut shad, and shrimp will do the job. A few flatheads are also caught from Hoover.

Bluegills in Hoover are of average size. Use wax worms and a bobber around brush and logs on the northeast side across from the Oxbow ramp.

There are record-size buffalo suckers in Hoover. Ohio state records in both the Hook & Line division and the Bowfishing division have come from these waters.

The shallow tailwaters can be accessed from roads off Sunbury Road and Central College Road and provide fishing for saugeyes in spring, fall, and winter and channel cat, largemouth, and smallmouth bass throughout the summer.

Special regulations: There is a 12-inch minimum on largemouth bass. Outboards are limited to 10 hp. Fishermen using pontoons or float tubes are required to stay within 25 feet of the shoreline.

Facilities/camping: Gas, food, and ice can be found at gas stations and convenience markets located at intersections near the south end. Camping is at nearby Alum Creek State Park campground, which has 289 sites.

Additional information: At the north end of the lake, near Galena, there is a boardwalk built over the shallow mudflats that is well worth the walk. Below the dam, you can observe an abundance of wading birds, gulls, and waterfowl. Several urban wildlife areas are located around Hoover Reservoir. The Old Dutchman, just south of the dam, is an old-style bait and tackle shop of which there aren't many of anymore.

Directions: Located northeast of Columbus, east of Highway 3.

11 Indian Lake

Key species: Saugeye, yellow perch, bluegill, white bass, channel catfish, and largemouth.

General description: Indian Lake has big bluegills in the spring and excellent saugeye fishing right from shore, but expect crowded fishing on this popular resort lake.

Overview: Indian Lake was originally a small natural lake. It became part of a larger impoundment called Lewistown Reservoir, which was built in the 1850s by impounding the North and South Forks of the Great Miami River to provide water for the Miami Canal. The enlarging of the lake began in 1856. Once completed, the lake covered 6,334 acres. After 1896 the lake was no longer used as a canal feeder; two years later the General Assembly created Indian Lake State Park. Today Indian Lake covers 5,800 acres and has over 30 miles of shoreline. The town of Russells Point, at the south end of the lake, has become a resort town of sorts, reflecting the general atmosphere of festivity that surrounds the lake during summer.

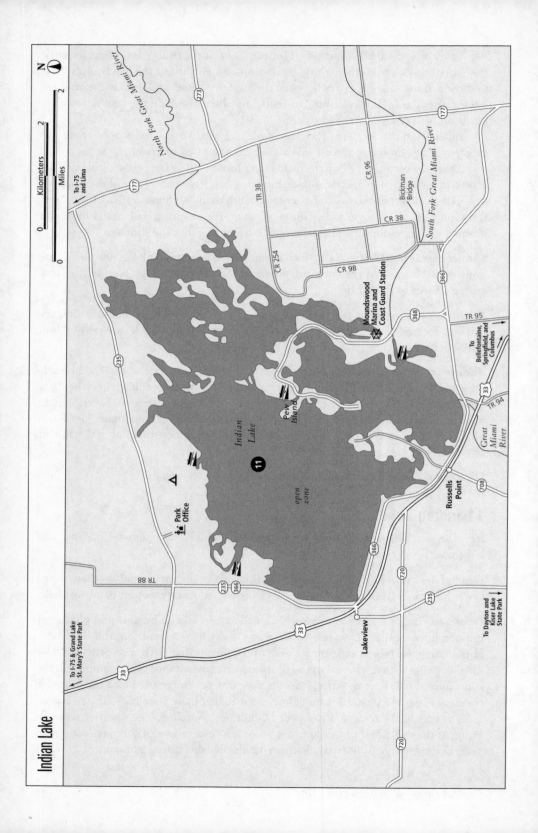

Summer cottages and high-dollar real estate surround Indian Lake. The resort-like atmosphere is further reinforced by numerous Jet Skiers, water skiers, and pleasure boaters who descend upon the lake during the summer months. You can pull your boat into a dock on one of the many canals at Russells Point and order a pizza, taco, or Big Mac. I understand one place will even deliver pizza to where you are fishing. Indian Lake is a lake of numerous small islands and peninsulas, miles of canals, and thousands of boat docks with thousands of boats attached to them. The majority of land around the lake is privately owned, and lakeside cottages dot the shoreline nearly everywhere. That's not to say the state park does not have its share of shoreline. Access for fishers is quite good at Indian Lake; with four boat ramps and many miles of shoreline access, whether you are a bank or boat fisher, this place has something for you.

There are numerous marinas, boat storage facilities, and repair shops on the water. There is wheelchair-accessible fishing at nearly every public area on the lake, numerous picnic areas right at the water's edge, and two swimming beaches. The campground is located at the northwestern edge of the lake, as is the park office—off Highway 235.

For the most part, the shoreline is covered with riprap rocks and boulders; some weed growth is present along the edges during summer, while patches of lily pads dot the headwaters. The water has a tint of green, making visibility a foot at best. Old underwater stumps are present in some parts of the lake, particularly at the upper end, and warning signs about them are posted at boat ramps. The lake is shallow with an average depth of 5 feet. The spillway is just east of Russells Point; below that spillway the Great Miami River begins.

The fishing: From all indications, fishing is not bad at Indian Lake. Saugeyes are perhaps the main draw, with most in the 15- to 18-inch range. Several whoppers in the 7- to 9-pound range have been turned in at various bait store contests across the lake. Most fishers just slowly troll the open flats or along the shorelines, picking up a few here and there. Shoreline fishers also have fairly good luck with the saugeyes. Fishing for saugeyes starts as soon as the weather breaks in spring and continues into the fall. When the lake freezes over, fishers cut a hole in the ice and continue to fish for them.

Bluegill fishing is very good. Many 9- to 10-inch 'gill are caught; a few that weigh over a pound have been caught during the spawn off any shoreline in late May and early June. Fishing through the ice is also productive for big bluegills. Red worms or wax worms under a bobber fished around dock and shoreline brush will catch bluegills.

Channel cat fishing is also good; nice eating-size channels make up the bulk of the catch. The occasional 10- to 12-pounder is found every once in a while. Most anglers fish from the shoreline anywhere on the lake with chicken livers and catch channels.

Ring perch up to a pound are caught, but most are much smaller. White bass are in the lake and provide a pretty good fishery. Some weigh as much as 2 pounds, with most averaging around 15 inches.

Bass fishing is fairly good at Indian Lake; numerous bass tournaments are held every month. Most bass average 12 to 14 inches; but 4- to 5-pounders are not that uncommon, and a couple that size will turn up at almost every tournament. For bass, fish the shoreline riprap, around docks and lily pads in the canals with spinner baits, plastics, and cranks.

Crappies are strong at Indian Lake, and some major crappie tournaments are held here every year. Crappies in the 12- to 15-inch range are caught around boat docks, old stumps, pilings, and piers during April and May.

There are fishing piers at Old Field Island and Pew Island. Some stream fishing to the upper South Fork of the Great Miami River is found at the Bickman covered bridge at County Road 38. It is possible that one could put in there and float down over a mile to the Moundwood boat ramp, where the stream enters the lake. Another stream opportunity is at the spillway just east of Russells Point, where the Great Miami begins. A parking area on Township Road 94 allows access to the tailwaters.

Special regulations: Unlimited horsepower, but complex no-ski and -wake zones; endless winding canals may be confusing for first-time Indian Lake boaters. Area maps don't show all the roads or canals, and I found myself consulting three different maps at certain times to find specific spots.

Facilities/camping: Russells Point has bed-and-breakfasts, cabins to rent, bait and tackle shops, a marina, and boat rentals, in addition to all the amenities you would need. There are also numerous small communities around the lake for gas, ice, bait, and groceries. Indian Lake State Park campground has 479 sites, a boat ramp, canals, docks, and a camp store.

Additional information: There is so much to see and do; I suggest you contact the Indian Lake Area Chamber of Commerce at (937) 843-5392 or visit their Web site at www.indianlakechamber.org.

Directions: Indian Lake is located approximately 10 miles northwest of Bellefontaine off U.S. Highway 33.

12 Kiser Lake

Key species: Channel catfish, largemouth bass, bluegill, hybrid striper, striper, crappie, some saugeye, yellow perch.

General description: Kiser is a wonderful little lake known to produce some big hybrid stripers.

Description: Kiser Lake is a small lake of 385 acres located in northeastern Champaign County. Kiser Lake State Park has a marina, boat rental, seasonal dock rental, two boat launches, hiking trails, picnic areas, shelters, a beach, and a primitive campground. The lake is weedy along the edges, with large lily pad fields covering a great deal of the shoreline. It is a shallow lake with an average depth of 10 feet. There are two gravel/rock fishing piers on opposite sides of the lake. Shoreline access is good.

Kiser Lake has boats available to rent, as do many state parks.

The fishing: Kiser Lake offers good fishing for just about everything contained in its shallow waters. Large hand-size bluegills and 14- to 15-inch black crappies are common catches in the spring. You can find crappies around the sailboat docks on the northern shore. The lake has a robust bass population that has been known to produce a few 5-pound-plus bass; fish for them around shoreline cover and the edges of lily pads and against the south bank.

Saugeyes were introduced, but fishing for them has not been productive.

The hybrid striper fishing has done well; a few 6- to 8-pound fish have been caught. A hybrid was caught in spring 2006 that was said to have weighed more than 15 pounds. Channel cat fishing is good. Some in the 6- to 7-pound range are caught, most with chicken livers or night crawlers fished off the piers and near the boat rental. Some fishing exists for perch, but the catch is generally few and small.

Kiser Lake is a no-motors lake, which means it is limited to canoes and row-boats. In 2006 the Division of Wildlife stopped stocking Kiser with hybrid stripers and began stocking pure striped bass with the hope of establishing a brood stock to be used for the future production of hybrid striped bass.

Special regulations: Nonmotorized craft only; no outboards or electric motors permitted.

ping: Kiser Lake State Park has 115 campsites, a dozen of which are
~~and park headquarters are at the marina located on Kiser Lake Road.
also at that location.

national information: The adjoining Kiser Lake Wetlands Preserve, administered
by the Ohio Department of Natural Resources Division of Natural Areas and Preserves, is worth a visit.

Directions: To get to Kiser Lake take U.S. Highway 36 west from Urbana 11 miles
to St. Paris, then north 3 miles on Kiser Lake Road.

13 Knox Lake

Key species: Largemouth bass, crappie, bluegill, channel and flathead catfish.

General description: A high-quality bass lake managed for trophy bass, with horsepower restrictions.

Overview: Impounded in 1954, Knox Lake covers 468 acres; depths range from 3
feet at the shallow east end to over 20 feet near the dam located at the west end. At
the east end of the lake, most of the standing timber was left during impoundment.
What remains today are a few old snags and acres of stumps. Three boat ramps, a
full-service marina on the lake's north side, and a combination boat rental/tackle
and bait shop is located at the lake's southwest corner. Stumps are thick at the east
end, which make boating difficult. Good wheelchair accessibility at the southwest
boat ramp is right at the good fishing spots.

The fishing: I'll go out on a limb here and say that Knox Lake is probably one of the
better bass lakes in Ohio. It is a joy to fish; it is remote, scenic, and has no water skiing or Jet Skiing. It is a lake built and managed for fishers. It offers high-quality fishing for bass and channel catfish and has produced a 38-pound lake record flathead.

The Division of Wildlife keeps the lake well stocked with channel cats. The lake
is popular with bass fishers but is not crowded. It is managed for trophy bass with
an 18-inch minimum size limit.

Channel cat fishing is excellent on Knox Lake, with a few reaching the 20-
pound range. Channels can be found in any of the lake's coves and at the stumpy
east end and are at times pesky.

The lake is best fished from a boat, but there is shoreline access at the lake's
southwest corner, at the boat ramps, at the dam, and along the county road at the
east end. Houseboat rental is available at the southwest marina, and that option is
popular with nighttime cat fishers.

Bass tournaments are held regularly at Knox Lake, but the 10-hp restriction limits most bass boats to electric-motor propulsion. Catches of bass are good, with fishers having 10- to 12-fish days. Most bass range from 12 to 16 inches, but 4- to
5-pounders are not uncommon. Bass fishers use brightly colored crank baits, Rapalas
worked on top, Slug-Go's, spinner baits, and plastics, and they pitch to shoreline

cover. In the spring most bass are concentrated at the stumpy, shallow east end, but gradually they move to the deeper waters in the center of the lake and toward the dam. The shoreline is rocky. There is very little weed growth, and a number of fallen trees, slips, and overhanging trees are found on the deep north bank, across from the boat rental. Bass are well distributed, and although there is not an abundance of shoreline access, a bank fisher could do well with what there is.

Bluegills are found everywhere, but they are average in size. Black crappies are caught in late March and April from the timber in the coves at the lake's west side. There is a minor tailwater fishery below the spillway for channel cats up to 5 pounds and smallmouth up to 13 inches. In all, Knox is a rewarding place to spend the day.

Special regulations: There is an 18-inch size limit on bass. Outboards are restricted to a maximum of 10 hp.

Facilities/camping: Boat rental for houseboats and V-bottoms, with or without motors, is available at the lake's southwest marina. There are no camping facilities at the lake.

Additional information: Nearby Fredericktown has all the amenities and a couple of fine old-style diners.

Directions: Knox Lake lies northeast of Fredericktown. It can be accessed off U.S. Highway 95. The lake's south side can be reached off Armentrout Road.

14 Kokosing Lake

Key species: Largemouth bass, channel and bullhead catfish, bluegill, crappie.

General description: A small, shallow lake good for channel cats and bass.

Overview: This is a minor lake of 150 acres impounded by the U.S. Army Corps of Engineers for flood control purposes on the Upper Muskingum River watershed. The impounded body of water is at the headwaters of the north branch of the Kokosing River and is managed by the Muskingum Watershed Conservancy District (MWCD). Its official name is the North Branch of Kokosing Lake. There is a MWCD campground, boat ramp, beach, and picnic area on the lake's south shore. Access is limited to the dam-spillway area and the Kokosing campground.

The fishing: Kokosing Lake is best fished from a boat, as most of the lake sits in the center of the Kokosing Lake Wildlife Area. The campground and boat ramp are the only close shoreline access areas. Access to the dam is more for the view, but it is possible to reach the shoreline with some effort.

Channel cats are the most sought-after catch here, and some 5-pound channels do turn up. Fish chicken livers, cut shad, or night crawlers from the dam or off the shoreline at the boat ramp and camping area. The best fishing is usually at night but late afternoons are productive too.

Kokosing Lake is a shallow lake that averages 6 to 8 feet in depth, with some 15-foot water at the dam. There are stumps and some remaining timber in the coves. Bass are found scattered throughout, but stick to the old creek channel, the deep point across from the campground, and the riprap along the face of the dam. Spinner baits and plastic night crawlers work well. At times bass fishing is considered good on Kokosing, and it occasionally ranks high on the list of productive tournament lakes.

Crappies are found around the many stickups, stumps, and fallen trees in April and May and can be caught with minnows and small tube jigs. Bluegills of average size are best found in the shallows during spawning time in early June and in the shoreline brush in summer.

With some effort you can access the upper Kokosing stream for smallmouth and rock bass by following the trail north from the parking area across from township road T-376 and again at á parking area east of Batemantown.

Special regulations: Outboards are limited to a maximum of 10 hp.

Facilities/camping: Kokosing Lake Campground has 46 sites. Ice, bait, snacks, and firewood are available at the campground headquarters.

Additional information: There is a large grassland and marsh area at the lake's north end that offers a variety of wildlife-viewing opportunities.

Directions: The lake is 3 miles northwest of Fredericktown on County Road C-6.

15 Kokosing River

Key species: Smallmouth bass, sunfish, rock bass, channel catfish.

General description: Fish by canoe or bike or wade on one of Ohio's most scenic streams.

Overview: Designated a State Scenic River in 1997, Kokosing is the kind of stream of which there are too few in Ohio. Flowing through rural farm country, steep wooded hillsides, and sandstone cliffs, the Kokosing is well worthy of its scenic river designation.

The Kokosing River starts west of the Morrow-Knox County line and continues for 48 miles downstream to its confluence with the Mohican River. While there are a number of public access areas downstream of Mount Vernon to the Mohican River, the access is limited upstream of town.

The Kokosing is part of the Ohio Water Trails, a joint venture by state, local, and private agencies to promote public canoeing, kayaking, and fishing along selected waterways and to encourage public access along those streams. For the canoe or kayak fisher, there are nine well-marked canoe launches on the Kokosing Water Trail.

A paved recreation path known as the Kokosing Gap Trail follows the old Pennsylvania Railroad line, paralleling the stream for 9 miles to the village of Howard. The recreation trail also provides fishing access to the stream either by walking or bicycling to various points along the stream. A rod tube strapped to a

The Kokosing River is a good smallmouth stream and has numerous canoe drop-offs, plenty of fishing access, and a bike trail that follows its course.

bike would allow fishing at locations on the stream that cannot be reached by car. Another option, should you decide to float, is to place a bike at a downstream location on the bike trail, eliminating the need for a second vehicle, and ride the bike back to your original starting point.

The fishing: Six government agencies have contributed to provide public access sites on the Kokosing River. As a result, there are numerous fishing options. Canoe launches are well marked and vary in distances, offering a variety of float options from short trips to overnighters. The Kokosing Gap Trail offers biker and hiker fishers approximately 12 miles of stream from which to fish. Parking at bike trail terminals is available at Phillips Park in Mount Vernon, at Laymon Road Bridge near Gambier, and at the Pipesville Road Bridge near Howard. If you like to park and fish, you can do so at any canoe launch or at pulloffs along the 4 miles of Lower Gambier Road east of Mount Vernon. The Gambier Road stretch is a mixture of small pools and long deep riffles and offers easy wading and a short scenic drive.

Smallmouth fishing is good all along the stream. Small crank baits, foxtail Mepps, and tubes fished in the deep runs and at the head and tail of pools in the evenings will bring solid strikes from 10- to 16-inch smallmouth. Kokosing is a good stream to wade and fish; long shallow riffles and easy wading along the shoreline allow an angler to leisurely fish from one pool to the next. Wide and open enough for fly casting, it is still a stream small enough to be intimate with as you get to know every rock and riffle. Olive or black bead-head Woolly Buggers, hoppers, and crayfish imitations worked in the deep riffles and chutes and at the head and tail of pools will grab any smallmouth's attention. The only mistake you can make is to not fish it. Good water exists throughout the Kokosing. Rock bass and sunfish are also in good numbers, as are channel cats in the slower pools near the Mohican River.

Access is in the town of Mount Vernon at Riverside and Phillips Park, on Lower Gambier Road, at the Laymon Road Bridge, at Big Run Road Bridge, at Pipesville Bridge, beneath Millwood Bridge at Millwood, at Riley Road Bridge, and at the end of Township Road 423 in Coshocton County.

Special regulations: State game and fish laws apply.

Facilities/camping: The towns of Mount Vernon and Gambier have all the amenities. There are two campgrounds on the Kokosing River near the village of Millwood. Kokosing Valley Camp and Canoe is located west of Millwood on US 36, and the Caves Campground is located southeast of Millwood on Austin Road.

Additional information: Take a minute to visit the old historic 1940 Alco locomotive and the 1924 Chesapeake and Ohio caboose next to the recreation trail at Gambier.

Directions: All public access areas on the Kokosing River can be reached east of Mount Vernon, off U.S. Highway 229, US 36, and Highway 715.

16 Mad River

Key species: Brown trout, smallmouth bass.

General description: Ohio's premier brown trout stream.

Overview: The Mad River in Champaign, Logan, and Clark Counties is Ohio's oldest man-made trout fishery; it is also arguably the state's most well known. The making of the Mad was one of Ohio's earliest attempts at channeling. The Mad has been altered, straightened, strangled, dammed, and domesticated. Evidence of its old channel is visible here and there, and every once in a while it tries to find it. Through the marvels of engineering, we created a trout stream. We cracked the bedrock of the river and unleashed its fountains of spring water. Perhaps a trout stream was there all along, we just had to uncover it. The substantial flow of groundwater that percolates through the gravel bed has kept the Mad River well under 65 degrees throughout the summer. The Mad is now a spring creek and ideal to support trout.

Records indicate that trout were first stocked into the Mad in the late 1800s. The Division of Wildlife began stocking rainbows before World War II and continued that practice until the mid-1980s. After that, brown trout were exclusively stocked, and this continues today. An estimated 15,000 6- to 8-inch brown trout are stocked into the Mad each fall, plus additional stockings of trout when available. To reach 12 inches, trout grow at an astonishing rate to double their size in a little over two years.

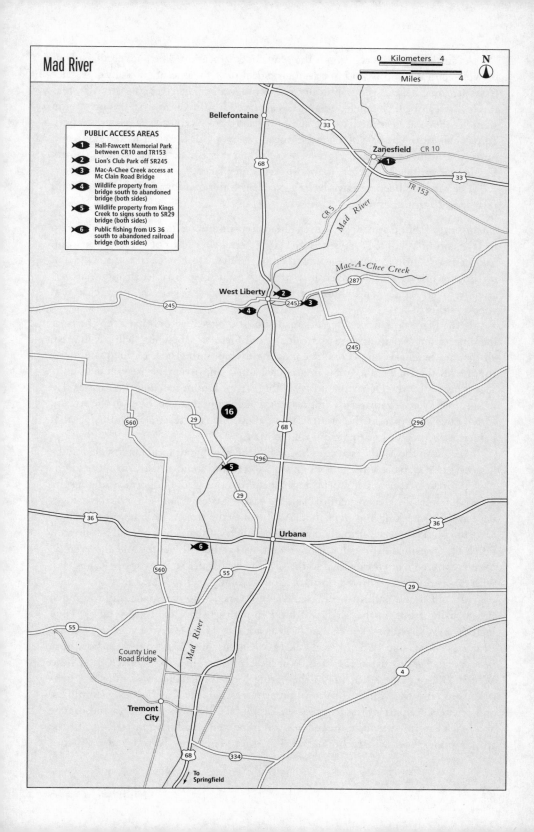

Mad River

Kilometers 0 — 4

Miles 0 — 4

N

PUBLIC ACCESS AREAS

1. Hall-Fawcett Memorial Park between CR10 and TR153
2. Lion's Club Park off SR245
3. Mac-A-Chee Creek access at Mc Clain Road Bridge
4. Wildlife property from bridge south to abandoned bridge (both sides)
5. Wildlife property from Kings Creek to signs south to SR29 bridge (both sides)
6. Public fishing from US 36 south to abandoned railroad bridge (both sides)

Bellefontaine

33

Zanesfield   CR 10

68   1

33

TR 153

CR 5

Mad River

Mac-A-Chee Creek

287

West Liberty   2

245   245   3

4

245

16

560   29

68   296

296

5

29

36   36

560   Urbana

6

55   29

55

Mad River

County Line Road Bridge

4

Tremont City

68   334

To Springfield

As surprising as its creation is the Mad River's location. The flat rural farmland of west-central Ohio would not seem a logical pick for one of the state's premier trout streams, neither geographically nor geologically. The river's mostly flat, featureless streambed, channeled straight as a surveyor's line, is at first an uncommon sight to those accustomed to the tumbling and rocky trout streams in southern Appalachia or the beauty of a western meadow river. But the river has strength and purpose as it flows over a firm gravel bottom, and it is as clear as a mountain stream. Cooled by springs and shade, it almost seems misplaced.

The Mad has been noted as having excellent water quality and fisheries' surveys revealed 120 trout per mile.

The fishing: Trout do grow large in the Mad. Ten-pound trout occasionally show up in Division of Wildlife studies; trout that size are believed to be 7 to 10 years old. Yet their seduction is not an easy matter and requires all the stealth and finesse that a roadside brown in a Pennsylvania stream would. Dependable, prolific hatches, aquatic invertebrates, and abundant mottled sculpins provide the prey base that supports this fishery.

If the Mad has a dark side, it is made up of the two factors that keep the river from becoming a truly first-class trout stream. First, the spawning habit is limited; all fish are hatchery supported. Second, the disappointing lack of adequate cover suppresses the Mad's potential. In-stream habitat improvements at various public access points by the Department of Wildlife, Trout Unlimited, and the various fly-fishing clubs have dramatically improved the fishing in those sections of the stream. Catch rates have increased tenfold in those areas. This is a testament to the fact that habitat is the key to locating trout on the Mad.

Access on the Mad has always been with the blessing of local landowners. Public access is at Urbana at the U.S. Highway 36 crossing and downstream at the Highway 55 Bridge. Access is at most bridges that cross the Mad, but permission must be secured. Some old Department of Wildlife easements exist and some of the bridges have areas for parking and steps that lead down to the stream. U.S. Highway 68 follows the Mad between Springfield and West Liberty, then County Road 5 follows it north to Zanesfield. Trout distribute themselves rather efficiently, and they can be found scattered from Springfield to the shallow headwater streams above Zanesfield, with most trout concentrated north of County Line Road to West Liberty.

My old friend and fly-fishing guide, Will Gray, who has spent way too much time chasing trout on the Mad, was kind enough to share his top fly picks. They include a Gold-Ribbed Hare's Ear bead head, size 12 & 14; Adams, size 14 & 16; Prince Nymph, size 12 & 14; and Elk Hair Caddis, size 12 through 16. For those deep-pocket big trout on the Mad, Will likes an olive, brown, or black bead-head Woolly Bugger, size 10 & 12. In the spring look for hatches of caddisflies, hendricksons, and blue quills. In the summer terrestrials such as beetles, caterpillars, and crickets are part of the trout's diet. Come fall, blue-winged olives and orange and black caterpillars make the menu. And in winter, small nymphs seem to be the trout's preference. Will recommends a 7½-foot, 4-weight fly rod and a 7½-foot leader tapered down to 4x for the close confines of the Mad. Spin fishers will find the trout attracted to small, brightly colored spinners. The stream averages 30 to 40 feet wide, and is 2 to 3 feet deep, with high, tree-lined, brushy banks. The Mad has long gravel runs, broken by occasional pools and riffles, and some undercut banks.

The Mad is a pure cold-water trout stream to a point, but once it enters the suburbs of Springfield, it is a warm-water fishery with all the usual suspects, including smallmouth bass, rock bass, and sunfish. In fact the Mad held the state record smallmouth bass for 51 years, a giant of a fish that weighed 7.5 pounds and was more than 24 inches long. Smallmouth fishing on the south Mad is considered fairly good. Access is still at most bridge crossings, the Old Ohio Edison Plant, Huffman Dam, Eastwood, and Deeds Park in Dayton.

In a state not known for its trout fishery, the Mad offers an outlet for the serious, dedicated fly-fisher. Fly shops have been named after it, as well as inspiring trout clubs. Books and articles have been written about it; committees have formed to preserve its welfare. The Mad has friends, and in these days, rivers need friends.

Special regulations: Minimum size for trout on the Mad River is 12 inches.

Facilities/camping: The Mad is floatable. Birch Bark Canoe Livery (937-652-2663), just west of Urbana, will rent canoes and provide shuttles and has camping for canoe-rental customers.

Additional information: Cedar Bog Nature Preserve is located south of Urbana and was the first nature preserve in Ohio, purchased with state funds in 1942.

Directions: Mad River can be easily reached from numerous county roads and highways west of US 68 north and south of Urbana.

17 Madison Lake

Key species: Largemouth bass, channel catfish, bluegill, crappie.

General description: A small, quiet lake limited to electric motors only.

Overview: Madison Lake was impounded in 1947 on land deeded to the state for the specific purpose of building a lake on Deer Creek stream. Lying within walking distance of a tiny village named after the lake, Madison Lake resembles a small, sleepy community lake at only 106 acres. The Madison Lake State Park that surrounds the lake has a boat ramp, picnic areas, a shelter house, a beach, and a small hiking trail. The park headquarters is located at Deer Creek State Park; however, a small office is maintained at Madison Lake at the park entrance off Cheseldine Road. Madison is a shallow lake, averaging 4 to 6 feet deep, with thick lily pads at the shallow north end and several small bays and inlets along its banks. There is good bank access at the lake's south end, but you need a boat to get to the north end. The lake is a little over a mile long and 1,000 feet across at its widest point. The boat ramp is located at the park entrance.

The fishing: Some good fishing for small 12- to 15-inch bass can be found by fishing right up against the banks of Madison Lake. Throw spinner baits and plastics to shoreline cover wherever it exists and to riprap along the face of the dam. In the shallow north end and in the backs of coves, fish the holes in the moss and around lily pads with lizards and weedless moss frogs. Some good bass have been taken this way. Madison is a shallow lake; work the shoreline for bass.

Some nice crappies have come from Madison; stringers of 12- to 16-inch white crappies are displayed on the bait store walls. In spring, fish shoreline cover on the west bank with minnows and minnow-tipped jigs. Fish around the small island located on the lake's west shore. There is good fishing right off the bank.

Plenty of bluegills of average size can be caught right off the shore using wax worms and a bobber.

There is very good channel cat fishing at Madison. On a good night, catches of 20 to 30 cats can be made, with some as big as 5 to 6 pounds. The best fishing is near the creek channel, off both banks, but any place on the shore will yield channels. Occasionally a nice flathead shows up, too. Use chicken livers and chubs for cats; the best fishing is always after dark.

On occasion hybrid striped bass show up in Madison Lake as a result of the fish washing over the spillway from the private Choctaw Lake. Choctaw Lake is stocked with hybrid stripers and is located several miles upstream from Madison Lake.

There is no public fishing in the tailwaters below the dam, as the area is on private property.

Special regulations: Electric motors only.

Facilities/camping: There is a small bait and tackle store on Payne-Thompson Road just west of the lake. Camping is at nearby Deer Creek State Park, with 227 campsites.

Additional information: If you're into snapping turtles, check out the collection of turtle shells at the local bait and tackle shop.

Directions: Take Highway 665 east from London to Spring Valley Road. Turn south to Madison Lake Sate Park.

18 Mount Gilead Lake

Key species: Largemouth bass, bluegill, channel catfish, some crappie, carp, trout in the spring.

General description: Two small, shallow, and weedy lakes; the lower lake is stocked with trout in the spring.

Overview: Mount Gilead Lake is actually two small lakes, totaling 30 acres, built between 1900 and 1930 and separated by an old concrete dam. The upper lake is more marsh than lake. The lower lake is also weedy but does harbor channel cats, bass, carp, small bluegill, and trout. The state park has a campground, boat rental, nature center, and picnic area. The old concrete boat ramp, located near the upper dam, is suitable only to hand launch a small boat.

The fishing: When the trout are gone by summer, there is an abundance of small bluegills, bass, and channel cats and some big carp. Surprisingly a few local anglers do quite well on bass. The lower lake is weedy and mossy along the south bank, but it is still fishable in the pockets and along the mossy edge, where you may pick up a nice bass or a bluegill. Try fishing over the moss with plastic worms and moss frogs; some 5-pound bass have been caught this way. Top-water fishing produces well both morning and evening.

The north shore of the lower lake is the deepest part of the lake, with its overhanging and downed trees, but you'll need a small boat to reach it. Shoreline access is on the south side of the lower lake and at both dams. Some nice channel cats can be caught off the dam at the lower lake. This is a good place to bring the kids to catch that first bluegill. Mount Gilead Lake is very popular with local fishers when it is stocked with 10- to 12-inch rainbows in late March.

Special regulations: Limit for trout is five fish per day. Only electric motors are permitted.

Facilities/camping: The campground has 65 sites; group camping is at the dam.

Additional information: Nearby Mount Gilead has all the amenities.

Directions: Take Highway 95, 1 mile east of the town of Mount Gilead.

19 Oakthorpe Lake

Key species: Largemouth bass, redear, sunfish, crappie.

General description: A little-fished, hard-to-find, high-quality bass lake.

Overview: One of a number of lakes impounded as a watershed project on the upper Hocking River watershed, Oakthorpe Lake covers 41 acres and has a primitive boat ramp. Thick lily pads cover the shallow northern end, but there are open pockets and an open deep channel that runs through the center of the growth. Access is at the dam off Pleasantville Road, which requires a steep climb up and down, but it is the only way to access any shoreline fishing. Fishing from a small boat is the best way to access the fishing.

The fishing: Oakthorpe is a high-quality bass lake. It is relativity clear, with 1 to 2 feet of visibility. This is probably one of central Ohio's best places to catch a bass worthy of the wall. Bass up to 7 pounds have come from here, with loads of bass in the 12- to 20-inch range. The best bass fishing is done along the west shoreline among the overhanging trees and shoreside timber. Some good bass are also caught along the deeper edge of the lily pads at the lake's south shore and across from the ramp in the channel. Lizards and worms worked deep against the shoreline seem to do the job.

Redear sunfish are found in the same places as the bass and are frequently caught by bass anglers. Oakthorpe is the only lake in central Ohio that contains redear sunfish. The best fishing for them is in May and June, with some fish getting up to 9 to 11 inches.

Oakthorpe Lake also offers good crappie fishing, with a few up to 12 inches caught on minnows and crappie jigs in the same cover as the bass every spring.

Special regulations: Electric motors only.

Facilities/camping: There are no facilities or camping. Rushville is the closest town.

Additional information: Rushville has some nice old-town shops worthy of a visit, and nearby Rush Creek Lake is a fine catfish lake.

Directions: Travel Highway 664 north to Pleasantville Road and turn east past the small town of Oakthorpe. A gravel lane leads north; there is an Oakthorpe Lake Wildlife Area sign just past the entrance. To get to the boat ramp, continue south past the entrance, turn north onto Indian Run Road, and turn east on Grubb Road, which dead-ends at the lake.

20 O'Shaughnessy Reservoir

Key species: Largemouth bass, saugeye, bluegill, crappie, channel catfish, white bass.

General description: One of three Columbus city reservoirs providing good bass fishing close to town with no horsepower restrictions.

Overview: Impounded by the city of Columbus in 1925, O'Shaughnessy is one of two early reservoirs created on the Scioto River for water usage and storage. Located 4 miles north of Griggs Reservoir, O'Shaughnessy is more than 6 miles long but less than a quarter mile wide, covering nearly 900 surface acres. Like Griggs, it resembles a river more than a lake and is administered by the City of Columbus Division of Watershed Management. The reservoir and dam are named in honor of Jerry O'Shaughnessy, who was superintendent of Columbus City Water Works at the time of his death in 1921.

O'Shaughnessy has three boat ramps and a number of city park shoreline access sites on the east shore off Highway 257. Like all Columbus city reservoirs, O'Shaughnessy flows in a nearly straight north-south direction. The water has good visibility and averages between 20 to 40 feet deep at the south end. The lake's primary boat ramp is located on the east shoreline, just south of the Home Road Bridge. Another smaller ramp is located at the O'Shaughnessy Twin Lakes Nature Preserve on the west side, and a third ramp is located near the headwaters at the village of Bellepoint, north of the intersection of Highway 745 and US 42.

The fishing: Bass in O'Shaughnessy are creatures of shallow water, relating primarily to shoreline cover, weeds, and riprap. One of the top bass tournament lakes in the state, O'Shaugnessy has an abundance of 12- to 16-inch bass. Pitch plastic worms, tubes, and lizards into fallen trees and shoreline brush on both banks. In the backwaters south of the US 42 Bridge, flip 4- to 6-inch watermelon lizards right to the edge of the water willows. Look for logs, bank slips, and riprap around the bridge to find bass. Small rocky, weedy points along the lake's southeast side produce well with crank baits. The coves are good in the spring, but concentrate on shoreline structures throughout the summer.

Almost a small lake in itself, the Twin Lakes Area on the lake's west shore can be accessed off Highway 745 at the O'Shaughnessy Twin Lakes Nature Preserve for a quiet day of bank or small-boat fishing. Bass, bluegills, crappies, and channel cats can be caught here. Boat access to the main lake is gained by going under the Highway 745 Bridge.

Saugeyes are found near the ledges and drop-offs south of the Home Road Bridge on the east bank. Like the other Columbus Lakes, night crawler harnesses do well. Some shallow points also exist just south of the US 42 Bridge on the east bank. Saugeye fishing is not great on O'Shaughnessy itself, due to the migratory nature of the fish. The best saugeye fishing is below the dam after periods of high water and during late winter and early spring runoff. Below the dam, tailwater access is gained on the west side of the dam, off Glick Road. For tailwater saugeyes, use brightly colored jigs and twister tail grubs in the big pool below the dam.

Fish for channel cats north of Home Road Bridge; pulloffs and shoreline access spots are readily available from Highway 257–Riverside Drive along the east shoreline. There also is good channel cat fishing below the dam during the summer, with channels ranging anywhere from 15 to 24 inches long. Fish the west side of the big pool immediately below the dam.

Bluegills are caught the usual way, by fishing shoreline brush and around the east bank coves with worms and a bobber. You can count on a good number of hand-size bluegills especially during the spring spawn in early June.

Crappie fishing is nothing to write home about, but there are some fish to be found. Fish the Twin Lakes area and several of the small east-side coves in early spring with minnows and a bobber. Main-lake shoreline brush and wood always hold crappies. Crappies in O'Shaughnessy range from 6 to 10 inches long.

White bass fishing in O'Shaughnessy is a spring sport practiced upstream north of the US 42 Bridge in late April and May. Fish white spinners where the Scioto River enters the lake at Bellepoint. Continue to fish upstream in the Scioto River along pulloffs on Klondike Road and farther north on River Road. Just south of the town of Prospect on River Road is a small lowhead dam with a pulloff and access next to it.

Special regulations: There is a 12-inch minimum length limit on bass. Fishers who use pontoons or float tubes are required to stay within 25 feet of the shoreline.

Facilities/camping: Gas stations and convenience stores are located at the south end of the lake. Camping is not permitted at the lake.

Additional information: The Columbus Zoo entrance is located on Highway 257 next to the dam.

Directions: Take the Sawmill Road exit north off I-270 to Powell Road and then turn west to Highway 257.

21 Rock Mill Lake

Key species: Largemouth bass, bluegill, channel catfish.

General description: A small remote lake best fished from a small boat or float tube.

Overview: Rock Mill Lake is one of several lakes impounded as part of the Upper Hocking Watershed Project. The lake covers 18 acres. Lily pads abound in the shallow east end of the lake. The water is deeper at the west end where the dam is. There is good shoreline cover on the north shore, consisting of overhanging and fallen trees.

The fishing: Rock Mill Lake has two parking areas; use the lower parking area to launch small watercraft. The upper parking area has a long footpath that leads to the dam, where shoreline fishing is available. There is good fishing for channel cats at the dam. Bass fishing can be done from shore, but a small boat would be of great benefit. The water is not very clear, but visibility is 6 inches to a foot. The best bass fishing is along the edges of the lily pads near deeper water and against the north shore. Plenty of cover exists along the steep and deep banks on the north shore. Access by foot to the north shore is problematic. Bass fishing is considered fair, but the lake is not heavily fished. Some good bass are bound to be hiding in the shore-line snags. Bluegills are also plentiful, but small.

Special regulations: Electric motors only.

Facilities/camping: There are no facilities; the nearest town is Lancaster.

Additional information: It is worth the side trip to see the Rock Mill Covered Bridge and the old gristmill. A very photogenic waterfall is there, and on hot summer days local boys jump 30 feet into the deep mill pool below.

Directions: Approximately 5 miles west of Lancaster on Highway 188, take Mount Zion Road north.

22 Rush Creek Lake

Key species: Largemouth bass, channel catfish, bluegill, crappie.

General description: Rush Creek Lake has timbered coves, stumps, good shoreline access, and excellent fishing for channel cats.

Overview: Impounded in 1983 as a result of the Rush Creek Watershed Project on the Upper Hocking watershed, the lake covers 302 acres and has 9 miles of shoreline. The lake averages 10 to 15 feet deep. There is one concrete boat ramp, which is wheelchair accessible. There is standing timber in the coves; stumps, cover, and riprap abound all along the shoreline. The Rush Lake Wildlife Area surrounds the lake. The shoreline near the boat ramp is trashy and spotted with old fire pits.

The fishing: Rush Creek Lake is highly regarded locally as a good catfish lake. Every summer night, anglers fishing for the whiskered fish are posted along its banks. Night crawlers, chicken livers, minnows, and chubs—and just about anything else that attracts catfish—will suffice as bait. The more popular spots are the parking area near the boat ramp and the first pulloff as you enter the wildlife area on Thornville Road.

There is some bass fishing, but most bass run small. However, I am told that some 6-pound bass are awaiting the right cast. The backs of timber coves and along the south bank across from the caretaker's house near the boat ramp are the right places to pick up a bucket mouth. Of course one needs a boat to access these spots. Crappies are present but not large. Fish for them around sticking-up and standing timber. Bluegills are here as well, with a few reaching the size of a hand. For the most part they are caught near the shore during May and June by anglers using wax worms.

Special regulations: There is a 10-hp limit and a 15-inch size limit on bass.

Facilities/camping: No facilities; the nearest small town is Rushville.

Additional information: Rushville has some interesting little shops and small-town dining establishments.

Directions: Take US 22 east from Lancaster approximately 12 miles and then turn north onto Thornville Road.

Northwest Ohio—Wildlife District Two

Northwest Ohio does not have nearly the same fishing opportunities that other parts of the state offer. That is not to say there are not some outstanding fisheries here. The whole area is relativity flat and drains slowly, thus many rivers and streams are slow moving and stay murky most of the time. The western basin of Lake Erie is the primary fishery in the northwest corner of the state. The small-mouth and walleye fishing put the place on the map. Each spring beginning in late March, when the walleye begin their spawning run up the Maumee and the Sandusky Rivers, an angling madness grips anglers from across Ohio. After the spring run, walleye fishing shifts to the big lake, and the harbor town of Port Clinton becomes the walleye capital of the world.

Outside of Lake Erie there is some fine bluegill and bass fishing in the far-west corner at the Lake La Su An Wildlife Area. A little south are some quarry ponds named after two influential northwest Ohio outdoor writers that offer superb bass, bluegill, and trout fishing. Throughout northwest Ohio there are a number of upground reservoirs that offer quality fishing. Clear Fork Reservoir is one of the top lakes in Ohio for muskies.

The upper Sandusky River is a very good smallmouth stream. The Maumee at Independence Dam is a top spot for big flatheads. The Vermilion River gets a spring run of steelhead. Clearfork is a beauty of a trout stream and one of the most scenic. On the other hand, Cold Creek at the Castalia Hatchery is like dying and going to trout heaven.

If I had to pick one place in northwest Ohio, I'd take North Bass Island and fish my life away for smallmouth bass.

23 Bible Park Lake

Bible Park Lake is located at small, nicely maintained Williams County Park southeast of Montpelier on County Road J. I estimate the lake at 8 to 10 acres; it contains bass, bluegill, and channel catfish. The park has picnic areas, shelter houses, restrooms, and carry-in boat access only. The lake is weedy, with some good shoreline cover along the south bank. The lake is primarily a small bluegill and bass pond where local folks gather for family reunions, picnics, and a little fishing.

24 Castalia Trout Hatchery—Cold Creek

Key species: Rainbow trout.

General description: Premier trout fishing on Cold Creek by drawing only.

Overview: In 1997 the Ohio Division of Wildlife purchased Castalia Trout Hatchery from a private concern. The hatchery came on line that fall, and the trout reared

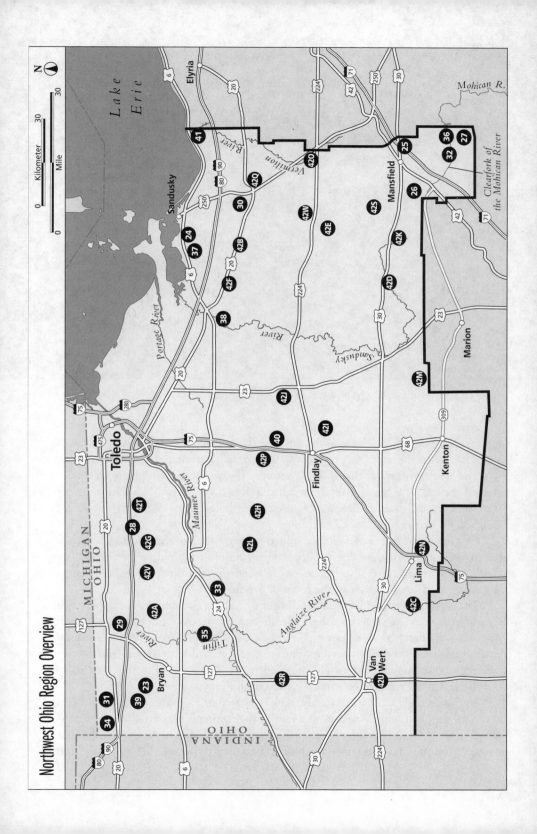

Northwest Ohio Region Overview

Cold Creek permits trout fishing by a special drawing only.

at this facility are the backbone of the catchable trout program and the steelhead program. Each year the hatchery produces 80,000 catchable trout and 400,000 steelhead.

The cold springwater that is used to supply the hatchery comes from an above-ground welling of a large spring hole called a blue hole. Several "blue holes" exist around the area; one of the more famous blue holes is located in the town of Castalia, known as the "Duck Pond."

Originally the blue holes simply spilled out over the ground, creating a marsh. But in 1810, channels were dug to supply a gristmill with running water. The entire Cold Creek stream system is a human-made, hand-dug stream that eventually empties into Lake Erie, just west of the town of Sandusky.

The water from the blue holes is devoid of oxygen and could not support fish if various devices and structures that generate oxygen were not placed in the stream. Water for the hatchery does not come from Cold Creek. Instead it comes from a blue hole located on the hatchery grounds that is enriched with oxygen and used in the raceway to support the hatchery-raised trout. The raceway water eventually ends up in Cold Creek at the hatchery entrance on Heywood Road.

Approximately 0.5 mile of Cold Creek is located on the hatchery grounds. It is kept well supplied with 2- to 3-pound rainbows. Fishing is permitted on the hatchery portion of Cold Creek by an annual lottery held in March. Anglers wishing to sample this one-of-a-kind trout fishing experience must submit an application

Cold Creek trout like these are the reason anglers enter the drawing.

between December 1 and January 31. A nonrefundable application fee of three dollars is required. If an angler is chosen, he or she receives a permit by mail; that successful angler may bring two other adults and three youths. A successful applicant or guest of that applicant may fish on the hatchery grounds only one time per year. Successful applicants are notified of the date. Fishing is from 7:00 a.m. to 12 noon, Monday through Friday only, except holidays. Nearly 4,000 to 5,000 anglers apply for the 128 available spots.

The fishing: The hatchery portion of Cold Creek looks like trout heaven. The gentle flowing stream serpentines through hatchery grounds, its pools and riffles loaded with large trout. It is a once-in-a-lifetime experience to fish here, and it's easy to forget that these are fairly dumb hatchery-reared trout, even if they are big. Most trout average 2 to 3 pounds, but there are a few that approach steelhead size. They will take anything from a delicately laid-out caddis fly to a gob of night crawlers. Most anglers take a five fish limit in less than two hours. There is no catch-and-release fishing; all trout caught must be kept.

Fishing is from the mowed banks; there is a shelter house and restroom along the way. For a while you can almost imagine being a member of a wealthy trout club, fishing on nicely manicured club grounds. Take it all in, and please, invite me along if you get drawn.

Special regulations: Anglers are limited to five trout; privilege to fish the hatchery portion of Cold Creek is by random drawing only. Applications are available online at www.ohiodnr.com/wildlife.

The hatchery is open to the public from 8:00 a.m. to 3:00 p.m., Monday through Friday, except holidays.

Facilities/camping: Other than a restroom and shelter house, there are no facilities and no camping on hatchery grounds. Nearby, the small village of Castalia has everything.

Additional information: Just west of Sandusky, Clear Creek empties into Lake Erie. There is a small private dock called Cold Creek Trout Camp that charges a small fee to fish from its dock. Anglers regularly catch plenty of trout there.

Directions: Castalia Hatchery is located on Heywood Road just north of Castalia off Highway 269.

25 Charles Mill Lake

Key species: Largemouth bass, crappie, hybrid striper, saugeye, bluegill, channel and flathead catfish.

General description: Another excellent tailwater fishery for saugeye.

Overview: Charles Mill Lake was impounded by the U.S. Army Corps of Engineers in 1935 for the purpose of flood control on the Upper Muskingum River watershed. The 1,350-acre lake is administered by the Muskingum Watershed Conservancy District (MWCD). The MWCD maintains the Charles Mill Lake Park, which has camping areas, a beach, a full-service marina, a boat ramp, a restaurant, and docking.

As a flood control lake, Charles Mill Lake is subject to fluctuating lake levels, with normal fluctuations generally 6 feet or less a year. The lake is lowered 3 feet on November 1, but is back up to normal levels by April. The lake is stained and murky with visibility less than 12 inches.

The lake has an average depth of only 5 to 6 feet. The shoreline is shallow, slopes gradually, and has abundant cover in the way of fallen trees, bank slips, old snags, and brush. Many peninsulas and islands are found in this lake.

Shoreline access is excellent for an MWCD lake, with access along Highway 430, at the bridge and boat ramp, and inside main park entrance. Below the dam is a park and access to the tailwaters.

The fishing: Bass fishing is fairly good at Charles Mill Lake. Most bass average 1 to 2 pounds, with a few 5-pound bass picked up every now and then. Most bass fishing is confined to the deeper east section of the lake. Chartreuse and white spinner baits work well in the stained water. Bass are taken from shoreline cover east of the South Peninsula Cottage Area and off the east bank of Fisherman's Point. Work the entire west bank of Mifflin Cottage Peninsula, throwing to every submerged tree and shoreline snag. The south end of the South Peninsula Bay has plenty of submerged timber, which you shouldn't overlook either. There are some rare lily pads at the mouth of the east bay near the dam that have started to attract bass as well. Plastics, worms, tubes, and buzz baits worked in the evening have produced some nice bass, too. If you stick with the shoreline cover on both shores between the marina and the south peninsula, you'll find bass.

The good or only hybrid striper fishing on Charles Mill is confined to two areas. The first area includes the deep holes found at the lake's east side. Fish between the Mifflin Cottage Peninsula and the Lower Campground Peninsula just past the marina; water there reaches 16 to 18 feet deep. The other area for striper fishing is the pool between the east side of the far-south end of the Lower Campground Peninsula and the east shoreline. The water there is the deepest in the lake, reaching over 25 feet deep. Most success comes from fishing a tight line on the bottom with chicken livers; some anglers use floaters and have success that way. Both holes can be reached from the shore at the Lower Campground–Beach Peninsula. Hybrids do not get overly large; a 24-inch fish is about as big as they get.

Crappies are abundant, but most average only 6 to 9 inches. Fish jigs and minnows on the east side of the lake along brush and boat docks and under pontoon boats. The east shoreline of Fisherman's Point is also excellent. Fishing starts in April, slows down during summer, and picks up again in September.

Bluegills are also plentiful; fish the shoreline around docks with wax worms and red worms. Most bluegills will only average 5 to 6 inches.

As with all Muskingum River watershed lakes, flathead catfish are present here. Fish the shallow far-north end near the two small islands off the shore of Sites Lake Cottage Area. Also fish the main lake from the Highway 430 Bridge south, drifting along the main creek channel and using cut shad at night. Flatheads are also caught from shore around the Highway 430 Bridge and the public boat ramp and from pulloffs along Highway 430 west of the bridge.

Channel cats are caught from basically the same areas as flatheads; fish the bridge, the boat ramp, and off the Lower Campground Peninsula. Chicken livers, cut shad, and night crawlers work well for channels. You can also pick up channels in the tailwaters below the dam. Most channels average 12 to 16 inches, with a few 5-pound cats present above and below the dam. A few flatheads are also taken below the dam.

Saugeye in flood control reservoirs do not do well. But those flood control reservoirs do provide an excellent tailwater fishery for the fish. Charles Mill Lake is no different. A few saugeye are picked up along the riprap at the dam, and some of the flats and points on the east side of the lake have given up a few. But few anglers target saugeye in the lake. Most saugeye fishing is done below the spillway. The best fishing takes place after high-water releases in early spring, but saugeye can be picked up all summer long below the dam. Good eating-size 2-pounders, and a few 6-pound fish, are caught regularly by anglers using red and white tubes, minnow-tipped jigs, and chartreuse curly tail grubs. Fish the long narrow pool below the dam for best results. Saugeyes can be picked up all along the stream below the riffles and in the pools. It is a popular area with local fishers and well worth the time to fish it.

Special regulations: There is a 10-hp limit on Charles Mill Lake. Minimum size limit on bass is 12 inches.

Facilities/camping: Charles Mill Lake Park has 350 camping sites, but a large number of them are taken by seasonal campers. Only 150 campsites are available for daily use. The marina has fuel and a boat rental. The nearest town is Mifflin, where you can find everything.

Additional information: Canoeing the Black Fork of the Mohican is popular during the spring and summer.

Directions: Take U.S. Highway 30 east of Mansfield for 6 miles.

26 Clear Fork Reservoir

Key species: Muskie, largemouth bass, crappie, bluegill, channel catfish, white bass.

General description: One of the five top muskie lakes in the state.

Overview: This 973-acre reservoir serves as the water supply for the city of Mansfield. It has one boat ramp, a marina, a campground, four picnic areas, and seasonal docking. The lake has a number of small islands, three springs that feed into the lake, and varying amounts of weed growth. Water visibility ranges from 1 to 2 feet under optimum conditions. Clear Fork is a popular lake on the tournament circuit with both muskie and bass clubs. It is fished heavily. However, because the lake has a speed restriction of 8 miles per hour, conflicts with water skiers and personal watercraft users are nonexistent.

Shoreline access is very good on the lake's south shore, from the four picnic areas along Highway 97 and at the bridge on Bowers Road. Access to the dam is restricted to both boats and bank fishers.

Picnic area 2 is accessible by way of a specially built pier to accommodate wheelchairs, and a parking area near that pier is set aside for those anglers.

The fishing: Clear Fork is one of the top muskie lakes in the state. It is also the lake that the Ohio Huskie Muskie Club has chosen for their annual Division of Wildlife and media day, when they take members of the outdoor media and high-ranking Division of Wildlife personnel out for some muskie fishing.

Come April, muskies can be found on the lake's west end near the point where the headwaters of the two feeder streams enter the lake. Fish the shallow flats on the lake's northeast shore with smaller size crank baits, tandem spinners, and bucktails. Fish the emerging weed beds in all the bays and around the lower islands. The lake produces for both casting and trolling. Troll slowly along the shoreline in 6 feet of water, off the points and edges of the shallow flats, making a complete circle on the lake's west end. It is not a big lake, and you can cover a lot of water in a short time. Work lower islands and the saddles between the islands.

Come summer the muskie fishing moves to the upper half of the lake. Work the north shoreline, where the springs enter the lake; around all the upper islands and

Clear Fork Reservoir

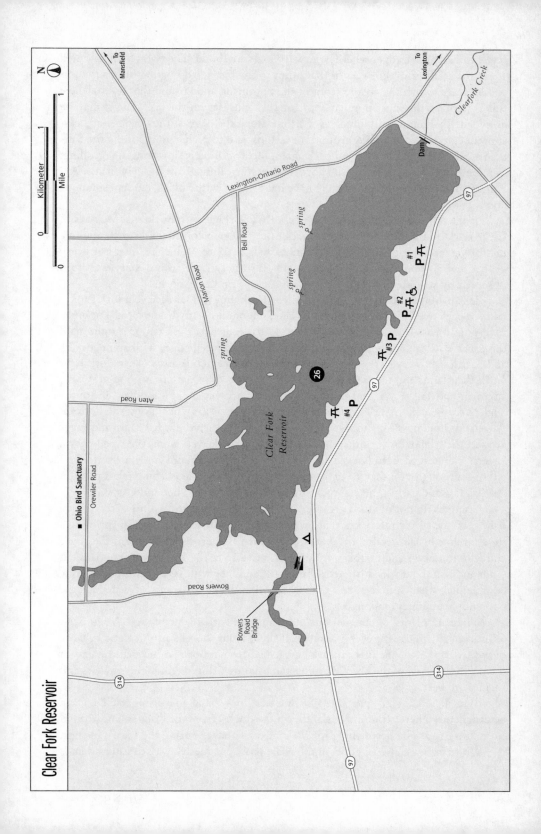

reefs; and along the edges where large weed beds are found. The point by picnic area 1 and the south shoreline east of that point to the restricted boating buoys is a top producer. Also fish the area in front of the big spring and around the three islands; this is perhaps the most popular spot for July muskies on the lake, and it may be crowded. Trolling usually involves working along the edge of the deeper northeast shoreline, to the spring hole, around the islands, and to picnic points along the Sailboat Club, along the buoys, and back again. Most trolling is slow long-line trolling, but some have had success with short-line speed trolling. Troll Beagely Shads, AC Shiners, and big Shad Raps. Casters have had success with Suicks, tandem spinners, and top-water baits.

In the fall fish the inlet at the Bowers Road Bridge with bucktails. Muskies in Clear Fork do not obtain great length, but they do gain considerable girth due to a diet of gizzard shad. Most muskies caught will be 32 to 36 inches long, but every year a few 30-pound-plus fish are caught. Fish near state record size have been observed by wildlife personnel doing fish surveys on Clear Fork.

Bass fishing is also very good on Clear Fork, but it does receive a lot of tournament pressure. It is not a trophy bass lake; seldom does any bass exceed 4 pounds. Five-pound bass is a rarity; most average 12 to 16 inches. Bass can be caught in all the usual ways by pounding the shoreline cover and weed edges with spinner baits and plastics. However, the most productive way to catch bass at Clear Fork is to work the islands and the saddles between the islands. This pattern is good in spring, summer, and fall. Rock and downed timber is present on the saddles, and most anglers fish plastic night crawlers and jigs with plastic crawfish along the bottom. All islands hold bass; stay in water 4 to 8 feet deep and fish the weed edges and snags around the island. In spring and fall, buzz baits work well along the weed edges. Several submerged islands exist in the lake, and these should not be overlooked either—although you may have to hunt for them. Good bass fishing takes place in April, May, and early June and picks up again in late September and October.

Crappies do not obtain a great size, but the lake is bountiful with 9- to 10-inch fish. It is one of the rare lakes that produce crappies all season long. In spring fish the shoreline brush, around the docks, and off the Bowers Road Bridge at the lower end with minnows and bobbers. In summer move up to the area around the Sailboat Club and fish the docks. Fish deep during the summer with small yellow and white crappie jigs, small spinners, and crank baits. Stay in 12 to 16 feet of water for the best shot at summer crappies.

There are plenty of channel cats, most in the 14- to 18-inch range. A few 5- to 6-pound fish are caught every summer. Fishing from shore is problematic because of weed growth, so channel cats are best fished from a boat on the shallow flats at the northwest side of the lake. Morning and evening fishing with night crawlers and shrimp are best.

Bluegills obtain a respectable size in Clear Fork, hand size or bigger. They can be caught anywhere around the islands, off the docks, from the bridges, and around shoreline cover. The best fishing for the nice-size ones is during the spawn in June.

White bass are also in good supply. The most productive way to catch them is by trolling white Rooster Tails for suspended fish off the islands and points from the middle of the lake toward the dam. Most white bass will average 10 to 14 inches.

Clearfork creek below the dam has some small stream fishing for bass, bluegills, and the occasional muskie. Parking is at the bridge on Lexington-Ontario Road.

Special regulations: Unlimited horsepower, but the reservoir is restricted to 8 miles per hour.

Facilities/camping: Limited camping is available at the Clear Fork Reservoir campground, while most campsites are occupied by seasonal campers. There are six tent sites and four electric sites available for public camping. At the ramp, there is a marina and bait store. Nearby, the town of Lexington has all the amenities.

Additional information: The Ohio Bird Sanctuary is located on Orewiler Road just north of the lake, and an eagle's nest is visible from the boat ramp.

Directions: Clear Fork Reservoir is located southwest of Mansfield on Highway 97.

27 Clearfork of the Mohican River

Key species: Brown trout, smallmouth, bluegill, sunfish, rock bass, muskie.

General description: Quality trout fishing on one of Ohio's most beautiful streams.

Overview: Located within the Mohican State Forest and Mohican State Park, the Clearfork branch of the Mohican River is one of the state's few high-quality trout streams. The section of stream below the Pleasant Hill Dam was designated a State Scenic River in 2006. It is a beautiful stream full of riffles and pools, with a gentle, easy flow that is as inviting to fish as it is to look at. Easy to wade, it is a popular stream with both fly-fishers and the weekend worm and bobber anglers. Two public state park campgrounds are located along the Clearfork. Hiking trails lead up and down the stream, making every pool available to fishers willing to hike the distance. The Clearfork is divided into two streams sections: one above Pleasant Hill Reservoir and one below the reservoir. Trout are in both sections. Above Pleasant Hill Reservoir is a small section of public fishing along Gatton Rocks Road that extends from the Stoffer Bridge to the Cutnaw Bridge between the towns of Bellville and Butler. Below the Pleasant Hill Dam, 5 miles of the Clearfork is open to public fishing. The area extends through both campgrounds and just past the Highway 3 Bridge. The portion of the Clearfork that runs through the state park campground has been improved by a number of stream enhancements.

The fishing: The fishing on the Clearfork of the Mohican is primarily devoted to the pursuit of brown trout. Upstream of Pleasant Hill Lake smallmouth, sunfish, muskie, and trout are available, but only about 1 mile of stream is open to the public. It is a beautiful stretch and well worth the time to explore the haunts where trout may be hiding.

The Clearfork of the Mohican River is one of the most beautiful places to fish in Ohio.

The primary stretch of river that attracts most anglers is below Pleasant Hill Dam. To reach the tailwaters of the dam, park at the covered bridge located at the entrance of campground B, or drive to the dam and walk the steps downhill. The tailwater section is considered the best fishing by some and perhaps the most popular section of stream. The hike in from the covered bridge is 0.75 mile and has much productive water. You can fish from the bridge up to the dam and hike the trail back, or vice versa. Perhaps the easiest ways to access the tailwater is to park at Pleasant Hill Dam and walk down. The only problem here is that you have to walk back up again. Another good fishing hike is the Hemlock Gorge Trail, which follows the stream between the two campgrounds. This stretch has some of the coldest water during summer, as several springs enter the stream along this section. The hike between the two campgrounds is said to be 2 miles long, but those that have done it said it is more like 3 miles. Some of the best stream fishing is along this stretch and is not heavily fished, as the waters close to the campgrounds are. Fishing pressure is greatest at both campgrounds and at the dam.

The trout like brightly colored bead-head nymphs and caddis flies. Blue-winged olives hatch in May, and tricos and caddis hatch throughout the summer. Terrestrials are always excellent during the summer, with grasshoppers, Woolly Worms, beetles, and ants rounding out a good selection. Don't overpower the

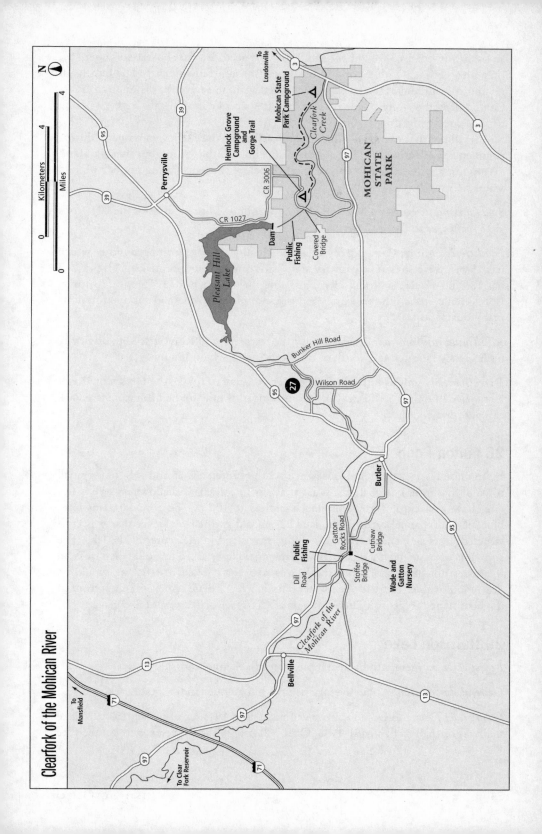

Clearfork of the Mohican River

N

Kilometers
0   4   4

Miles
0   4

To Loudonville

3

Mohican State Park Campground

Hemlock Grove Campground and Gorge Trail

Clearfork Creek

97

MOHICAN STATE PARK

3

CR 3006

Perrysville

39

95

39

CR 1027

Dam

Public Fishing

Covered Bridge

Pleasant Hill Lake

Bunker Hill Road

Wilson Road

95

27

97

Butler

Gatton Rocks Road

Public Fishing

Cutnaw Bridge

Dill Road

Stoffer Bridge

Wade and Gatton Nursery

97

Clearfork of the Mohican River

95

To Mansfield

71

13

97

Bellville

13

To Clear Fork Reservoir

97

71

trout; a four- to five-weight fly rod is all you need. If you chose a spinning rod, then arm yourself with a good selection of Rooster Tail spinners. The best trout fishing is early May through early June, then again in early fall, although trout are caught all winter long. Annual trout stockings occur in mid-fall, with a few big brood-stock trout thrown in.

Smallmouth are in good supply in Clearfork below the impoundment; during summer, anglers are more likely to catch smallmouth than trout, but that shouldn't disappoint anyone. Saugeyes are also taken below the dam during periods of high water releases.

Special regulations: Minimum length for all trout on both sections of the Clearfork is 12 inches, with two fish per day.

Facilities/camping: Camping is free at the Hemlock Grove Campground B, which has 25 primitive sites. The primary state park campground located off Highway 3 has 186 full-service sites and 25 cabins along the stream's edge. The nearest town, Loudonville, has all the amenities and is a nice place to stop and snoop around its many quaint stores.

Additional information: Be sure to visit the restored Wolf Run Grist Mill, originally built in 1831, located just south of Mohican State Park on Highway 3.

Directions: Six miles south of Mansfield on Interstate 71, take the Highway 97 exit east; drive 14 miles to Highway 3, then turn north 1 mile to the Mohican State Park campground entrance.

28 Fulton Pond

Fulton Pond is a small, secluded lake just south of Interstate 80 and west of the small town of Swanton. I estimate the pond at about 15 acres; it is shallow and weedy but does have a blacktop boat ramp and is limited to 10 hp. The pond contains bass, bluegill, and channel catfish. The lake has an old earthen-rock pier that was constructed years ago, and there is a small brushy island in the center of the lake. The shoreline consists mostly of small overhanging willows and a few old fallen trees on the lake's northeast shore, but the lake is so weed choked that fishing would be nearly impossible. There is open water only in a few isolated pockets and in front of the boat ramp. To get to Fulton Pond, take County Road 3 west of Swanton.

29 Harrison Lake

Key species: Largemouth bass, crappie, bluegill, channel catfish.

General description: About average fishing, but an outstanding state park.

Overview: Harrison Lake Dam was completed in 1941, creating the 105-acre lake that was opened to fishing in 1946. Over 300 fishers and 75 boats were on the lake that opening day. In 1975, Harrison Lake lost all its fish, because the old gate malfunctioned due to age. The gate was repaired and the lake was filled that year, but the lake was again drained in 1976, because the gate repair was not satisfactory. Once the gate was repaired, the lake was poisoned to remove the rough fish. The lake was finally restocked in 1977 with bass, bluegill, crappie, and channel catfish.

The Harrison Lake State Park was established in 1950; today it is a fully modern first-class state park with camping, hiking trails, a beach, a boat rental, picnic areas, shelter houses, and a boat ramp. In addition to campers, the park is used by many local residents, schools, and community groups.

The lake is stained with less than a foot of visibility at best, with a shoreline that consists of some riprap, overhanging and fallen trees, some brush, and old snags. The lake averages anywhere from 4 to 16 feet deep. Shoreline access is good by way of a trail that encircles the lake.

The fishing: Most bass on Harrison Lake will average only 1 to 2 pounds, with a 3- to 4-pound bass making a rare appearance. Fish chartreuse spinner baits, crank baits, and black or purple plastic night crawlers tight against the shoreline cover along the south bank near the south campground. Another good shoreline is the north bank around the water tower. The riprap around the footbridge has produced a few bass as well. The bass fishing starts the end of May or the first of June, depending on weather.

Crappie fishing starts as early as the end of March but reaches its peak on Mother's Day weekend. The entire east shoreline from the footbridge, in front of the beach, and around the spillway is where most crappies are caught. Minnows, jigs, and wax worms take most crappies that average 8 to 10 inches, with a few larger, into the teens, taken by some lucky anglers.

Channel catfish do fairly well on Harrison Lake, with 9 pounds about tops. Most channels will be small, in the 12- to 14-inch range, but they are plentiful. Fish the west end from the south or north shore and around the boat ramp. Fishing near the bridge at the lake's inlet is always productive. Use chicken livers or night crawlers for bait. A few bullheads are also in the lake.

Bluegills are only so-so; most are small. Fish the small bay and around the lily pads in front of the old park office. Use red worms and a bobber.

At one time a few northern pike were in Harrison Lake, but the last pike reportedly caught from the lake was in the late 1980s.

Special regulations: Harrison Lake is limited to electric motors only.

Facilities/camping: Harrison Lake State Park has 175 campsites and 1 cabin. The nearest town is Archbold, which has everything.

Additional information: Sauder Village, located about 7 miles south of Harrison Lake, is a reconstructed pioneer village and nonprofit historical center.

Directions: From Archbold take Highway 66 north 8 miles.

30 Huron River—Milan Wildlife Area

The Milan Wildlife Area, located a couple of miles north of Norwalk, was acquired in 1932 and was originally used to propagate raccoons. The wildlife area contains a couple of miles of the upper Huron River within its boundaries. A small dam was constructed on the stream called the Coho Dam. The river was once a part of the Division of Wildlife's effort to stock coho salmon into Lake Erie.

The section of river that runs through the wildlife area is a beautiful stream, full of riffles, pools, and gravel runs. The old dam is gone, but its remains are still evident. The stream has excellent fishing for smallmouth, rock bass, sunfish, and small channel cats. That section of the Huron also receives a little known, minor run of steelhead in the fall and spring. One angler informed me that small rainbow trout are occasionally caught from the stream, indicating perhaps some steelhead reproduction may occur in the stream's cooler tributaries.

To access the stream, take Lovers Lane off Highway 113, east of Milan. There is a parking area at the bridge. From the parking area, anglers walk the old roadway downstream to the old dam.

Upstream of the Milan Wildlife Area is the small town of Monroeville, which has a city park on the Huron River. From here anglers can access the stream and the tailwaters of the old city dam.

The Milan Wildlife Area is located 2 miles north of Norwalk on Highway 113.

31 Lake La Su An Wildlife Area

Key species: Bluegill, redear sunfish, pumpkinseed, ring perch, hybrid sunfish, and largemouth bass.

General description: Best bluegill fishing in Ohio; the bass fishing isn't bad either. A permit is required.

Overview: The Division of Wildlife manages all ponds on the Lake La Su An Wildlife Area for high-quality bluegill fishing. Nearly 5,000 anglers visit the wildlife area every year to sample this one-of-a-kind fishery. Bass anglers can catch 50 to 70 bass a day, but 90 percent of visiting anglers fish the areas 14 ponds for bluegills, redear, and pumpkinseed.

Located in the northwest corner of the state in Williams County, the ponds were originally small natural lakes that had dikes constructed across the outlets. The resulting lakes were part of a private enterprise called Dreamland Acres. The Division of Wildlife acquired the property in 1981 and has since added to the wildlife area as funds became available. The previous private fishery was of such high quality that the Division of Wildlife enacted a specific set of regulations designed to preserve that quality under public-fishing pressure. The wildlife area ponds were finally opened to anglers in 1983.

At 82 acres the largest lake and perhaps most popular is Lake La Su An. It has a boat ramp and wheelchair-accessible pier and is limited to 10 hp. Lake Lavere is 15 acres, has a boat ramp, and is limited to 10 hp. Lake Sue is 12 acres, has a boat

Each bluegill caught and kept at Lake La Su An Wildlife Area must be weighed and measured by wildlife officials.

ramp, and has a 10-hp limit. Lake Ann is 4.6 acres, has a ramp, is wheelchair accessible, and is limited to 10 hp. Lake Us, which is for youths only, and Lake Mel are accessible by vehicle. Jerry's, Hogback, Lou's, and Clem's Ponds are walk-in ponds. Lake Teal and Lake Wood Duck require a short walk from the parking area.

The ponds on Lake Lu Sa An Wildlife Area are perhaps the most micromanaged fisheries in Ohio. Each bluegill, sunfish, perch, and bass kept is weighed to the gram and measured to the millimeter. Specific quotas and bag limits are set on each lake, which can vary from year to year depending on monthly summaries and lake surveys. After a lake quota is reached, the angler is required to use artificial bait only. If any bluegills are kept after a lake quota is met, it must be a minimum length of 9½ inches. This minimum length limit is set because a bluegill of that size is approximately five to eight years old and at the end of its life span.

Reservations are required one week in advance to obtain a free one-day permit to fish Lake La Su An, Lake Ann, Lake Lavere, Lake Sue, Lake Mel, and Lake Us. Reservations are accepted on Monday only from 8:00 a.m. until 12 noon. A free permit is required to fish the walk-in ponds, which may be made in advance or picked up on that day at the wildlife area fisheries office located at Lake La Su An. Only a specific number of anglers are permitted on the larger lakes per day. Lake La Su An is limited to 16 anglers, Lavere is limited to 6 per day, Lake Sue and Lake Ann are

Brock and Bill Thorp caught this limit of bluegills from Lake La Su An.

limited to 10 per day, and Lake Mel is limited to 5 per day. Two different permits are issued: a bluegill permit, which is good for all sunfish and perch, and a bass permit, which allows the angler to fish only for bass. Of the 16 daily permits allowed for Lake La Su An, 4 are reserved for bass fishing.

Permits are in high demand; within the first hour on Monday, all reservations are filled on the larger lakes. The six walk-in ponds still require a permit, but permits are unlimited and may be either picked up at the fisheries office or reserved ahead of time.

The peak demand is summer and weekends. If, on a rare occasion, the quota for the number of anglers is not met on a specific lake, then an angler can pick up a permit for that lake on that day. Permits are good for only one day and only one lake.

An angler is allowed one permit every 21 days to fish Lake La Su An, and every 10 days on the remainder of the lakes.

Lake Us is reserved for youths 15 years or younger. The lake is limited to groups of 10 youths or fewer accompanied by an adult. Reservations for youth groups are preferred but not mandatory, but a permit is still required.

Fishing is allowed every day except Tuesday and Wednesday, when the lakes are closed. Lake La Su Ann Wildlife Area is open to fishing from the second week in April through October 9 and remains closed until December 31. Ice fishing is permitted as long as the ice is safe; a signed liability release is required before ice fishing.

Anglers must check into the fishery station at the conclusion of fishing. A daily creel summary of all fish caught is recorded, a work sheet on every lake from which fish are harvested is kept, and the creel information form on the back of the permit must be filled out. After the permit form is turned in, the angler's fishing license is returned, which must be surrendered to obtain the actual permit.

The fishing: To say fishing is excellent on these lakes is somewhat of an understatement; it is as good as it gets. The primary draw to Lake La Su An Wildlife Area is the premier bluegill fishing, but the bass fishing is no second string.

Bluegills are bountiful, plentiful, and big. Every pond has bluegill fishing equal to every other pond. Bluegills average a healthy 7 to 10 inches, with a 10-inch fish a very good one. Fishing holds up all year long; red worms, wax worms, small spinners, and jigs will take a limit of big bluegills usually by noon. Fish weed edges, around any structures, off any shoreline or bank; the bluegills are not hard to find. There's no science to it. Once you get the permit, the rest is easy.

Redear and pumpkinseed sunfish are caught from Lake La Su An, Jerry's Pond, Lou's Pond, and Clem's Pond. Redears are taken from near the bottom with wax worms, crickets, and small beetle spins, and you can catch plenty out in the shallows with a fly rod and rubber spiders. Most redears average 9 to 11 inches. Late May and early June are the best time to fill a stringer. Pumpkinseed are about equal to the redears in number and average 7 to 8 inches in length. They, too, can be caught right along with the rest of the panfish. Usually wax worms, a pinch of night crawler, and a bobber are all that is required to catch them.

Lake Us, the youth-only fishing lake, also contains hybrid sunfish. They are easy to catch and can average over 9 inches.

Lake La Su An has a small population of yellow perch, which on occasion can

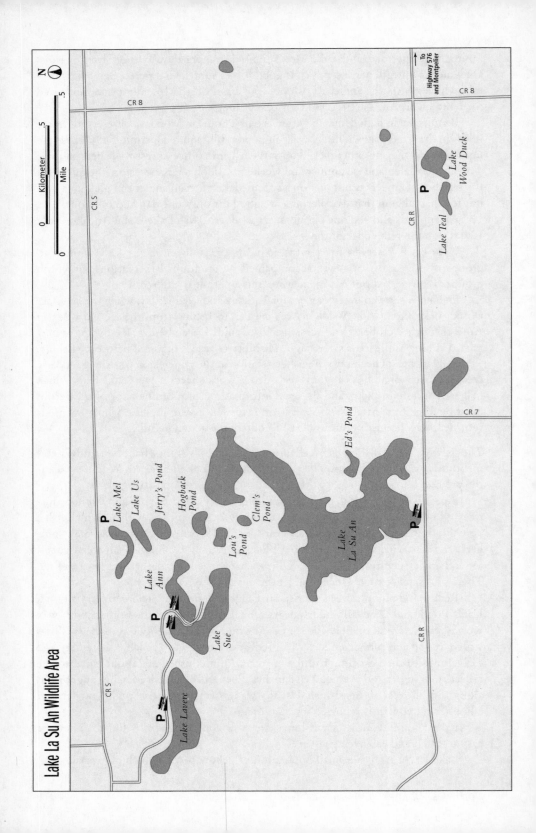

Lake La Su An Wildlife Area

yield some good catches. Most perch average 11 to 13 inches and are caught from the deeper areas of the lake. Fish the deeper north bay and in the middle of the lake off the east shore. Stay in about 10 feet of water and fish the bottom with red worms or night crawlers and a slip bobber. June is the best month for perch.

The bass fishing here is something to experience. I haven't had this kind of fishing since I was a kid sneaking into local farm ponds in Clermont County. The bass are plentiful and eager to nail anything thrown their way. It's no trick to catch bass here. Most average 12 to 14 inches, but plenty of 16- to 18-inch bass can be found. An angler can easily catch 30 bass a day—on a good day, 60 to 70. Some real hawgs in the 5- to 6-pound range do come from these lakes. Fish weed edges, shoreline cover, and around floating patches of moss with spinner baits, buzz baits, Rapalas, and plastics. Lake Lavere is the best bass lake in the wildlife area in terms of size. Bass there are bigger and healthier and the lake produces more 6- to 7-pound bass than any of the other lakes. Fly-fishermen can score on hair bugs, poppers, and big terrestrials such as grasshoppers and rubber spiders. Only 10 percent of the anglers who visit Lake La Su An Wildlife Area fish for bass.

All ponds have excellent populations of bass. Some of the smaller ponds can be fished from shore. Other lakes can be fished from docks and piers. The larger lakes, however, require a boat to fish effectively.

Ice fishing is permitted as long as the ice is safe; the best months are January and February. Most fish caught through the ice are bluegills.

Special regulations: A free permit is required to fish all the lakes in the Lake La Su An Wildlife Area. To obtain a permit, call (419) 636-6189 one week in advance on Monday only from 8:00 a.m. to 12 noon. Some regulations and bag limits are subject to change depending on survey results and creel census.

Regulations are as follows:

- **Lake La Su An, Lake Lavere, Ed's Pond, Clem's Pond, Lou's Pond, Lake Wood Duck, and Lake Mel:** Largemouth bass 17 inches or longer. Bluegills and sunfish, a daily bag limit of 15, of which only 5 may be 8 inches or larger.

- **Lake Sue:** Largemouth bass, 17 inches or longer. Bluegills and sunfish, a daily bag limit of 10, of which only 2 may be 8 inches or longer.

- **Hogback Pond, Jerry's Pond, and Lake Teal:** Largemouth bass must be 15 inches or longer. Bluegills and sunfish, no special regulations.

- **Lake Us (youths only):** Largemouth bass, 17 inches or longer. Bluegills and sunfish, a daily bag limit of 10.

- Minnows are not permitted as bait.

- Fishing is permitted only on Monday and Wednesday through Sunday during daylight hours.

- All anglers must check into the fishery office located at Lake La Su An.

For updated regulations contact the Ohio Division of Wildlife District Two office at (419) 424-5000.

Facilities/camping: There are no facilities other than restrooms at Lake La Su An. Camping is not permitted at the wildlife area. Private campgrounds are available at nearby Nettle Lake. The nearest town is Montpelier, which has everything.

Additional information: Lake La Su An Wildlife Area is open to youths-only turkey hunting in late April and May, which can be combined into a father-and-son hunting and fishing outing.

Directions: From Montpelier take Highway 576 north to County Road R. Turn west approximately 3 miles.

32 Malabar Farm

Home of the late Pulitzer Prize–winning author Louis Bromfield, Malabar Farm State Park has a number of small farm ponds that allow public fishing. The ponds contain bluegill, channel catfish, crappie, and bass. The pond below the Bromfield house has a wheelchair-accessible dock. Primitive camping is available at the 917-acre state park, which has 15 sites. During the last weekend in September, Ohio Heritage Days are held, and after a fisher has had his or her fill of homemade apple butter and hayrides, he or she can drop a line into any of the ponds and catch nice bluegill.

Malabar Farm is located on Pleasant Valley Road, off Highway 603, west of Pleasant Hill Lake.

33 Maumee River

Key species: Walleye, white bass, smallmouth and largemouth bass, channel and flat-head catfish, crappie, bluegill, sunfish.

General description: The spring walleye run is a phenomenal event that attracts thousands of anglers.

Overview: The Maumee River begins in Fort Wayne, Indiana. Flowing eastward, the river is joined by the Auglaize and Tiffin Rivers at Defiance, nearly doubling its size. The Maumee arrives at Lake Erie 60 miles later. In Ohio, only two low head dams impede the river's progress to Lake Erie: Independence Dam and Providence Dam. Providence Dam was originally built in 1838. Independence Dam was built in 1924, replacing an old dam that was built during the 1840s. The last Indian battle in Ohio, the Battle of Fallen Timbers in 1794, took place just north of the river and west of the town of Maumee. That battle settled the conquest of Ohio, opening up the northwest frontier to commerce and settlements. The Maumee River played a vital commercial role during the 1800s. Today the lower river is used primarily for recreation purposes; all commercial river traffic is confined to the industrial ports at Toledo.

The Maumee is a state-designated scenic river. Its first public stream access is at a canoe launch west of Defiance off U.S. Highway 24 on Bend Road. Downstream of Defiance numerous public boat-launching facilities are available.

Independence Dam on the Maumee River is a top spot for smallmouth bass and flat-head catfish.

The primary public access areas on the Maumee of interest to fishers are at Independence Dam State Park, Mary Jane Thurston State Park, Providence Metro Park, and Side Cut Metro Park. There are boat ramps at both state parks.

The fishing: At Independence Dam State Park, anglers fish for flathead and channel catfish, white bass, smallmouth, crappies, and a few resident walleyes. Fish the pool immediately below the spillway for channels and flatheads. Some of the Maumee River's biggest flatheads, weighing up to 50 pounds, come from this pool. Use stout tackle, heavy sinkers, and strong line. Fish from the railing around the small overlook into the white water below the dam with big chubs, bluegills, and shad. If you hook a large flathead, you must walk down to the river's edge in order to land the fish. If the water is low and you're feeling brave, you can walk out on the dam to the center "steps" and fish for flatheads there. There is no public access at the dam's south end, but some anglers will beach a boat above the dam, walk around the side of the dam, and fish the whitewater pool from that side. The fishing holds up fairly well all summer, but the best flathead fishing is on rising water. Most anglers fish tight line on the bottom, but some do well with floaters, suspending the bait off the bottom and letting it drift with the current.

White bass also make a run up to Independence Dam, but they are low in numbers compared to Providence Dam. In spring the run starts in mid-April and lasts until the end of May. Another fall run takes place in mid-September. The spring run averages bigger fish. In the fall, white bass average 10 to 12 inches. Most white bass are caught on jig and curly tail grubs and white spinners.

Crappies can also be caught from Independence Dam. Fish the small pool below the overlook out of the main current with minnows and jigs. Most crappies run small, but occasionally a few nice ones are caught.

In the river below Independence Dam, a small resident population of walleyes stay mostly within sight of the dam. A few are picked up throughout the spring and summer by anglers fishing for smallmouth or panfish below the dam. Jig and curly tail grubs, night crawlers, and crank baits catch a few below the dam every year.

Smallmouth bass can be caught in the riffles and pools and around the small islands below Independence Dam. Most smallmouth reach from 12 to 14 inches, but 15 inches and larger is not uncommon. Fish small crawdad-colored crank baits, Mepps spinners, and watermelon seed tubes at the head of pools and below riffles and eddies. In summer there is easy wading below the dam, and it's shallow. If you discover the right pools to fish, you can have a field day.

Providence Dam is actually two dams with an island in the center. So an angler can access the tailwaters from two sides. The north dam can be accessed from Providence Metro Park; the south dam from Mary Jane Thurston State Park.

Flathead catfish can also be caught from the tailwaters below Providence Dam, but these do not reach the size of the flatheads that come from Independence Dam. However, anglers using shad, chubs, and cut bait have caught some 10- to 25-pound flatheads from the tailwaters of Providence. Fish both pools immediately below the dams, again using stout tackle, and expect a long, drawn-out fight should you hook one.

Good catches of big channel cats come from the tailwaters below Providence Dam. Fish the many pools and riffles below the dam with floaters and chicken livers. There is easy wading in the water below the dam when at summer pool. Channel cats from 1 to 10 pounds are common catches at Providence.

White bass make good spring and fall runs up to Providence. Starting in mid-April, during the peak of the run, anglers can catch 60 white bass a day. Use jigs and curly tail grubs in the white water below the dam and in the riffles and pools below the dam. Starting in mid-September, there is a fall run of white bass that lasts about four weeks. The fish run smaller during the fall run, but they are just as eager to bite.

There is good smallmouth fishing around the many islands, pools, riffles, and eddies below the tailwaters. Some nice 3- to 4-pound smallmouth show up every summer for anglers who know where to look. There is so much good smallmouth water here that pinpointing a specific spot is impossible. To catch smallmouth, fish below either dam. Anglers can also access the broad expanse of riffles below the south dam from the community park at Grand Rapids. Small crank baits, tubes, or "Slurpies" will fool most smallmouth. Most fish will average 1 to 1.5 pounds, but plenty of bigger ones have been caught.

Walleyes normally do not make a spring run up this far. The bulk of the

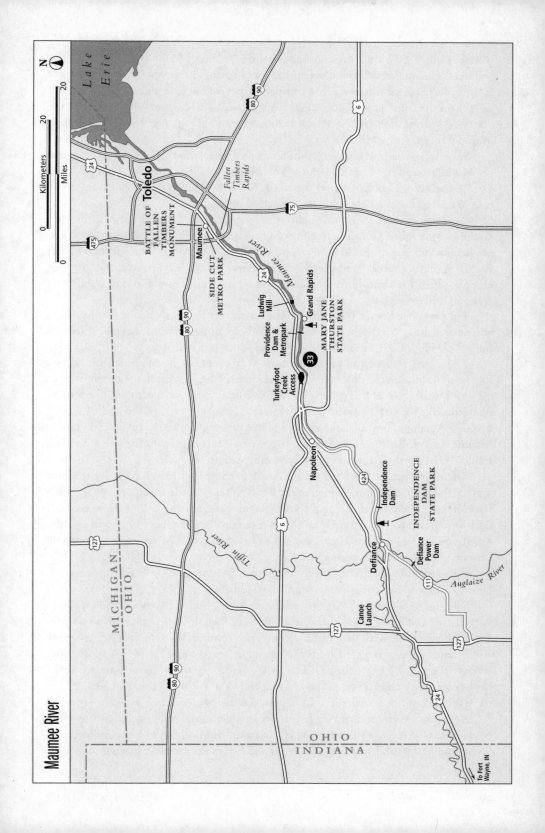

Maumee River

Lake Erie

N

Kilometers
0   20   20
0   20
Miles

MICHIGAN
OHIO

127

80 90

127

OHIO
INDIANA

To Fort
Wayne, IN

24

127

Canoe
Launch

Defiance

Defiance
Power Dam

Auglaize River

111

424

Independence
Dam

INDEPENDENCE
DAM
STATE PARK

6

Tiffin River

Napoleon

6

33

Turkeyfoot
Creek
Access

80 90

Providence
Dam &
Metropark

Ludwig
Mill

Grand Rapids

MARY JANE
THURSTON
STATE PARK

24

Maumee River

75

Fallen
Timbers
Rapids

80 90

475

BATTLE OF
FALLEN
TIMBERS
MONUMENT

Maumee

SIDE CUT
METRO PARK

24

Toledo

6

walleyes find spawning ground long before reaching Providence Dam. Some walleyes are caught at Providence in the early spring, however. Whether they are from Lake Erie, or simply a few resident river walleye, is debatable. Most are caught on the usual jig and grubs and Sassy Shads by a few local anglers below the dam and in the riffles in late March through April and again in the fall beginning in mid-September.

Surprisingly, a few northern pike are also caught out of the slow off-channel pools and around old logjams below Providence Dam. To catch northern pike, use 4- to 6-inch creek chubs around the old Ludwig Mill at Grand Rapids. Ten to 20 pike are caught every year, with some over 30 inches.

Crappies are also taken throughout the year; the best months are April, May, and mid-September. Crappies like the old canals, the creek mouths, tributaries, and any backwater along the Maumee. The marina bay at Mary Jane Thurston State Park, Turkeyfoot Creek, and the old canal at Grand Rapids are productive spots for crappies. Fish for them with a jig and minnows, or minnows and a bobber; most crappies will average 9 to 12 inches.

The Defiance Power Dam on the Auglaize River below Defiance also has some tailwater fishing for flathead, channels, and smallmouth bass. Access is from a pulloff on Highway 111 and off River Road south of town.

The spring walleye run up the Maumee is an event like no other in Ohio. If you like fishing shoulder to shoulder with thousands of anglers, catching a limit of 3- to 5-pound walleyes every day, then this is for you. It is a hectic, carnival-like atmosphere during the run's maddening four weeks. Every spring at the end of March through April, millions of Lake Erie's walleye make an annual spawning run up the Maumee River. By the end of April, the walleye run is over and white bass from Lake Erie begin their annual spring spawning run up the river.

The prime area to get in on this event is the Side Cut Metro Park, located just west of the town of Maumee. Fish the Fallen Timbers Rapids area. Park at the Metro Park; it can get crowded. Bring a pair of warm waders, a can full of ¼- to 1-ounce lead-head jigs, a bag full of curly tail, twister tail grubs, and plenty of line and you're set. If you find a good location among the crowd, you had better stay there. If you leave, someone will take your spot.

Be warned: It is cold, the river current can be strong, and wildlife officers will be watching and ticketing fishers with snagged fish.

The jigs you use will vary in weight depending on the current; the idea is to keep the jig bouncing along the bottom, not allowing it to get stuck or be stationary on the bottom. With the proper jig and grub combination, the current will carry and bounce the jig along the bottom. Getting snagged on rocks is part of the deal, so have plenty of jigs in all sizes. The local anglers say color doesn't matter; other anglers swear by chartreuse, orange, white, and yellow. Once you get the hang of it, the fishing is not that difficult; it's the patience that wears out.

Beginning at the end of April, as soon as the walleye run concludes, the white bass make a spring run up the river. It's popular, but nothing like the walleye run. Use white Mepps and white jig and grubs and fish in the same areas where the walleye fishers pounded the week before. You should be able to catch 30 to 50 white bass in an afternoon. Most white bass will average 12 inches; seldom will anything exceed 2 pounds.

Special regulations: Smallmouth bass cannot be kept or harvested between May 1 and June 23 from Providence Dam to Lake Erie. Minimum size limit is 14 inches, with a limit of five.

Between March 1 and April 30 from Providence Dam to Lake Erie, the walleye minimum length is 15 inches, with a daily limit of four.

From March 1 through May 1, fishing from Providence Dam to Lake Erie is allowed only from sunrise to sunset when signs are posted. No fishing with more than a single hook. The hook cannot be larger than 0.5 inch from shank to barb. Treble hooks are prohibited.

Facilities/camping: Camping is available at Mary Jane Thurston State Park, which has 35 campsites. There are other private campgrounds in the area. Motel and other lodging are available at Maumee and Perrysburg. Nearby towns can supply all amenities.

Additional information: A monument to the Battle of Fallen Timbers is located at the Side Cut Metro Park.

Directions: Defiance Power Dam is south of Defiance on Highway 111, off River Road. Independence Dam is 3 miles east of Defiance on Highway 424. Providence Dam is off US 24 at Grand Rapids. Side Cut Metro Park is located off the Interstate 475 and US 24 exit on River Road, west of the town of Maumee.

34 Nettle Lake

Key species: Largemouth bass, crappie, channel catfish, bluegill, and some northern pike.

General description: One of Ohio's natural lakes with good crappie and bass fishing.

Overview: Nettle Lake is a natural lake of 94 acres, hewed out by glaciers that reached well beyond northern Ohio. Summer homes, cottages, and seasonal campers surround the lake; the only public access is at a single boat ramp on the lake's southwest end. The lake is weedy around the edges and in the few bays; lily pads cover a large amount of shoreline and spread into the human-made channels. That said, most of the shore of Nettle Lake is taken over by boat docks. There is some depth to the lake, with some pockets close to 30 feet deep. Nettle Lake is a resort lake, and during the summer water skiers and jet boats are in heavy use. There are no horsepower restrictions on the lake. And because the lakeshore is private property, it can only be fished by boat.

The fishing: Bass fishing is good on Nettle Lake. Most bass are caught from boat docks and shoreline cover, although some are taken from lily pad edges as well.

Using spinner baits, crank baits, and plastic night crawlers, work the shoreline cover, weed edges, old docks, and the few points on both sides of the lake and in the backs of bays. On the north end of the lake there is still some undeveloped shoreline that has good bank cover; many fishers prefer this section. The bass seem evenly spread out, with one end of the lake about equal to the other end. Most bass run small, about 12 inches, but some 20-inch-plus bass show up regularly enough to make it interesting.

Crappies are also in high numbers here, usually in the 7- to 9-inch range. Most are caught in spring around the boat docks. In summer, fish deep pockets and boat docks in 9 to 10 feet of water. Again, crappies like to hide in boat docks and under pontoon boats. Jig and minnows worked slowly along the dock edge will pick up most crappies. Some nice crappies up to 12 inches do appear in the spring, but you have to hunt for them.

Channel cats are also in good numbers at Nettle Lake, with several in the 6- to 7-pound range caught on chicken livers and night crawlers. One of the best ways to catch channels is to let the boat drift across the shallows on a summer evening after the boat traffic has gone. Locally, most cat fishing is done right off the private boat docks.

Bluegills are so-so at Nettle Lake, with most being small. But every June during spawning season, a few 6-inch fish do end up on someone's stringer.

Northern pike are present here, but in low numbers. In summer a few are caught, some up to 30 inches, but these are mostly incidental catches by bass or crappie fishers. The pike like cold water; fish weedy coves in March and the deep pockets during summer, and you may catch one. A longtime resident told me that his father-in-law caught a northern pike over 5 feet long from Nettle Lake back in the early 1940s. He said the old black-and-white photo hung on a wall in a lakeside shop for many years until it closed sometime ago. The gentleman attempted to recover the photo after the place closed, but the photo was lost.

Special regulations: Horsepower is unlimited, but idle speed only from 6:00 p.m. to 10:00 a.m., and no wake anytime at all in the north bay area.

Facilities/camping: At times a private marina with fuel and bait is open on the south end. There are a few private campgrounds, but most are filled with seasonal campers. The lake's largest private campground is at the north end and has 45 sites available for public use.

Additional information: On the east side of the lake, overlooking a small stream running into Nettle Lake, are four Hopewell burial mounds. You can visit them from May through mid-November, courtesy of the Williams County Historical Society.

Directions: Take Highway 576 north of Montpelier approximately 6 miles, then turn west on County Road R and go 5 miles.

35 Oxbow Lake Wildlife Area

Key species: Largemouth bass, crappie, channel catfish, yellow perch.

General description: A favorite with local anglers, Oxbow Lake Wildlife Area produces a quality fishery.

Overview: Oxbow is a small lake of 40 acres with riprap dams at both ends. The main feeder stream enters in the center, thus creating an oxbow lake. It is part of the Oxbow Lake Wildlife Area, which also allows public hunting. The Division of Wildlife used to operate a satellite fisheries research station from the wildlife area. The small lake has a boat ramp, a dock, and plenty of parking areas. There are four gravel piers from which to fish. They are level and covered with grass and appear wheelchair accessible. The lake averages 5 to 10 feet deep.

Oxbow has an abundance of shoreline cover including overhanging trees, stumps, old snags, and riprap.

There is also a smaller impoundment just east of the lake that is fishable and can be accessed from a parking area.

The fishing: Oxbow Lake is a favorite haunt for retired General Motors workers who like to come out in the morning and evening to fish for bass and catfish.

The lake supports a good bass fishery. Most are in the 12- to 14-inch range, but enough 2- to 3-pound bass are caught to make it a worthwhile endeavor. The Division of Wildlife has imposed a size limit on the lake to enhance the bass fishing.

Oxbow is a good spring and fall bass lake. The fishing slows down considerably during summer. The months of May, June, September, and October are its best months.

Fish shoreline cover, brush, and especially around the four rock/gravel piers with spinner baits, watermelon tubes, plastic night crawlers, and top-water baits during the evening. Good shoreline access around the lake allows shoreline anglers plenty of opportunity to tangle with some good bass. The two piers from the west parking areas are favorite spots. Fish the riprap dams at both ends, near the shoreline stumps on the lake's south side, and at the mouth of the small inlet on the lake's south-central shore.

Channel cats weighing up to 6 pounds are caught regularly by nighttime cat fishers. Most cat fishing is done during the summer off the stone piers with chicken livers and night crawlers. The majority of cats will be only 12 to 15 inches, but enough good channels are caught to make an evening here rewarding.

Perch are available, but in low numbers. Most are caught in spring by fishers looking for bluegills off the banks.

Some good crappies in the 10- to 12-inch range are taken from the lake in late April and May and again in the fall. Fish the cover and old snags from shore with jigs and minnows.

Bluegills are also in good numbers here. Most run small, but when spawning occurs in June, some nice bluegills up to 8 inches materialize from the lake's depths.

A small impounded pond of about 5 acres lies just east of Oxbow Lake. It is full of stumps and old trees and has been known to give up a nice bass or two. You can reach the pond by taking a short walk south from a parking area located at the end of a lane on the east side of the lake.

Special regulations: Oxbow Lake is limited to 9.9 hp. Minimum length for kept bass is 18 inches. The sunfish and crappie daily bag limit is 10 fish. White amurs were stocked to control weed growth. If caught, these must be immediately released unharmed.

Facilities/camping: There are no facilities at the lake, and camping is not permitted. South of Oxbow Lake is the town of Defiance, which can supply all amenities.

Additional information: A small community nature preserve is located just south of Oxbow Lake along Highway15.

Directions: Oxbow Lake is located 6 miles north of Defiance off Highway 15.

36 Pleasant Hill Lake

Key species: Largemouth and smallmouth bass, saugeye, channel and flathead catfish, white bass, bluegill, crappie, muskie.

General description: There is a smorgasbord of good fishing in this lake.

Overview: Impounded in 1938 by the Corps of Engineers, Pleasant Hill Lake covers 850 acres and is administered by the Muskingum Watershed Conservancy District (MWCD). The MWCD Pleasant Hill Lake Park has a campground, a marina with fuel and boat rental, and a beach. Just outside the park, the MWCD maintains the only public boat ramp and a wheelchair-accessible fishing pier.

The lake's primary function is flood control, and water levels can vary as much as 9 to 20 feet after prolonged periods of rain.

As with all MWCD lakes, shoreline access is limited. A boat is the only practical way to fish this lake. The lake has no horsepower limit, but is divided on the Richland-Ashland County line between a 6 mph zone and a ski zone.

The fishing: The bass fishing here is fairly good. There are not many lunkers, but a good number of 1- to 2-pound bass find their way into live wells. Tournament fishing is as popular here as it is anywhere. Most bass fishing is done in the eastern portion of the lake toward the dam. Fish both banks and all the coves near the dam. Much downed timber is in those coves and along the edges. Fish the shoreline cover, the slips, and fallen trees along the east and west banks from the dam north to the bend in the lake. Chartreuse crank baits, plastic tubes, and worms are the choice of locals. The lake's smallmouth also come from the rocks and points in this stretch. The deep bank just west of the lodge is excellent during the summer. The old stream channel swings tight against this bank, and bass suspend 6 to 12 feet in over 20 feet of water just off of it. Use Rattle Traps to catch suspended bass, as gizzard shad is the primary forage in the lake. On summer evenings use buzz baits around shoreline cover and along the edges of boat docks on the lake's south shoreline directly across from the marina. The best fishing is from April through May and again in September.

Crappies can be caught all year, but the prime months are mid-April through early June. Fish the boat docks and shoreline brush on the lake's east side. The docks on the south shore are also excellent. Use minnows and a bobber, small jigs and grubs. Crappies are widespread; any shoreline brush will hold crappies. Crappies range from 10 to 12 inches, but a few 14-inch fish show up every spring.

Bluegills are healthy here, and many hand-size fish are caught just about anywhere close to the shoreline. The biggest bluegills are caught in early June. Fish the cover in 2 to 4 feet of water, and you will catch your fill. Wax worms and red worms do the job.

Saugeyes are very good at this lake; an occasional 10-pound fish can be caught. Fish curly tail jigs and jigs with minnows in front of the beach and boat ramp just outside the marker buoys. Slow trolling works best in this area. On the east shoreline, fish the rocks and points with small crank baits and curly tail jigs. Fish the flats across from the wheelchair-accessible area at the end of Forbes Road. Fishing for saugeyes is good in the lake from March through May and again in September, until the lake freezes over. Evenings and cloudy days are best. Fish can also be caught from the headwaters in Clearfork in early spring. During periods of high water, saugeyes are also caught from the tailwaters with ⅛-ounce jigs and chartreuse curly tail grubs. Saugeyes over 10 pounds have come from the Pleasant Hill tailwaters.

Channel cats obtain a great size in Pleasant Hill; channels 10 to 15 pounds are caught often. Fish the northwest end of the lake around the small island and off the shoreline west of the boat ramp. Also fish the creek channel where it enters the lake from the west end. The shallow flat on the southwest shore is also a top producer. If fishing from shore, the bank around the wheelchair-accessible area is hard to beat for night fishing. Use night crawlers and shrimp.

Flatheads are well distributed throughout the lake and could likely be caught anywhere. Fish up to 35 pounds have been caught from the same creek channel as channel cats—at the west end of the lake, but just south of the island. Use shad and a tight line or just drift; both work well.

White bass are common throughout the lake. I was told to follow the schools of shad to find them. Beginning in mid-April the white bass begin a spawning run up the Clearfork, and catching 30 to 40 fish a day is not unusual at this time. During the spring run, use white Rooster Tails, white Mepps, and small white bucktail jigs. Later in June and July, the bass start suspending under the shad and can be observed in the jumps. The best action is across from the boat ramp on the south shore and around the dam. White curly tail jigs and small rattle traps work well for summer white bass.

Muskies are an interesting study at Pleasant Hill. The lake was never stocked with muskies, yet several nice muskies come from the lake every year. Muskies originally stocked in Clear Fork Reservoir wash over the dam during high-water events and enter Clearfork Creek. Some 17 miles downstream, muskies eventually find their way into the headwaters of Pleasant Hill Lake. In early spring, starting in mid-March, muskies making a spawning run up the stream are observed in Clearfork Creek at the bridge east of Newville. This activity occurs for about three weeks; the muskies return to the lake by mid- to late April. Muskies are caught in July and August where the Clearfork Creek channel enters the lake. I suspect the stream is cooler, and this is why muskies are located there during the summer months. I've seen this occur in Kentucky muskie lakes during the summer. Muskies are caught trolling big Shad Raps and Bagley's Shads.

Special regulations: Minimum size on bass is 12 inches. Unlimited horsepower, but the lake is divided into two speed zones.

Facilities/camping: The Pleasant Hill Lake Park has 280 camping sites, 10 vacation cabins, and 3 small camper cabins. The Mohican State Park lodge has 96 rooms and a dining hall. Perrysville is east of the lake, which has gas, ice, and groceries.

Additional information: Visit Malabar Farm State Park, which is the farm of Pulitzer Prize–winning author Louis Bromfield. The park is located just west of Pleasant Hill Lake on Pleasant Valley Road.

Directions: Take Highway 95 north of the small town of Butler, located on Highway 97 approximately 8 miles east of I-71.

37 Resthaven Wildlife Area

Key species: Bass, bluegill, crappie, redear sunfish, channel catfish.

General description: Resthaven Wildlife Area has 13 ponds available for fishing.

Overview: Resthaven is a large wetland wildlife area of 2,272 acres. It has a number of ponds totaling more than 400 acres of water. Most ponds have carry-in boat access; pond 8 has a concrete ramp and wheelchair-accessible pier and is limited to 10 hp. Access is off the county roads; some shoreline access is available, but most spots require a small boat to fish efficiently.

The fishing: The ponds on Resthaven are bog-type marsh ponds with brushy islands, backwater channels, standing timber, stumps, and logs throughout. Obviously some ponds are better bass ponds, some are better bluegill ponds, some have good crappies, and a few have channel cats. For bass, fish the brushy bank and around the old stumps and logs with spinner baits and plastics. Bluegills can be picked up anywhere along the shore and around the brushy islands on small jigs and wax worms. In spring and fall, crappies can be found around the deeper holes with timber; a minnow and bobber is all you need. Channels can be caught from a few ponds using chicken livers and night crawlers. Most run small, but some 2- to 3-pound channels have been caught.

Special regulations: Pond 8 has a minimum length limit of 15 inches for bass and a 10-hp limit. Other limits may apply to other area ponds; check current regulations.

Facilities/camping: There are no facilities or camping at the wildlife area. The nearby town of Castalia has all the amenities.

Additional information: Located a couple of miles east on Heywood Road is the Castalia Trout Hatchery, open for public visitation from 8:00 a.m. to 3:00 p.m. weekdays.

Directions: Resthaven Wildlife Area is located approximately 5 miles southwest of Sandusky on Highway 269.

38 Sandusky River

The 65-mile stretch of the Sandusky River that runs between the towns of Upper Sandusky and Freemont was designated a State Scenic River in 1970. The river has an excellent spring walleye run in late March, and between Freemont and Tiffin, the stream has some of northwest Ohio's best smallmouth fishing.

Walleyes make an annual spring run up the Sandusky from late March to the end of April. The primary area to catch the spring run is in Freemont between the West State Street Bridge and Ballville Dam. Most walleye fishing is done from the Roger Young Park, located on the south side of town off South Front Street. Anglers have to climb the dike and down the riprap on the other side to access the river. Walleyes are caught from the Sandusky River, like they are from the Maumee, with jig and curly tail grubs.

Sandusky County Wolf Creek Park is approximately 4 miles south of Freemont. The park is divided into two sections. At Wolf Creek, the park has a public canoe launch with stream fishing for smallmouth, rock bass, sunfish, and channel catfish. Some 2- to 3-pound smallmouth have come from this stretch of water. Approximately 1 mile south of the Wolf Creek access is the other half of the county park, which has a very nice public campground where anglers can spend the night for a modest fee.

Approximately 2 miles north of the town of Upper Sandusky is the Indian Mill State Memorial. The old mill was built in 1820 on the Sandusky River, and during its time it turned out about a dozen bushels of grain a day. Across the bridge from the old mill is the Indian Mill Scenic River canoe access to the upper Sandusky River. From this access, you can launch a canoe or fish. Smallmouth, rock bass, sunfish, and channel catfish are what you'll most likely encounter here during the summer.

To get to the Indian Mill Scenic River access, take Highway 67 north 2 miles from the town of Upper Sandusky. Turn east on County Road C47.

39 St. Joseph Wildlife Area

Key species: Largemouth bass, crappie, trout, bluegill, northern pike, channel catfish, perch.

General description: Two large quarry ponds that offer excellent fishing for trout and bass.

Overview: The St. Joseph Wildlife Area is one of the Division of Wildlife's more recent purchases, consisting of 95.8 acres bordered on both sides by the St. Joseph River. The centerpiece of the purchase is two large quarry lakes, named in honor of two of northwest Ohio's most influential outdoor writers and past presidents of the Outdoor Writers of Ohio: the late Hobart "Hob" McKarns and the late Ted Barton. I knew both gentlemen well; they were devout conservationists and leading sportsmen who influenced a generation of hunters and fishermen.

There are few facilities at the lakes at this time. McKarns Lake does have a boat ramp and pier, and in the future Barton Lake will have one as well. The Division of Wildlife has moved the District 2 Fisheries Work Unit from Oxbow Lake into a new building constructed at the wildlife area.

The fishing: Both quarry ponds offer excellent bass, bluegill, and channel cat fishing.

In early spring, the Division of Wildlife stock trout into McKarns Lake. McKarns has depths of 70 to 80 feet, which enable trout to survive year-round. The visibility on McKarns Lake is over 6 feet; it has a number of small gravel reefs, weedy shallows, rock points, brush, and some timber. The lake also contains a few large northern pike. When the Division of Wildlife fisheries personnel sampled the lake shortly after the purchase, a couple of 40-inch pike turned up.

Barton Lake, which averages 35 to 40 feet, resembles a large farm pond with a gentle sloping bank and some weed growth along the edges and in the shallows.

The St. Joseph River, which runs between McKarns and Barton Lakes, will flood into both lakes during periods of high water, bringing with it a fresh supply of fish.

Both lakes can be fished from shore, although McKarns Lake is a more typical quarry pond with steep banks and a loose-rock shoreline. Both lakes are within walking distance of each other.

Just northwest of McKarns Lake, in the wildlife area, are a couple of small quarry ponds that contain bass, bluegill, and channel catfish.

Special regulations: Outboard motors are limited to 10 hp. Bag limits are 5 trout, 10 sunfish, 10 crappies, and 5 bass 18 inches or longer.

Facilities/camping: There are no facilities or camping areas at this time.

Additional information: Hob McKarns lived in the nearby town of Bryan and wrote his outdoor column for the *Bryan Times* for more than 30 years. Ted Barton is from the Toledo area.

Directions: St. Joseph Wildlife Area is located just southwest of Montpelier, east of Highway 576, on County Road J.

40 Van Buren Lake

Key species: Largemouth bass, bluegill, channel catfish, bullhead.

General description: A small, shallow lake with limited fishing opportunities.

Overview: The dam over Rocky Ford Creek was constructed in 1939, impounding a 45-acre lake that was named after the eighth U.S. president, Martin Van Buren. Van Buren State Park was established in 1950. Today it offers a campground; picnic areas and shelter houses; hiking, biking, and bridle trails; and a primitive boat ramp.

The fishing: Van Buren is a shallow, murky lake, not much more than 6 feet deep. Shoreline access is along the entire north shore by way of the park road; to reach the south bank you would need a boat.

Van Buren Lake has abundant shoreline cover in the way of overhanging trees, old trunks and logs, and brush. There are some weeds in the shallow bays, but I would avoid them when fishing.

Bass are not large, 12 to 13 inches, nor are they plentiful. Work the south shore cover with chartreuse and yellow spinner baits; white buzz baits may get their attention on summer evenings.

Channel cats are in good supply but barely reach 16 inches. Most use shrimp or chicken livers. Fish from the south shore; there are plenty of locations along the bank.

Bluegills are small but can be readily caught with just a pinch of night crawler.

Smallmouth, bluegills, and channel cats can also be caught from Rocky Ford Creek south of the campground. A trail from the campground leads to the creek and follows the stream to the lake.

Special regulations: Electric motors only.

Facilities/camping: The state park has 38 campsites. You can pick up groceries and ice at the interstate gas and convenience store located at the Interstate 75 and Highway 613 intersection.

Additional information: The tiny village of Van Buren has a wonderful little ice-cream bar located in the center of town that is open during the summer.

Directions: From Findlay, take I-75 north 6 miles to the Highway 613 exit, turn east, and go 2 miles.

41 Vermilion River

The Vermilion River is one of the more recent additions to the state's list of steelhead streams. The Division of Wildlife first stocked the river in 2002 with 66,199 steelhead smolts. Years before the first steelhead were ever officially released, migrating Lake Erie steelhead had already established the stream as an excellent steelhead river. Normally by mid-October, depending on temperature, steelhead enter the river and anglers start picking them up at the Vermilion boat ramp and dock and from under the U.S. Highway 6 Bridge. Anglers catch steelhead from under the bridge throughout fall. In winter, holes are cut into the ice and the anglers keep catching them. Any rainfall that raises the river a few inches is all it takes to send the steelhead upstream to the Lorain County Metro Park holdings along the upper Vermilion, where stream anglers can find them holed up in the deeper river pools. By March, steelhead are found throughout the entire Vermilion River, their upstream spawning migration blocked only by the dam at the town of Wakeman.

The Lorain County Metro Parks have a number of parks and various park properties on the upper Vermilion River known as the Vermilion River Reservation that anglers can use to access the stream. Mill Hollow and Bacon Woods Park are adjoining parks with picnic areas, shelter houses, restrooms, and ample parking. Schoepfle Gardens is a smaller park with some facilities, but its gates are closed at 8:00 p.m. The rest of the park areas from which anglers can access the stream are simply gravel parking areas.

From the town of Vermilion, going upstream or south, the first public access is just north of the Vermilion Road and Highway 2 overpass by way of a small pulloff on the west side of the road. From there it is a short hike downhill to the river. Just past that pulloff going south are two gravel parking areas at the Vermilion Road–Jerusalem Road intersection, from which there is a well-worn path across a guardrail that leads downhill to the river.

The next access is at Bacon Woods and Mill Hollow County Parks, located on North Ridge Road on both sides of the river. This section of stream includes a series of nice riffles and pools and is a popular steelhead spot. Anglers from here can easily access a couple of miles of stream.

If you prefer the company of wild turkeys and deer over crowds of anglers, the access at the end of Peaseley Road should be suitable. To get to Peaseley Road, take Portman Road west off Vermilion Road just before the I-80/Interstate 90 overpass. Go 0.5 mile, turn north on Peaseley Road, and follow it to a gravel parking area on the left; the road dead-ends just ahead. Walk the old county road through the beautiful woodlot down to the stream, which is on the left. It is a long walk to this upstream location on the Vermilion River but worth every step.

There is also a listed access area off Gore Orphanage Road, about a mile west of Peaseley Road, but the access there is questionable. An old county road dead-ends next to a residence from which there are posted ROAD CLOSED and NO PARKING signs. I wouldn't feel comfortable parking that close to a residence. Perhaps a better option is to access the old Gore Orphanage dead-end road from Sperry Township Road off Highway 60.

Farther upstream, access is located at the Highway 113 Bridge at the Schoepfle Garden Metro Park. Anglers are allowed to fish there only until the gates close at 8:00 p.m. A pathway from the parking area leads down to the stream.

The farthest upstream location where anglers can find steelhead on the Vermilion River is at the Wakeman Dam located at the U.S. Highway 20 Bridge in the town of Wakeman. Access there is also questionable, as the parking area next to the bridge had a NO TRESPASSING sign posted next to a well-worn trail that led downhill to the stream.

The Vermilion River is home not only to steelhead but to smallmouth, bluegills, sunfish, and channel cats. The river is a beautiful place to fish and spend the day. Enjoy your time there.

The Vermilion River is located south of the town of Vermilion. From Highway 60, anglers can easily access the Lorain County Metro Park's Vermilion River Reservation.

42 Upground Reservoirs of Northwest Ohio

Drought conditions in Ohio during the early 1960s led to the establishment of a comprehensive water development plan. The first such plan was the Northwest Ohio Water Plan, which recommended the construction of "upground" reservoirs to meet the water-supply needs of local and regional communities. Because of the relatively flat terrain in northwest Ohio, impounding streams was not feasible or possible in most cases. Instead, large upground reservoirs were built to meet those needs.

Upground reservoirs are the second most common type of water reservoir in Ohio. They are typically large excavated ponds or lakes built aboveground, embanked on all sides, and usually rectangular in design. Some reservoirs were built large enough to hold more than 600 surface acres of water. They typically have a flat clay bottom, the sides are lined with limestone rock or boulder, and water is pumped in from a nearby water source. The upground reservoir is designed as a water-holding structure that must be periodically replenished. Most communities have a number of upground reservoirs, and new ones are built as demands on the water supply increase. In addition to supplying water, upground reservoirs also provide recreational benefits to northwest Ohio communities, such as fishing and boating, and many serve as community parks. Use restrictions vary with each reservoir, and regulations are generally posted at the entrance.

The Division of Wildlife stocks the reservoirs with bass, bluegill, and channel catfish; and most are stocked with saugeye or walleye on a semiregular basis. A majority of the reservoirs have boat ramps, and some have wheelchair-accessible fishing piers.

42-A. Archbold Reservoirs

The town of Archbold has two upground reservoirs. They are located on the east side of town behind the Sauder industrial buildings. Both are nearly impossible to find; only one street, Reservoir Street, leads to the reservoirs.

Archbold Reservoirs allow only carry-in boats with electric motors; no boat ramps are available. Both reservoirs are stocked with bass, bluegill, channel catfish, and saugeye. The smaller Reservoir 1 has yellow perch. Of the two, Reservoir 1, which is only 20 acres, is the most interesting. It has grassy banks, some large rock structures, and a number of other shoreline features that make for good fish habitat. I am told both reservoirs have on occasion produced some nice bass.

Archbold Reservoirs are easily accessed from a single parking area behind the town's waterworks plant. Additional parking areas for the larger Reservoir 2 are on an access road that runs between the two.

Bob Orewiler with a channel cat from Bucyrus Reservoir, one of many he regularly catches during the summer.

42-B. Bellevue Reservoirs

The city of Bellevue has a number of upground reservoirs. The first is located just southeast of town in a residential neighborhood off Bauer Road. A small gravel lane next to a residence takes you right to the foot of the reservoir. No boats are permitted; fishing is by shoreline only. Shoreline cover consists of small willow trees and a small amount of brush and rock. This reservoir is approximately 20-plus acres and contains bass, bluegills, and channel cats.

The other Bellvue Reservoir is south of town, 5 miles off Highway 547, and is the most unusual upground reservoir I have ever seen. Instead of having the rectangular shape that most upground reservoirs have, this reservoir is perfectly round. It is a large reservoir of more than 100 acres. Boats are not permitted on this reservoir, and anglers have to climb up the steep grade to get to the water's edge. Fishing for bass, bluegill, crappie, channel catfish, and saugeye is allowed from the shoreline only.

42-C. Bresler Reservoir

At 610 acres, Bresler is one of the largest upground reservoirs in northwest Ohio. The lake averages 20 to 35 feet deep, but there is a large reef on the reservoir's southeast corner that ranges from 10 to 15 feet deep. The reservoir contains white bass, largemouth and smallmouth bass, bluegill, walleye, crappie, channel catfish, and perch. The lake is popular with bank walkers who like to walk the 3.5 miles around the reservoir. There is a concrete boat ramp; only electric motors are permitted.

Bass fishing is good at Bresler Reservoir. Some 3- to 4-pound fish have been caught from the shoreline late and early in the morning. To pick up walleyes and bass, slow troll along the edges with deep-diving crank baits. For walleyes, drift or slow troll the shallow hump or reef with night crawlers or jigs and minnows. Catch perch off the boat ramp dock with worms; get channels from the shoreline with chicken livers or night crawlers suspended under a floater. You can catch some nice channels from Bresler Reservoir; some may even be in the 15-pound-plus range.

Bresler Reservoir is located approximately 4 miles west of Lima off Highway 81.

42-D. Bucyrus Reservoirs

The city of Bucyrus has four reservoirs: two are upground reservoirs and two are older impounded reservoirs. All have bass, bluegill, and channel catfish. The largest upground reservoir, named Paul R. Outhwaite Reservor, also has crappie, saugeye, and perch and is said to have flathead catfish as well.

Reservoir 1, called Robert Clark Neff Reservoir, is an older impounded reservoir of 40 acres with parking and a primitive boat launch. It has a lot of shoreline cover, timber, brush, weeds, and cattails and is located just off Plymouth Road northeast of town. The reservoir is limited to electric motors only.

Reservoir 2 is also an older impounded reservoir. It is 38 acres, has a primitive boat ramp, and is limited to electric motors only. Its shoreline cover consists of downed timber and brush. It is located at Stetzer Road east of town.

Reservoir 3, called Riley Reservoir, is an upground reservoir of 30 acres. It is very clear with a limestone rock shoreline. There are two parking areas but no boat ramp. Riley Reservoir is located on Kiess Road northeast of town. Small watercraft can be carried in but are limited to electric motors only.

The largest upground reservoir is Reservoir 4, Outhwaite Reservoir, and is 150 acres. It has a boat ramp and three parking areas. Boats are limited to electric motors only. The reservoir averages 30 feet deep at full capacity. The water is very clear with visibility as far as 6 to 7 feet. It too has a limestone-rock shoreline, which is typical in this type of upground reservoir. Channel cat fishing is very good at Outhwaite Reservoir, with channels reaching upwards of 5 to 6 pounds. Chicken livers with a touch of garlic work well here. Baja Boat Company, which manufactures their line of boats in Bucyrus, has special permission from the city to test run boats in this reservoir. The reservoir is located northeast of town, on Plymouth Road.

There is a small public fishing pond of about 10 acres at the industrial park north of town off US 30. It is known as Crossroads Industrial Pond and contains bass, bluegill, and catfish. It can be reached from the Highway 4 exit off US 30.

42-E. Celeryville Reservoir

The Celeryville Reservoir is located about 4 miles south of Willard, off Highway 103 behind a small community church. I estimate the reservoir at 65 to 75 acres. It contains bass, bluegill, and channel catfish. There is no boat ramp and only a small gravel parking area that has a path that leads up the dike to the water's edge. The reservoir is used primarily for water irrigation.

42-F. Clyde City Reservoirs

The city of Clyde has a couple of upground reservoirs that permit public fishing. Both reservoirs are stocked with bass, bluegill, channel cat, and crappie.

Raccoon Creek Reservoir is located just south of Clyde off Highway 101. I estimate the reservoir is about 25 acres. It has a boat ramp and is limited to electric motors only. The reservoir also serves as a community park. Unlike typical upground reservoirs, Raccoon Creek has a big limestone-rock shoreline and broken concrete pieces along the banks that provide plenty of shoreline cover.

The larger reservoir, called Beaver Creek Reservoir, is also an upground reservoir with a concrete ramp and pier. It is limited to electric motors only. It too has a big limestone-rock shoreline and good shoreline cover. It yields some nice catches of bass, crappie, and channel catfish. It can be reached 4 miles south of Clyde on Highway 101.

42-G. Delta Reservoirs

The town of Delta in Fulton County has a couple of very nice reservoirs for residents to fish. Reservoir 1 is a dug and impounded reservoir of 39 acres. The newer Reservoir 2 is a large upground reservoir of 50 acres. Both have boat ramps and are limited to electric motors only. A community park is located at the reservoirs, with picnic tables, a shelter house, and restrooms. There is ample parking and good access to both lakes. Both reservoirs contain bass, bluegill, and channel catfish.

The older Resevoir 1 has an abundance of shoreline cover, overhanging trees, and brush, resembling an ideal fishing lake more than a municipal water supply.

The larger Reservoir 2 is very clear, with 6- to 7-foot visibility, a large limestone-rock and boulder shoreline, and a double concrete boat ramp and pier. The reservoir averages 30 to 35 feet deep, with some deep 50- to 60-foot pockets. There are a few shallow rock reefs in the lake, and over the years fish structures were anchored to those reefs and at specific locations along the shoreline.

Nice bass have been taken from both reservoirs; I wouldn't hesitate to fish either of them. They are located north of town on County Road H.

42-H. Deshler Reservoirs

The small village of Deshler has three small upground reservoirs that allow public fishing. They are located south of town. Unlike the majority of upground lakes, these reservoirs contain a variety of shoreline structures, overhanging trees, riprap, and old snags that provide excellent cover for game fish. All reservoirs are part of the Community Crossroads Park.

The largest reservoir has a primitive boat ramp and is limited to electric motors only. It has been stocked with bass, bluegill, crappie, and channel cats. The reservoir has produced some big channels; most are caught on chicken livers, shrimp, and night crawlers. In spring some 4- to 5-pound bass have been caught on spinner baits and plastic night crawlers. Fish the south bank against the tree line roots and riprap for summer bass. Crappies and bluegills are taken from the shoreline brush.

Just across and to the north of the main reservoir is a smaller upground reservoir that has a number of old snags, fallen tree cover, and brush. It too has bass, bluegill, and channel cats and can be reached from the boat ramp.

North of that is yet a smaller reservoir that has weeds and shoreline cover. The small pond is popular with the town fishers and youngsters who like to fish for bluegills off the dike. The town of Deshler has Fishing Fun Days on the reservoirs every so often. Deshler is located just inside the Henry County line on Highway 18.

42-I. Findlay Reservoirs

Findlay has two very nice upground reservoirs that are part of the Riverbend-Findlay Recreation Area. Reservoir 1 is 187 acres and is stocked with walleye, channel catfish, and perch. Reservoir 2 is the largest upground reservoir in northwest Ohio at 640 acres. It contains largemouth and smallmouth bass, walleye, crappie, channel catfish, white bass, perch, and bluegill. Both reservoirs have boat ramps and fishing piers. Reservoir 1 is limited to electric motors only; Reservoir 2 is limited to 9.9-hp motors. Both allow ice fishing.

Reservoir 2 has had fishing structures placed at several locations near shore and at the boat dock pier. Bass can be caught early in the morning and during the evening off the rock banks. During the day troll along the rock shoreline. Deep-diving crank baits and spinners produce for all species. Channel catfish do well in both reservoirs; some 20-pound-plus catfish have been reported. Fish chicken livers and shrimp for catfish. Walleyes in the 6- to 8-pound range are caught, and some good largemouth and smallmouth are occasionally caught.

The reservoirs are popular recreation areas with walkers, joggers, and local fishers. Riverbend Park has a small pond called Giertz Lake, which is a favorite fishing hole for youngsters. Every spring the pond is stocked with trout. Riverbend Park also has primitive tent camping available.

Findlay Reservoirs and Riverbend Park are located 2 miles east of Findlay off Highway 568.

42-J. Fostoria Reservoirs

Fostoria anglers have a number of nice reservoirs from which to fish. In remembrance of Fostoria's veterans, all the town's reservoirs are named after soldiers who lost their lives in war.

The newest is Reservoir 6, Veterans Memorial Reservoir. It is a large upground reservoir that covers 160 acres. It is stocked with crappie, perch, saugeye, bluegill, and bass. The reservoir has a boat ramp and is limited to 9.9-hp outboards. The reservoir was constructed somewhat differently than other upground reservoirs in that large limestone boulders line the lake's edge. This makes it difficult to walk on, but the crevices and cavities created between the boulders make good shoreline cover for bass and other game fish. As a result, bass fishing is excellent along the banks; several bass in the 4- to 5-pound range have been caught. Spinner and crank baits work well; night crawlers and wax worms will get the bluegills and perch. Occasionally a saugeye will come to the net, and minnows will get the crappies.

Reservoir 5, Lake Lecomte, in addition to bass, bluegill, and channel cats, has been stocked with walleye. For whatever reason, the banks along this upground reservoir have poured concrete over a large part of the shoreline rock. This eliminates the rocky banks typically found in upground reservoirs and makes shoreline walking and fishing difficult and dangerous. It also has a boat ramp and small wooden dock.

Reservoir 4, Lake Mosier, is a smaller upground reservoir that appears to be slowly drying up. There is an island with a transmission tower in the center and good shoreline cover in the way of small trees, brush, and rock. The reservoir has been stocked with bass, bluegill, and channel cats. The boat ramp is no longer usable, but it is still possible to launch a small boat.

Reservoir 1, Lake Daugherty, is a nice-looking, older in-ground or "dug" reservoir, with grassy and rocky banks and some minor shoreline cover. It too has bass, bluegill, and channel cats. No boats are permitted on this reservoir, but the fishing is easy, as you can walk around the mowed banks.

The two other Fostoria reservoirs are located in the city at the waterworks plant. Both are older inground reservoirs. Reservoir 2, Lake Mottram, is a fishy-looking lake, with rock and weedy banks and some shoreline cover in the form of small willow trees and brush. Reservoir 3, Lake Lamberjack, has a boat ramp and grassy, brushy, and rocky banks. The lake is limited to 10-hp motors. Both are well supplied with game fish.

Reservoirs 1, 4, 5, and 6 are located just south of town. Reservoirs 2 and 3 are located in Fostoria on the west side.

42-K. Galion Reservoirs

The town of Galion has a number of reservoirs, three or four depending on how you count them. Two are upground reservoirs and one is an impounded lake that serves as a city park. That lake has two spillways; one lake leads into the other.

Powers Reservoir is the older of the two upground reservoirs and is located just south of town on Railroad Street. It has a boat ramp and dock; boats are limited to electric motors only. The reservoir is stocked with bluegills, bass, and channel catfish.

South of Galion off Highway 61 is Amann and Amick Reservoirs, one of which is a newer upground reservoir. Both are located within the city park. Both are stocked with bass, bluegill, and channel catfish. Each reservoir has a boat ramp; boats are limited to electric motors only.

The old impounded Galion Reservoir serves as a city park lake. It is a small lake, about 45 acres, with plenty of shoreline cover and fishing access. It is a popular spot with the local fishers. It too has bass, bluegill, and channel catfish. The city park is located south of Galion on Crawford-Morrow County Line Road.

42-L. Hamler Pond

The little village of Hamler, located at the intersection of Highway 18 and Highway 109, has a small community pond right off Highway 18 on the north side of town. It has a shelter house and parking. The pond is no more than 2 acres and has bass, bluegill, and some channel catfish.

42-M. Killdeer Reservoir

Killdeer Reservoir is a large upground reservoir of 285 acres, located 9 miles south of the town of Upper Sandusky on Highway 67, near the small town of Marseilles. It is different from other upground reservoirs in that it was designed with fishing in mind. It has 18 rock reefs, a number of rocky points, and an island. It is stocked with smallmouth, walleye, bluegills, and channel catfish. When the reservoir was at full capacity, it was over 35 feet deep. The reservoir has one boat ramp (no longer usable as of this writing) and four parking areas. The lake is limited to 10 hp. The shoreline is large limestone rock and boulders. Normally the water is very clear, with visibility 6 feet or better. Fish the reefs, points, and island for smallmouth and walleyes. Some reefs have old tires and wooded structures anchored on them. Bluegills are along the banks; the channels can be located in the open water and on the reef edges. Fish crank baits and tubes for smallmouth; jigs and minnows or spinners and night crawlers worked slowly along the bottom of the reefs will pick up walleyes.

Killdeer Reservoir has developed several leaks in the dikes over the years, and the water level will never again be what it was when it was first created. I estimate the water level on the reservoir to be at least 15 to 20 feet lower than when it was first constructed. There are no plans to repair the leakage, and damage to the concrete pier was substantial.

East of the reservoir is the Killdeer Plains Wildlife Area. The area has a number of ponds, some of which are quite large and have never been stocked. That said, pond 33, 0.25 mile east of Killdeer Reservoir, is fishable. The pond covers 10 acres and has a new boat ramp. Anglers can expect to catch bass, bluegill, and channel catfish. Pond 30, at the east end of the wildlife area, also has bass, bluegill, and channel catfish.

42-N. Lima City Reservoirs

The city of Lima has four large upground reservoirs located on the east side of town: Lima Reservoir, Ferguson Reservoir, Metzger Reservoir, and Lost Creek Reservoir. Combined they offer more than 670 acres of public fishing water. Ice fishing is permitted on all reservoirs.

Lima Reservoir, or Lima Lake as it is called, covers 85 acres and contains crappies, largemouth bass, saugeyes, bluegills, channel cats, white bass, and trout. Trout are stocked in the spring and fall. The lake has a city park that includes picnic areas, a shelter house, a swimming pool, a campground, a wheelchair-accessible pier, and a concrete boat ramp with dock. Lima Lake is limited to electric motors only. There is some shoreline structure in the way of overhanging trees and a few old logs along the north shore, but the majority of shoreline is limestone rock. Most bass run small, from 12 to 13 inches, but occasionally a nice 3- or 4-pound fish shows up for some lucky angler. Trout fishing is popular, and most are taken with cheese, Power Bait, mealworms, and Rooster Tails. Channels up to 16 inches are caught using chicken livers; most are caught from the shoreline.

Ferguson Reservoir is the largest Lima City Reservoir at 305 acres. It contains walleye, bluegill, channel catfish, white bass, largemouth and smallmouth, and yellow perch. It has a primitive gravel boat launch and is limited to electric motors. It too has a typical limestone shoreline, with some limited bank cover on the south and east banks. Fishing for walleyes is fair, with some 6-pound fish showing up on occasion. Most anglers drift-fish along the shoreline with spinners and night crawlers or night crawler harnesses. Occasionally a nice smallmouth makes an appearance. To catch one, fish crawdad-colored crank baits or watermelon tubes off the rock shoreline mornings or evenings. Cat fishing in the reservoir is good, with some nice channels over the 10-pound mark. Most channel anglers fish from the banks using cut shad; in the evening or at night, they use night crawlers fished on the bottom.

Metzger Reservoir covers 167 acres and is located right next door to Ferguson Reservoir. A fisher can easily fish both from the roadway that separates the two, or drag a small boat over the gravel roadway and fish both at the same time. Metzger has saugeye, bass, bluegill, channel catfish, and perch. The reservoir has a gravel boat ramp and is limited to electric motors only. Saugeye average 15 to 20 inches and are caught the same way that anglers catch walleyes in Ferguson, with spinners and night crawler harnesses. A few are picked up off the limestone banks with crank baits in the evening. Channel cats are also nice, with some in the 20- to 22-inch range caught frequently on chicken livers.

Lost Creek Reservoir is the nicest-looking reservoir in the bunch. The reservoir covers 120 acres, has carry-in boat access only, and is limited to electric motors. Lost Creek has a nice brushy, weedy shoreline; some big limestone rocks provide good cover all the way around the lake. Lost Creek contains crappie, saugeye, largemouth bass, bluegill, perch, and channel catfish. Crappies range from 8 to 9 inches; bass don't get too big, but some 3-pound fish are caught; channels do well, with most in the 12- to 20-inch range; and saugeyes up to 18 inches are caught.

Lima Reservoir is located east of Lima on Highway 81. Ferguson, Metzger, and Lost Creek are all located along East High Street, east of town.

42-O. New London Reservoir

New London has one of the nicest upground reservoirs in northwest Ohio. The water is clear, with 5 to 6 feet of visibility, and there are numerous fish-holding structures such as reefs, points, and weed beds. The land around the reservoir has been made into a popular community park with camping, picnic areas, a beach, shelter houses, cabins, and three parking areas for fishers outside the park. The reservoir is popular with fishers, windsurfers, sail boaters, and canoers and kayakers. New London Reservoir is a large reservoir of 220 acres. It has a concrete boat ramp and is limited to electric motors only. The lake contains largemouth and smallmouth bass, rock bass, bluegill, walleye, saugeye, crappie, yellow perch, and channel catfish. The water can reach depths of over 30 feet when filed to capacity, although most of the reservoir depths average 20 feet.

This is not your typical upground reservoir. It was constructed in 1975 with the cooperation of the Division of Wildlife, which incorporated a number of fish-holding structures and six reefs of varying sizes into its design. The reefs contain a mixture of rock, gravel, boulders, and stumps.

There is a limestone-rock shoreline around most of the reservoir, with little bank cover except for some standing grass beds at the east end of the lake. Most cover is submerged structure consisting of points, reefs, and weed beds. Most of the weeds are floating-leaf pondweed.

Some nice largemouth come from New London, with a few in the 5- to 6-pound range. Most, however, average 12 to 14 inches and are taken from the stone shoreline and weed edges with spinner baits, buzz baits, and top-water and plastic night crawlers. Smallmouths are taken from the rock reefs with crank baits, crayfish, and tubes.

Crappies up to 10 inches are taken off the reefs with white jigs and minnows. Yellow perch are caught in about 10 feet of water with minnows. Most perch are 8 to 10 inches. Some nice channels up to 7 to 8 pounds are taken at night from the shoreline with chicken livers. Walleyes up to 7 pounds and saugeye weighing in at 3 to 4 pounds are taken off the reefs and points by drifting night crawlers and casting deep-running crank baits. Rock bass and bluegills are common and can be found practically anywhere, especially around the weeds.

The campground at New London is open from April 15 through October 15 and is mostly occupied by seasonal campers. Approximately 60 to 70 sites are open to public camping.

A $15 annual permit and ID sticker must be obtained before launching a boat at New London Reservoir. To receive a permit and sticker, inquire at the camp office.

The reservoir is located southwest of the town of New London off Town Line Road.

42-P. North Baltimore Reservoirs

The town of North Baltimore has two new upground reservoirs located just off Highway 18, south of town. Named North Baltimore Reservoir 1 and 2, they are located side-by-side so an angler can park at one and fish both. There are no boat ramps on either reservoir. Both are stocked with largemouth bass, bluegill, and channel catfish.

Both reservoirs can be reached from the I-75/Highway 18 intersection, 8 miles north of Findlay.

42-Q. Norwalk Reservoirs

The city of Norwalk has three upground reservoirs, which are part of the Veteran's Memorial Lake Park complex. In addition to fishing, there are picnic areas, shelter houses, and walking trails. All reservoirs have boat ramps and are limited to electric motors only. The largest reservoir, Veteran's Memorial, also has a fishing pier, which is wheelchair accessible. The reservoirs contain largemouth and smallmouth bass, crappie, bluegill, saugeye, some walleye, channel catfish, and perch. The lower Reservoir 1 is stocked with trout in spring and fall.

The Norwalk reservoirs are not typical upground reservoirs. They are part upground and part impounded. Reservoirs 1 and 2 have irregular shorelines, abundant bank cover, overhanging trees, downed timber, and riprap on the dikes.

In 2006 Veteran's Reservoir was partially drained as a result of an early summer flood that threatened to overflow and damage the dike.

Reservoirs 1 and 2 are excellent reservoirs to fish; they have plenty of bank cover and yield good catches of bass in the spring and fall—some up to 5 pounds. Channels reach a respectable 18 to 20 inches, and some nice bluegills are caught in early June. Crappies can be caught off the shoreline brush and fallen trees starting in April. Trout fishing is popular, and area anglers look forward to the spring and fall stockings. Most trout are taken right off the banks with wax worms, Power Bait, cheese, and small Roster Tails. The reservoirs have good shoreline access, but steep banks on the south side of Reservoir 1 limit reaching the good bank cover except by boat.

Most anglers work the shoreline cover and riprap for bass with spinner baits, plastics, and crank baits. Old fisher trails lead up and down the shoreline of most reservoirs, allowing anglers to get a cast in just about anywhere on the lake. These are very nice reservoirs; fishers in Norwalk are lucky to have such fine lakes in their backyard.

42-R. Paulding Reservoir

The town of Paulding has one new upground reservoir, located south of town. It covers 63 acres and is stocked with bass, saugeye, bluegill, perch, and some crappie. It is limited to carry-in boats with electric motors. The reservoir is part of a county park system that has ball diamonds, walking trails, and a nature center.

Paulding Reservoir produces good bass in the 2- to 3-pound range that are caught with spinner and crank baits. Saugeyes are caught with curly tail jigs and minnows; most are 15 to 16 inches long. Perch, bluegills, and the occasional crappie are caught with night crawlers, small spinners, and minnows.

Just north of the reservoir is an old but small low-head dam that has impounded a small portion of Flatrock Creek. Channels, bluegills, and small bass are caught from the backed-up waters. The small pool has plenty of cover and lily pads and a place to launch a small boat.

The Black Swamp Nature Center is within the park. From there you can view a small wetland swamp that is loaded with waterfowl and shorebirds.

42-S. Shelby Reservoir

The town of Shelby has one large upground reservoir, which is located south of town off Highway 61. The reservoir, called Shelby Reservoir 2, has an all limestone shoreline. The water is very clear, with visibility better than 6 feet. The reservoir has bass, bluegill, walleye, and channel catfish. While visiting, I observed a bass I believe was better than 4 pounds. There is a single parking area, which provides steps leading to the top of the dike. I saw no posting restricting the use of watercraft.

Another reservoir, Reservoir 3, is said to be north of town, near the industrial park. All I could locate was a large dug pond with cattails along the edges. It looked inviting to fish, but there was no parking available. A well-worn path leading from London West Road to the pond was evident, however.

42-T. Swanton Reservoir

The village of Swanton has one nice upground reservoir located about a mile south of town on Highway 64. It has a gravel boat ramp and is restricted to electric motors and boats 14 feet or less. The reservoir contains bass, bluegill, and channel catfish. It is a nice-looking reservoir with a riprap shoreline of big limestone rock and broken concrete slabs. A thick stand of cattails grows along the west end shoreline. I estimate the reservoir to be approximately 45 acres. It was mowed and well maintained during my visit, making for easy walking and fishing along the banks.

42-U. Van Wert Reservoirs

The city of Van Wert has a couple of nice reservoirs located south of town, both of which are 65 acres and serve as the center of a city recreation area. The reservoirs are popular with residents, who like to walk or jog around the lakes. Each reservoir has a blacktop jogging path around it. There is no boat ramp on either reservoir, but each allows carry-in access for boats or canoes under 17 feet. Electric motors are permitted. Ice fishing is also allowed, but fishers younger than 16 years of age must be accompanied by an adult over 21 at all times.

The reservoirs are upgrounds, with a big limestone-rock shoreline providing some limited shoreline cover. The reservoirs are located within rock-throwing distance of each other. The reservoirs contain saugeye, walleye, channel catfish, smallmouth bass, bluegills, and trout. Trout are stocked in Reservoir 1 in early spring. Some trout are able to survive all year long in the reservoir, making for some nice catches later on.

Saugeyes average from small to 16 inches, nice channel cats are caught from both reservoirs, and smallmouth bass average 10 to 14 inches. Most smallmouth are caught by anglers using tubes, jigs and grubs, and small crank baits along the riprap shoreline. Saugeyes are also caught this way, but drifting or slow trolling a night crawler harness is usually more effective. Trout are caught all the usual ways, including with Power Bait, worms, and corn and casting small ⅛-ounce Rooster Tails. The channels, like channels everywhere, prefer chicken livers over anything, fished under a floater 6 to 10 feet deep.

Both reservoirs are located just south of Van Wert on U.S. Highway 127.

42-V. Wauseon Reservoirs

The town of Wauseon has two large upground reservoirs that sit side-by-side just south of town on County Road C off of Highway 108. Neither reservoir provides much parking, but a lane leading to the top sits between the two, which allows for carry-in boat launching. Only electric motors are allowed. The Wauseon Reservoirs are stocked with bass, bluegill, channel catfish, saugeye, and crappie. Both shorelines have plenty of rock structures, broken-up concrete slabs, and some shoreline grass and brush to provide enough bank cover to make the fishing interesting, if not productive. The older reservoir contains more shoreline structure and also has a few shallow rocky/concrete slab points that would probably hold a fish or two. The larger reservoir is 45 acres and contains some nice saugeye and channel cats up to 4 and 5 pounds. Most channels are caught using chicken liver and night crawlers. The saugeyes are taken off the rock banks with jigs and chartreuse curly tail grubs.

42-W. Willard Reservoir

The Willard City Reservoir, located east of town off Highway 61, covers 215 acres. It has a concrete boat ramp, a wheelchair-accessible fishing dock, and a small parking area with water and restrooms. The reservoir is limited to electric motors only and has been stocked with largemouth bass, crappie, channel catfish, bluegill, walleye, and perch. In all, the Willard Reservoir is a nice place to fish.

Willard is a typical upground reservoir that averages 30 to 40 feet deep. The visibility in this reservoir is exceptional, averaging 6 to 7 feet.

Some nice bass come from the reservoir, weighing 3 to 4 pounds; most are taken along the shorelines in early morning and evening and by offshore trolling. Channels average 15 to 25 inches and are caught by fishing off the banks and boat dock and pier using night crawlers and chicken livers suspended under a floater. Saugeye are taken off the bank and by trolling, with most weighing 2 to 3 pounds.

Northeast Ohio—Wildlife District Three

The northeast part of Ohio has the most fishing opportunities found anywhere in the state. From hybrid stripers below the locks and dams on the Ohio River to yellow perch fishing on Lake Erie, anglers living in the snowbelt part of the state have it all.

From the ports of Conneaut, Fairport, Cleveland, Ashland, and Lorain, Lake Erie offers steelhead, walleye, smallmouth, and yellow perch to any angler with or without a boat. Shoreline fishing opportunities abound, and the harbors offer charter boats and private boat owners a place to launch and fuel up for a day of fishing.

South of the Great Lake, the Ohio River has some of the state's best smallmouth fishing, second only to the bass fishing on Lake Erie, and a chance at walleye, sauger, hybrid stripers, and big flathead catfish below the locks and dams.

Some of the state's best muskie fishing is in Pymatuning, Leesville, and West Branch Reservoirs. If it's big saugeyes you're after, then you'll be happy to know that Clendening is one of the best bets in the state to land a state record. Some of the biggest flathead catfish in the state come from the Muskingum watershed lakes and Mosquito Lake. Mogadore and LaDue Reservoirs are both outstanding fisheries for everything from channel cats to crappies. If stream fishing, then Little Beaver Creek is a wonderful place to float and fish for smallmouth.

I saved the best for last, and that's the steelhead fishing in the Lake Erie tributaries. Conneaut, the Grand, the Chagrin, and the Rocky River come alive in early spring with the silver bullet of sport fish, the steelhead. No other fishing compares, and that's my pick of the best of the best in northeast Ohio.

43 Aquilla Lake

Key species: Largemouth bass, bluegill, channel catfish, a few northern pike.

General description: A beautiful and scenic little lake to fish.

Overview: Aquilla Lake is a small 29-acre natural lake that is the cornerstone of the Aquilla Lake Wildlife Area. The lake has a boat ramp and parking. Lily pads and aquatic vegetation are thick on the lake, which is typical of natural lakes. White amurs have been introduced to control the weeds. There is little shoreline access; the lake is best fished from a boat.

The fishing: Aquilla Lake is a nice weedy lake with a fair number of bass. Most average 10 to 12 inches, but an occasional 2- or 3-pounder shows up. Fish the weed edges and lily pads with plastic worms and spinner baits. In summer try buzz baits around the shoreline. Bluegills are numerous; most are around 5 to 6 inches. Catch

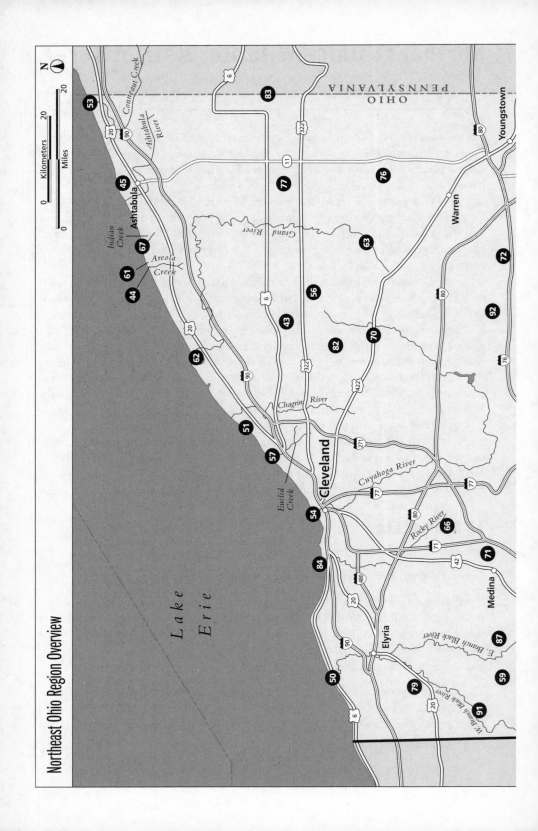

Northeast Ohio Region Overview

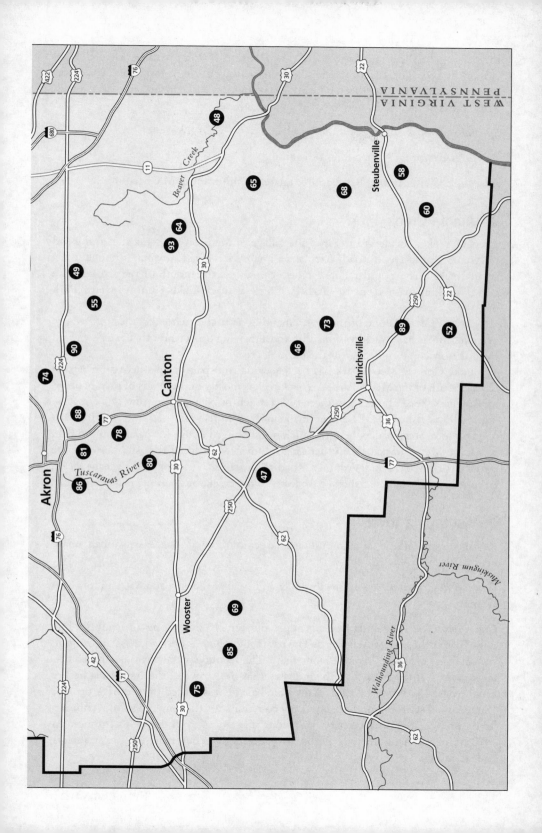

them along the shore and weed edges. The Division of Wildlife has stocked channel cats, most averaging 12 to 18 inches. Fishing on the bottom is tough because of the weed growth. A few northern pike are also caught in early spring; most run small. This lake is at the headwaters of the Cuyahoga River.

Special regulations: Electric motors only.

Facilities/camping: No facilities or camping.

Directions: Take Aquilla Road approximately 3 miles south of Chardon.

44 Arcola Creek

Arcola Creek is located just east of the village of Madison-on-the-Lake, at the end of Arcola Creek–Dock Road. Arcola is a quality steelhead stream. Although it is a small creek, it is a popular one. Anglers can access the mouth of the stream via a gravel walking path from the Arcola Creek Estuary–Lake County Metro Park parking area.

Arcola Creek is one of the few remaining natural estuaries on the south shore of Lake Erie. It has a variety of birdlife and a thriving osprey nest that can be viewed from the observation deck near the parking area.

Lake County Metro Park has been seeking to expand angler access on Arcola Creek. South of the Metro Park, Arcola Creek is mostly in the hands of private property owners. Several years ago there was a much-publicized shooting of a trespassing steelhead fisherman. The fisherman survived to fish another day, but after that incident local steelheaders became much more obliged to ask for permission to fish.

Lake Metro Park has another small unmarked holding that sits between the estuary parking area and Vrooman Road to the south. It looks like a vacant lot on Arcola Creek. A telltale fishers' path leads to the creek, but parking is questionable.

45 Ashtabula River

Key species: Steelhead, smallmouth and largemouth bass, rock bass, sunfish, channel catfish.

General description: A fine steelhead river, but also the site of a $50 million EPA cleanup.

Overview: The Ashtabula River is approximately 40 miles long and empties into Lake Erie at the city of Ashtabula. The name *Ashtabula* is derived from an Iroquois Indian name meaning "river of many fish." The Iroquois were obviously much better stewards of the river than the industry that has crowded the Ashtabula harbor for the past 150 years. In 1983, Ashtabula harbor was placed on the EPA priority "Superfund list" for containing industry contaminants that entered several tributaries by unregulated discharges of hazardous substances from the 1940s through the 1970s. Contaminants include PCBs, low-level radioactive material, heavy metals, and chemicals.

Fishing at the Lowhead Dam crossing on the Ashtabula River is popular during the fall.

In 2006, cleanup of the contaminated sediments from the harbor began, and it is expected to take two years. Since 1997, fish from Ashtabula harbor have been under a "do not eat" advisory issued by the Ohio Department of Health from the U.S. Highway 20 Bridge to Lake Erie.

While the Ashtabula River has significant problems in the harbor, upstream is another story. East of Highway 11, the Ashtabula is a beautiful shale bank stream with small waterfalls, covered bridges, and water as clear as if it were poured from the tap. The Department of Natural Resources is considering designating that eastern section of the Ashtabula River as a State Scenic River. This part of the river seems like an entirely different river than the one declared a Superfund site at the industrial center of town.

The fishing: The Division of Wildlife has not stocked the Ashtabula with steelhead due to the contaminants and the river's listing as a Superfund site. But neither the contaminants nor the EPA's listing has deterred the steelhead from utilizing the river for their own purposes. The Ashtabula has some very fine steelhead fishing and offers a generous amount of public access to boot.

The Ashtabula Township Park Commission has two parks from which anglers can access the Ashtabula River: Cedarquest Park and Indian Trails Park.

Cedarquest Park, which is the town ballpark, is located just west of the inter-section of Columbus Avenue and Harmon Hills Road. Anglers can park at either side of the bridge or at the park to access the river. A nice collection of deep pools and riffle water is found in this section and can be easily waded. The pool under the bridge is a local steelhead favorite.

Farther upstream is the Indian Trails Park, which encompasses 369 acres and over 3 miles of river. The river can be accessed in town from North Main, East 51st Street, and West 58th Street. Perhaps the best access to the Ashtabula, however, is at Indian Trails Park's South State Road entrance. At one time State Road went from Plymouth Ridge into the southeastern end of town. But the old bridge was deemed unsafe, and the road has been closed just beyond the entrance to the park. From the South State Road access, anglers can fish miles of river with plenty of deep holding pools, gravel spawning bars, and broad riffles.

Off Plymouth Road, west of Highway 11, there is a pulloff on the north side of the road that allows access to a small tributary stream of the Ashtabula River.

The last fishers' access point on the Ashtabula is at the old low-head dam on Hadlock Road. This is the farthest upstream point that steelhead can go on the river; it is also among the most scenic places to fish. Handlock Road fords the river at the old dam, which blocks the upstream migration of steelhead. During periods of high water, the road is impassable. A sign alongside the road reads:

PRIVATE PROPERTY, FISHING PERMITTED BY THE LANDOWNER,
DO NOT FISH IN FRONT OF THE HOUSE, STAY IN THE RIVER WHEN
WALKING UP OR DOWNSTREAM, PLEASE CARRY OUT ALL TRASH WITH
YOU, RESPECT ALL LANDOWNERS PROPERTY.

There is some talk that the old Hadlock Road dam may eventually be removed, which would allow steelhead to migrate farther upstream. But a few small waterfalls upstream of the Dewey Covered Bridge would be the limit of any steelhead migra-tion. It would also be a crime to deprive fishers of such a beautiful place to fish.

After the steelhead have gone in April, smallmouth, rock bass, and sunfish take over the stream. You can find them in the same pools that once held steelhead.

Special regulations: All trout, including steelhead, caught from the Ashtabula River must be a minimum length of 12 inches.

Facilities/camping: There are motels and restaurants at the intersection of Interstate 90 and Highway 11. The nearest camping is at Geneva State Park, which has 100 campsites, 12 cabins, and a state park lodge with 109 rooms.

Additional information: Ashtabula County is famous for its covered bridges.

Directions: Take Highway 11 north of I-90; exit east on Seven Hills Road. Go 0.5 mile and take State Road north to Plymouth Ridge Road. Continue on State Road and go downhill to the Indian Trails Park south entrance.

46 Atwood Lake

Key species: Largemouth bass, saugeye, crappie, bluegill, white bass, channel and flathead catfish, a few northern pike.

General description: Atwood yields good catches of saugeyes during the fall, winter, and early spring.

Overview: The U.S. Army Corps of Engineers impounded Atwood Lake in 1937 for the purpose of flood control on the Muskingum River. The lake is part of the Muskingum Watershed Conservancy District, which consists of twelve impoundments on the Upper Muskingum Watershed.

Atwood Lake covers 1,550 acres, averages 15 to 20 feet deep, and is a little over 6 miles long and on average 0.5 mile wide. The lake has a number of residences and summer cottages along its banks, as well as the Atwood Lake Park and Atwood Lake Resort and Lodge.

The Atwood Lake Park has picnic areas, cabins, a camping area, hiking trails, a beach, boat rental, and concessions. The Atwood Lake Resort and Lodge has a golf course, tennis courts, dining facilities, overnight accommodations, and lakeside cabins.

There are two marinas on Atwood Lake: Marina West is located on Atwood Lake Road, and Marina East is located off Highway 542. Both marinas have a launch ramp, fuel, and boat rental. There is also a public ramp off Highway 212, just south of the dam.

Shoreline access is good along Highway 542 on the northeast side of the lake and at Atwood Lake Park.

The fishing: Bass fishing at Atwood is like bass fishing at most lakes, which consists of working shoreline cover and riprap with spinner baits, plastics, and top-waters. Most bass will average 12 to 15 inches, with a few reaching up to 6 pounds. Work the riprap and stump bed along the shoreline just north of the dam; the rocky points, drops, and shoreline just west of the boater's beach on the north shore; and the slips and downed timber just south of Cemetery Bay. The rocks at Schoolhouse Point are good areas to find bass, as is the riprap along the Highway 542 roadway west of Elliott Run Creek. About 0.5 mile east Schoolhouse Point on the south shore is some timber shoreline, which is a good place to pick up a few bass. Fish right on the rock shoreline with chartreuse spinner baits, crawdad crank baits, brown or black plastic twin tails, and jigs. In the evening, work the timber and wood with jitterbugs and buzz baits. Bass fishing begins in early April in the coves at the east end and slowly moves west as the lake warms up. Stick with the riprap along the roadways, rocky points, and downed trees along the timbered shoreline.

Saugeyes are easy to find at Atwood, with most averaging 16 to 24 inches and topping out at around 6 pounds. Start at the east end and slow troll or drift jigs and night crawlers along the old railroad bed located in 4 to 6 feet of water off the south shoreline just east of East Marina. Just west of East Marina is an island; work the rock bank on the west shore of that island. Slow troll gold Hot 'n Tots or jointed

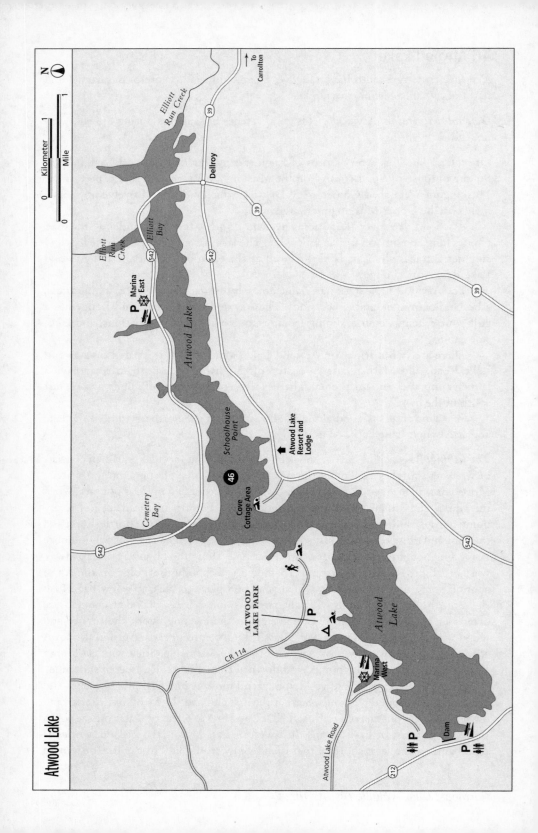

Atwood Lake

crawdad-colored Shad Raps around the reefs and underwater islands at the mouth of Cemetery Bay. Troll the west shoreline of the Cove Cottage Area, the point just west of the campground beach, and the points and islands around the boater's beach. Another good saugeye shoreline to cast or troll is the north shoreline east of Cemetery Bay, at the Arrowhead Cottage Area. Look for shallow flats 4 to 10 feet deep and rocky points, around islands, and near any old roadbed that will hold saugeyes. Jigs with minnows, worm harnesses, and small quarter-ounce crank baits will take saugeyes from Atwood. Saugeye fishing starts in early spring and continues through June. Fishing picks up again in mid-September and continues until the lake freezes. Then anglers catch saugeyes through the ice.

Crappie fishing is average at Atwood, with some good years and some not so good. Both black and white crappies can be found in Atwood. In good years, 14- to 17-inch crappies are caught; in bad or average years, 9- to 11-inch crappies are caught. While plenty of crappies can be taken from the downed timber and riprap, the best crappie fishing is around the 1,400 private boat docks found throughout the lake. Boat docks come in a variety of sizes and shapes, with the oldest and most dilapidated docks holding the most fish. Docks are spread out all over Atwood Lake; finding just the right one shouldn't be a problem. Look for docks in water 4 to 10 feet deep. The docks just west of Schoolhouse Point are good, as is the timber shoreline across from the East Marina. Crappie fishing starts in late March and remains good through Memorial Day, picking up again in October. Most crappies fall for minnows fished under a slip bobber or small crappie tubes.

Some nice channel cats come from Atwood, with a few reaching 12 to 14 pounds. Most of the cat fishing is done from the pulloff and parking areas off Highway 542 on the east side of the lake. The mouth of Elliott Bay is popular, as is the parking area about a mile west of East Marina and at the pulloffs around the Highway 542 Bridge at Cemetery Bay. If fishing by boat, try the coves east of Atwood Lake Lodge on the south shore. Catfish are caught in June, July, and August and mostly at night with chicken livers and night crawlers. Anglers also catch a few flathead catfish from Atwood using bluegills, creek chubs, and goldfish. While most flatheads will average 10 to 12 pounds, a few 20-plus-pound fish are occasionally taken.

Bluegills in Atwood run small, but during the spring spawn a few hand-size 'gills are caught close to the banks on red worms and wax worms.

White bass are common and widespread throughout the lake. Most white bass caught are incidental catches, as most anglers do not fish for them. Look for them under schools of shad during the evening and early morning at the mouth of coves.

A few nice northern pike are taken from Atwood right after ice-out in late February. Fish the headwaters in Indian Run Creek, east of the Highway 542 Causeway, with shiners and tru-turn hooks, 18 to 24 inches under a bobber. Most pike will average 20 to 30 inches, but a few pike up to 38 inches have been caught.

Below the dam is a tailwater fishery for saugeye, bass, and crappies; occasionally some northern pike are caught here in February and March. The parking area to access the tailwaters is just south of the dam on Highway 212.

Special regulations: Atwood Lake is limited to 25 hp. The minimum length limit on bass is 12 inches.

Facilities/camping: Atwood Lake Park has 300 campsites, 10 family vacation cabins, and 2 camper cabins. Atwood Lake Resort has a 104-room lodge with dining facilities and 17 cabins. Marina East and West are full-service marinas with fuel and boat rental. The nearest town is Dellroy, located at the east end of the lake at the junction of Highway 542 and Highway 39, which has gas, ice, and groceries.

Additional information: The Atwood Queen Cruise Boat operates out of Marina West from Memorial Day through Labor Day and offers an hour-long leisurely cruise around Atwood Lake.

Directions: From Carrollton take Highway 39 8 miles west to Dellroy. From Dellroy take Highway 542 north or east to access either the north or south shore.

47 Beach City Lake

Beach City Lake was originally an impoundment of 420 acres constructed by the U.S. Army Corps of Engineers in the mid-1930s for the purpose of flood control on the Lower Muskingum Watershed. The Muskingum Watershed Conservancy District manages the lake. Surrounding the lake and the headwaters is the 1,912-acre Beach City Wildlife Area, which has public hunting and is administered by the Division of Wildlife.

The lake is more marsh than lake, as sediments have almost totally filled in the upper reaches of the reservoir. Why the Division of Wildlife keeps stocking 10,000 to 20,000 saugeye a year is beyond me; however, the stocking does provide for a minor tailwater fishery below the dam during periods of high-water discharges. Most saugeyes caught below the dam will average 12 to 16 inches; occasionally some 22-inch-plus saugeyes are caught. Use ⅛- to ¼-ounce jigs with chartreuse twister tails.

48 Beaver Creek State Park

Located only a few miles from the Pennsylvania state line, Little Beaver Creek is one of the most beautiful streams in Ohio. It 1974 it became the first stream to be designated a State Wild and National Scenic River. Nearly 11 miles of Little Beaver Creek are within the Beaver Creek State Park. In 1949 Beaver Creek was among the first state parks to be dedicated with the creation of the newly formed Division of Parks and Recreation.

Beaver Creek State Park has picnic areas, a pioneer village, a historic operational gristmill, canoe rental, a camp store, miles of hiking and bridle trails along the Little Beaver, and a class "B" campground with 53 sites. However, the campground is located on a ridgetop so far away from the stream that it requires a quarter-mile downhill hike just to reach it.

The stream flows past sandstone cliffs, old gristmills, and remnants of the Sandy Beaver Canal built during the mid-1800s. It offers excellent fishing for smallmouth, rock bass, sunfish, and channel catfish. The stream is a popular canoe and kayaking stream, and there are several canoe liveries outside the park.

The stream is easily fished by either wading or floating, and at times it is clear enough to sight fish. Deep rocky pools, riffles, and mild rapids best describe a stream that begs to be fished with a fly rod. Woolly Buggers, Crystal Buggers, crayfish imitations, and big terrestrials are what the smallmouth goes for. Rock bass and sunfish will also be added to the day's catch, and even if the fishing is slow, any day spent here is reward enough. May, June, and late September are the best months to catch smallmouth. Channel cats are in the deeper pools downstream toward the river and are taken in July and August with night crawlers and crayfish. Smallmouth don't get overly large in Little Beaver Creek; a 15- to 16-inch smallie is a good one. Occasionally, if you're lucky, you may tie into an 18-inch bass. The Little Beaver has a 15-inch minimum size limit on smallmouth bass.

The Gretchen's Lock Trail follows the Little Beaver for almost 4 miles between Hambleton's Mill and Gaston's Mill. From Hambleton's Mill, an anglers' path follows the Little Beaver downstream 0.75 mile to the end of park property. From the parking area north of the old iron bridge, an angler can hike the Dogwood Trail a mile along the Little Beaver to the upstream edge of the state park.

Additional state park access is at Lusk Lock, which is located a couple of miles northwest on Middle Beaver Road. It's a rough-and-tumble lane to Lusk Lock that requires a stout truck to navigate. Once at the parking area at the end of the lane, Little Beaver Creek is a short hike in either direction from a couple of hiking trails. There is a state park canoe launch at the little village of Elkton west of Lusk Lock. One mile past Elkton there is another pulloff access at the bridge where Scroggs Road meets Middle Beaver Road. Access to the lower Little Beaver Creek is at the Beaver Creek State Forest, located northeast of East Liverpool. Take Grimm's Bridge Road east of Calcutta to reach the state forest.

Beaver Creek State Park is located approximately 6 miles north of East Liverpool on Highway 7.

49 Berlin Lake

Key species: Largemouth and smallmouth bass, walleye, channel catfish, white bass, muskie, bluegill, crappie, yellow perch.

General description: This is one of the few lakes in Ohio where natural reproduction of muskies occurs.

Overview: The U.S. Army Corps of Engineers completed the dam on the Mahoning River in 1943, impounding 3,321 acres for the purpose of flood control.

The Corps maintains the Mill Creek Recreation Area, located on the east side of the lake. There are picnic areas, shelter houses, day-use areas, campgrounds, and a boat ramp. A small fee is charged for use of the recreation area and boat ramp. Two other boat ramps are located at private marinas, which also charge a nominal fee. The state has one public ramp located off Bonner Road at the north end of the lake next to the Division of Wildlife Berlin Lake Wildlife Area Headquarters. There is also a youth fishing pond stocked with bass, bluegill, and catfish at that location.

Outside the U.S. Army Corps of Engineers' recreation area, there is fair amount of shoreline access from unimproved gravel pulloffs, dead-end roads, and around bridges. Although none of the access areas are marked, they are easy to spot by the well-worn paths leading to the lake's edge.

The lake has a confusing, if not complicated, set of open and no-wake zones that are marked by buoys and signs located at the boat ramps. Lake depths can vary considerably, from 10 feet to 30 feet, in the blink of an eye. Long shallow points can end abruptly into 40 feet of water. Locating these drops is the key to finding fish on Berlin Lake.

Summer pool on the lake is 1,024.7 above sea level. By winter the lake drops approximately 8 feet.

The fishing: Walleye is the game fish that generates the most interest here, and Berlin Lake is fished heavily for them. Newcomers to the lake are often frustrated by the walleye fishing, but local fishers who know the lake like the back of their hand do quite well.

Outside the bridges, fishing Berlin Lake for walleye is pretty much confined to main lake structures such as points, drops, reefs, and shallow bars. Walleye fishing is good from April through the end of June and again in the fall. In spring look for walleye in 3 to 5 feet of water; come July, 8 to 12 feet is where they will be. In summer walleye fishing is best in the morning and evening. Shoreline fishers can do well at the Highway 224 Bridge and Causeway using night crawlers, crank baits, and leeches, casting around the riprap and into the main channel. In the lake, fish the shallows adjacent to the lake drops. The shallow main lake flats just north of the creek channel between the Highway 224 Bridge and the railroad bridge are good areas. Fish the flats next to the drops by drifting or slow trolling night crawlers, jigs with twister tails or Sassy Shads, or size 6 Rapala Husky Jerks.

Other good areas for walleye are the flats just north of the Highway 224 Bridge on the east side of the channel and west of the railroad bridge, where two shallow flats lie on each side of the channel. Vertical jigging over the flats and edges with blade lures like Sonics, Silver Buddies, and Vib"E"s and jigging Rapalas are popular and productive methods for catching walleye. Most will average 15 to 23 inches; occasionally a fish up to 30 inches is caught. In summer walleye are more apt to suspend; spring and fall walleye are just off the bottom. Berlin is a walleye brood-stock lake for the Division of Wildlife and is stocked yearly.

Crappies can be found pretty much anywhere along shoreline brush or downed trees at Berlin Lake. Good crappie cover is widespread here. A couple of good areas are around the Highway 224 Bridge and at the south side of the public boat ramp around the Christmas tree structures placed in the water. In spring anglers wade the shoreline at the boat ramp, fishing the brush piles to catch crappies. In spring fish the Price Street "Crappie Bridge" and the south shoreline east of that bridge. Most crappies average 7 to 9 inches, with some years producing better fish than others. Crappies start hitting in April, and fishing is good through May and then again in the fall. Most anglers catch crappies on the usual minnows and bobbers and crappie jigs.

Bass fishing is good at Berlin Lake, with most averaging a good 12 to 15 inches. Bass don't get overly large, topping out at 3 to 4 pounds. Smallmouth do as well, with several 3- to 4-pound smallies reported annually. Most smallmouth are incidental catches by walleye fishers and shoreline-casting bass fishers fishing rock points and riprap. There is good smallmouth shoreline with plenty of rocks and drops at the south shore, west of the Highway 14 Bridge.

There is also some good bass fishing off the rocks and shoreline near the dam and in the east bay at the dam. Only electric motors are permitted near the confines of the dam. The point just off the Wildlife Area Headquarters is good for bass, as are both banks in upper Mill Creek. Any rocky points, steep shoreline with slips and timber, and the creek arms east of the railroad bridge are good. On the west end of the lake, stick to the channel as it hugs the banks. Just west of the railroad bridge, fish the steep west shore of the big island. Crank baits, plastics, tubes, and chartreuse spinner baits are the preferred baits.

Channel cats are widespread, and anybody who fishes for bass, walleye, crappies, and bluegills catches them. Good channels average 3 to 5 pounds; a few 10-pound cats are caught occasionally. Most cat fishing is done at night from the various gravel pulloffs, from parking areas at boat ramps, and at the recreation and day-use areas during July and August. Anglers fish off the bridge causeways at Highway 14 and Highway 224 and the Price Street Bridge. Crayfish do well for bait during the fall, as the catfish move into the rock points. In summer fish chicken livers and night crawlers on the bottom.

White bass are common but average only about 9 inches; they are hardly big enough to mess with. In spring anglers catch them in the creek arms and up the Mahoning River. Come summer they are widespread throughout the lake; most are caught by anglers targeting other species.

There are a few yellow perch. Most are surprise catches caught by crappie fishers in spring and fall.

Muskies are not plentiful. They are there as a result of some natural muskie reproduction from earlier stocking efforts by the Division of Wildlife. Muskies average 30 to 40 inches; a few 50-inch muskies have been seen by fishery personnel conducting studies. Most anglers troll the drops, flats, points, and creek channels for suspended muskies between the Highway 224 Bridge and the railroad bridge. Probably the most popular spot is the mouth of Mill Creek and back into the creek, as well as the shoreline and flats east of Mill Creek in front of the Mill Creek Recreation Area. Another place is the flats northeast of the railroad bridge. As with most Ohio muskie, Bagley's Monster Shad trolled deep and slow gets the fish.

Below the dam at Berlin is an excellent tailwater fishery for smallmouth, walleye, and catfish. Fishing for walleye is best during spring and periods of lake releases. Access the tailwaters from a parking area off Bonner Road.

Special regulations: There is a five-fish, 15-inch minimum length limit on walleye. Minimum size for kept bass is 12 inches.

Facilities/camping: There is a full-service marina at the mouth of Mill Creek. Groceries, gas, and ice can be purchased from various convenience stores located around the lake. The U.S. Army Corps of Engineers Mill Creek Recreation Area has camping with over 300 sites and is open from late May through mid-September.

Additional information: At the south end of the lake, located just off Highway 183, is a small impoundment of 314 acres named Deer Creek Reservoir that serves as the water supply for the village of Alliance. There is some fishing for bass, bluegills, channel catfish, and crappies at the county park. Only electric motors are allowed.

Directions: Berlin Lake is just north of Alliance on Highway 225.

50 Black River

The Black River, located almost entirely within the town of Lorain, has fishing for largemouth and smallmouth bass, crappies, bluegills, perch, white bass, sheepshead, and steelhead. The river was never stocked with steelhead, but rainbows have adopted the Black River as a spawning stream, as they have every river, stream, creek, and small tributary east of the Huron River.

At the mouth of the river, access is gained at the Eastside Boat Launch and Riverside Park and Marina. Farther downstream, access is gained at city and county Metro Parks and reservations.

At the mouth of the Black River, anglers can catch crappies, largemouth bass, channel catfish, sheephead, and steelhead during late fall and winter. When it freezes over, perch and steelhead are caught through the ice.

Good largemouth bass fishing is at the mouth of the river around the old boat dock, piers, and walls. Fish plastic night crawlers, tubes, crawfish, and rig them Texas style, or with a bead to create some noise, and fish the old city dock remains along the east wall. Crank bait works well too; some anglers prefer the darker color crank baits. Fish around the docks; any harbor structure will hold a bass, of which there are plenty. Most bass average 10 to 14 inches, but 3- to 4-pound bass are caught with some regularity.

Seldom do you get any smallmouth bass inside the river mouth. For smallmouth, fish around the stone break walls that are in Lake Erie, just outside the river mouth, with brown and olive tubes. Farther upstream a couple of miles on the Black River, you will begin to find a good supply of stream smallmouth. They tend to be much smaller than their Lake Erie counterparts, averaging only 10 to 14 inches, with some 2- to 3-pound fish occasionally caught. In spring, from late April through May, smallmouth caught from the stream tend to run larger, resulting from a small number of Lake Erie smallmouth migrating up into the Black River to spawn.

Crappies can also be taken from the river mouth docks and structures from April through May by all the usual ways, including small jigs and minnows suspended under a bobber. Fishing from a boat would get you into a lot of water that is otherwise off-limits, but at the Riverside Park, shoreline access is easy, if not comfortable.

Downstream access to the Black River is through the Lorain County Metro Parks. At James Day Park, a small city park, access is easily gained to French Creek, a tributary of the Black River, which also gets a small run of steelhead in early spring. From James Day Park, anglers can walk the stream up to the Black River.

The easiest access to the Black River is at the Burr Oak Reservation. The stream is an easy walk from the parking areas. Access can also be gained from the Day's Dam Reservation, but it is a hike and at times a steep and risky downhill climb.

In summer, anglers find a good mix of smallmouth, rock bass, sunfish, and channel catfish on the upstream portions of the river. Come fall and early spring, steelhead inhabit the upper reaches.

To reach James Day Park, take East River Road south of Highway 611; the park is just south of this junction. From East River Road, anglers can reach Day's Dam Reservation, which is across the bridge on East 31st Street. The Burr Oak Reservation is farther south off Ford Road at the junction with Highway 254.

51 Chagrin River

Key species: Steelhead, smallmouth bass, rock bass, sunfish, channel catfish.

General description: The Chagrin is another excellent Lake Erie steelhead stream.

Overview: Chagrin River is an urban fishery, flowing through downtown Eastlake and Willoughby with a number of city parks, ball fields, and recreation areas within those towns providing access to the stream. Once the river crosses U.S. Highway 6, and into Cuyahoga County, Cleveland Metro Parks provide access as far south as Mayfield Road.

The East Branch of the Chagrin was originally designated a scenic river in 1979. In 2002 the upper Chagrin headwaters were included, bringing the total to 71 miles of stream designated a State Scenic River.

The name Chagrin originated from an Indian word meaning "clear water," of which it has plenty when conditions are right. It is an excellent steelhead stream with a bounty of public access points. The upper watershed of the East Branch contains the only known native population of brook trout in the state and also holds the state record brook trout, which weighed over 2 pounds and was caught in 1955. Future listing of any brook trout into state records has been closed by the Outdoor Writers of Ohio due to the species' addition to the state endangered species list.

The fishing: While the Chagrin River lies within the city limits of major metropolitan areas, the valuable green space that several city and county parks have established allows plenty of fishing and elbow room for steelhead fishers. A couple of parks exist off Highway 283 and Erie Road near where the road meets or crosses the river. One of the better locations is at Chagrin River Park, located off Reeves Road. Anglers here have plenty of good water from which to choose, and there is also a footbridge across the river, restrooms, and picnic areas.

Anglers like to go after steelhead in November at the old Daniels Park Dam on the Chagrin River.

South of US 20 at the bridge is Todd Field and Daniels Park, which is more or less one continuous mile-long park from US 20 south to I-90. At Daniels Park on the north side of Highway 84 are the remains of an old dam that washed out after heavy rain and an ice melt in 2005. Daniels Park was one of the more popular fishing areas on the Chagrin when the dam was intact. The old dam acted as a temporary barrier, and a lot of fish stacked up at its base. Local fishers can still remember watching steelhead after steelhead jump the old dam on their way upstream. At the far south end of Daniels Park, just above the old dam, the East Branch joins the river.

Upstream, just past Chardon Road, is the start of the Cleveland Metroparks' 2,140-acre North Chagrin Reservation, which extends to Mayfield Road. The river from Chardon Road upstream is as nice a stretch of water as there is in northeast Ohio. It has beautiful crystal-clear ripple water, pools, gravel runs, and a stream that is easy to negotiate and wade. The North Reservation extends more than 7 miles, with public access and parking areas at a number of the various parks and picnic areas along Chagrin River Road.

From Mayfield Road south, public access is spotty but perhaps possible. About 2 miles south of Mayfield Road is the Gates Mills Dam, which stops all upstream migration of steelhead. In Gates Mills there is a quaint little fly shop, and behind it is a footbridge over the river. Just upstream of the footbridge is the old mill dam. I am told an angler can access the stream from the few but crowded public parking areas along the road, for which there is a set time limit. If fishing causes an angler to park over the time limit, a fine is assessed. But fishing here is worth it, even if it costs a day in court.

Like all central basin tributaries, steelhead begin showing up here in late September, and by late October steelhead have pretty much settled in at every pool in the river. Fishing is good from October through April for steelhead; late March and early April are the top months to find steelhead on the riffles and shallow gravel runs.

Beginning in May smallmouth, rock bass, sunfish, and a few channel catfish can be found in the same pools that held steelhead during winter.

Special regulations: All steelhead must be 12 inches to keep. For the Chagrin River downstream of the Highway 283 Bridge to Lake Erie, the minimum size for smallmouth is 14 inches. The minimum size for walleye is 15 inches. Possession of brook trout is prohibited.

Facilities/camping: For the most part the Chagrin River is an urban stream. Lodging and dining facilities can be found at nearly every exit on I-90.

Additional information: The Spring Brook Sanctuary on the upper East Branch is where the state's only remaining native brook trout population is found.

Directions: The Chagrin River is just east of Cleveland and can be accessed from I-90 exit 189 or exit 193. To get to Chagrin River Park, take the Lost Nation Road exit north of Highway 2, then head west on Reeves Road. Todd Field and Daniels Park can be accessed at the bridges on US 20 and Highway 84. From Highway 84 head south Highway 174, also known as Chagrin River Road, to Cleveland Metroparks' North Chagrin Reservation and Gates Mills Dam.

52 Clendening Lake

Key species: Saugeye, flathead and channel catfish, largemouth bass, crappie, and white bass.

General description: A top trophy saugeye lake and state record producer.

Overview: The U.S. Army Corps of Engineers impounded Clendening Lake in 1937 on Brushy Fork Creek for the purpose of flood control on the Muskingum River. The lake covers 1,800 acres and is part of the Muskingum Watershed Conservancy District (MWCD), which owns the lake and the surrounding property.

Clendening is one of the most beautiful lakes in Ohio. The shoreline is completely forested and uninhabited, and the lake has been designated by the MWCD to remain in a natural, undeveloped state.

There are three boat ramps and a full-service marina on Clendening Lake. The marina offers camping, a boat launch, and boat rental. One boat ramp is located on Kova Road approximately 4 miles south of Deersville off Highway 799. Another is located at the Clendening Marina off Highway 799, and a third ramp is at the west end of the lake on Norris Road, off Highway 800.

Shoreline access is limited to pulloffs and parking areas along Highway 799 and Kova Road at the east end of the lake and off Norris Road at Hefling Bay near the boat ramp.

The fishing: Clendening is a state record lake that I believe holds potential new state records in saugeye and possibly flathead catfish. Clendening currently holds the state record flathead, which at 76.5 pounds is possibly the largest fish ever taken with a rod and reel in Ohio. Clendening also held a state record saugeye that weighed 12.83 pounds. Both of these catches are testament to the quality fishing that awaits anglers at Clendening.

Clendening was the only lake in Ohio I visited where anglers were not just fishing for saugeyes—they were fishing for big saugeyes. It is hard to place an average size on the saugeyes in Clendening. While most anglers catch 16- to 22-inch saugeyes, a lot of 6- to 9-pounders come from the lake, and several 10-pound fish appear every year, too.

The best saugeye fishing is from March through May, and again from late September through December. Fish the old roadbeds, rocky points, and flats throughout the lake. While the lake has a considerable amount of excellent saugeye habitat, a majority of saugeye fishing takes place east of the marina to the Highway 799 Causeway and bridge.

Across the marina on the north shore are a couple of points that should be slow trolled or drifted with night crawler harnesses or minnows. The west point of the two has an old roadbed just offshore, while the east point has a shallow flat between the bends in the old stream channel. North of that point, troll or drift the west shoreline along the old stream channel that is 10 to 12 feet deep to the Highway 799 Causeway. From the causeway, turn south and troll the rocky east bank to Huff Bay. Small chrome and gold crank baits and ¼-ounce Hot 'n Tots are excellent trolling or casting baits for Clendening saugeyes. West of the marina work the point and old roadbed just east of Musky Bay on the north shore. Farther west troll or cast the old roadbed and rocks at Long Point. At the dam fish the riprap with crank baits or jigs and minnows.

In late fall and winter, the best place to find big saugeyes is at the bridges across Brushy Fork Bay and Huff Bay. Anglers stand off the roadway and vertical jig chartreuse and red blade lures like a Vib"E" and local favorite Mike's Saugeye Slayer right off the bottom in front or under the bridge. At the same time, the angler throws another rod rigged with a minnow into the creek channel. Other good jigging lures are ⅛-ounce white jigs with tubes or twister tails in chartreuse or white. If you want to catch the saugeye of your life, fish at night, preferably during November, off the rocks and riprap along the causeway across Brushy Fork Bay with ¼-ounce Rattle Traps. You may just catch the next state record saugeye.

Bass fishing is also excellent at Clendening. Fish the plentiful downed timber, under the overhanging trees, rocky shoreline and points, and weeds. One end of the lake is about as good as the other. Most bass average a healthy 12 to 15 inches, with many 2- to 3-pound bass caught. While occasionally a 7-pound bass will turn up, bass as big as 9 pounds have been reported from Clendening. Bass particularly like crayfish in Clendening, so double twister tails and plastic crawls in watermelon seed or pumpkinseed do well. Also fish Rapalas, plastic night crawlers on a drop-shot rig, tubes, chartreuse spinner baits, and crank baits in crawfish or brown. Bass fishing starts in late April in the coves around the downed timber and bank cover. By midsummer start working the steep creek bank west of Long Point on the north shore and the big rocks on the main lake points.

Crappies are plentiful at Clendening. You will find them from mid-April through the end of May around treetops in 6 to 8 feet of water. You will also find them off the creek channel across from Huff Bay and just south of Huff Bay on the east bank; in both banks in Deersville Bay; in McConnell Bay; and in any downed timber along the main lakeshore. Use a thin, size 6 Aberdeen hook with a minnow and slip bobber. Adjust the depth until you find crappies. They also are caught on crappie tubes and small Rooster Tails. Most crappies will average between 10 to 14 inches.

Small perch and bluegills are everywhere. Catch them close to shore around brush or weeds with wax worms and red worms.

Channel cats average anywhere from 12 to 24 inches; 10-pound channels are not too hard to find. Most fishing for channels is done at night from pulloffs and parking areas along Highway 799 at the east end of the lake and from Norris Road in Hefling Bay. The best cat fishing in the lake is said to be from the marina east into Brushy Fork Bay. Use chicken livers or night crawlers dead-lined on the bottom, or drift the area in front of Huff Bay or at the mouth of Brushy Fork Bay with floaters and chicken livers or cut bait. The best fishing is during June, July, and August.

Flatheads, or shovelhead catfish as they are called in southern Ohio, grow big in Clendening. Fifty- to 60-pound flatheads are not uncommon. To catch flatheads of that size requires tackle suitable for saltwater use and bait such as bluegills, goldfish, or shiners fished near the bottom. Some of the best places for flatheads in Clendening are Brushy Fork Bay, Deersville Bay, Colman Run Bay (Long Bay), and Hefling Bay. A lot of big flatheads are caught at night in summer, fishing from pulloffs and parking areas along Highway 799 at Deersville Bay and from the causeway across Brushy Fork Bay and Huff Bay.

Below the dam, a minor fishery for saugeyes occurs while water is being discharged after periods of rain or in late fall during drawdown. In early spring a few pike up to 30 inches are caught in Stillwater Creek on chubs and minnows.

Special regulations: Clendening is limited to 10 hp. Minimum length on bass is 12 inches. Only one flathead catfish 35 inches or longer may be kept. Only one channel catfish 28 inches or longer may be kept.

Facilities/camping: Clendening Lake Marina is a full-service marina with docking, fuel, supplies, ice, bait, tackle, boat ramp, and boat rental. Camping is available at the marina with 50 to 60 sites; 9 cabins are also available to rent.

Additional information: At one time the Clendening Lake Marina had the mounted state record flathead catfish displayed, but the old fish got moldy with age and had to be taken down. Now there is a 55-pound flathead catfish mounted on the wall.

Directions: From Uhrichsville, take Highway 800 11 miles south to the small town of Tippecanoe. Drive an additional 3.5 miles to Highway 799; turn east and drive approximately 1 mile to Clendening Lake Marina.

53 Conneaut Creek

Key species: Steelhead, smallmouth bass, rock bass, sunfish, occasionally salmon.

General description: Conneaut is one of the top steelhead streams in the state.

Overview: Conneaut Creek is roughly 50 miles long and starts in western Crawford County, Pennsylvania, where the Pennsylvania Game Commission stocks it with trout, muskies, and steelhead. In fall the Division of Wildlife adds an additional 80,000 fingerling steelhead where the stream enters Ohio. The stream empties into Lake Erie at the small harbor city of Conneaut, the most northeasterly town in Ohio.

The 21-mile stretch of Conneaut Creek from the Ohio-Pennsylvania border to the city of Conneaut was designated an Ohio State Wild and Scenic River in 2005.

The name Conneaut comes from an Indian word meaning "place of many fish," or "place where snow lays in spring." I would have to agree with both descriptions. Not only is Conneaut filled with fish, but winter arrives early and leaves late on this stream.

The stream is also known for its historic covered bridges, clear water, steep shale banks, and scenic rural location. It is among the handful of most beautiful streams in the state, and I fish it every chance I get.

The fishing: Fishing for steelhead starts in September at the mouth of Conneaut Harbor on the west break wall. The break wall can be reached from the beach at a township park, but perhaps a better way is to drive to it from Conneaut Harbor on a two-track sand road that leads right up to the break wall just west of the boat ramp. The break wall has a nice flat top, which makes for easy walking; but use common sense and don't be out there when the wind kicks up, as waves easily top the wall. Steelhead are caught with quarter-ounce blue and silver Little Cleos, small quarter-ounce spinners, and jigs with maggots. Smallmouth, walleye, and perch are all caught from the break wall throughout the summer fishing season.

Largemouth and smallmouth bass, perch, bluegill, channel catfish, and some crappies are taken from the harbor itself. Conneaut Harbor has ample fishing facilities, such as benches, lighting, restrooms, a wheelchair-accessible fishing pier, bait and tackle, boat launch, and docking. Several charters operate from the harbor. Tom Harbison caught a 20.49-pound state record lake trout from Lake Erie from the port at Conneaut.

Starting in early October, steelhead begin to enter central basin streams such as

Conneaut and winter out in the river, spawning in the early spring. By the end of April, most steelhead have returned to Lake Erie.

Unlike the other major steelhead streams in northeast Ohio, Conneaut does not have an abundance of public access. Access for the most part is limited to a few areas within town and at one bridge on Center Road south of town. Other access is wherever an angler finds it. Conneaut is held for the most part in private hands; however, at many bridges anglers can usually find their way into the stream. In the early days of steelheading, there was rarely a NO TRESPASSING sign posted along a stream or at a bridge, but nowadays it has become quite common.

In Conneaut, anglers can access the stream at the Woodworth boat ramp, located at the end of Woodworth Road, through an old tunnel under a railroad track that was built in 1906. Not much wading can be had at this location, but you can launch a small boat from the primitive ramp. A better location is at the railroad crossing at the junction of South Liberty and Old Main Street. Parking is at the bridge on both sides, and although there are a few outdated posted signs, there seems to be a truce in effect between the railroad and the local fishers who use this site to access the stream. Another access point is at the old Mill Street Bridge and across the road on Welton Road. There is a small tributary stream off the Conneaut along Welton Road, along with a parking place on the left where steelheaders can access the tributary.

The next public access is at the old concrete bridge on Center Road south of town. Access is on the west side of the bridge; after that an angler is on his or her own.

On cold days anglers will find steelhead in the deeper pools. Occasionally there will be some activity on the riffles and runs, but for the most part steelhead fishing is confined to the deep pockets of water found within the streams. Undercut banks, deep cuts in the shale bottom, and creek bends are all places where steelhead hole up before they spawn. In mid-March it's a different story and an almost altogether different fish.

While "hole" fishing anglers use spawn sacks, maggots, minnows, salmon eggs, and even Power Bait on size 6, 8, or 10 bait-holder salmon hooks gently drifted through the pools and deep pockets. Fish steelhead right in the current, stay in the foam lines, and fish the deepest part of the pool. Allow your bait to drift naturally and right along or near the bottom by using just enough split shot to get the bait down. Use a small, brightly colored balsa floater to suspend the bait just above the bottom and to act as a strike indicator. Fine diameter, 4- to 8-pound-test fluorocarbon leaders are preferred, but not always necessary. I use stiff 2x to 5x dark brown chameleon Maxima tippet; I like its abrasive resistance and sheer strength for its size.

Fly anglers use a variety of flies, from size 16 nymphs to size 8 streamers. Yarn flies, such as sucker spawn, are easy to tie, and the yarn hangs up in the fine teeth of a steelhead, which makes hooking a lot easier. Some fly anglers use dropper flies, but I find that success is determined more by persistence and stealth than any other factor.

In March look for steelhead to be on the move up the riffles and onto the gravel spawning beds called redds. A few dark, cloudy pockets usually indicate the presence of redds with active steelhead. Every fly fisherman's dream is to be on a steelhead stream while the fish are actively engaged in romance. At times Conneaut is so clear that it's possible to sight-fish for cruising and spawning steelhead. It is times like these that make all the cold, wet, and miserable days spent steelhead fishing worth it.

When winter has finally left Conneaut Creek, anglers can find rock bass, sunfish, and smallmouth bass in the same pools and riffles that held steelhead in March.

Conneaut is an easy stream to wade. It clears up quickly after a rain, and in summer it is a perfect canoe stream. There is nothing I don't like about Conneaut, except that it's so far away from where I live.

Special regulations: All trout from Conneaut must be 12 inches in length, and anglers are limited to two steelhead per day.

Facilities/camping: No public campgrounds exist on Conneaut Creek, but several bed-and-breakfasts, cabins, rooms, and motels are found in the towns of Conneaut and Kingsville. The nearest public camping is at Geneva State Park, which is located approximately 25 miles west of Conneaut.

Additional information: Both Conneaut and Kingsville have quaint, local eateries where a steelheader can get a hot cup of coffee and a warm meal to chase away the chill.

Directions: To get to Conneaut, take I-90 east of Cleveland, almost to the Pennsylvania state line.

54 Cuyahoga River

Key species: Smallmouth, rock bass, sunfish, bluegill, channel catfish, northern pike, steelhead, yellow perch, white perch, crappie, and some largemouth bass.

General description: The Upper Cuyahoga has good pike and smallmouth fishing.

Overview: The Cuyahoga will never live down its reputation as the river that caught fire, but the river in Cuyahoga Valley National Park and at it headwaters at Eldon Russell Park is a different river than the one that flows through the industrial heart of Cleveland.

The last fire that plagued the river in 1969 led to the creation of the Clean Water Act and the Environmental Protection Agency. Although improvements in water quality have been significant, the river is not without its problems. A series of dams on the river between Akron and Cuyahoga Falls has contributed to lower dissolved oxygen content and the buildup of possibly hazardous sediments in the river. Wastewater overflows continue to be a problem from the sewage treatment plant just upstream of the national park.

The old 57-foot-high Ohio Edison Dam, built in 1912 in Cuyahoga Falls to generate electricity, was decommissioned in 1958. But renewed interest in generating hydropower from the dam has sparked a local controversy. There are parties who want Edison Dam removed, but the cost of removing contaminated sediments built up behind the dam is estimated to be $70 million. When the Edison Dam was built, it flooded the waterfalls for which the town of Cuyahoga Falls was named.

Public access on the Cuyahoga starts in the upper reaches at Eldon Russell Park in Geauga County, where there is a canoe launch. Another canoe launch is 5 miles downstream at Hiram Rapids. The village of Mantua has a small town park with public access on the Cuyahoga. The city of Kent, Cuyahoga Falls, and Summit County Parks have several community parks with access on the river. Northeast of Cuyahoga Falls is the 33,000-acre Cuyahoga Valley National Park, which places 22 miles of the river under the protective umbrella of a cooperative arrangement between national and county Metro Parks.

The Upper Cuyahoga from just north of the Eldon Russell Park to Rockwell Lake in Geauga and Portage Counties was designated a State Scenic River in 1974. It's a beautiful stream.

The fishing: The Upper Cuyahoga from the village of Burton to Lake Rockwell, which is an Akron City reservoir that does not allow fishing, is the primary pike water on the river. It is a beautiful stretch of river that varies from 30 to 60 yards wide with weeds and brushy shorelines. The Upper Cuyahoga River can be accessed at the Geauga County Park District's Eldon Russell Park, located on Rapids Road a few miles south of the small village of Burton. From the park a canoe or kayak can be launched at Horwaths Landing at the end of the road. There is excellent smallmouth fishing from that landing downstream, and northern pike are fairly bountiful.

Canoes can also be launched from a small pulloff on the south side of Highway 87 east of Burton, where it crosses the Cuyahoga, 4 miles upstream from the park.

Hiram Rapids, a popular takeout and launch location, is 5 miles downstream from Horwaths Landing off Highway 82. Another 5 miles downstream off Highway 44, there is a small village park in Mantua that also provides access to the river and is another takeout site on the upper Cuyahoga.

For northern pike fish the shoreline brush and weed edges with spinner baits from September through November. In March and April, use shiners, chubs, or suckers fished under a bobber in the same shoreline brush and emerging weeds near deeper water.

In Kent, Silver Creek, and Cuyahoga Falls, northern pike are still in good numbers, as are smallmouth and rock bass. Fish spinners or live bait in current breaks around timber and brush in 5 to 6 feet of water. Chubs and shiners still produce well in the early spring after ice-out for northern pike. Most northern pike will be between 15 to 28 inches long. For smallmouth, use small crawdad-colored crank baits, Mepps spinners, and pumpkin tubes around the weeds, current breaks, and rocky areas.

In the town of Kent, almost 2 miles of the river can be accessed at the Kent City Park. West of Kent there is access at Brust Park, which is the site of the old Munroe Falls Dam, which was removed in 2005. Some good riffle water exists here, as well as a natural waterfall that was discovered while removing the dam.

Angler fishing the Cuyahoga River at the Brecksville Dam and Highway 82 bridge.

Downstream in Cuyahoga Falls, Water Works Park has a boat ramp, wheelchair-accessible fishing piers, and a boat dock. Here the water is flat with brushy banks that average 5 to 6 feet deep. This is also a good section for catching pike. A bike and hiking trail follows the river for almost 3 miles from Brust Park to Fisher Park, which is located just upstream of Water Works Park; some fishers opt to bike and fish along the trail.

River Front Park offers some limited fishing, although the banks are steep and the drop to the water's edge should discourage anyone from being careless. It could also be slippery and dangerous during or after a rain.

The Gorge Metro Park north entrance has fishing at the small impoundment created by the Edison Dam. A wheelchair-accessible fishing pier is located on the lake below the shelter house. Launching a small boat on the impoundment might be possible at the old power plant located across Front Street, but probably not advisable. Bluegills, a few bass, and some channel cats are caught from the old lake. Trails lead down into the gorge below Edison Dam and the tailwater looks inviting to fish, but the park restrictions warn users to stay on the trails. Trails also lead upstream of the impoundment, though fishing is limited. From the Gorge Metro Park south entrance, the trail leads into Cascade Valley Metro Park, which has excellent access to the Cuyahoga River and allows fishing. You can also drive to Cascade Valley; it is located on Cuyahoga Street.

Just west of Cascade Valley Park is the Ohio and Erie Canal Towpath Trail, which skirts the Cuyahoga River for more than 30 miles to Harvard Avenue in Cleveland. Anglers can walk or bike the trail to access various pools and riffles on the Cuyahoga.

In the Cuyahoga Valley National Park anglers have more than 20 miles of river to fish. The most prominent species are smallmouth, rock bass, sunfish, and channel cat. I'm told the fishing is average at best, and anglers are loath to keep and eat any fish from the river due to the Akron Water Pollution Control Station outlet within sight of the national park's south boundary. In fact, the National Park Service recommends against water sports such as swimming, canoeing, kayaking, and wading because the water quality in the park is questionable.

The river through the park is beautiful, with several old historic villages and must-see sites along the river's edge. It's a crooked river, deriving its name from an Indian name meaning "crooked," with bends and turns; plenty of riffle water and deeper holding pools make the stream inviting to fish. The park also has a number of small ponds and lakes which offer fishing too. Most ponds require a hike to get into, and some big bluegills have been reported out of a few of the ponds.

Steelhead also make a run up the Cuyahoga but are stopped at the Becksville Dam, located at the Cleveland Metropark's Brecksville Reservation. Fishing is popular at the tailwaters for smallmouth, rock bass, sunfish, channel catfish, and for steelhead in winter and early spring. From the trailhead parking area at Brecksville Station, anglers are free to hike, bike, or ride a horse as far up or down the stream as the towpath leads.

Upstream about 4 miles, Tinkers Creek, a medium-size tributary that enters from the east, gets a minor steelhead run during March. By summer, Tinkers Creek is too small to be of interest to anglers.

Metro Parks and community parks, bridges, and the towpath located between Tinkers Creek and the Ohio and Erie Canal Reservation 7 miles to the north offer some fishing access from which anglers are more likely to encounter better numbers of steelhead.

Special regulations: Minimum length for steelhead is 12 inches. From the mouth of the Cuyahoga downstream to Harvard Road Bridge, smallmouth must be 14 inches to keep; minimum length for walleye is 15 inches.

Facilities/camping: At the Cuyahoga Valley National Park there are a couple of nice restaurants at the small village of Peninsula. Lodging is available at the inn at Brandywine Falls. Outside the park, lodging and dining facilities are widely available.

Camping is not permitted in the park.

Additional information: In Cuyahoga Falls there is a bronze statue of a Native American holding a canoe over his head and a plaque marking the start of the 8-mile portage used by the Indians to get from the Cuyahoga River to the Tuscarawas River, thereby linking a canoe route from Lake Erie to the Ohio River.

Directions: Interstate 80 south of Cleveland crosses both the Cuyahoga Valley National Park and the Upper Cuyahoga. Exit at Highway 8 to reach Cuyahoga Valley National Park. Exit at Highway 44 to access the Upper Cuyahoga.

55 Deer Creek Reservoir

Key species: Largemouth bass, channel catfish, bluegill, crappie.

General description: A nice place to catch a few bass and to do some shore fishing with the family.

Overview: Deer Creek Reservoir is located at the southwest end of Berlin Lake and serves as a water supply for the city of Alliance. The lake covers 314 acres and is administered by the Stark County Park District.

There is a boat ramp at the county park with picnic areas and restrooms. Shoreline access is good on the north shore along Price Road and at the park grounds, where there is also a fishing pier.

The fishing: Bass fishing is fair at Deer Creek. Most bass average 10 to 14 inches; a few in the 15- to 16-inch range show up occasionally for local anglers. Fish the shoreline cover and downed timber on the south bank and the riprap along Price Road with plastic night crawlers and jigs.

Crappies are caught in the spring, but they tend to run small. Most anglers will fish nearby Walborn Reservoir for crappies. Catch crappies from the brush and downed timber on the south bank using ⅛-ounce jigs and minnows.

Bluegills are everywhere, but small, and can be caught from the shoreline around the park and off the pier with red worms and maggots.

Channels are plentiful and can be easily caught from the pulloffs along Price Road at the west end of the lake. Most cats are caught using chicken liver and night crawlers fished on the bottom.

Anglers can access the dam via a walking trail from the park.

Special regulations: The lake is limited to electric motors only. Catfish limit is six daily.

Facilities/camping: Other than restrooms, there are no facilities or camping at Deer Creek Reservoir.

Directions: Take Highway 183 for 4 miles north of Alliance; turn east on Price Road.

56 East Branch Reservoir

Key species: Largemouth bass, crappie, bluegill, northern pike, white perch, ring perch, a few channel catfish.

General description: The fishing is excellent, but shoreline access is restricted to specific locations.

Overview: East Branch Reservoir covers 420 acres and was previously an Akron City reservoir. The lake is now administered by the Geauga County Parks District and is known as Headwaters Park. The park has a small number of facilities including hiking trails, picnic areas, restrooms, a boat ramp, and fishing platforms. The park is open from 6:00 a.m. to 11:00 p.m. Shoreline fishing is restricted to board-walk platforms constructed at three locations along the bank and at the U.S. Highway 322 Causeway. Short trails from the parking area near the boat ramp lead to the fishing platforms.

East Branch is so weedy that anglers find it difficult to fish, and in summer the lakeshore in front of the fishing platforms is usually choked with heavy weed growth.

The fishing: Fishing at East Branch is restricted to three fishing platforms, the cause-way, and by boat (electric motors only). The lake is a typical northwest Ohio reservoir with aquatic vegetation, lily pads, and brushy and woody shorelines. It is surrounded by trees and several islands, creating the illusion of a northwoods lake.

Bluegills are abundant, reaching a respectable hand size and bigger, and are found near any shoreline, along the weed edges, off the platforms, around the brush, and off the islands. They can be caught year-round with a simple bobber and wax worms. Late May and early June during the spawn are the best times to catch the bigger panfish.

Black and white crappies are also present in good numbers and can be found around woody structures and fallen treetops and off the islands throughout the lake. Most crappies average 10 to 12 inches; in good years some 14-inch-plus crappies are caught from late March through May and again in fall. Fish the brush and bank cover around the three islands north of the boat ramp and off the causeway at the north end with minnows and a bobber and small crappie jigs.

Some nice northern pike from 30 to 35 inches have been taken from East Branch. They are caught in early spring from ice-out through March in the weedy headwaters north of the US 322 Causeway and under the causeway bridge. Use shiners, chubs, or big minnows suspended under a bobber. A few pike are also caught from the tailwaters below the dam. Though access is restricted from the Highway 608 Bridge to the dam, there is a pulloff on the south side of the road just past the bridge from which anglers can access a small portion of the tailwaters.

White perch are common catches in East Branch. How the perch got into the lake is a mystery, and Geauga Parks and the Division of Wildlife do not appreciate their introduction. The perch are caught with a simple worm and a bobber. Ring perch are also present; most are small, although a few are caught upwards of 10 inches. Catch ring perch off the shore along the weed beds in spring and fall and off the bottom around the channel between the islands and the causeway in summer.

Bass fishing is excellent on East Branch and can be found throughout the lake. Work the shoreline cover on both banks from the middle to the south end of the lake. Fish the weed beds, the saddles between the islands, and the weedy humps and islands north of the boat ramp. Fish the rocks where you can find them and the weedy points in the middle of the lake on both shores. The old streambed that runs between the islands is as good a place as any to take bass that average 12 to 15 inches. Every year anglers take several bass in the 3- to 4-pound range. Spinner baits, tubes, and buzz baits are preferred by bass all over East Branch.

Channel cats are also present in East Branch, but in low numbers. Most average 12 to 15 inches. The majority of the cat fishing is done from off the end of the causeway near the stream channel under the bridge with chicken livers and night crawlers.

Special regulations: Shoreline fishing is restricted to the platforms and causeway. Only electric motors are permitted on the lake. Outboards and gas tanks must be removed prior to launching. The park is open from 6:00 a.m. to 11:00 p.m.

Facilities/camping: Park facilities include a restroom and picnic areas. No camping is permitted. The nearest town is Chardon, which has everything.

Additional information: The Buckeye Trail runs along the west side of the reservoir.

Directions: From Chardon, take Highway 44 south to US 322, then go south on Highway 608 to Headwaters Park.

57 Euclid Creek

Euclid Creek is a small, shallow, but very scenic Lake Erie tributary in eastern Cleveland that usually contains a fair population of steelhead in winter and early spring. Thankfully Cleveland Metroparks has set aside 345 acres along the stream. The area is known as the Euclid Creek Reservation. Fishing is allowed on the small stream, but wading is prohibited—which is not much of a problem for fishing, but the creek banks are so steep that staying on them without getting your feet wet tests one's balance. There are not more than 2 miles of productive fishing stream in the park, if that.

Probably the best chance for a steelhead would be the few deep holes north of the Highland Road Bridge downstream to the end of the reservation at US 20. To get to Euclid Creek Reservation, take US 20 to East Cleveland, head south on Highland Road, and then turn west on Euclid Creek Parkway. In addition to fishing, the reservation has parking areas, hiking and walking trails, restrooms, and picnic areas.

58 Fernwood State Forest

Fernwood State Forest is located southwest of Steubenville, south of U.S. Highway 22, off County Road 34. It offers fishing in several small quarry ponds for bass, bluegill, and some channel catfish. In addition to fishing, there is a trap, rifle, and pistol range, some scenic views in the eastern section, several picnic areas, and a campground with 22 sites. The 3,023-acre forest consists mostly of reclaimed strip-mine land and has a number of strip-mine and beaver ponds available for anglers, some of which must be hiked into to fish. There is some limited public access on Cross Creek, which appears to be a pretty good smallmouth stream.

59 Findley Lake

Key species: Largemouth bass, channel catfish, crappie, bluegill.

General description: Another excellent lake to catch a limited number of channel cats.

Overview: Findley is a beautiful lake of 93 acres surrounded by the forest of Findley State Park. The park offers camping, a beach, hiking and mountain bike trails, two boat ramps, and boat rental at the marina.

The donated parkland was originally known as the Findley Forest, but it was transferred to the Division of Parks and Recreation in 1950. Findley Lake was created in 1956 by impounding Wellington Creek. When the lake was finally impounded, one of the last landowners left behind a 1950s Crown Victoria that was not running. It is still here, located off the north side of Picnic Point under 15 feet of water. There is also an old wooden rowboat that sank many years ago just south of Picnic Point.

In June a youth fishing derby is held on Findley Lake; the lake is stocked with approximately 500 channel catfish for the event.

The lake contains an abundance of shoreline structure in the way of fallen trees, bank slips, brush, and rock. The lake averages 5 to 15 feet, with some 20-foot water at the dam.

The fishing: Cat fishing is the primary draw at Findley Lake, with most channels averaging 12 to 20 inches. Most fishing is done from the shoreline at the dam and at Picnic Point with chicken livers and night crawlers, but the fish are evenly spread out and can be found anywhere. Prime fishing is on summer nights and evenings.

Crappie fishing is also good here, but most run a smallish 6 to 8 inches. If you know where to look, 30 to 40 fish days are not uncommon in April and May. Fish the shoreline brush and stumps along the old creek channel on the lake's southeast side and at the old beaver lodges. Also fish the north bank of Picnic Point, where several fish structures have been placed. But don't stop there; the entire rocky shoreline of Picnic Point is good for crappies. Using minnows suspended 3 feet under a bobber is the most productive way to catch crappies.

Bluegills are common, reaching a respectable 6 to 8 inches. Anywhere around the shoreline will yield good catches with wax worms and floaters. The most popular spot for bluegills is among the rocks at Picnic Point.

Bass fishing is tough at Findley Lake, but fairly good, with plenty of bass averaging 8 to 14 inches; a 3-pound bass would be considered a very good one. Some 6-pound bass have been caught here in the past. Some say the bass fishing was much better before the introduction of weed-eating white amurs, which cleaned the lake of weeds. To catch bass now, fish the shoreline cover on the east bank across from the beach and the west bank near the dam, and the old creek channel shoreline cover on the southeast side of the lake. There is plenty of shoreline cover along these banks that consists of fallen trees, brush, and big rocks. Several years ago the Division of Wildlife felled a number of trees to provide shoreline habitat. Chartreuse, white, or yellow spinner baits thrown into bank cover and around the rocks work best; plastic night crawlers work well also. During the spring spawn work the shallow flats on the east shore just south of the dam with tubes and jigs and plastic crayfish.

In spring and fall a few yellow perch are also caught off the deep point just south of the dam off the east shoreline. Most perch caught are incidental catches by crappie fishers using minnows.

At one time the lake was stocked with northern pike. The last stocking took place in 1991. The last known pike caught from Findley Lake was in 1996.

Special regulations: A special slot length limit is in effect on bass: Bass between 12 and 15 inches must be released. Anglers are also limited to six channel catfish per day. The lake is limited to electric motors only.

Facilities/camping: Findley State Park does have a small camp store at the campground. A gas station/convenience store is located a couple miles south of the state park. The park has 273 campsites.

Additional information: The 200-acre Wellington Wildlife Area is adjacent to the park grounds. There is one small, but fishable pond in the wildlife area that can be reached from the parking area off Griggs Road across from the park.

Directions: From Wellington take Highway 58 south 2 miles. Findley Lake State Park is on the east side of the road.

60 Friendship Lake Park

Key species: Largemouth bass, channel catfish, bluegill, walleye, trout.

General description: Friendship Lake was once an old strip-mine lake, which now serves as a county park.

Overview: The 100-acre Friendship Lake is the centerpiece of Jefferson County Park, which also includes the fairgrounds and county airport. The reclaimed strip-mine land was donated to the county by the Hanna Coal Company and the Cravat Coal Company. In 1972 a dam was constructed across one of the strip-mine ponds, creating Friendship Lake. In addition to fishing, the park has a campground, picnic areas, shelter houses, and the very interesting Fort Friendship Veterans' Museum, which includes several pieces of old military hardware.

The lake is easily fished from the entry road on the north side of the lake. The Choogie Trail encircles the lake, and anglers can access the south shore of the lake from this trail. There is a gravel ramp just below the campground, and the lake is limited to electric motors only.

The fishing: Friendship Lake is a beautiful lake tucked away in the hills of Jefferson County; just finding the place is an adventure. The lake is very clear, with the type of shoreline and deep structure nominally associated with quarry and strip-mine lakes. It averages well over 30 feet deep in the center. Over the years, hundreds of fish attractors were placed into the lake at various locations along the shoreline. The lake is not very fertile due to the presence of marl along the lake bottom, which one biologist said tends to absorb all the nutrients from the lake. This means nutrients aren't available for fish growth, which was reflected in Division of Wildlife studies conducted in the early 1990s. To counter the lack of nutrients, there have been regular stockings of fathead minnows to provide forage. There is a healthy presence of small bluegills and some nice bass up to 4 or 5 pounds that roam close to the shoreline rocks. Occasionally the county stocks rainbow and brown trout in the lake, and there are said to be walleyes in the lake as well. Nice channel catfish in the 2- to 5-pound range are caught from Friendship Lake, as is a 40-pound-plus flathead catfish that has been caught and recaught several times. Small perch and crappies are also taken from the lake.

At the headwaters to Friendship Lake is another large strip-mine pond of about 25 acres located directly across from the main entrance. It is said to contain bass, bluegill, and channel catfish. Around the park vicinity and along a few nameless township roads are several old strip-mine ponds that are well worth exploring and fishing.

Special regulations: Special limits are posted at the entry to Friendship Lake. Trout are limited to three per day, walleye two per day, channel cats two per day, and all bass must be over 10 inches to keep. Friendship Lake is limited to electric motors only. The park is open from March 31 through November 1; gates are open from 8:00 a.m. through 4:00 p.m. However, fishing is permitted all year and ice fishing is allowed.

Facilities/camping: The Friendship Park campground has 15 sites, which overlook the lake.

Additional information: Be sure to visit the outdoor display of old military hardware at the Veterans' Memorial Museum; everything from tanks to jets are located at the entrance to the fairgrounds.

Directions: From Steubenville, take Highway 151 west 9 miles to Smithfield and watch for signs.

61 Geneva State Park

Key species: Steelhead, smallmouth and largemouth bass, walleye, perch, bluegill, channel catfish.

General description: This park has public boat launching, camping, and fishing on the central basin.

Overview: Geneva State Park is the only state park east of Cleveland on Lake Erie to offer a boat launch, docking, camping, and fishing. The park also has two fine steelhead streams within the park boundaries and a couple of other steelhead streams close by. Geneva State Park has a new lodge with dining and overnight accommodations, a beach, cabins, golfing, picnic areas, and shelter houses.

The fishing: In spring, summer, and early fall, the Geneva State Park is a busy headquarters with walleye, steelhead, smallmouth, and perch fishermen. Fishing can be had off the rock fishing pier and break wall that line the entrance to the marina. Off the break walls anglers catch smallmouth, perch, sheepshead, and at times walleye and steelhead. Inside the marina panfish, largemouth and smallmouth bass, channel catfish, and, after November, a few steelhead are taken. However, 99 percent of the fishers who visit Geneva launch a boat and fish offshore for walleye, perch, and smallmouth.

Geneva State Park also has a couple of small ponds that offer fishing for bass and bluegills. Two small Lake Erie tributary streams within the park, Cowles Creek and Wheeler Creek, offer excellent steelhead fishing in fall, winter, and early spring.

Cowles Creek can be accessed from the marina parking area and also at the service road bridge that crosses the creek. From the bridge, anglers can park and walk upstream on a fishermen's path and wade back to the bridge or vice-versa. Cowles Creek can also be accessed from a pulloff on Highway 534, east of the park.

Wheeler Creek can be accessed from the west side of the park off Lake Road West. Anglers can pull off alongside the bridge, but a better approach is to park just west of the bridge at a service road entrance and walk the path upstream to the creek. The mouth of Wheeler Creek can be accessed from a northbound, dead-end road at the western edge of the park boundary.

Just outside the state park to the east is Indian Creek, and to the west of the park is Arcola Creek. Both are excellent steelhead streams, with Arcola Creek having public access from a Lake County Metropark parking area.

Special regulations: Steelhead and trout must be 12 inches to keep, with a daily limit of two fish. There is a 14-inch minimum length limit in effect on smallmouth bass, and a 15-inch length limit on walleye.

Facilities/camping: Geneva State Park has 100 campsites, 12 cabins, and a 109-room lodge with dining facilities.

Additional information: Approximately 2 miles west of Geneva State Park is the Arcola Creek Estuary, one of only two remaining natural estuaries on the south shore of Lake Erie.

Directions: From I-90 southwest of Ashtabula, take Highway 534 north 6 miles.

62 Grand River

Key species: Steelhead, smallmouth bass, rock bass, sunfish, channel catfish, muskie, northern pike, walleye, and stocked trout.

General description: Public access aplenty on one of Ohio's top steelhead streams.

Overview: The Grand River is approximately 103 miles long. It flows north out of Trumbull County into Ashtabula County, then west, emptying out at Fairport Harbor in Lake County. Fairport Harbor is a busy port with boat launching, docking, fishing, restaurants, bait and tackle, charter services, and overnight accommodations that are not far away. Every September, Lake County hosts an annual Perch Fest, which draws thousands of visitors and fishers into Fairport Harbor.

The Grand has the most aquatic diversity of any Ohio Lake Erie tributary and was designated a State Wild and Scenic River in 1974. The Upper Grand above Harpersfield Covered Bridge is a slow-moving stream bordered by swamp and a wetland forest of maple, pine, and white oak. It is home to some of the first reintroductions of river otters by the Division of Wildlife. Below Harpersfield, the Lower Grand is an entirely different river, with enough strength and flow to create a fast-paced stream of broad riffles, pools, and gravel runs. It is ideal habitat for smallmouth and steelhead and great for canoes and kayaks.

Flowing through one of the most populated regions of Ohio, the Grand has so far survived the developmental pressures placed upon it by a burgeoning population, in part by a local community that recognizes its value. Through the cooperation of community and local government, more than 14 miles of the Grand River have been incorporated into a string of Lake County Metroparks that provides picnic and recreation areas, green spaces, hiking trails, natural and wild areas, boat launching, and fishing access. In all more than 5,250 acres of Grand River Watershed are protected by the Lake County Metroparks.

In 2006 a devastating flood that resulted from a 48-hour downpour caused the Grand River to reach over 11 feet above flood stage. Damage to homes and infrastructure along the river and its tributaries was so great that the area was declared a federal disaster area. Many of the Metro Parks and public-access areas along the Grand suffered severe damage, causing a number of the riverside parks to close until structures and roads could be either be repaired or replaced.

The fishing: The Grand River is perhaps the most popular steelhead river in northeast Ohio. Steelhead migrate as far up as the Harpersfield Covered Bridge and dam, which is approximately 50 miles upstream from Fairport Harbor. At Harpersfield Covered Bridge, access is provided by the Ashtabula County Metroparks. Fishing

The Grand River at the Harpersfield Covered Bridge is good for smallmouth during the summer and steelhead in the spring.

at the old scenic bridge is an experience unlike any other in Ohio. Built in 1868, the old bridge and adjoining steel bridge span 230 feet across the river. The water downstream of the bridge is easy to wade and a popular and productive fishing area for steelhead, smallmouth, and rock bass. Anglers can also fish from the bridge walkway, and if a steelhead is caught, they simply walk the rod over to the north side of the bridge, go down the bank, and attempt to land it.

The pool above the dam has been known to produce a few muskies, as the Grand River is one of the few natural muskie streams in the state. Tandem spinners, bucktails, and crank baits thrown into brush, timber, and deep pools will occasionally produce a follow, and perhaps a strike, from muskies that range from 28 to 36 inches. One of the better spots on the Grand for muskies is the big hole of water just upstream from where Paine Creek joins the river at the Indian Point Metro Park. I have heard credible reports of anglers who have observed muskies feeding on suckers in the riffles just above the pool. Catching muskies from Grand River is not uncommon, and several are taken every year. Every once in a while, a muskie is caught at the mouth of the river at Fairport Harbor and from the waters in Mentor Lagoon about 3 miles west of the harbor.

Walleyes do make a small run up the Grand, as far as Helen Hazen Wyman Park, in late March. But the run goes unnoticed, as steelhead steal the spotlight.

Smallmouth do well in the Grand, with plenty of 12- to 15-inch smallies caught from the same pools that held steelhead in March. The best smallmouth fishing is May through early July, with some of the best water from Paine Creek upstream to Harpersfield.

The Grand is the steelhead river in Ohio. Beginning in September, steelhead are caught from the break walls and harbor mouth; by the end of October the fish have already migrated the 50 miles upstream to Harpersfield. Anglers have benefited greatly from the various parks and pulloffs along the stream.

Some of the more popular spots are the Kiwanis Club Park off East Main Street in Painesville. The next upstream access is at the Helen Hazen Wyman Metro Park, which also provides access to the mouths of Big and Kellogg Creeks. Smaller Grand River tributaries like Big, Paine, Kellogg, and Mill Creeks often clear quickly and offer fishing within a day or two after heavy rain or snowmelt has muddied up the Grand.

Upstream from Helen Hazen Park is Mason's Landing and Indian Point Park on Paine Creek. At Mason's Landing, anglers can launch a canoe or small boat and float downstream to the Grand River Landing boat ramp in Fairport. Paine Creek is an excellent small scenic stream that clears quickly and contains several small but deep pools. Nearly the entire creek can be fished in a long afternoon. Upstream from the bridge that spans Paine Creek are a couple of pools under the I-90 ridge and then a waterfall that impedes the migration of steelhead. At the other end, where Paine joins the Grand, is another excellent area. Fish for steelhead from the broad set of riffles on the Grand downstream of that junction. Upstream from where Paine Creek enters the Grand is a big pool that is one of the best muskie holes in the river. In April 500 trout, weighing from 1 to 2 pounds, are stocked in Paine Creek by Lake County Metroparks.

The next upstream access on the Grand is off I-90 at Madison. Take Highway 528 south, then head east on River Road, and then south on Bailey Road, which will lead right to the river's edge. Walk the path down to a good set of riffles. Back on Highway 528, go south across the high bridge over the Grand and then turn west on Klasen Road down to Hidden Valley Metro Park. From Hidden Valley, anglers can access miles of the river and launch a canoe or small boat and float down to Mason's Landing. It's a day's trip but an unforgettable experience. From Hidden Valley anglers can also walk the path downstream a mile to Talcott Creek, which is a small stream at the foot of a very scenic waterfall that usually contains a few steelhead.

Upstream from Hidden Valley is Hogback Ridge Metro Park, located at the end of Emerson Road. Take Highway 528 south of Klasen Road; turn east on Griswold Road, then north on Emerson Road. From Hogback, anglers can access Mill Creek via a set of long steps or a downhill path that leads to the mouth of the stream. Mill Creek is one of the finest tributaries on the Grand; it clears quickly and holds good-size fish.

Upstream from Hogback, there are a few access points at the end of county and township roads. The next public access is at Harpersfield Covered Bridge, located

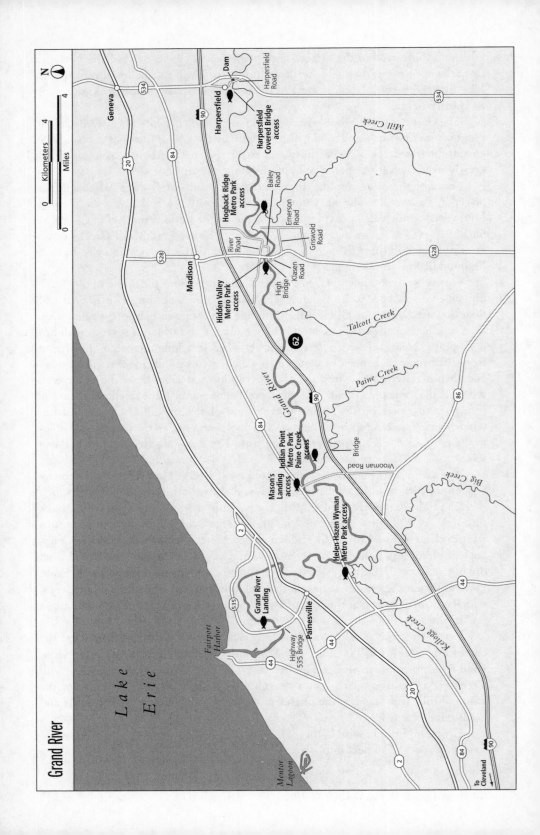

Grand River

south of I-90 exit 218, off Highway 534 on Harpersfield Road. Parking is on either side of the covered bridge. There is also a small bait and tackle shop. A canoe or kayak can be launched from here as well, and anglers can fish and float down to Hidden Valley.

Steelhead fishing on the Grand starts in earnest in late October and continues through the winter until the end of April. Prime time is probably the last two weeks in March and the first two weeks in April, when steelhead start seeking out the gravel runs to spawn. Because the watershed is so large, the Grand is often high and muddy as a result of snowmelt or spring rains. You should check ahead when planning a visit to the Grand. Contact one of the local bait and tackle shops or visit the Lake County Visitors Bureau Web site at www.lakevisit.com.

Special regulations: Steelhead and trout must be 12 inches in length, except on Paine Creek, where special regulations apply during the annual trout stocking. From the mouth at Fairport Harbor to the Highway 535 Bridge in Painesville, bass must be 14 inches; walleye must be 15 inches.

Facilities/camping: Painesville, Fairport Harbor, and Madison have all the amenities, as do the intersections and exits off I-90. At various Metro Parks, anglers can find ample parking, restrooms, picnic areas, shelter houses, and boat launching. Geneva State Park has 100 campsites, 12 lakeside cabins, and the 109-room Geneva State Park Lodge. Lake County Metroparks also has cabins at Hogback and Hidden Valley.

Additional information: Lake County is known for its vineyards and wineries.

Directions: From I-90 east of Cleveland, take exit 200 north on Highway 44 to Fairport Harbor. Take exit 205 north on Vrooman Road to Mason's Landing and Indian Point. Take exit 212 south to Hidden Valley Metro Park and Hogback Ridge Metro Park. Take exit 218 south to Harpersfield Covered Bridge.

63 Grand River Wildlife Area

The Grand River Wildlife Area, located about 10 miles northwest of Warren on Highway 534, has a number of small ponds that have bass and bluegill. These are small weedy ponds managed primarily for waterfowl, but most contain a population of game fish. One of the ponds at the southeast corner along Highway 88 contains a few small chain pickerel, resulting from a stocking by the Division of Wildlife that took place years ago.

64 Guilford Lake

Key species: Largemouth bass, channel catfish, crappie, bluegill, yellow perch.

General description: An old canal lake that provides excellent bass and channel cat fishing.

Overview: Guilford Lake was originally constructed in the 1830s to provide water to the Sandy and Beaver Canal. The dam on Guilford Lake is named after Edward H. Gill, the chief engineer of the Sandy and Beaver Canal System. The lake covers approximately 396 acres and averages 10 to 15 feet deep.

The lake is virtually surrounded by lakeside homes, cottages, and boat docks; what isn't private property is part of the 93-acre Guilford Lake State Park.

The newly renovated Guilford Lake State Park has a beach, three boat ramps, picnic areas, a wheelchair-accessible pier, boat rental, and lakeside camping. There is plenty of good shoreline access from the park grounds.

The fishing: Let's keep this between you and me: There is some fairly good bass fishing at Guilford, and it's probably one of the better-kept secrets around. While most bass average 12 to 15 inches, plenty of 3- to 4-pounders are caught. I know of one 8.5-pound bass that came from the lake by a fellow fishing from his own boat dock. Bass are caught off the dam, from the riprap around the camping area, from the County Road 411 Causeway, off the shoreline of the few brushy islands, in the backs of the coves, and from around the few stands of cattails. Throw spinner baits and Rapalas during the day, and in the evening switch to jitterbugs. Live bait works well: Bass-size minnows, shiners, and leeches fished under a bobber next to cover pick up plenty of nice bass as well. The best bass fishing takes place in late April through June, and again in late September and October. Most of the shoreline is taken over by private docks, but some shoreline cover is found on the southeast corner and in the back of Little Beaver Creek Cove.

Channel cats do just fine on Guilford, and the cat fishers know it. Channel cats average 12 to 18 inches, but 8- to 10-pounders show up every month at local catfish tournaments. The cat fishing is done at night with stink bait, chicken livers, and night crawlers. Fish for channels from the dam, the campgrounds, the southside picnic areas, and the pier. The best catfish are caught in July and August.

Crappie fishing is so-so on Guilford, with most crappies averaging only 7 to 10 inches at best. Fish the boat docks, the coves, the causeway, and around the brushy island and cover in Little Beaver Cove. Crappies are caught in early spring from late March through May and again in mid-September. The crappies are taken with minnows, maggots, and 1/16-ounce yellow, chartreuse, and hot-pink twister tail jigs.

Bluegills are everywhere but seldom make 5 inches, except during the early June spawn, when a few hand-size bluegills come out of hiding.

Yellow perch are also caught from Guilford, but they are small, hardly reaching 6 or 7 inches.

Special regulations: The lake is limited to 10 hp.

Facilities/camping: The small but historical town of Lisbon, founded in 1803, is 5 miles east of Guilford Lake and has everything. Guilford Lake State Park has 41 campsites.

Additional information: After a day's fishing, have dinner at Marks Landing, located on the south shore of the lake since 1946. It can be reached as easily by boat as it can by car.

Directions: From Lisbon, go 5 miles east on Highway 172.

65 Highlandtown Lake Wildlife Area

Key species: Largemouth bass, bluegill, redear sunfish, pumpkinseed, channel and bullhead catfish, and crappie.

General description: A popular local lake for channel catfish, bass, and crappie.

Overview: Highlandtown Lake was completed in 1966, impounding 170 acres on the upper drainage of Little Yellow Creek. The lake is part of the 2,265-acre Highlandtown Wildlife Area, which also includes two other wildlife area ponds that contain bass, bluegill, and catfish. The lake has two concrete boat ramps, wheelchair access, and four parking areas around the lake. The wheelchair-accessible pier is located at the Osbourne Road boat ramp. The lake averages 5 to 15 feet deep, and a thick growth of spatterdock pads crowds the headwaters at the west end.

Over the years, the Division of Wildlife has sunk numerous fish attractors along the shoreline. To find their exact location, inquire at the Wildlife Area Headquarters located north of the lake on Spring Valley Road.

The fishing: Around 1999, gizzard shad got into the Highlandtown Lake. As a result, the bass got fatter and the bluegills smaller. There was an attempt to exterminate them, but the gizzard shad won. A few local anglers say the bass fishing was so good years ago when the lake was full of weeds that catching 20 to 30 bass a day from the weed beds was not unusual. But since the introduction of white amurs to control the weeds, the perfect bass cover disappeared. Catching bass now requires much more work. As a result of the gizzard shad and white amurs, the bass appear fewer but heavier. There is still a lot of good bass fishing at Highlandtown. While anglers still catch plenty of smaller bass, 2- to 3-pound bass are fairly routine; every now and then, a 6- or 7-pound fish turns up.

Most anglers work the shoreline cover with spinner baits and plastics. Come evening, jitterbugs and buzz baits turn the bass on. Work the riprap at the dam and the rock reef just south of the Osbourne Road ramp. Another good area is the underwater structure on the south bank opposite the Osbourne boat ramp; a depth finder can help you find it. There are plenty of spatterdock pads at the west end of the lake near the Clarks Mill Road ramp. Work the weed edges and channels between the spatterdock with spinner baits and weedless rigged plastic night crawlers. The north shoreline in front of the Clarks Mill ramp is worth a going-over as well. There are a few remains of standing timber off the southwest shore, and more than a few bass have come from there. The old roadbed from Steubenville Pike Road crosses the lake to the north parking area, and on that road are the remains of a submerged bridge that once crossed the channel. If you can locate it, you will find

Wheelchair-accessible piers like this are located at most wildlife areas and lakes throughout Ohio.

bass there as well. Fish the creek arms and coves early in spring, and stick to the main lake and submerged structure in summer. The best bass fishing takes place in late April through June. It drops off in summer, but gets good again in mid-September.

Channel catfish do well at Highlandtown. Over the years the Division of Wildlife has sunk 25-gallon plastic barrels, called tubs, to encourage the spawning of channels, which look for cavities in which to spawn. While plenty of small 12- to 15-inch catfish are caught, a lot of channels between 20 and 28 inches are caught as well. Bullheads usually run up to 12 inches. The most popular bait is chicken livers, followed by night crawlers. The best cat fishing is done on summer evenings and at night from the north side of the dam, from the parking area at the end of Steubenville Pike Road, and off the shoreline east of the Osbourne ramp. Also off the parking area across from Osbourne ramp, there is the old roadbed that crosses the lake to Steubenville Pike Road. Catfish are well distributed; an angler will find plenty of channels and bullheads at all locations.

Crappies are fairly plentiful and reach a good 14 to 15 inches. Look for them around the piles of sticks that beavers gather together for their winter food supply and around the many fish structures. Any woody structure along the lakeshore and off the riprap at the dam will also hold crappies in spring. Minnows and a slip bobber are all that is needed to catch crappies from Highlandtown. Most crappies are caught during April and May.

Bluegills are small, but a few hand-size ones are caught during the spring spawn in late May and early June. Some nice redear sunfish approaching 9 inches also are caught in the spring. A few nice pumpkinseeds are caught this time of year, too. A fisher can catch bluegills off the shore from any boat ramp or parking area, and the pier is an especially good place. Red worms, wax worms, and small jigs with maggots do the job.

Special regulations: Highlandtown Lake is limited to electric motors only. A special slot length limit is in effect on bass; all bass between 12 and 15 inches must be released. The daily limit of channel catfish is six.

Facilities/camping: There are no facilities or camping at the wildlife area. The nearest town is Wellsville, which is only a hot cup of coffee away.

Additional information: If you get skunked at Highlandtown Lake, Ismond Pond is just north of the lake on Steubenville Pike Road.

Directions: From Wellsville take Highway 39 west approximately 6 miles to Highlandtown Lake. Look for WILDLIFE AREA signs.

66 Hinckley Lake

Key species: Largemouth bass, channel catfish, crappie, bluegill.

General description: Some minor fishing for channel cats and small bluegills.

Overview: Hinckley Lake is a small 90-acre lake on the east branch of the Rocky River. It is owned and operated by Cleveland Metro Parks as part of the 2,682-acre Hinckley Reservation. The park has a swimming beach, concessions, a primitive boat launch, a marina with boat rental, and miles of hiking, walking, and biking trails. The boat launch is located off State Road.

The fishing: Fishers have a few choices when fishing in the Hinckley Reservation. There is a small tailwater fishery in the pool below the dam, and anglers also can access a couple of miles of the east branch of the Rocky River for some small stream fishing for smallmouth and sunfish. Below the dam anglers catch a few channel cats and small bluegills, but in summer they have to share the tailwaters with swimmers and waders. Above the lake the east branch of the Rocky River has a fair population of small bass, sunfish, and some channel cats in the deeper pools. Access to the stream is via two gravel roads: one off State Road, the other off Parker Road.

Hinckley Lake offers fishing for channel cats, bass, crappies, and bluegills. Crappies are caught in early spring from shoreline brush along the north and west shores with minnows and a bobber. Most crappies average only 8 to 10 inches; a few larger ones do show up, and some as big as 17 inches have been caught.

Bass usually run small, but some 2- to 3-pound fish have been caught in spring and fall. Most anglers fish the shoreline cover at the north end of the lake, the slips, rocks, and downed trees with spinner baits and plastics. The best fishing is in May before all the paddleboats are turned loose on the lake.

Channels are caught with some regularity, and a few nice ones in the 3- to 4-pound range are caught by anglers fishing on the bottom with chicken livers. Catfish can be found all over the lake, but the east shallow end is better on summer evenings. The largest channel cat ever reported to have come from the lake was a whopping 36-inch fish that weighed over 27 pounds.

Bluegills are plentiful, but they are small and can be caught from brush and cover near the shore and from the headwaters.

Bank access is good by way of the Lake Loop Trail that encircles the lake.

Special regulations: Electric motors only.

Facilities/camping: Food, ice, beverages, and boat rental are available at the Hinckley Lake Boathouse off West Drive on the south side of the lake. No camping is allowed on the reservation.

Additional information: Every Ohioan is aware of the Hinckley buzzards that arrive like clockwork in early spring.

Directions: Hinckley Lake is located just southeast of the town of Hinckley off Highway 606.

67 Indian Creek

Indian Creek is a small Lake Erie tributary located on Highway 531 about 1 mile east of the small summer village of Geneva-on-the-Lake. Indian Creek is an excellent steelhead stream with very limited access. The stream north of the Highway 531 Bridge is heavily posted. There is a small pulloff on the southeast side of the bridge, and a path leads to the creek south of the bridge. I would strongly suggest seeking landowner permission before fishing here so that posted signs don't magically appear on the south side of the bridge as well.

68 Jefferson Lake State Park

Jefferson Lake is a small, but beautiful lake of 17 acres approximately 10 miles northwest of Steubenville off Highway 43. The lake is surrounded by the 945-acre Jefferson Lake State Park, which has picnic areas, shelter houses, miles of hiking and bridle trails, a beach, a boat ramp, and a 67-site camping area. The Civilian Conservation Corps built the Jefferson Dam during the Depression in 1934. In 1950, the lake and area surrounding it became a state park.

Jefferson Lake contains largemouth bass, bluegill, and channel catfish and is stocked with trout every spring by the Division of Wildlife.

Most bass average 8 to 12 inches; occasionally a 2- to 3-pounder is caught out of the cover and downed timber along the steep bank opposite the boat ramp with spinner baits or a floater and night crawler. Channels are stocked on a semiregular basis, and most caught will average 12 to 16 inches. The catfish are usually caught with red worms and night crawlers. Bluegills are plentiful but small, and a container of wax worms will get young anglers plenty of action. Trout are the biggest draw at Jefferson Lake. In early April approximately 2,500 rainbow trout are released into the lake. The trout are taken with corn, Power Bait, cheese, wax worms, and sometimes yellow or chartreuse Rooster Tails. The trout fishing, though usually good, lasts only four to six weeks. The lake is easily fished from shore.

69 Killbuck Creek Wildlife Area

Key species: Bullhead, channel cat, bowfin, northern pike.

General description: A good place to catch northern pike in spring.

Overview: Killbuck Creek is a small, slow-moving stream surrounded mostly by marshland in the 5,521-acre Killbuck Marsh Wildlife Area. The 151-acre Lower Killbuck Creek Wildlife Area is approximately 12 miles downstream from the main wildlife area. Access to the stream is at several county and township road bridges within the wildlife area and at wildlife parking areas near the stream. There are numerous marsh ponds in the wildlife area, but they are managed primarily for waterfowl, not fishing. Headquarters for the wildlife area is located on County Line Road east of the town of Shreve.

The fishing: Fishing at Killbuck Creek is primarily composed of rough fish, small channel cats, bullheads, and 10- to 12-inch bowfins. These fish are caught with minnows, night crawlers, and wax worms throughout spring and summer. Starting in early spring right after ice-out, usually in early March, anglers using suckers or creek chubs under a floater will catch northern pike in the 18- to 24-inch range. Occasionally some 8- to 10-pound pike are caught. A few pike are caught from the stream in the Killbuck Marsh Wildlife Area, but the best fishing is at the Lower Killbuck Creek Wildlife Area south of the town of Killbuck off U.S. Highway 62. From the parking area just south of US 62, anglers can access the old original Killbuck Creek stream channel. Killbuck Creek has been channeled away from its original course, but pike still return to the old channel to spawn after ice-out. Most of the pike fishing is done in early spring in that original stream channel.

Killbuck Creek is hardly big enough to put a canoe in; most fishing is done from the banks.

Special regulations: None; state game and fish laws apply.

Facilities/camping: There are no facilities or camping at Killbuck Wildlife Area. The nearest towns are Shreve and Killbuck at the lower wildlife area.

Additional information: The Killbuck Wildlife Area is popular for waterfowl hunting.

Directions: The Killbuck Wildlife Area can be reached on any county or township road east of the small village of Shreve. The Lower Killbuck Creek Wildlife Area is located 6 miles south of Millersburg at the junction of Highway 520 and US 62.

70 LaDue Reservoir

Key species: Largemouth and smallmouth bass, channel catfish, crappie, northern pike, walleye, bluegill, and ring perch.

General description: One of the best fishing lakes in northeast Ohio; home of two state record fish.

Overview: LaDue Reservoir covers 1,500 acres and is one of a number of Akron City Water Department reservoirs in northeast Ohio. As with all Akron City reservoirs, this too has a number of restrictions regarding shoreline access, outboard motors and gas tanks, and access to the tailwaters.

The lake has two rough, primitive boat ramps: one off Highway 44 at the south end of the lake and another just east of Highway 44, off Valley Road at the crossroads village of Auburn Corners. Improvements to the boat ramps and some limited shoreline access are planned for the reservoir. As it stands now, anglers can fish LaDue by boat only, as shoreline access is restricted, and the reservoir is limited to electric motors only.

LaDue is a large reservoir that can get windy and rough. The lake has numerous weed beds, and several small islands are scattered at both ends.

The fishing: LaDue is an excellent lake for bass, bluegills, crappies, channel catfish, and walleye. In 1992 a state record channel catfish weighing 37.65 pounds was caught, and in 2006 a state record warmouth sunfish weighing 1.19 pounds was also taken from LaDue.

Bass fishing starts south of the U.S. Highway 422 Causeway in early April, and as the water warms, the fishing gradually moves north of the causeway. Most bass average 12 to 15 inches, with many living long enough to top out at the 5- or 6-pound mark. Fishing for bass is primarily composed of finding and fishing the numerous weed beds that grow in 2 to 5 feet of water along the shoreline. Shoreline structure and brush are also productive, but they play second fiddle to the big weed beds. Bass are also taken from the causeway riprap and at the dam. An angler is just as likely to catch smallmouth from the riprap as largemouth. The smallmouth in LaDue grow just as large as the largemouth.

There are a couple of large weed beds off the east and west shore, south of the Highway 422 causeway. Work the outside weed edges and pockets with plastic night crawlers and spinner baits. Work any weed beds off the points on the east bank and around the islands. A couple of points southeast of the causeway are also good locations for spring bass.

In summer the weed beds north of the causeway get the most attention. There are large weed beds just south of the dam on the east and west shoreline about 0.5 mile south of the dam. There is also some riprap in that area along Valley Road.

Only electric motors are allowed on LaDue Reservoir and many other large reservoirs in Ohio.

Chartreuse and black jigs and buzz baits produce well in the summer. A local favorite is the Chatter Bait Jig and the weedless Barney Spoon. Even though bass relate to weeds throughout the summer and into fall, don't pass up rocky points and the islands' brushy shorelines. Like most reservoirs in this area, the shorelines have a gradual slope.

Walleye fishing is also excellent at LaDue Reservoir, with most keeper fish averaging 1 to 3 pounds. It takes an 8-pound fish to raise any eyebrows at the local bait and tackle. Again, it's the weeds that are the key to walleye location in LaDue. In spring, work the weed edges, tops, and pockets with quarter-ounce weight-forward spinners tipped with half a night crawler. Fish the riprap along the causeway edge and dam with small crank baits and jigs and minnows. Come summer, troll along the edge of the old streambed from the causeway to the dam with Hot 'n Tots and Rapalas. Also drift or troll the shoreline, flats, and weeds along the west bank north of the causeway with night crawler harnesses, weight-forward spinners, or jigs and minnows. Fish the flats around the islands south of the causeway and the weed beds along both shores. A 0.5 mile south of the causeway are a number of stumps along the creek channel; this area is also good for walleye.

LaDue is a great crappie lake; most crappies are in the 10- to 14-inch range, with a few 16-inch slabs. Fish both sides of the causeway, the stumps along the old streambed south of the causeway, around the north islands, and any shoreline brush or wood along the banks. Use minnows and a slip bobber, fish off the bottom, and adjust the depth until you find crappies. Early spring from late March through May and again in fall are the right times to find crappies at LaDue.

Bluegills are also a nice hand size and bigger. Fish the south stream channel stumps, around the two small north islands, and anywhere along the shoreline. The best fishing is in May and during the spawn in early June, which is when the biggest bluegills are caught. Jigs and maggots under a bobber are the ticket.

Nice ring perch also come from LaDue, averaging 10 to 12 inches. The best fishing for perch is off the causeway near the bridge from both sides. Minnows fished on the bottom are best.

Channel cats average 15 to 24 inches, with 10-pound cats not uncommon. Use night crawlers, stink baits, and chicken livers on the bottom. Some of the best areas to catch channels are off the causeway and under the causeway bridge. Channels are spread out, so drifting bait over the bottom anywhere will produce fish.

Northern pike are caught from LaDue in early spring right after ice-out. Fish the far-south end along the old streambed with spinners and golden shiners or chubs under a bobber. Pike range in size from 24 to 36 inches. After spring the pike scatter and are caught incidentally by bass and walleye fishers from the weeds.

Ice fishing is permitted and popular on LaDue. Walleye, bluegills, and yellow perch are caught through the ice.

Special regulations: LaDue Reservoir is limited to electric motors only. All outboards and gas tanks must be removed before launching. Shoreline access is restricted, but that may change. Minimum length for bass is 12 inches.

Facilities/camping: There are no facilities or camping at the lake. A bait and tackle shop is located just west of the reservoir in Auburn Corners.

Additional information: There are a number of bald eagle nests near LaDue Reservoir, and eagle sightings are common during spring and early summer.

Directions: LaDue Reservoir is located east of the Highway 44 and US 422 intersection, 15 miles north of the town of Ravenna.

71 Lake Medina

Previously the Medina city water supply, Lake Medina was taken over as a county park in 2003. Fishing is permitted, but no fishing license is required to fish the reservoir. I estimate the lake at 65 acres. There is no posting to indicate if the lake permits boats or not. If a canoe or kayak were to be used, it would have to be carried a considerable distance from the only parking area to the lake. The lake is popular with walkers and joggers, as there are walking paths on the west side of the lake. Shoreline fishing is limited to the west side; access to the east shore is unavailable because it is privately owned and posted as such.

The west shoreline consists of riprap and concrete poured over rocks with some brush, making shoreline fishing difficult if not dangerous. On the east private side, a considerable amount of shoreline cover and structure are present, but one would need a boat to reach it. I am told a few nice bass have come from the lake by fishing along the shoreline rocks in the morning and evening with crank baits.

The only access to the lake is by a parking area on the east side of Medina off Highway 18. From there you have to walk to the lake. For additional information contact the Medina County Park District at (330) 722-9364.

72 Lake Milton

Key species: Largemouth and smallmouth bass, walleye, crappie, white bass, bluegill, pumpkinseed, channel catfish, perch, and muskie.

General description: A sleeper muskie lake.

Overview: Impounded in 1913 by the city of Youngstown as a water supply for the city's steel mills, the lake was completely drained in 1986 due to safety concerns about the dam. The dam was repaired and reopened as a state park in 1988. Lake Milton covers 1,685 acres and is almost completely surrounded by residential housing. State parks have several picnic areas and fishing access locations around the lake that provide excellent shoreline fishing opportunities. The Lake Milton State Park has a beach, walking trails, picnic areas, shelter houses, and three boat ramps.

As expected with any lake with a large amount of residential housing around its shoreline, Lake Milton gets plenty of jet boaters and water skiers in summer.

The fishing: Bass fishing is fairly good on Milton. Most bass average 12 to 14 inches; rarely is one caught over the 4-pound mark. Smallmouth are also common, with a few reaching into the 16-inch range. Most anglers work the shoreline structure, weeds and cattails, boat docks, riprap at the dam, and Mahoning River at the south end of the lake. There are several grassy, weedy points across from the Mahoning Avenue boat launch where anglers take bass. Also work the small creek on the east side of the lake where the park headquarters are located. The east shoreline from the Interstate 76 Bridge and north is good wherever there is shoreline cover and docks. A lot of bass are also taken from around the boat docks off Jersey Street. However, perhaps the best bass fishing is at the south end of the lake. Work the shoreline along the old stream channel across from the Pointview boat ramp and south along the east bank. Most anglers use spinner baits, plastics, and buzz baits on late summer evenings. Bass fishing begins in April in the few coves and at the shallower south end. In summer and when boat traffic is down, bass are caught from the points, islands, and shoreline structure in the middle of the lake near the two bridges and from the causeway.

Beginning in early April crappies are caught from the docks, brush, and shoreline cover. One end of the lake is as good as another. The Mahoning Road Causeway is an excellent place, as is the bridge pillars under I-76. Quite a few are also taken from the shore access at the east end of the dam. The crappie population and size fluctuate from year to year, with most fish averaging 6 to 9 inches. Most crappies are caught the old-fashioned way, with minnows and a bobber.

Walleyes are what every fisher is after at Lake Milton. Slow trolling, drifting, and vertical jigging with jigs and twister tails are how they get them; although a fair amount are caught by bank sitters fishing night crawlers on the bottom. Fish the shallow reef about a quarter mile north of the I-76 bridge next to the old streambed, the area between the two bridges, the Mahoning Road Causeway, and the sandbar southwest of the causeway. About 0.5 mile south of the causeway is another large sandbar that produces good walleyes, but it is so stumpy and filled with logs that vertical jigging is the only practical way to fish it. Anglers sometimes slow troll or drift crawler harnesses dressed with half a night crawler or leeches, use jigs tipped with minnows or night crawlers, or leeches on a bottom bouncer. Walleye average 15 to 18 inches; anglers catch lots of undersize fish. The walleye fishing begins in March, continues through June, and picks up again in fall. In fall, the flats in front of the beach produce well.

Bluegills are common and of good quality, averaging hand size or bigger; nice-size pumpkinseed sunfish are caught, too. Anyplace during the spawn from mid-May through June is a good place to fish. Fish around the docks and shallow shoreline with wax worms and a bobber, and you will find a bucketful of panfish.

Channel catfish are also well distributed. To catch cats, fish the causeway, off the east end of the dam, from the docks at the beach, the mud flats south of the Pointview boat ramp, and in the Mahoning River at the south end of the lake. Chicken livers are the preferred bait, but night crawlers do pretty well, too.

White bass and perch are also caught from the causeway, with white bass being the more common of the two. Most perch run small and are caught by fishers who are bank fishing for anything that bites off the causeway. White bass are caught in the same way, and from under the I-76 bridge. In spring white bass can be caught up the Mahoning River as far as the dam to Berlin Lake.

Muskies are the king of game fish at Lake Milton; several behemoths over the 40-pound mark have been taken. Trollers take summertime muskies suspended over the 12- to 15-foot flats between the two bridges and from the outer edge of the big sandbar 0.5 mile south of the causeway. Also troll the old stream channel where it brushes up against the east bank south of the causeway. From the Pointview ramp and south, troll the old creek channel into the river. In the Mahoning River, cast deep divers, big tandem spinner baits, and Crain baits to logs and bank cover. Plenty of shad are in the lake, which is the primary forage for muskies. Troll Bagely Super Shads or Tuff Shads slow and deep; some success has come from trolling baits in the prop wash.

The tailwaters at Lake Milton are also excellent for walleye, channel cats, and smallmouth. Most fishers vertical jig a night crawler or minnow off the concrete walls for walleye. Access the tailwaters from a parking area on the west side of the dam. You can fish for muskies, walleyes, bass, and catfish at a low-head dam 5 miles downstream on the Mahoning River. The dam is in a Rotary Club Park in the town of Newton Falls.

Special regulations: Walleye must be 15 inches to keep; there is a limit of five. Minimum length on bass is also 15 inches.

Facilities/camping: There are plenty of grocery stores, gas stations, and bait and tackle shops on Lake Milton. There is no camping at Lake Milton State Park; the nearest campground is at West Branch State Park, 8 miles west of Lake Milton, with 198 campsites.

Additional information: Eagles, ospreys, and an abundance of waterfowl are frequently seen on the lake.

Directions: From Youngstown, take I-76 west 11 miles to the Highway 534 exit. Head south to the village of Lake Milton.

73 Leesville Lake

Key species: Muskie, largemouth bass, crappie, bluegill, channel and flathead catfish, saugeye.

General description: The premier muskie lake in Ohio.

Overview: Leesville Lake was impounded in 1937 for the purposes of flood control on the Upper Muskingum River Watershed by the U.S. Army Corps of Engineers. The lake covers 1,000 surface acres and is managed by the Muskingum Watershed Conservancy District.

The lake is, for the most part, surrounded by woodlands. It makes an excellent setting for the various 4-H, Boy Scout, and church camps that dot the hillsides around the lake. The same is true for the lucky fishers who get to fish Leesville on a regular basis. The serene setting and quality fishing are all too rare on most public lakes.

The lake is served by two full-service marinas; both have public boat launches, boat rental, and small campgrounds. Petersburg Marina, located on the North Fork, has a restaurant that is open in summer. Clow's Marina is located near the dam on the South Fork.

There is no easy way to get around Leesville Lake by vehicle; numerous county and township roads wind around the hillsides leading into the various camps, cottage areas, and marinas. A good map is recommended for the first-time fisher to Leesville. That said, there is very little public shoreline access except at the dam; plan on bringing a boat or renting one. The lake is limited to 10 hp.

The fishing: Leesville is a muskie lake, plain and simple. Eighty percent of the fishers who visit Leesville are muskie fishing. And with good reason: Leesville leads the state in virtually every category related to muskie fishing, with the most "huskies" (fish over 42 inches) caught, the most 30-inch fish caught, and the most muskies caught from any Ohio lake. Leesville at one time held the state record muskie and state record tiger muskie.

Muskies in Leesville average 30 to 40 inches, with plenty of 42-inch-plus muskies caught. While most are taken during summer trolling, a few hearty anglers venture forth in early April to work the backs of coves and emerging weed beds

Leesville Lake muskie stocking takes place every fall when the muskies reach 10 to 11 inches. Muskies are stocked one fish per acre.

with big tandem spinner baits, jerk baits, and Belivers. Work all the west-side bays on the North Fork, from the Petersburg Marina to Doctors Bay. Pay particular attention to Leavittsville Bay or, as it's called locally, Muskie Bay. Work both sides of the bay, but double your efforts on the west side, where the creek channel and old roadbed meet halfway back.

Early summer trolling starts to kick in, and anglers find muskies outside weed edges and stream channels from Rockwood to Camp Aldersgate. The water just south of Camp Muskingum off the east shore is well worth several passes. Smaller crank baits and Bagley Shads are trolled with good success.

From midsummer on, troll the deep weed edges and stream channels from Camp Muskingum to the dam, the south shoreline east of Clow's Marina on the South Fork, and the stream channel in front of Clow's Marina. When trolling in summer, let out 50 to 55 feet of line, using 20-pound test, and troll at approximately 2 mph. Bagley's Super Shads will enable the lure to reach depths to 15 feet. In summer muskies will suspend 12 to 15 feet between the creek channels and weed edges. Popular lures for Leesville muskies are shad and silver foil Bagley's Super Shads and Lee Sisson crank baits in shad, tiger muskie, and orange. In late July and August, get a good topo map and troll along the edges of the creek channels.

Trolling is not the only way to catch muskies at Leesville. Casting works well all summer long, but trolling still produces bigger fish. Cast the outside weed edges and work over the top of weeds and pockets with big spinner baits, jerk baits, and top-water lures such as the Creek Chub Knuckle Head. Weeds are plentiful in Leesville. You should look for the largest and longest weed beds to hold muskies. But that doesn't mean you should pass up small pockets of weeds, particularly if the weeds happen to be growing in water 6 feet or deeper. Muskie fishing is best on gray overcast days and in front of approaching storm fronts. Bigger muskies seem to show up from late September through October on Leesville.

Bass fishing is also good on Leesville, but it is overshadowed by the muskie fishing. Most bass average 10 to 12 inches; 3- to 4-pounders are considered good ones and a few 5-pound bass are occasionally caught. Bass fishing starts in mid-April in the backs of coves. Use spinner baits and plastic lizards worked tight against the shoreline structure and any timber or emerging weeds. Later work heavy shoreline cover and thick weeds, but stay in the coves until late May. Bucktail jigs and plastics work well during this time. After May, start working the main lake weed beds, rocky points, and rock shorelines with crank baits and buzz baits. Bass anglers can expect to hook a few muskies in these locations, as well. Top-water baits do well in Leesville; chartreuse buzz baits, Pop-Rs, and jitterbugs are popular. Bass are pretty well spread out, but fishing seems best in the middle half of both the North Fork and South Fork. July and August are slow months, but fishing picks up again in September. Crawfish-colored crank baits, chartreuse spinner baits and buzz baits, and watermelon lizards are what most bass anglers throw.

Crappies can be caught off any boat dock or from downed timber in the backs of coves from late March through June. Crappies will average 10 to 11 inches, but sometimes anglers can find a school of nice slabs that contain a few 15- to 16-inch fish. Look for crappies in downed trees and in the deeper coves with feeder streams like Muskie Bay. Fish the downed trees across from the Petersburg Marina and the next cove west. Crappies are also found along both banks around Camp Musk-ingum and in the brush just south of the boaters' swim area in the North Fork. In the South Fork, find crappies east and west of Frog Hollow. There are between 900 to 950 boat docks on Leesville, and these always hold crappies during the spring. Use minnows under a slip bobber 5 to 8 feet deep or $\frac{1}{16}$-ounce jigs with white or chartreuse twister tails.

Leesville offers some excellent fishing for channel cats. While shoreline access is limited to the dam area, and perhaps to a few small areas known only by local anglers, most cat fishing is done from pontoon boats at night. Channel cats will reach 15 to 24 inches, with several over the 30-inch mark being caught. Fish the shallow bays and rock shelves with chicken livers, night crawlers, and shrimp. The stretch of water from Petersburg Marina to Rockwood on the North Fork is excel-lent, as is the water between Frog Hollow and Big Rock Canyon on the South Fork. Some say the cat fishing on the South Fork is better. Occasionally, a flathead upwards of 30 pounds is caught using chubs or bluegills.

Bluegills are plentiful in Leesville Lake and are caught anywhere during the spring spawn from late May through June. A nice one will be a least hand size or

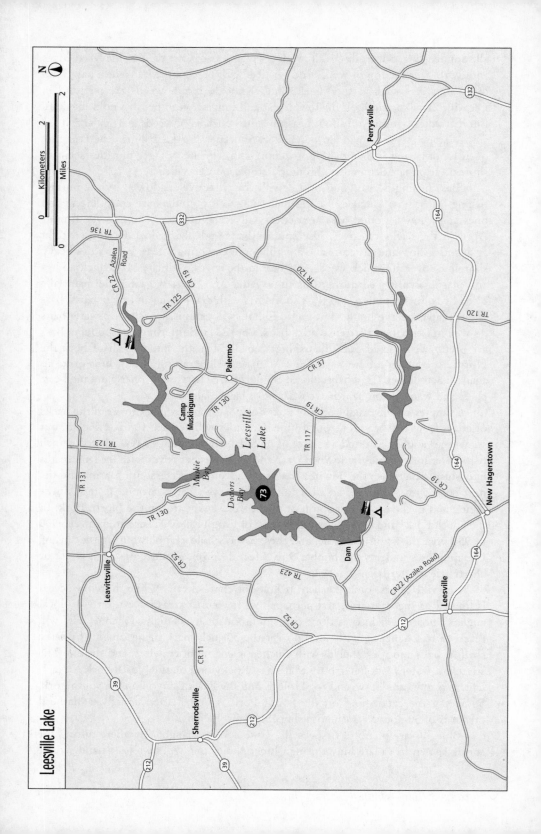

Leesville Lake

bigger, and a bucketful shouldn't be hard to come by. Most are caught using maggots, wax worms, and red worms. There are also some nice redear sunfish at Leesville that will run anywhere from 9 to 11 inches.

Saugeyes are also in good numbers, but anglers seldom target them. Most saugeyes are caught in fall; some reach up to 27 inches. Jigs and small crank baits take most saugeyes off the rocky points and shallow flats in the upper lake near the dam. Slow troll or drift the old roadbed in front of Clow's Marina. Work the east bank in front of the dam and the flats and points north of the dam at Thornhill.

A few yellow perch are caught from Leesville; most are caught accidentally by bluegill or crappie fishers. You can find perch around the deeper shorelines and in the weeds. Once in a while a few perch up to 11 inches are caught with minnows or red worms.

Special regulations: Leesville Lake is limited to 10 hp. Minimum size for kept bass is 12 inches.

Facilities/camping: Clow's Marina and Petersburg Marina both have campgrounds with between 20 to 30 campsites each. Facilities are few and far between, so bring it with you.

Additional information: An angler can get a fine breakfast at the Western Grill in downtown Bowerston, located about 10 minutes east of Leesville Lake.

Directions: From Carrollton take Highway 332 south 4 miles to Azalea Road, turn west to Petersburg Marina, or continue south on Highway 332 to Highway 164, head west to Highway 212, and then go north. Look for signs to Leesville Lake Dam and Clow's Marina.

74 Mogadore Reservoir

Key species: Largemouth bass, bluegill, redear sunfish, crappie, channel catfish.

General description: The best bluegill and sunfish lake in northeast Ohio.

Overview: Mogadore Reservoir is managed by the City of Akron Water Division and is used primarily as a backup reservoir for the city. Impounding the Little Cuyahoga River in 1939, the reservoir covers 1,000 acres and is surrounded by woodlands and small bogs. The city of Akron has provided six primitive boat ramps and a marina with boat rental, which is open from April to mid-November. The lake has a number of boating and access restrictions. Shoreline access is limited, but the Buckeye Trail follows the north shore of the lake, allowing anglers access to the shoreline. Most of the lake can be reached only by boat.

Mogadore Reservoir looks like a north woods Minnesota lake. A moose is all that's needed to make the resemblance complete. The lake is surrounded by a mixed hardwood-coniferous forest; it has numerous small brushy wooded islands, countless weedy bays and coves, backwater marshes, and an atmosphere of a thousand miles away. All of this contributes to the excellent fishery that this lake has within it.

Mogadore Reservoir is a beautiful body of water that offers superb fishing for panfish.

The fishing: The bluegills and redear sunfish in this lake are something to brag about. Bluegills average 7 inches, with many going into the 8- and 9-inch range. The redears, on the other hand, easily reach into the double digits, and many, if not most, sunfish average 10 to 12 inches and are as thick as a boy's wrist.

The good panfishing begins in mid-April, but it picks up steam as spawning time approaches in late May and early June. Fish the shoreline brush and along the weed edges in 1 to 4 feet of water with wax worms and red worms. Come spawning time, concentrate on spawning beds in the coves and along the shallow sheltered shorelines from Congress Lake Road and east. Fish the beds with wax worms, a pinch of night crawler, or red worms, with or without a bobber. The sunfish are aggressive and will attack anything that gets close. Good areas to fish are the shorelines east and west of the marina and off the marina dock; but any shallow shoreline will hold plenty of redears and bluegills. After spawning time, fish the shoreline weeds, lily pads, timber, and under low overhanging brush and trees. Morning and evening are best in summer; fishing does slow down during the hottest months, but quickly picks up again in mid-September and continues until November. Ice fishing is permitted.

Channel cats also do well here, with many reaching into the 8- and 9-pound range. The catfish are so evenly distributed that any shoreline or shallow flat will provide good cat fishing. One popular area is the shoreline west of the marina, which can be accessed from the Buckeye Trail that runs along the entire north shore of the lake. Most cat fishers use the standard stuff—chicken livers and night crawlers. Bullheads are also present in the lake, and they are healthy, averaging 11 to 13 inches.

Crappies are also in good supply here, with most averaging 9 to 12 inches. Fishing for them begins at the end of March; it tails off toward the end of May and picks up again in late September. The deeper edges off the islands, the wooded cover around the north dike, and Crappie Bay at the north end are all excellent places to find a stringer of crappies. Look for water at least 8 to 15 feet deep with logs, downed timber, and brush. Stay in the deeper west half of the lake, from the Highway 43 Causeway and east. Crappies in this lake are caught with a simple minnow and bobber.

Perch are also in the lake, although they are not in any great numbers and are usually caught by crappie fishers in early spring at the west end of the lake.

Bass fishing is excellent here, with a few 6- and 7-pound fish coming into local bait shops every spring. In the past, some 10-pound bass have come from Mogadore. Bass fishing begins the first of March, with anglers working the shallow bays and shorelines on the east side of the lake, throwing tight against shoreline brush with jig-and-pig combos and jigs and plastic crawls. Most of the 6- and 7-pound bass that come from Mogadore are caught this way in early spring; on a good day, 5-pound bass are common.

Summer is perhaps the best time to catch bass in Mogadore around the weeds, lily pads, islands, and points. Work the brush around the islands from the Highway 43 Causeway and east and around the north islands with tubes, plastics, and spinner baits. Work the saddles between the islands and any weed growth around the islands, as well as any humps, points, or underwater islands or reefs. On summer mornings and evenings, you might find some top-notch top-water action around the thousands of lily pads and grass beds using buzz baits and spinner baits. The culvert under the Congress Lake Road Causeway is a good place for a shore-bound angler to pick up a nice bass.

Occasionally a muskie or two is caught from Mogadore, even though the lake hasn't been stocked since the 1960s. This leaves one to speculate that some natural reproduction is occurring within the lake.

Special regulations: Gasoline motors are not permitted on Mogadore, nor are gas tanks. Outboards must be removed before a boat can be launched. The lake is limited to electric motors and watercraft of 18 feet or less. Shoreline access is severely restricted; the only shoreline access is at the boat ramps and the marina and from portions of the Buckeye Trail on the lake's north side. Fishing is not permitted within 500 feet of the dam or spillway.

Facilities/camping: Facilities are few, but a number of bait and tackle shops and convenience stores are in the area. Countryside Campground is located just north of the marina on Highway 43.

Additional information: The Buckeye Trail follows the north shore of Mogadore for more than 7 miles from its headwaters to the dam.

Directions: From Kent, take Highway 43 south for 5 miles.

75 Mohicanville Dam

The Mohicanville Dam offers some limited tailwater fishery for channel catfish, an occasional flathead, smallmouth, bluegill, and sunfish.

The dam was constructed between 1935 and 1936 by the U.S. Army Corps of Engineers for the purpose of flood control on Lake Fork Creek of the Mohican River, which is part of the Upper Muskingum Watershed. Mohicanville is unusual in that the dam is a dry dam, used strictly for flood control; it holds water back only during times of heavy rain and periods of flooding. There is no impounded lake at the dam.

Fishing at the dam occurs during water releases in early spring—usually April and May—and periodically throughout the summer as the weather warrants. Anglers catch mostly channels, but I am told some nice flatheads are also taken. Fish right up in the chute with chicken livers, shad, creek chubs, and night crawlers. Farther downstream in summer, smallmouth, sunfish, and rock bass are caught from Lake Fork Creek.

Mohicanville Dam is located on County Road C 175, approximately 10 miles northeast of Loudonville off Highway 179.

76 Mosquito Lake

Key species: Largemouth bass, crappie, walleye, bluegill, northern pike, channel and flathead catfish, ring perch.

General description: Good walleye fishing and some big pike, but the flathead catfish are huge.

Overview: Mosquito Creek Lake is Ohio's second-largest inland lake at 7,850 acres. The reservoir was impounded in 1944, upon completion of the dam by the U.S. Army Corps of Engineers. The primary function is flood control; summer pool is at 901.4 feet above sea level. The lake averages 8 to 15 feet deep; along the old streambed, depths can reach 20 to 25 feet at the south end toward the dam. North of the causeway, lake depths average only 4 to 10 feet. The lake is more than 9.5 miles long and 0.75 mile wide.

At the far-north end of the lake, the Division of Wildlife has set aside the upper headwaters of Mosquito as a waterfowl refuge. No boats or fishing are permitted in refuge waters; the area is clearly marked with buoys.

The rest of the lake is encompassed by the 3,278-acre Mosquito Lake State Park, which offers hiking, biking, and bridle trails; picnic areas; a beach; boat rental; docks; and a marina with fuel, five boat ramps, and camping.

Mosquito Lake is infested with zebra mussels. As a result, the water is very

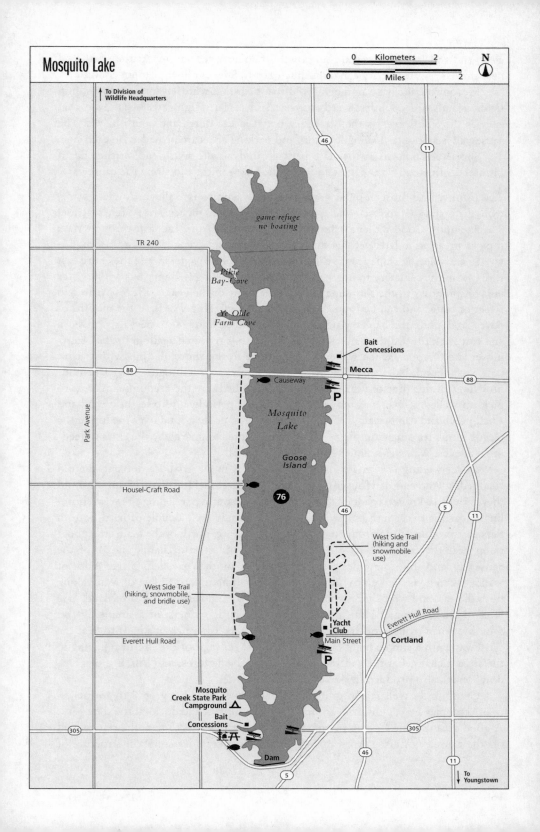

Mosquito Lake

Kilometers
0   2

Miles
0   2

N

To Division of
Wildlife Headquarters

46

11

TR 240

game refuge
no boating

*Pikie
Bay-Cove*

*Ye Olde
Farm Cave*

Bait
Concessions

88

Mecca

88

Causeway

P

*Mosquito
Lake*

*Goose
Island*

76

46

West Side Trail
(hiking and
snowmobile
use)

5

11

Park Avenue

Housel-Craft Road

West Side Trail
(hiking, snowmobile,
and bridle use)

Yacht
Club

Everett Hull Road

Cortland

Everett Hull Road

Main Street

P

Mosquito
Creek State Park
Campground △

Bait
Concessions

305

305

11

Dam

5

46

To
Youngstown

clear, and this has encouraged the growth of aquatic vegetation. At the south end near the dam, water clarity can be as much as 4 to 5 feet under optimum conditions.

Mosquito Lake has a number of old roadbeds that were left intact, a few stump fields, islands, and countless weedy bays and inlets. The Highway 88 Causeway that crosses the lake serves as the boundary between the north and south halves. The causeway is a popular fishing location, and parking areas are provided on each side.

Shoreline access is at the state park grounds at the south end, at the end of Housel-Craft Road on the west shore, at the boat ramps, and along the causeway.

The fishing: The most popular game fish on Mosquito is walleye. Anglers wade, troll, drift, and cast to catch walleyes averaging 15 to 20 inches, with a few reaching 8 to 9 pounds. Good walleye fishing begins the first of April and lasts through May; it picks up again in late October and continues through the ice-fishing season.

In early spring walleye move in close to the banks. Anglers wade the entire east shore from the cemetery to north of the causeway, casting ⅛-ounce jigs with twister tails or minnows to the shoreline flats. At that time of the year, walleyes are in 1 to 5 feet of water and can be found near rocks and emerging weeds, at the mouths of coves, and along the banks. Anglers will sometimes wade 40 to 50 yards offshore and cast back toward the bank. This same pattern is repeated again in the fall, starting in late October, when walleyes again move to the shoreline. Jigs with twister tails, small crank baits, and weight-forward spinners with a night crawler or minnow do well this time of year. Also by fall, weed beds are the predominant areas to pick up walleyes. Walleyes move into weed beds periodically to feed on shad and small perch and can be caught by fishing the edges, pockets, and over the top of the weeds. Look for small jumping shad or feeding gulls to give away the clues to feeding walleyes. Walleyes seem to run bigger in the fall.

After wading is over in spring and walleyes move offshore, look to the old roadbeds at the end of Housel-Craft Road and Everett Hull Road. I am also told there is a little-known roadbed that runs north to south, paralleling the west shoreline. Near the two south boat ramps on the east side are a couple of hard-bottom flats that produce. One productive flat is just offshore, north of the main street boat ramp near the cemetery. Also drift or troll the old stream channel north of the causeway, and the riprap along the causeway is another excellent place. A lot of walleyes can be picked up by slow trolling or drifting in 8 to 12 feet of water along both the east and west shores south of the causeway and around Goose Island. Use worm harnesses, small Hot 'n Tots, weight-forward spinners, or a simple jig and minnow when trolling or drifting. For shorebound fishermen, it's hard to beat the causeway with a simple night crawler fished just off the bottom. Vertical jigging in the stream channel at the causeway bridge with blade lures, like Vib"E"s or Heddon Sonars, also produces walleyes in fall and winter.

Crappies do well at Mosquito Lake, most averaging between 8 to 15 inches. Many crappies are caught from around the shore, riprap, and docks at the state park. A good area is Pikie Bay on the northwest corner of the lake near the refuge, and off the causeway during April through May. Most crappies come off structure of some sort, whether it be stumps, brush, docks, or downed timber. Crappies are not hard to find; every bay over 3 feet deep has a few in the spring and early fall.

Perch are common, with some nice ones reaching up to 12 inches. The best way to catch perch is to fish a few inches off the bottom with minnows anywhere around the causeway.

Bass fishing is not bad here, and the pattern is simple. Fish the weeds, the weeds at the mouths of coves and in the coves, and along the riprap at the causeway, dam, and state park. In early spring, Pikie Cove and Ye Olde Farm Cove are hot, as are most of the other coves along the west shore. In spring spinner baits, plastics, and jigs take most bass averaging 12 to 15 inches. As early summer arrives, buzz baits and weightless, but weedless plastic worms produce. Later, in early fall, anglers have luck with rattle traps over weeds. Bass anglers should try the submerged islands northwest of the causeway and the rocky points west of the big island. Anglers also take a few bass off the banks around the yacht club just north of the dam. Bass in Mosquito Lake seem to top out at around 4 pounds.

Bluegills are common and reach hand size and a bit bigger. A small jig with a maggot or a pinch of red worm is all an angler needs. Fish anywhere close to shore at the state park, at the boat ramps, and any brushy shoreline. Early June is the best time to catch a stringer of big bluegills.

Northern pike are well entrenched in Mosquito Lake. I suspect most spawn in early March in the restricted headwaters at the refuge. Fish any of the shallow bays north of the causeway right after ice-out with chubs and shiners. After spawn the pike scatter, and most are caught by fishers fishing for other species. This would be great territory for an angler to explore if seeking a state record pike. Most pike average 25 to 35 inches, but a few 40-inch, 20-pound pike are also caught. Can a 23-pound pike be far behind?

Channels are common and fishing from any boat ramp, off the causeway, and from the state park will guarantee a catch of nice channels in the 3- to 5-pound range. A few 10-pound channel cats are taken from the causeway every year.

Mosquito Lake could also produce the next state record flathead catfish. Flatheads weighing 45 to 55 pounds are regular catches to the small fraternity who know how to fish for them. Fishing at night off the causeway with bluegills is the best way for a shorebound angler to find one. One angler says the north end is best, another says the south end near the dam is best. One thing's for sure: They are widely distributed in Mosquito. Use stout saltwater tackle, 30- to 50-pound line, and live bait fished just off the bottom. Flatheads weighing 65 pounds have come from here. If 65-pound flatheads swim in Mosquito Lake, then a 77-pound catfish is probably there as well.

Below the dam is a small tailwater fishery for walleyes, bass, and catfish. Parking is at the U.S. Army Corps of Engineers parking area just off Highway 305, behind the dam.

Special regulations: Minimum size for bass is 12 inches, with a five-fish limit. North of the Highway 88 Causeway, boats are limited to 15 mph. There are no horsepower restrictions on Mosquito Lake.

Facilities/camping: The small town of Cortland just east of the lake has all amenities. Camping is at the Mosquito Creek State Park campground with 234 sites.

Additional information: The Mosquito Creek Wildlife Refuge is great place to view eagles, ospreys, waterfowl, and shorebirds.

Directions: Take Highway 11 north of Youngstown approximately 12 miles, exit west on Highway 305.

77 New Lyme Wildlife Area

New Lyme Lake is one of those little out-of-the-way places that you have to get lost to find. Sitting at the back end of a dead-end township road, the lake is part of the 720-acre New Lyme Wildlife Area, which at one time was an experimental ruffed grouse refuge.

Not many grouse take refuge there nowadays, but the beautiful little lake of 43 acres offers a quiet refuge for the angler seeking bass, bluegills, and channel cats.

The lake is weedy with aquatic vegetation, cattails, bulrushes, and lily pads and has brushy shorelines and deadfalls that provide plenty of fish habitat.

New Lyme Lake offers some quality bluegill fishing, with nice hand-size or bigger 'gills that can be caught just about anywhere around the weeds and brushy banks. Channel catfish are stocked semiregularly and obtain a size of 12 to 16 inches; catch them with red worms or night crawlers. It's a beautiful lake to fish for bass around the deadfalls and lily pads with a small buzz bait on a summer evening. Most bass are small, around 12 inches, but there are a few that reach 15 to 18 inches hiding around the marshy edges and islands. It would be a nice lake to take a fly rod and some bluegill or bass poppers.

Access to the shoreline is virtually impossible from the south end because of the thick growth; it is best fished from a small boat or canoe that can be easily launched from the parking area. The lake is limited to electric motors.

The best way to find New Lyme Wildlife Area is to take US 6 8 miles west of Andover and then head south on Peck Road. Turn east on Dodgeville Road to access the north end. The south end is accessed at the end of Brownville Road.

78 Nimisila Reservoir

Key species: Largemouth bass, bluegill, channel catfish, crappie; walleye and saugeye were stocked, but stocking was discontinued in 2005.

General description: A good catfish lake and an excellent bass lake.

Overview: There are not many lakes in Ohio like Nimisila. It is full of brushy islands, weedy backwaters, and lily pads, and it is overgrown with shoreline brush and so much cover it is hard to know where to start fishing. The reservoir is approximately 800 acres and was originally developed to supply water to Portage Lakes, which in turn served as a water supply to various Akron industries since the 1930s.

Nimisila is part of the 466-acre Portage Lakes State Park, which offers all the usual park amenities, including a beach, picnic areas, shelter houses, 6 miles of hiking trails, and a total of eight boat ramps on the various lakes. Nimisila itself has four of those ramps. Nimisila Lake also has the state park campground. It is the only lake in the Portage chain of lakes that is encircled by public state park land.

The lake averages depths of 6 to 15 feet; the shorelines are relativity shallow, making wading along the shore an easy task. The lake is limited to electric motors, one park ranger suggesting it takes two fully charged batteries to fish Nimisila.

The fishing: Nimisila is a quality bass lake, with the majority of bass averaging 12 to 14 inches. Plenty of 2- to 3-pounders are caught, and a few approaching the 5-pound mark have also been caught. Work the shoreline cover and islands, the cattail stands, and the edges of the lily pads. Bass fishing begins about mid-April, and the points, islands, and bays around the campground peninsula are good places to start. Jigs and pigs and spinner baits do well in the spring.

Because of the electric motor restriction, Nimisila doesn't receive the pressure the other Portage Lakes get. Anglers like to wade around the edges of the lake near the campground and cast to lily pad edges and overhanging brush. In the hot summer, bass are found in the lily pads. Although bass fishing is good, it is tough because the forage base is so abundant.

In summer bass fishing is a little better at the south end, the southeast end toward the dam, and the west shoreline where there is some deeper water; look for the submerged island with weeds, cattails, and bulrushes. Also fish the riprap along the roadways. The points on the northwest corner of the campground peninsula are a good area; just hammer the brushy points, islands, weeds, and riprap wherever you find it, and you'll find bass.

Bluegill are plentiful, but seldom reach anything over 6 inches. Consider the bluegills forage for the bass.

Channel catfish do real well in Nimisila, with most averaging a respectable 14 to 20 inches. A few 5-pound cats are not that hard to find. Fish chicken livers, shrimp, or night crawlers from the banks around the campground and from the parking areas and boat ramp off Christman Road on the northeast corner of the lake and around the dam.

At one time the Division of Wildlife stocked saugeye and walleye into Nimisila, but the fishery proved so unproductive that the stockings were discontinued in 2005. A few walleyes may still be caught, and if you find any, they will likely be along the edges and points along the west shoreline near the edge of the 15- to 20-foot water.

Crappies are in fair numbers at Nimisila; most average only 7 to 8 inches. Catch them around the shoreline brush and old downed snags and trees on the west and south banks. Crappies appear in mid-April through May and fire up again in late September. Jigs and minnows work as well as anything.

Special regulations: Electric motors only.

Facilities/camping: The southern end of Akron is just outside the park boundaries, where you can find everything. The Portage Lakes State Park campground with 74 campsites is located at Nimisila.

Additional information: Nimisila Reservoir is a good place to observe white swans.

Directions: From Akron, take Highway 93 south approximately 5 miles and then turn east on Center Road. Center Road dead-ends on South Main Street at Nimisila Reservoir. Turn north or south on South Main Street to access either end of the lake.

79 Oberlin Reservoir

The city of Oberlin has an upground reservoir open to public fishing. It is a typical upground in that it is rectangular in shape; has a generally featureless, flat bottom; and has a limestone-rock shoreline. The reservoir contains largemouth bass, channel catfish, and bluegills. Carry-in boats are permitted, but motors are not. The only way to launch a boat is to carry it up the steps from the parking area located next to the waterworks plant. The reservoir is located 1 mile east of Oberlin on Parsons Road. The reservoir is open to fishing during daylight hours.

80 Ohio-Erie Canal at Canal Fulton

At the village of Canal Fulton, located south of Akron, anglers can fish along the old Ohio-Erie Canal that was constructed in the 1830s. Access is at the Canal Fulton Community Park at the bridge over the Tuscarawas River. Anglers can walk the old tow road and fish the 5 miles from Canal Fulton to Crystal Springs. Largemouth bass, channel catfish, and plenty of bluegills are among the species anglers will most likely encounter. Although most fish run small, I did encounter a young fisher who said he caught a 15-inch catfish from the canal. Canoes and kayaks are permitted in the canal, if you wish to fish it that way. A couple of old historic canal locks are also located on this stretch of the Ohio-Erie Canal.

The Tuscarawas River can also be accessed from the park for some stream smallmouth, sunfish, rock bass, and channel catfish. Canoeing and kayaking are popular on the Tuscarawas; a canoe livery is located across the bridge.

If you get tired of fishing, you can always take a ride on the horse-drawn canal boat stationed at the park.

The Village of Canal Fulton is located approximately 7 miles south of Akron on Highway 93.

81 Portage Lakes

Key species: Largemouth bass, bluegill, redear sunfish, channel catfish.

General description: One exceptional chain of bass lakes and home to three state record fish.

Nimisila Reservoir has gorgeous sunsets and excellent bass fishing.

Overview: The Portage Lakes is a chain of 12 reservoirs all linked together by a series of canals built during the 1830s to provide water to the growing city of Akron, founded in 1825. The reservoirs were originally lowland bogs, swamps, and small natural lakes that were dammed, diked, dug, and channeled. The name Portage came from the 8-mile portage between the Cuyahoga and Tuscarawas Rivers that connects Lake Erie to the Ohio River. Of those twelve lakes, anglers can access the following seven by boat through the old canal system: West Reservoir (115 acres), East Reservoir (250 acres), Cottage Grove Lake (70 acres), Miller Lake (60 acres), Rex Lake (100 acres), Mud Lake (115 acres), and Turkeyfoot Lake (450 acres). The other lakes are North Reservoir (160 acres), Nimisila Reservoir (825 acres), Nesmith (80 acres), Long Lake (180 acres), and Summit Lake (115 acres). All together the total Portage Lakes chain provides more than 2,500 acres of fishing water.

In 1949 control of the lakes was turned over from the Department of Public Works to the newly formed Division of Parks and Recreation. Today the Division of Parks is responsible for the nearly 3,000 acres that make up Portage Lakes State Park; of that, only 466 acres are land on which the park has a beach, picnic and shelter houses, a campground, and eight boat ramps. The remaining shoreline is privately owned by residents and businesses, the only exception being Nimisila Reservoir.

Outside of Nimisila, shoreline access to the 11 other lakes is limited to the primary state park ground, which is located off Highway 93; at the boat ramps and five other small public holdings at the old canal locks; and at various picnic and recreation areas. A wheelchair-accessible pier is located at the North Reservoir, but access is relatively easy from any of the park grounds. Boat ramps are located at Nimisila, Turkeyfoot, North Reservoir, and Long Lake.

Private marinas are located at several locations throughout the various lakes, where fuel and boat rental are available.

The fishing: The Portage Lakes were subject to several different stocking efforts throughout the years, and at one time they contained a natural population of chain pickerel. Over time the Division of Wildlife has stocked northern pike, muskies, tiger muskies, channel cats, saugeye, and walleye; today, the lakes are stocked only with channel catfish.

Three state record catches have come from the Portage Lakes: a state record chain pickerel caught by Ron Kotch, a tiger muskie also caught by Ron Kotch, and another tiger muskie caught by Matt Amedeo. Both state record tiger muskies came from the same small bay located off Turkeyfoot Lake during the spring. Ron Kotch tells me that catching 10 to 15 muskies a day while bass fishing was not uncommon during the 1980s and early 1990s.

Today the primary focus is on largemouth bass, of which there is a robust and healthy population that feeds primarily off the abundant gizzard shad.

The chain of lakes is popular with the local bass tournament circuit, yielding catches that average 9 to 15 pounds for the five-fish limit. Most bass average a healthy 1 to 3 pounds, with many 3- to 5-pound bass being weighed in on tournament scales. The top bass average over 5 pounds, with 6 pounds about tops.

Bank cover, which consists of downed timber, brush, and the over 2,000 private boat docks that dot the shoreline, is the primary focus of bass anglers. Deep weeds over shallow humps and lily pads are also prime areas to find the chain of lakes' abundant bass. Although weed beds are hard to find because private owners attempt to kill off the weeds, they are the gold mine for the angler who finds them.

In spring fish the shallow west bays off Turkeyfoot and Miller Lakes, the east bay off East Reservoir, and Swigert's Pond south of Mud Lake. In summer many bass are caught under the shade of pontoon boats and from under boat docks. Many of the docks in Turkeyfoot and Mud Lakes have sunken Christmas trees around them, placed there by dock owners. If you can locate them, you'll find bass. Look for water averaging 4 to 8 feet deep.

In spring fish plastic tubes and crawls and jigs and pigs. As summer progresses anglers still fish plastics, but spinner baits, jerk baits, and Rapalas are added to the arsenal. One local favorite is the Lucky Craft Pointer Minnow, a suspending jerk bait that no self-respecting Portage Lakes bass angler would be without. In fall, as the water cools, the boat docks are less important, and anglers look for deep weeds over humps and shoreline brush, fishing primarily with spinner baits, jerk baits, and Rattle Traps for suspending bass over weeds, humps, and points.

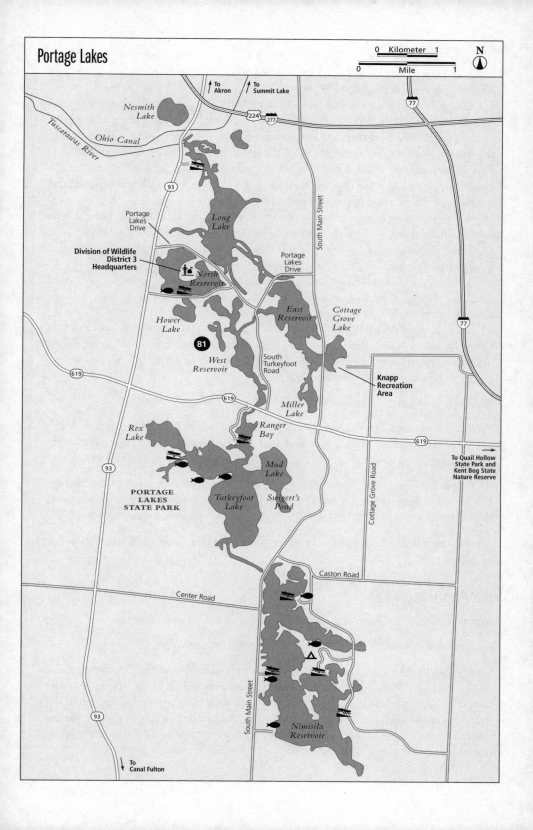

The fishing for bass in all the Portage Lakes is about equal, with the local favorites being Long Lake, Miller Lake, Ranger Bay, and Turkeyfoot Lake; the same patterns are constant in all the lakes.

Bluegills run small, about 6 inches is tops, but the redear sunfish is the top pan-fish in Portage Lakes. Most redears average 7 to 9 inches, with a few in the 10- to 11-inch range. The best time to catch redears is late May through early June, during the spawn. Redears can be caught in all the lakes, but Mud Lake, Turkeyfoot Lake, East Reservoir, and around the concrete break walls north of West Reservoir are excellent places. Look for shallow water 1 to 3 feet deep; fish with wax worms, and the redears will be there for the catching.

Crappie fishing is widespread, and any cover will contain crappies. But the boat docks in late April, May, and September are when you will find the lion's share. Minnows work well, as do small crappie jigs with curly tails. Crappies here are not large, with most reaching 6 to 7 inches.

Channel cats are plentiful, and any of the shoreline access locations will yield good cat fishing. Channels average 2 to 3 pounds, with most caught on shrimp, chicken livers, and night crawlers.

At the Division of Wildlife District Three Headquarters, located off Portage Lakes Drive on North Reservoir, there are a number of youths-only fishing ponds open during the summer. The youth fishing is limited to catch and release, with a young angler allowed to keep one fish per day.

Special regulations: There is a 400-hp limit on the Portage Lakes.

Facilities/camping: The Portage Lakes are surrounded by various businesses, lodging facilities, marinas, restaurants, and bait and tackle shops. Portage Lakes State Park campground, located on the east side of Nimisila Reservoir, has 74 sites.

Additional information: At the village of Canal Fulton, 6 miles south of the Portage Lakes on Highway 93, the Canal Fulton Heritage Society offer horse-drawn canal boat rides along the old Ohio-Erie Canal during the summer, except on Monday.

Directions: The Portage Lakes can be easily reached by taking Highway 93 south of Akron.

82 Punderson Lake

Key species: Trout, bluegill, largemouth bass, channel catfish, crappie.

General description: A beautiful lake with great trout fishing.

Overview: Punderson Lake is one of three small lakes within the Punderson Lake State Park. The park is popular for winter sports, including snowmobiling, cross-country skiing, sledding, and ice fishing. In summer the snowmobiling and skiing trails double as hiking and walking trails. The state park has picnic areas, a shelter house, a beach, a golf course, an archery range, campgrounds, cabins, and a wonderful lodge that was completed in 1948.

The fishing: Punderson State Park has three lakes from which an angler can choose: Pine Lake, Stump Lake, and Punderson Lake. All three are natural glacial lakes with aquatic weeds, shoreline brush, timber, and lily pads and bass, bluegill, and crappies. The lakes also are popular for ice fishing. Pine Lake and Stump Lake require a short hike to reach; however, you can access the north end of Stump Lake from a pulloff on Highway 87, just east of the park entrance. Stump Lake is a good early spring bass lake, and Pine Lake has a natural population of chain pickerel.

Punderson Lake is 101 acres and more than 70 feet deep in the center. The lake has two fishing piers, a boathouse with boat rental, and a boat ramp. The primary draw at Punderson is the twice-a-year stocking of trout by the Division of Wildlife—once in early spring with 10- to 13-inch rainbows, and again in late fall with big brood stock trout. Because of Punderson's depth, some trout survive all season. Trout fishing is best from late March, April, and May and again in fall, especially around Thanksgiving, when the big trout are stocked. Anglers use a variety of baits including corn, Power Bait, maggots, minnows, and small Rooster Tail spinners.

Trout aren't the only fish that anglers catch at Punderson Lake. Nice crappies are caught along the shoreline brush in spring, as are hand-size bluegills, bass from 10 inches to 4 pounds, and channel cats that range from 12 to 20 inches.

After you catch a limit of trout, reward yourself with dinner at Punderson Lodge.

Special regulations: Trout are limited to five fish per day. Only electric motors are permitted.

Facilities/camping: The state park lodge has 31 rooms, plus dining facilities. There are also 26 cabins and 194 campsites.

Additional information: The nearby small village of Burton has a number of unique little shops and some quaint eateries that are well worth a visit.

Directions: From Chardon, take Highway 44 south approximately 7 miles, then turn west on Highway 87.

83 Pymatuning Lake

Key species: Walleye, largemouth and smallmouth bass, muskie, channel and flat-head catfish, crappie, ring perch, bluegill, white bass.

General description: An excellent bass lake, overshadowed by walleye, muskie, and crappie. The lake is limited to 10 hp.

Overview: Pymatuning Lake, located on the Ohio-Pennsylvania state line, was impounded in 1933 on the Shenango River. The lake is an inland sea at 17,088 acres, with numerous islands, wetlands, bays, coves, and the Highway 85 Causeway that splits the lake almost in the center and crosses into Pennsylvania. The lake is 14 miles long and nearly 2 miles wide, averages 10 to 18 feet deep, and is shallower at the north end, which averages less than 10 feet.

Debbie Kent with the biggest perch of her life caught near a state park campground on Pymatuning Lake.

The lake is host to four state park campgrounds, three of which are Pennsylvania Department of Conservation and Natural Resources parks. On the Ohio side, the Ohio Division of Parks and Recreation has the 3,500-acre Pymatuning State Park, one of the crown jewels among Ohio state parks. The park has hiking trails, picnic areas, shelter houses, a beach, a marina with boat rental and fuel, five boat ramps, campgrounds, and cabins. The Ohio state park campground is an ideal home base for the camping angler. It has a boat ramp, dock, lakeside campsites and is located right in some of the best areas for muskies, walleye, and bass. Excellent fishing is only a short boat ride away, and with only a 10-hp limit, that means more time can be spent fishing than moving between locations. Shoreline access is good from all state park grounds, and there is a parking area with access to the causeway on the Ohio side of Highway 85 as it crosses the lake.

Ohio and Pennsylvania have a reciprocal agreement that allows anglers to fish either state's waters from a boat with an Ohio or Pennsylvania fishing license.

The primary forage base in Pymatuning is gizzard shad, small ring perch, and alewife.

The fishing: Bass fishing is pretty good at Pymatuning. Although most bass average 12 to 16 inches, enough 3- to 5-pounders are caught to make the effort a worthwhile endeavor. There are also nice smallmouth in the reservoir, with some reaching 16 to

18 inches; some anglers say that smallmouth slightly outnumber largemouth. The largemouth and smallmouth receive little pressure at Pymatuning. Most anglers prefer walleye, crappies, or muskies over bass. Bass fishing at Pymatuning consists of fishing weeds, bays, boat docks, rocky points, islands, and shoreline structure.

In spring work the bays with spinner baits, crank baits, and plastics, throwing to shoreline structure and any emerging weed beds. Most bays on the west shoreline are good producers. Come summer, continue to fish the bays, but work the weeds with plastics and buzz baits. Start fishing points and cover around islands. You will pick up smallmouth off rock points and along riprap. Good bays for bass are the south bay at the state park campground, the bay at the water treatment plant, Black Creek Bay at the main park office, and the bay just north of the causeway on the Ohio side.

Along the main lake, fish the weedy shoreline north and south of the causeway on the west side with rattletraps worked over the top of weeds. Largemouth are more abundant on the north end; smallmouth like the deeper south end.

Walleye is everybody's favorite fish at Pymatuning; most fish average 15 to 22 inches, but occasionally a 28-inch, 8-pound fish will be caught. In early April, walleye are close to shore in 2 to 4 feet of water. Anglers wade the west shoreline and points from the camping area to the causeway, casting ⅛-ounce jigs with either minnows or twister tails or Rapalas. Any point or sandbar will have fish. When you start to catch more smallmouth than walleye, you know it's time to move to the weed beds in 6 to 8 feet of water and fish jigs and minnows around the edges and in the pockets. Also fish the deeper sandbars and points with jigs, leeches, or night crawlers.

In May and June, slow troll or drift the flats, points, and sandbars with crawler harnesses or jigs and leeches. Tuttle Point on the Pennsylvania side is good, as is the flat just north of the causeway on the Ohio side. South of the beach on the west side is a long sandbar that runs east and west that produces well. There is also a narrow bar that appears to be an old roadbed that runs out from the campground toward the island, directly east of the campground. You can see it from the end of the campground.

Come hot summer, start trolling on the river channels with chrome and black-back Hot 'n Tots, Shad Raps, and Wally Divers. Some fishers troll with lead-core line in order to get a ¼-ounce Hot 'n Tot down to 19 feet, where the old river channel is. Anglers also troll or drift the outside of weed edges with weight-forward spinners and worm harnesses.

In fall, once the water temperatures dip back down, generally around late October, fish return to the banks and anglers can again reach them by wading and using jigs and minnows and crank baits. Plenty of walleyes are caught from the causeway with night crawlers or minnows fished on the bottom. Also fish the river channel at the causeway bridge with Vib"E"s and blade lures by vertical jigging off the bottom in late fall and winter.

Muskie fishing in Pymatuning was at its heyday during the 1970s and early 1980s, when many 40-pound, 50-inch muskies were caught. At one time it was

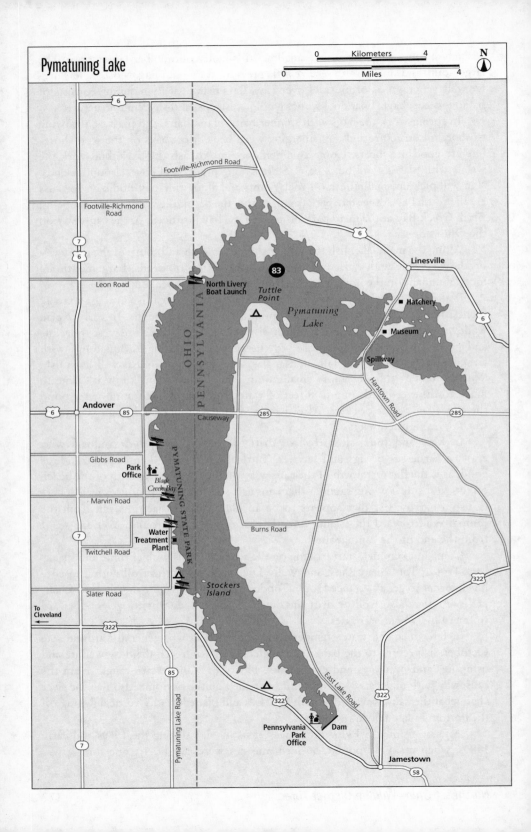

probably the best place in the United States or Canada to catch a 40-pound muskie. Those days are gone, but muskie fishing is still very good at Pymatuning. A few local fishers who know the water still catch 20 muskies a year. A good muskie now though reaches 45 to 47 inches and weighs close to 30 pounds. Most muskies average 34 to 35 inches, the bulk of which are caught in July and August.

Muskie fishing begins in late April in the backs of bays and feeder creeks in the same coves you find bass. In fact bass fishers will hook muskies on crank baits while bass fishing in April and May. Start in the coves, casting big tandem spinner baits to emerging weed beds and any downed timber or rocks. The bays just north and south of the causeway are good, as are the bays on either side of the campground. Forty-One Bay is just across the state line at the south end; it's a good bet for spring muskies. North of the causeway at the Padanarum Area boat launch, which is also known as the North Livery boat launch, is another good area for early muskies.

In early summer start fishing for muskies in weeds in 5 to 7 feet of water; look for rock bars, points off islands and shorelines, and shallow humps. A good area to troll is from the campground to 41 Bay, around Stockers Island, and along the edge of the islands south of the North Livery boat launch, and the big point at Tuttle Camp on the Pennsylvania side. Don't pass up trolling along the weed edges that run north and south of the causeway. Troll Bagely's Monster Shads, Bagely's DB-08, Grandmaws, and Swim Whizz's 15 to 20 feet back, going 4 to 5 mph. During the dog days of August, troll long line, 14 to 15 feet deep, in the old river channel south of the causeway.

Crappie fishing is excellent at Pymatuning Lake, and they can be caught anywhere around the state park, in the bays, off boat docks, around timber, around stumps, around brush, and from the fish attractors placed on both sides of the causeway. There is a big stump field south and east of the North Livery boat ramp that is loaded with good crappie cover. Any west-side bay has crappies in spring. The crappies here are big, with most averaging 10 to 15 inches. The lake has both black and white crappies, with black crappies more common north of the causeway and white crappies more common farther south toward the dam. Most crappies are caught with a simple slip bobber and minnow, 1 to 3 feet deep. April through May is the best crappie time.

Bluegills are everywhere and can be found just off the shoreline at any park picnic area, boat dock, ramp, or pier. Use wax worms suspended about 18 inches under a bobber. The biggest bluegills come in late May and early June during spawn; they average hand size and at times bigger.

Channel cats are common, too. Catch them in the evening and at night in summer from the causeway or any shoreline access along park grounds. Most channels average 12 to 20 inches; several in the 8- to 9-pound range are caught as well. Use chicken livers or night crawlers fished on the bottom.

Perch are also plentiful here; catch them with minnows or red worms from the shoreline in spring and fall and from the causeway in summer. Most perch will be small, but enough 12- to 14-inch perch are caught to make the fishing worthwhile.

There are also some big flatheads in Pymatuning, but nobody fishes for them.

If you want to catch one, use stout tackle and small bluegills for bait and fish at night off the bottom from the causeway.

Special regulations: Minimum size for walleye is 15 inches, with a six-fish daily limit. Minimum size for bass is 12 inches, with a five-fish daily limit. Muskies must be 30 inches to keep, with a two-fish daily limit. Outboard motors are limited to 10 hp.

Facilities/camping: The small town of Andover is located just west of the Highway 85 Causeway and can provide all the amenities. Numerous bait and tackle shops are also located along Highway 7 on the lake's west side. Pymatuning State Park has 60 cabins and a campground with 370 campsites.

Additional information: A nice side trip is to visit the Pennsylvania Game Commission's State Fish Hatchery located on the northeast corner of the lake on Harstown Road. The hatchery is open from 8:00 a.m. to 3:30 p.m. seven days a week.

Directions: Located off US 6 in northeast Ohio on the Pennsylvania state line, approximately 20 miles southeast of Ashtabula.

84 Rocky River

The Rocky River is one beautiful stream—a true treasure in northern Ohio and, thankfully, almost completely protected by the Cleveland Metroparks. The Rocky has a short, if not abrupt mouth, turning into a small stream within a mile of its confluence with Lake Erie. Located within the town of Rocky River, a western suburb of greater Cleveland, over 10 miles of Rocky River is under the protective umbrella of the 2,572-acre Cleveland Metroparks' Rocky River Reservation.

The string of parks that join together starts at the Emerald Necklace Marina and continues south along Valley Parkway, offering anglers an unbroken chain of access sites along the entire stream.

In summer anglers find a good supply of smallmouth, rock bass, and sunfish. Beginning in late September, steelhead begin moving into the stream, and anglers start picking them up at the mouth at the Emerald Necklace Marina with $\frac{1}{16}$-ounce white jigs tipped with maggots or minnows; later, spawn sacks and a variety of steelhead flies take the lion's share. The Rocky has a number of low-head dams along its course through the reserve, but these have proven to be no obstacle to steelhead as they move upstream. Lagoon Dam on the east branch has been an obstacle that stops most upstream migration on the east branch of the Rocky, except during periods of high water.

Rocky is one on the state's premier steelhead streams. By November, steelhead fishing is in full swing and doesn't stop until late April. It is a popular stream, easy to wade and fish. Access is readily available from any of the parking areas along Valley Parkway; no one location is any better than another, as the entire stream is full of 25- to 30-inch steelhead. It's a sight to witness if you're a first-time steelheader.

Public boat launching is available only at the Emerald Necklace Marina. To get to the boat launch and to the Rocky River Reservation, take Valley Parkway south, which is located on the east side of the river, at the Highway 254 Detroit Road Bridge.

85 Shreve Lake Wildlife Area

Key species: Largemouth bass, crappie, bluegill, channel catfish, some yellow perch.

General description: Shreve Lake yields good catches of channel cats.

Overview: Shreve Lake is the centerpiece of the 228-acre Shreve Lake Wildlife Area that was acquired in 1958. Previously a marsh, the 58-acre lake was created by the construction of a dam and the diversion of a small stream. The lake has a concrete boat ramp, parking area, restrooms, and a wheelchair-accessible pier. The lake averages 4 to 10 feet deep, contains the remains of old standing timber and stumps, is weedy at the shallow west end, and has some limited riprap rocks along the south and east banks.

White amurs were released into the lake to control weed growth. If caught, they must be released immediately.

The fishing: Fishing at Shreve Lake is primarily devoted to summer fishing for channel cats. There is good shoreline access, and most anglers are content to fish from the banks with chicken livers and night crawlers, catching nice 2- to 3-pound channels and an occasional 5- to 6-pounder. The Division of Wildlife stocks channels every other year.

Crappies are caught in spring and fall from the deeper south end, around the old stumps and shoreline brush. Most crappies run a small 7 to 9 inches and are taken with jigs and minnows.

Bluegills are plentiful and caught everywhere close to shore with red worms or wax worms; most average around 6 inches.

Bass fishing is only fair here. Several years ago 3- to 4-pound bass were taken, but nowadays most bass run small, with some 15-inch bass occasionally showing up. Fish the shoreline cover with spinner baits and plastic night crawlers. In the evening, some top-water action can be had around the south shore stumps with hula poppers and buzz baits. The best bass fishing is in spring and early summer.

Every now and then, someone catches a nice ring perch, but these are mostly incidental catches by bluegill or crappie fishers.

Local lore has it that there is a 50-inch muskie in the lake. Whether it's true or not, anglers should be on the lookout for this brute. What a catch that would make.

Special regulations: The limit on channel cats is six per day. The lake is limited to electric motors only.

Facilities/camping: Other than restrooms, there are no facilities or camping at Shreve Lake. The town of Shreve can supply all amenities.

Additional information: Shreve Lake is an excellent place to view a variety of shorebirds and waterfowl.

Directions: Shreve Lake is not easy to find. From Wooster, go southwest on Highway 3 for 7 miles, turn south on Elyria Road, go 3 miles, and then turn east onto Brown Road.

86 Silver Creek Lake

Key species: Largemouth bass, crappie, bluegill, channel catfish, perch; trout are stocked in spring.

General description: Good numbers of small bass, and a popular trout fishing lake.

Overview: Silver Creek Lake is a small lake of approximately 50 acres and the centerpiece of the Silver Creek Metro Park. It is one of several community parks within Summit County. The park has a beach, boat rental, hiking trails, and shelter houses.

Fishing on the lake is subject to several restrictions: Anglers are not permitted to launch their own boats, boats must be rented from the boathouse marina, minnows are not allowed to be used as bait, and bank fishers are restricted to the designated east and west shorelines and boat dock only. The entire north end of the lake is closed to fishing and boats.

The fishing: Despite the restrictions, bass anglers do well at Silver Creek Lake, catching and releasing dozens of small bass daily in spring and summer. A 15-inch minimum size limit is in effect. Most bass average 9 to 14 inches; seldom are any caught over the 15-inch mark. Most bass anglers will fish from shore along the big rocks that line the east and west shorelines. Outside the rocks and some overhanging brush, there is not much shoreline cover. Tubes, plastic worms, and spinner baits work well for the small bass.

Bluegills and ring perch are plentiful but both run small. Bluegills seldom exceed 3 or 4 inches; ring perch might reach 6 or 7 inches if you're lucky. Perch fishing picks up in fall, and fishing from the boat dock is about as good a place as any. Use red worms for perch, suspended about 3 feet under a small bobber. Do the same for bluegill, except substitute wax worms.

Channel cat fishing is okay; most average 12 to 15 inches, and a few will hit the 2-pound-plus mark. Evenings are best; use chicken livers or night crawlers.

Trout are the big draw at Silver Creek. The lake is stocked with 2,500 10- to 12-inch rainbow trout in late March. Use Power Bait, mealworms, maggots, and small Rooster Tail spinners and concentrate on the south end.

Special regulations: Shoreline and boat anglers are restricted to designated sections of the lake. No minnows are permitted, and fishers wishing to use a boat must rent one from the marina. The marina is open from Memorial Day through Labor Day. All bass less than 15 inches must be released.

Facilities/camping: In summer, refreshments are available at the marina and beach concession stand. Camping is not permitted at the park.

Additional information: The park is only open during daylight hours.

Directions: Silver Creek Metro Park is located southwest of Akron, off Highway 585, east of the Highway 21 intersection; take Hamertown Road north to the park entrance.

87 Spencer Lake Wildlife Area

Key species: Largemouth bass, channel catfish, bluegill.

General description: An excellent bass and catfish lake.

Overview: Spencer Lake is the centerpiece of the 618-acre Spencer Lake Wildlife Area. The lake was impounded in 1961 by the construction of dikes and dams. After a severe storm in 1969, the north dam had to be rebuilt and the lake was enlarged to 78 acres. The lake was drained in 1985 for reconstruction and was finally opened again to fishing in 1986. The lake is actually two lakes, with a dike built across the center and a concrete walkway between the two parking lots to accommodate wheelchairs. There is a wheelchair-accessible pier and a concrete boat ramp on each lake. Walking paths around the lake make for good shoreline access.

The fishing: Bass fishing is good on Spencer Lake, with most bass averaging 12 to 14 inches and many caught above that mark. Fish the standing timber and stumps on the south lake's west side, the riprap causeway and dams, and around the rock peninsulas with crank bait, spinner baits, and plastic worms and tubes. Good cover exists throughout most of the lake's shoreline. Some weeds are present along the shallow shoreline, and several bass are taken from around the weed edges in the evening. Fishing is good from early May through late June, picking up again in September. Most bass anglers work the riprap and timber. Pick your lake, as a boat is not able to pass from one lake to the other unless you carry it.

Bluegills are so-so. Most are small, seldom exceeding 6 inches.

Channels are plentiful, and that is perhaps the most popular game fish in the lakes. Most average 12 to 15 inches, but some nice 3- to 4-pounders are fairly common. Most cat fishing is done from the two peninsulas within easy walking distance of the parking areas, but anywhere along the shoreline is productive. Chicken livers and night crawlers are the preferred bait on summer nights.

Anglers can also access the east branch of the Black River from the wildlife area for some stream fishing for smallmouth and sunfish. Parking areas off Foster Road and at Highway 162 allow access to the stream.

Special regulations: Bass less than 15 inches must be released. The daily limit on channel catfish is six, and the lake is limited to electric motors only.

Facilities/camping: There are no facilities other than restrooms, and camping is not permitted at the wildlife area. The nearest small town is Spencer, which has gas, ice, beverages, and food.

Additional information: Findley State Park, located about 7 miles west of Spencer Lake Wildlife Area, has 273 campsites.

Directions: From Wellington, travel 4 miles south on Highway 58, turn east on Highway 162, go 7 miles, and then turn north on Foster Road and watch for signs.

88 Springfield Lake

Springfield Lake is located between the communities of Sawyerwood and Lakemore just east of Akron off U.S. Highway 224. The lake covers 291 acres and serves as the center of the Springfield Township Park. The park has picnic tables, restrooms, a fishing pier, and plenty of shoreline access on the north end. Outside the park the lake is surrounded with various private residences and businesses. The lake contains largemouth bass, bluegill, crappie, channel catfish, and walleye.

The lake has a fair amount of weeds along the shoreline and some minor shoreline structure in the way of brush, riprap, and boat docks.

Most bass in Springfield Lake average 12 inches; there are a few 3- to 5-pound fish if you know where to look. Fish the weed edges and any shallow humps that contain a patch of weeds. Spinner baits, tubes, and Rapalas worked over the weeds will place a few bass in the live well.

Bluegills are small; most are 3 to 5 inches. Crappies run small, too; about 6 to 7 inches is average. The crappie fishing is just fair; most are caught in spring around the docks. Walleyes have been stocked into the lake, but walleye fishing is regarded as poor. If there is one bright spot, it's the channel catfish, which average in the 12- to 18-inch range. There is a six-fish limit on channel cats. Most cat fishing is done from the township park on the north end of the lake.

Fishing is permitted on the north end at the park, where there is also a primitive boat launch. The lake has a 250-hp limit. Only boats engaged in skiing, jet boating, and speed boating are allowed inside the designated speed zone; the area outside the speed zone is restricted to 6 mph.

89 Tappan Lake

Key species: Largemouth bass, saugeye, channel and flathead catfish, crappie, bluegill, white bass.

General description: Popular with bass tournaments and recreational users during the summer, but also a top flathead catfish lake.

Overview: Tappan Lake was created in 1936 with the impounding of Stillwater Creek on the Upper Muskingum Watershed. Primarily built for flood control, the lake covers 2,350 acres and is heavily used by recreational boaters in summer. The lake was named after the village of Tappan, which now sits under 25 feet of water, about 0.75 mile east of the dam off the north shoreline. Several of the old noteworthy buildings from Tappan were moved, including the Pleasant Valley Church, now located about 4 miles east of its original site.

Tappan Lake Park, located off Deersville Ridge Road, has camping, a beach, picnic and shelter houses, hiking trails, a boat ramp, and cabins. Two public boat

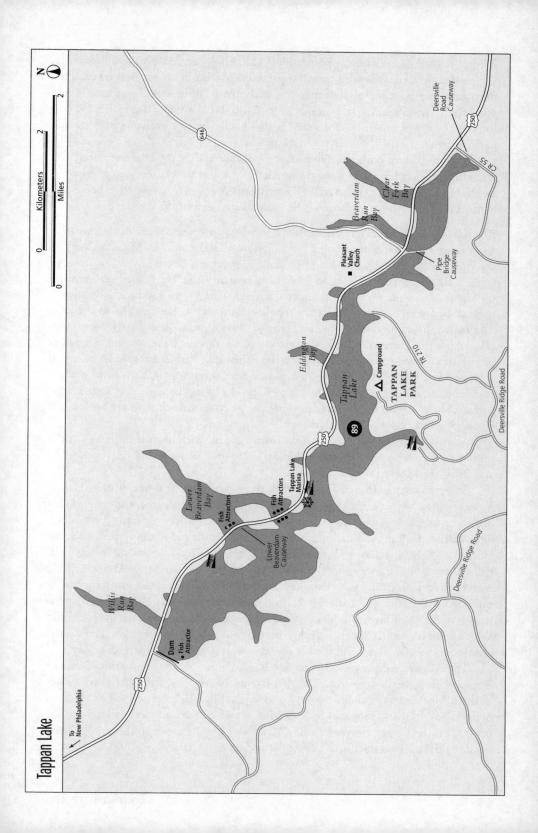

ramps are located on Tappan; both are off U.S. Highway 250 on the north shore. One is located across the road from Tappan Lake Marina in Lower Beaverhead Bay; the other ramp is located about a mile east of the dam. Public shoreline access is very good for a Muskingum Water Conservancy District (MWCD) lake, as US 250 follows the entire north shore for more than 14 miles with numerous pulloffs and parking areas.

Over the years both the Division of Wildlife and MWCD have placed fish attractors at select locations along the north shore and at the causeway across Lower Beaverhead Bay. In 1995 the MWCD airdropped 110 tree stumps by helicopter about 100 feet offshore of the roadside park located east of the dam.

The fishing: Tappan Lake is fished hard for bass, every weekend with tournaments and during the week with evening "working man" tournaments. Most anglers fish the riprap along the US 250 roadway and the shoreline cover in the big coves of Clear Fork, Beaverdam Run, and Lower Beaverdam Run. The bass are taken from the riprap, shoreline timber, and under the overhanging trees and brush. Be sure to fish the riprap and bank cover at the pipeline causeway at the east end of the lake. The rocky shoreline east of the campground is good, too. Most bass fishing takes place from the Deersville Road Causeway to the Tappan Lake Marina. There are plenty of downed trees and slips along the banks that harbor bass. Most bass will average 12 to 15 inches, with a 4- to 5-pound bass about tops. Chartreuse or white spinner baits, small crank baits, and Shad Raps in a bluegill pattern work well. Tappan is a big lake with no shortage of shoreline structures. Stick with the bank cover and rocks, and you will find bass.

A few smallmouth are also caught from Tappan, with most being taken at the deeper west end from the rocks and riprap along the causeway and dam with tubes and small crawdad-colored crank baits.

Saugeyes are plentiful in Tappan, with some fish reaching upwards of 30 inches; however, most will average 18 to 24 inches. It's a good saugeye lake, and it's good for big saugeyes, but it can be tough. Saugeyes are caught a variety of ways—vertical jigging, casting, trolling, and drifting. Slow troll or drift the old shallow roadbed at the mouth of Clear Fork Bay with small Hot 'n Tots or jigs and minnows. Moving west, fish the pipeline causeway shoreline and at the end of the causeway. About 0.5 mile west of the pipeline causeway, fish the flats and old roadbed off the south shore. On the north bank, fish the flats east of Eddington Bay and the old roadway at the mouth of the bay. Slow troll the shoreline west of Eddington Bay. Fish the point and shoreline across from the camper beach on the south shore. Another good area is the saddle between the shore and the big island just west of Lower Beaverdam Bay.

The saugeye fishing picks up come fall and winter. As the U.S. Army Corps of Engineers lowers the lake from October to mid-November, saugeye fishers gather at the bridges between the causeways and vertical jig blade lures, such as Heddon Sonars, Vib"E"s, and Hopkins Spoons, and jigs with night crawlers or leeches. The bridges on the Lower Beaverdam Bay Causeway are the most productive, but any of the bridges across the north bays will produce some saugeyes.

White crappies average 9 to 10 inches, but 12- to 13-inch crappies are relativity common on Tappan. Any downed tree next to deeper water will hold crappies in spring. Look for downed timber over 6 to 8 feet of water, and fish at the deep end of the treetop. The best crappie fishing is from late March through late May, using crappie tube jigs and minnows and a bobber.

Bluegills are common; nice ones will reach hand size, with a few bigger during the spring spawn in early June. Red worms and a floater are all an angler needs.

A few perch are caught, some up to 10 or 11 inches. For perch try fishing off the old roadbed south of the big island at the mouth of Lower Beaverdam Bay.

White bass are caught in the jumps, busting schools of shad early in the morning in summer near the dam. Once in a while, some angler lands one as big as 15 inches on a Rooster Tail or white Mepps.

Channel catfish are widespread with a few reaching upwards of 10 pounds. Most cat fishing takes place in the shallower east end, from Beall Bay to the Deersville Road Causeway. There is plenty of good shoreline access from parking areas along US 250 and at the Deersville Road Causeway. Other good areas include the west shoreline of Lower Beaverdam Bay and the east shoreline of Willis Run Bay. Most channels are taken at night with chicken livers and night crawlers. At the end of the pipeline causeway is an excellent spot, as is off the Deersville Road Causeway.

What is going to put Tappan on the map is that the next state record flathead catfish may come from these waters. Flathead over 60 pounds are caught from Tappen every year by anglers who know where they are and know how to land a monster catfish that acts more like a tractor than a fish. When fishing for flatheads use stout tackle, bluegills, suckers, or goldfish for bait, and fish at night. Try fishing for flatheads in, or just off, the old stream channel from Beall Bay and Clear Fork Bay. The water is shallow there, usually less than 8 feet. Also fish off and at the end of the pipeline causeway. Some 50-pound flatheads have come from the end of the pipeline causeway.

Below the dam is a fairly good tailwater fishery for smallmouth, saugeyes, and channel catfish. Some excellent saugeye fishing is available when the lake is drawn down, from November 15 through December 20, but it is rumored that saugeyes have an odd taste from the Tappan tailwaters. From May through September, fishers are restricted from the walkway directly above the tailwater discharge pipe and around the stilling base because of high concentrations of H_2S (hydrogen sulfide) that are emitted from the tailwater discharge that builds up under the thermocline, which is 15 to 18 feet deep in the lake in summer. The buildup is so strong that the H_2S levels are between 200 to 300 parts per million directly above the discharge pipe, which is nearly lethal. If you doubt the strength of the H_2S, then look at the corroding railing around the stilling base.

Special regulations: Tappan is limited to 299 hp. Minimum size for bass is 12 inches. For crappies, a 9-inch minimum length limit is in effect.

Facilities/camping: Tappan Lake Park has 250 campsites and 11 cabins. The nearest store with ice and groceries is located in the small village of Deersville, just west of the campground entrance.

Additional information: Tappan Lake Park is so busy during the Fourth of July week that it doubles the population of Harrison County and becomes the biggest community in the county during that time.

Directions: From New Philadelphia, take US 250 east approximately 16 miles.

90 Walborn Reservoir

Key species: Largemouth bass, channel catfish, crappie, bluegill, ring perch, walleye.

General description: An excellent spring and fall crappie lake.

Overview: Dale Walborn Reservoir covers 651 acres of water and is part of the Stark County Park District. The Walborn Reservoir Marina Park is popular with hikers, horseback riders, weekenders out for a scenic drive, and fishers. The marina has boat rental, a boat ramp, docks, and a wheelchair-accessible fishing pier. Numerous pulloffs along the causeways and parking areas provide excellent shoreline access. From the marina, access to the dam and tailwaters is only a short walk away.

Boats are limited between the German Church Causeway and the Reeder Avenue Causeway, because passage is not possible through those causeways. However, canoes and small boats could be carried across the causeways with little trouble.

The fishing: Bass fishing is popular at Walborn, with most bass taken from the riprap at the causeways and around the shoreline cover on the southeastern banks. Bass average 12 to 16 inches, with a few reaching above 3 pounds. Bass are not in great numbers, but what fish are here reach a respectable size. Spinner baits and crank baits worked around the causeways account for the majority of taken bass. Stumps are also found along the old streambed; if you can locate them, you will find bass there as well. Most bass taken will be small; in some years small bass are more numerous than in other years. The majority of bass fishing takes place between the Price Street Causeway and the Reeder Avenue Causeway. Most of the reservoir is shallow, so caution is advised to keep from running aground—especially in the north end.

Channel cats are plentiful. Most are 12 to 18 inches; a few upwards of 24 inches are taken every summer from the German Church Causeway, the Stroup Road Causeway, and the pier at the marina. Try fishing for channel cats with night crawlers or chicken livers on the bottom in the evening in late June, July, and August.

Bluegills are plentiful and can be caught close to the shore from any location. Occasionally some nice hand-size 'gills show up during the spawn in early June.

Crappies are the big catch at Walborn, averaging 12 to 15 inches or better. Locate the stumps along the old stream channel between the Price Street Causeway and Reeder Avenue Causeway, and you will catch crappies big enough to brag about. Also fish off the German Church Causeway and around any shoreline brush that is in water 3 to 5 feet deep. Several fish structures have been placed in Walborn over the years, and these too hold crappies in spring. Structures have been placed just offshore on the west side of Price Street Causeway, to the north of the fishing

Anthony Collins and his father had a good day of crappie fishing in September on Walborn Reservoir.

pier, off the Reeder Avenue Causeway, and around the shoreline near the spillway. The best time to catch crappies is late March through May, and again in October. Use minnows and a slip bobber and small crappie tubes.

Ring perch are present here but run small, usually less than 8 inches. Most are caught by bank fishers with a simple red worm. There are also a few walleye in the lake, but they seldom receive much attention.

Special regulations: Walborn Lake is limited to 10 hp and boats under 21 feet. Bass must be 15 inches to keep. Channel cats are limited to six fish a day. The park closes at 7:00 p.m.

Facilities/camping: The Walborn Reservoir Marina has bait, food, beverages, and boat rental. There is no camping at the reservoir.

Directions: Located on Price Road northwest of Alliance off Highway 183.

91 Wellington Reservoirs

The town of Wellington has two reservoirs open to public fishing; both are located south of town off Highway 58, west at Jones Road. The reservoirs contain bass, channel catfish, and bluegills.

The south reservoir is an older impounded reservoir of 21 acres. It has a concrete boat ramp and is limited to electric motors only. The reservoir is now part of the Lorain County metro parks. With a new nature center, walking trails, and free use of paddleboats, the lake is a park pond more than a fishing lake.

The south reservoir still has excellent shoreline cover, including overhanging trees and brush, and occasional rock and riprap along the banks. It was a nice little bass lake at one time. Most bass averaged 10 to 12 inches, but enough 15- to 16-inch bass showed up to make fishing a worthwhile endeavor. Fish the shoreline brush with plastic worms, watermelon lizards, and white spinner baits. In the evening buzz baits worked along the brushy banks do well. The south reservoir has a 15-inch minimum length limit on bass.

Channel catfish are also good here, but most run 12 to 15 inches, with a few 2- to 3-pound fish. Fish night crawlers, red worms, or chicken livers off the banks anywhere, and you'll catch them.

Bluegills are common catches but tend to run small. Wax worms and a bobber are all you need to catch a few.

If you tire of the paddleboaters, then fish the Wellington Upground Reservoir across the street. It's a nice clear reservoir. I estimate it to be at least 100 acres, with 4 to 5 feet of visibility. It has a concrete boat ramp but is limited to electric motors only. The reservoir is a typical upground—rectangular in shape with a generally flat, featureless bottom and a limestone-rock–boulder shoreline. The clarity of the water has encouraged a healthy growth of coon tail weeds along the banks, which provide good shoreline cover. The majority of the bass and bluegills are caught along the outer edge of these weeds, with plastic night crawlers, spinner baits, crank baits, and wax worms.

92 West Branch Reservoir

Key species: Muskie, largemouth and smallmouth bass, northern pike, walleye, crappie, bluegill, channel and flathead catfish, striped bass.

General description: A popular lake for muskie, bass, and walleye.

Overview: West Branch Reservoir, or the Michael J. Kirwan Reservoir as the U.S. Army Corps of Engineers calls it, was completed in 1965, impounding a 2,350-acre lake on the West Branch of the Mahoning River. The lake averages 25 feet deep; the water clarity is around 12 to 18 inches, at best. The lake is characterized by numerous deep coves; weedy bays; long, shallow rocky points; and countless downed trees along the banks—ideal habitat for muskie, bass, and walleye.

At the west and south ends of the lake is the West Branch Wildlife Area. On the north and east ends is West Branch State Park. The newly renovated state park offers hiking, biking, and bridle trails; numerous picnic areas and shelter houses; a beach; a campground; five boat ramps; and a marina with boat rental and fuel. A wheelchair-accessible pier is located at the marina.

Normal fluctuations in the lake are usually less than 5 feet, but that can vary according to the weather. At summer pool the lake level is 985.5 feet above sea level. Beginning in July the lake is slowly dropped to winter pool, reaching 980.5 feet above sea level by November.

You can access the tailwaters from the U.S. Army Corps of Engineers parking area located on Wayland Road. From the parking area is it about a 0.5-mile hike to the dam. Shoreline access to the lake is good on the south side from the various boat ramps, picnic areas, and the marina.

The fishing: Over the years West Branch has been stocked with tiger muskie and striped bass, both of which have been discontinued. Now the lake only receives channel catfish, walleye, and muskie. Some big remnant stripers are still caught, and I did talk to a fellow that recalls catching a small tiger muskie a long time ago.

The crappie fishing is pretty good on West Branch, and like most lakes, some years are better than others. Most crappies average a respectable 9 to 11 inches; in good years 14- to 16-inch slabs are caught. April, May, and late September through October are the good months. Jigs and minnows or minnows and a bobber work well, as do small jigs and twister tails. Fish the shoreline brush and around the old bridge pillars in Jay Lake Bay. Also fish Silver Creek Bay and the next bay west on the south side of the lake. Crappies are also good along the south shore of the west end and at the Rock Spring Road Bridge. Fish the culvert at Cable Line Road in the west end. Plenty of crappies are caught off the pier at the marina and also from the marina boat docks. Look for any downed timber, beaver huts, slips, logs, or brush in any of the bays, and you'll fill a basket. No secret to crappies here.

Walleyes are usually caught from the points and flats in the main lake, east of Rock Spring Bridge. Most walleyes average 15 to 20 inches, but several in the 6- to 8-pound range are caught every year. Anglers use small Hot 'n Tots; dressed jigs with minnows, night crawlers, or leeches; and blade lures such as Silver Buddies and

Jim Worley shows off a basket of nice crappies caught from West Branch Reservoir.

Vib"E"s. Cast, jig, or slow troll the points and flats on the north shoreline from Rock Spring Bridge to the campground. At Rock Spring Bridge, plenty of walleyes are caught from the causeway and from under the bridge. The point at the south end of Goose Island is particularly good. The area in front of the beach has been known to produce, as has Water Tower Point. Toward the dam on the north shore, the long point just east of Jay Lake Bay, and the south side of Hickory Island are good areas. In early spring work the Hinkley Creek mouth at the west end of the lake. Good walleye fishing begins in late April and lasts through May, and it picks up again in fall. Through the ice, anglers jig blade lures and jig and minnows to catch walleyes.

A few stripers are still caught at West Branch, and most are caught around the dam by fishing chicken livers 4 to 5 feet deep under a floater. Occasionally a striper will chase a school of shad against the dam, and anglers will catch them in the jumps with Rapalas or Rattle Traps. The causeway at Rock Spring Road has also produced a few good stripers.

They also get some nice bluegills at West Branch. Most are caught during the spawn from May through mid-June with maggots, red worms, and wax worms. Just fish the beds from any shore, and bluegills averaging hand size to 10 inches will be waiting.

Largemouth and smallmouth are both in pretty good supply at West Branch, with largemouth outnumbering the smallmouth two to one. Every year some nice

4- to 5-pound largemouth bass come from the reservoir, with most averaging 13 to 15 inches. Smallmouth will average close to the same; a 4-pound bass is a very good one.

Most smallmouth come from the rocks, riprap along the dam, and the rocky shoreline around the camping area on the north side of the lake. Another good area is Water Tower Point. Look for smallmouth around rocky points and drop-offs in the eastern half of the lake. May is the best time for smallmouth, followed by mid-September and through fall. Fish jigs with twister tails, crayfish, and tubes.

Largemouth are much more widespread than smallmouth. In summer most are caught off the weeds and downed timber at the creek mouth and bays using Carolina rigs, tubes, crawls, spinner baits, and buzz baits. Good spring bass can be caught from Silver Creek Bay, Jay Lake Bay, and the south shoreline of the west end of the lake. Any weedy bay, point, or creek mouth will hold some bass; look for weeds in 3 to 4 feet of water and fish the downed trees along both shores from the campground and east and from the west ramp toward the marina. In fall continue to fish the weeds; as water drops, bass will be on the deeper outer edge.

Northern pike are caught in early spring using creek chubs and shiners from the creek mouths at Silver Creek Bay, Hinkley Creek, and Bixon Creek Bay off Cable Line Road. Pike usually run 20 to 30 inches in West Branch, but a few 34-inch-plus pike do show up every year.

Muskies are something special at West Branch, and every spring some crappie fisher hooks a whopper using a crappie minnow. In summer most muskie anglers simply troll Bagely's Super Shads and big Hot 'n Tots, 10 to 15 feet deep off the points at the west end of the lake in search of suspended fish. In spring, work the creek mouths with big tandem spinners. Some of the best spring creeks are Silver Creek, Jay Lake Bay, Hinkley Creek, and Bixon Creek Bay at the west end. Muskies can be found in the weeds all summer long. Fish the weedy bays with spinners, buzz baits, and jerk baits. In late summer and fall, troll the main creek channel at the west end of the lake, west of Rock Spring Road. Fish any weeds off the main lake islands and the big cove north of the dam. Several "huskies" come from West Branch every year; 30- to 40-pound muskies are not uncommon.

Cat fishing is good at West Branch, and an occasional flathead is also caught. Some nice channels that weigh up to 9 pounds are taken from the lake; a few 20-pound flatheads are caught as well. Catfish can be taken from any shoreline; the gravel boat ramp off Rock Spring Road is good, as is the bridge on that road. The bay at Hinkley Creek is also good. Channels are also caught from the picnic area near the marina and from the marina pier. If you're in a boat, fish the creek channel at the west end using chicken livers, dough balls, or night crawlers. Most channel cats average 15 to 18 inches.

The tailwaters provide a good chance at taking muskies, walleyes, channels, bluegills, or bass. Six miles downstream on the West Branch, at the village of Newton Falls, anglers also take muskies and walleye from the tailwaters of the West Branch Dam located at the Highway 534 Bridge. Another dam is located on the Mahoning River at a Rotary Club park at the north end of Newton Falls, where they also take muskies, walleye, and bass.

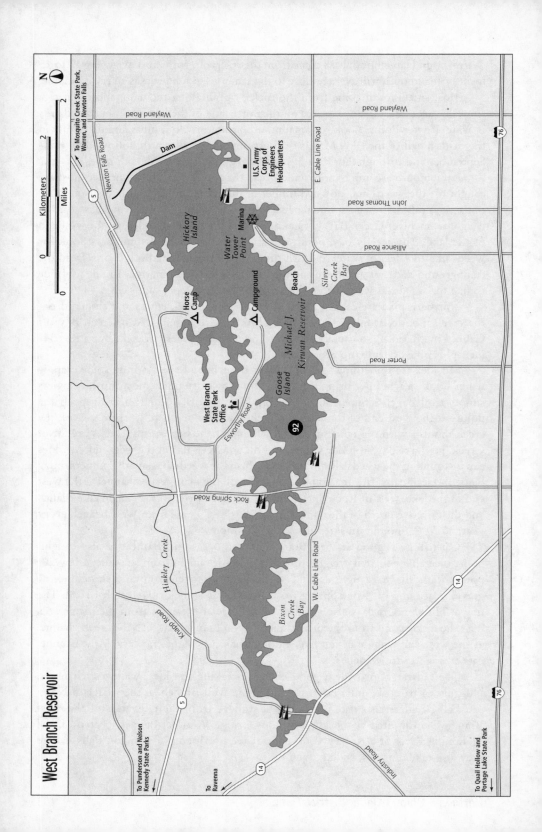

West Branch Reservoir

N

Kilometers
0   2

Miles
0   2

To Mosquito Creek State Park,
Warren, and Newton Falls

Wayland Road

Newton Falls Road

5

Dam

Hickory
Island

Water
Tower
Point   Marina

U.S. Army
Corps of
Engineers
Headquarters

E. Cable Line Road

Wayland Road

76

John Thomas Road

Alliance Road

Horse
Camp

Campground

Beach

Silver
Creek
Bay

Porter Road

West Branch
State Park
Office

Esworthy Road

Goose
Island

Michael J.
Kirwan Reservoir

92

Rock Spring Road

W. Cable Line Road

Hinkley Creek

Knapp Road

Bixon
Creek
Bay

5

14

To Punderson and Nelson
Kennedy State Parks

To
Ravenna

14

Industry Road

76

To Quail Hollow and
Portage Lake State Park

Special regulations: Unlimited horsepower, but idle speed only within 300 feet of shoreline and at the west end past Rock Spring Bridge.

Facilities/camping: Facilities outside the state park are few; the nearest town is Ravenna, which has everything. West Branch State Park has 198 campsites.

Additional information: There is an osprey platform near the dam.

Directions: From Ravenna, take Highway 5 east 5 miles.

93 Zepernick Lake Wildlife Area

Zepernick Lake Wildlife Area is located south of Alliance approximately 12 miles on Highway 172. The wildlife area contains two weedy ponds from 5 to 7 acres stocked with bass, bluegill, and channel catfish and the 39-acre Zepernick Lake, which also has crappies.

Zepernick Lake has a boat ramp and is limited to electric motors only. The lake is weedy with lily pads and coon tail, has a few old standing snags, and has four earthen piers from which to fish. Shoreline access is good, as paths encircle most of the lake. It's an absolutely beautiful lake and the centerpiece of the 518-acre wildlife area.

Bass fishing is good at Zepernick Lake; a number of nice bass from 4 to 5 pounds are caught here every year, including possibly a lake record 7.5-pound large-mouth taken by a local angler. The best bass fishing is from April through May; fish the north and northeastern shoreline weeds with spinner baits and plastic night crawlers. Come June and through summer, most bass are taken in the evening using buzz baits along the weed edges.

Bluegills tend to run small, one local fisherman told me. But during the spring spawn, a few nice hand-size bluegills are caught from around the shoreline.

Years ago there was a good population of chain pickerel in Zepernick, but from what locals tell me, there are few caught nowadays. There are a few small ones in the tailwaters down by Conser Run Stream.

Channel catfish are excellent on the lake. Most average between 12 and 22 inches; a few reach the 28-inch mark. In summer channels are usually taken at night by fishers from the earthen piers using night crawlers and chicken livers. Another good area to catch catfish is the old streambed channel. The Division of Wildlife stocks catfish every other year.

Crappie fishing is fairly good here, with most averaging 9 to 11 inches. Fish the old stump remains at the northwest side of the lake, around the old standing snags, and off the brushy east point. Crappies are caught in April and May with minnows.

Southeast Ohio—Wildlife District Four

Southeast Ohio has some of the most varied fishing opportunities in Ohio; it also has some of the most beautiful. The Ohio River dominates the fishing in this part of the state, with sauger, flathead catfish, and hybrid striper fishing below the locks and dams. In the Muskingum River, the old historic dams offer some of the best river and stream fishing found in Ohio. Plus, the flathead fishing on the Muskingum would rival flathead fishing on any river in the United States.

The AEP ReCreation Land has no equal when it comes to pond fishing for big bass and bluegills. Southeast Ohio is full of old strip-mine and quarry ponds that hold some of the biggest bass and bluegills in the state. Thousands of acres of old strip-mine properties have been opened to public fishing and hunting in southeast Ohio.

Many smaller reservoirs such as Barnesville and Hammertown, though off the beaten path, harbor some big largemouth. Salt Fork and Piedmont are both top muskie lakes, and Seneca Lake offers anglers a shot at a pure striper at the only striper fishery left in Ohio. Smallmouth fishing in the Upper Hocking River is regarded as some of the best in the state. Little Clear Creek Preserve offers some quiet and beautiful trout fishing. When stocked in early spring, Rose Lake, Wolf Run Lake, and Turkey Creek Lake have excellent trout fishing and are deep enough to have carryover trout throughout the year.

If there were a crown jewel in southeast Ohio, it would be tough to call, because there are so many fine fishing spots and opportunities here, but the Muskingum River and Piedmont Lake would certainly rank among the top of everyone's list.

94 AEP Ohio Power Lakes

Key species: Largemouth bass, bluegill, and channel catfish.

General description: One of the most popular fishing areas in southeast Ohio. A free permit is required.

Overview: The American Electric Power ReCreation Lands is one of the top recreation areas in Ohio. More than 42,000 acres of reclaimed strip-mine land is open to public hunting, hiking, horseback riding, mountain biking, sightseeing, and camping. In addition, it has more than 350 ponds, making it an angler-gone-to-heaven fishing experience. The area hosts a variety of outdoor programs, from Wheelin' Sportsmen hunts to youth fishing events. In 1998 the AEP ReCreation Lands were recognized by the Department of Natural Resources as the single largest outdoor recreation facility in the state. In addition to fishing, the area has seven campgrounds with restrooms, water, and picnic tables, located at various locations that are available for public use free of charge.

The Central Ohio Coal Company began extracting coal from the hills of Musk-ingum and Morgan Counties in 1947, moving more than 2 billion cubic yards of earth and mining over 110 million tons of coal. Today coal extraction still continues on the land, but much of the area has been reclaimed and hundreds of the old strip-mine ponds have now become a bonanza of high-quality fishing lakes. The Division of Wildlife has stocked nearly every pond with largemouth bass and bluegill, and some ponds have received channel catfish. A few ponds also got a limited stocking of saugeyes, and some ponds have populations of crappies and redear sunfish.

A wheelchair-accessible pier is at pond MB 72, located off Highway 83, west of Hook Lake campground. Several lakes have gravel boat ramps, others are carry in. A free permit is required to fish, hunt, or camp on AEP lands; those permits are available online at www.aep.com/environmental/recreation/recland/requestpermit.htm, or you can contact the Division of Wildlife District Four headquarters in Athens. The permit must be carried at all times and is good on all AEP lands that allow public hunting and fishing, including the Conesville Coal Lands and Avondale Wildlife Area.

The fishing: This is about as good as it gets in Ohio. Anglers have over 350 ponds to choose from that vary in size from 0.5 acre to over 100 acres. The quality of fishing varies from pond to pond, with the most remote and least fished ponds offering the best fishing.

Bass fishing kicks off early at AEP; some of the heaviest bass catches are reported in March and April. Thick, heavy bass, which look as though they swallowed a baseball, are taken from some of the more remote ponds. It takes a 7- to 8-pound bass to raise eyebrows around here. A few local anglers who know the backwoods trails to the better bass ponds swear there are 10-pound bass in some of those lakes. Not all ponds are created equal; some ponds offer better fishing for numbers, some ponds contain a lot of small bass, and others are true trophy ponds.

A float tube is the best way to explore the virtually unlimited amount of fishing, as shoreline access to 95 percent of the ponds is via a small, single entry point. These ponds are deep, so such little shoreline access makes fishing difficult without a small boat or float tube. Many lakes are clustered in groups, and a canoe or kayak can be portaged from one pond to another if an angler knows his or her way around. Trails and rough footpaths lead to most lakes, but a number of lakes can be easily reached from the Buckeye Trail on the east side and from miles of bridle and hiking trails located throughout the rest of the area.

Any campground can serve as a base camp to explore the backcounty. A good map is advisable, as is a compass, bug dope, water, and energy snacks. The best fishing is from mid-March through June; during the summer it's hot and the weeds and foliage are nearly impenetrable. I'd pick April and May as the most desirable time to fish and explore the AEP lands. Spinner baits, jigs and pigs, plastic lizards, and night crawlers are good early season bets; later it's hard to beat buzz baits. Six lakes have a slot-length limit on bass, and those lakes are clearly posted, advising anglers of the special regulations.

Southeast Ohio Region Overview

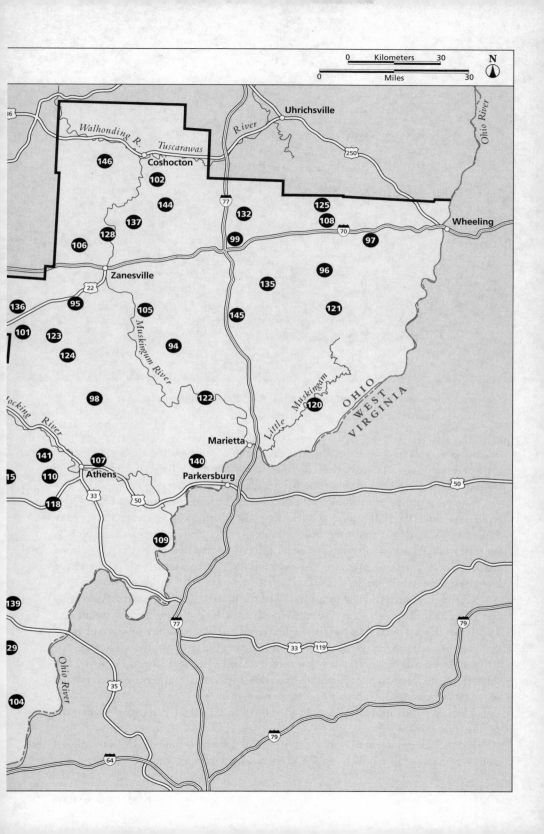

Camping is permitted on several ponds in the AEP ReCreation Lands.

Anglers will find most ponds very clear with some standing timber and varying amounts of aquatic vegetation. With so many ponds it's hard to find company; on most days an angler will have the fishing all to him- or herself.

The AEP ponds offer some of the best bluegill fishing in southeast Ohio. Nice hand-size bluegills are found in nearly every pond during spring spawn in late May and early June; also at that time bruiser bluegills 7 to 10 inches are caught on wax worms, rubber spiders and flies, and small spinners. Some of the more remote ponds that receive little fishing pressure still yield 1-pound bluegills. Big redear sunfish are also present in many ponds.

Channel cats are stocked in nearly all of the more accessible ponds. Most average 15 to 20 inches, although several channels are taken in summer that weigh 8 to 10 pounds. Every pond that can be reached from a gravel road has good numbers of channel cats, with the bigger lakes usually harboring the largest catfish. The best catfish ponds are off the gravel road that runs between Highway 83 and Highway 284 near the Sand Hollow campground. Chicken livers and night crawlers are what most cat fishers use on summer evenings and nights.

There is some limited ice fishing for bluegills, bass, and yes, catfish, when the ponds freeze over.

Hook Lake is a youths-only fishing pond for those anglers 15 years old or younger that is full of big bluegills, fat bass, and hungry catfish. Conveniently

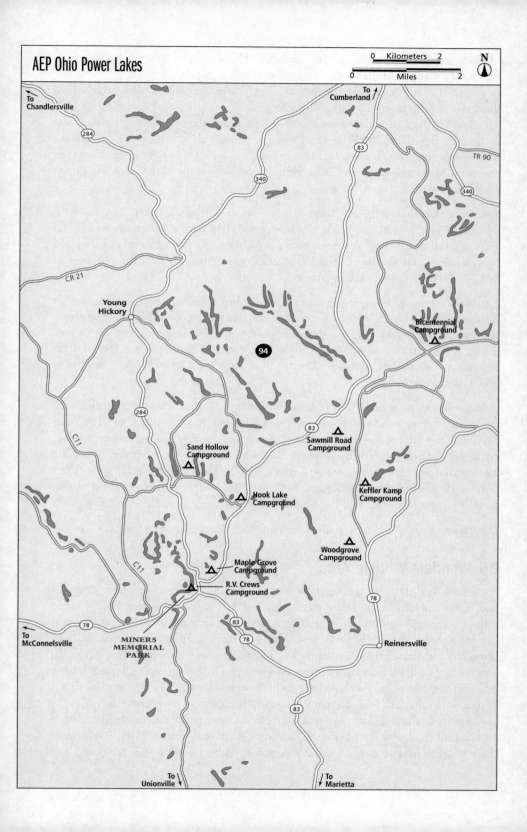

located next to Hook Lake campground, it is the location of an annual youth fishing event usually held the first or second weekend in May.

Several of the larger lakes near roads have gravel boat ramps; all AEP lakes are limited to 9.9-hp motors unless otherwise posted.

Some of the AEP Lakes were closed in 2006 due to dam removal or repair. Concerns were raised about the safety of some impoundments, and ongoing construction may limit access or close entirely the use of some lakes in the future. However, those few impoundments constitute only a small percentage of the lakes and ponds available to fishers.

Special regulations: All AEP lakes are limited to 9.9-hp outboard motors. AEP lakes MB40, MB41, MB42, MM29, MM34, and NB43 have a special 12- to 15-inch slot-length limit on bass. A permit is required to use AEP lands. Permits are good for a lifetime and can be obtained free of charge online or from the Division of Wildlife District Four office in Athens.

Facilities/camping: Camping is currently available at seven campgrounds; Keffler Kamp was closed in 2006 due to construction, but may reopen. There are approximately 380 campsites available for free public use. Facilities include restrooms, water, picnic areas, and shelter houses. Gas, ice, and groceries are few and far between in this remote area of southeast Ohio. The closest town is McConnelsville, which has everything.

Additional information: Miners Memorial Park, located in the center of the AEP lands, at the intersection of three roads, Highway 83, Highway 284, and Highway 78, is dedicated to the men and women who worked the mines in southeastern Ohio. At Miners Memorial Park the massive 220-cubic-yard bucket from the famed Big Muskie dragline power shovel is on display. Big Muskie could move 325 tons of dirt in a single bite and was used from 1969 to 1991. Despite efforts to preserve the world's largest power shovel, Big Muskie was completely dismantled in 1999.

Directions: From McConnelsville, take Highway 78 8 miles east to the AEP lands.

95 Avondale Wildlife Area

Avondale Wildlife Area is roughly 6 miles long and 2 miles wide and is a rough-and-tumble place of abandoned strip-mine ponds, rugged landscape, hollows, and hills. There are 70 old mining ponds that range in size from 1 to 10 acres that you can hike, hack, and crawl your way into, each with its own population of bass, bluegills, and some channel catfish. The terrain is rugged, there are copperheads, and the bugs will eat you alive during the summer. Old grown-up hull roads lead to most ponds, but some you will have to find on your own. The best way to fish is with a float tube, but you can manage to get a few casts in from shoreline.

Access to the interior is best gained from the two parking areas at either end of an old hull road that runs between Lewellyn Road and Fulton Rose Road. From there you can hike to over 25 fishable ponds. Getting a good map is advisable, and a free permit from American Electric Power is required. You can get the permit online at www.aep.com/environmental/recreation/recland/requestpermit.htm, or by contacting the Division of Wildlife District Four office at Athens.

Avondale Wildlife Area is bordered on the west side by U.S. Highway 22 and Highway 345, on the east side via Highway 93, and to the south on Highway 669. Access is from any of the five township roads that run through the wildlife area. Avondale Wildlife Area is located southwest of Zanesville off Highway 93 and US 22.

96 Barnesville Reservoirs

The town of Barnesville has four city reservoirs; one is a city park lake that offers some minor fishing for city residents. All contain bass, bluegills, and channel catfish. Reservoir 3 is stocked with trout in early spring.

Reservoir 1 is 36 acres and located off Township Road T-25, south of town about a mile. It has some limited shoreline access at the dam above the water treatment plant. It is devoid of any shoreline cover, and boats are not permitted.

A better option is to fish Reservoir 2, which appears much larger than its 13 acres, located a short distance away on the same township road as Reservoir 1. The only parking for this reservoir is on top of the hill, with a short hike to the spillway. There are no boating restrictions posted at this reservoir, which is good because you need a small boat to fish it effectively. You could fish from the bank on the spillway, which is the only shoreline access. The reservoir is a much nicer looking body of water than Reservoir 1, with an abundance of shoreline cover in the way of overhanging and downed trees. One can only imagine the bass that this reservoir hides. The water is clear, and there is some weed growth along the edges.

The best known of these city reservoirs is Reservoir 3, also known as Slope Creek Lake, a large body of water at 98 acres. It has boat ramps at the dam off Township Road T-12 and another located at the headwaters off T-514. The reservoir is limited to electric motors only. Shoreline access is limited to the two boat ramps, but some old fishers' footpaths lead up and down the bank. This is a well-known big bass reservoir; a reported 11-pound bass is said to have come from here. There is lots of cover in the way of coon tail weeds, water willows, and shoreline trees and snags. The Division of Wildlife has imposed a special slot-length limit on bass; all bass between 12 and 15 inches must be released. To find this reservoir, take Highway 800 5 miles south of Barnesville, then take Township Road T-514 or T-33 west.

97 Belmont Lake

Key species: Largemouth bass, channel cat, bluegill, saugeye; trout in spring.

General description: Popular for trout, but the fishing doesn't last long.

Overview: The 117-acre Belmont Lake, impounded in 1963, is part of the 1,005-acre Barkcamp State Park, which gets its name from Barkcamp Creek, site of a former logging camp. The state park offers camping; a beach; hiking, biking, and bridle trails; several picnic areas; shelter houses; a boat ramp; docking; and boat rental.

Over the years numerous fishing enhancements have been done at Belmont, including the felling of some 20 trees to provide shoreline cover and, more recently, the submersion of fishing crib structures at 10 locations in the lake. Belmont is fairly clear with a visibility of 18 inches. Some good rock and gravel structure are along the south shore, while the overhanging and downed trees are on the deeper north shore.

Shoreline access is good on the lake's south side, which is also wheelchair accessible, but you need a boat to reach the bass cover on the north shore.

The fishing: Bass fishing is reputed to be good at Belmont, with an abundance of shoreline cover in the way of downed and overhanging trees and old shoreline snags. Fish the north shore cover, the backs of the small north shore coves, and weed beds with plastic night crawlers, crank baits, and spinner baits. Both feeder arms are shallow but offer excellent cover by way of weeds and old timber. A lot of smaller bass are caught, but many in the 3- to 4-pound range are taken as well. Sampling by the Division of Wildlife has indicated the presence of some heavy 6- to 8-pound bass. There is a special slot-length limit in place at Belmont to hopefully improve the trophy bass potential.

Channel cats are in good numbers here. Fishing for cats is done from the parking areas along the south shore toward the beach. Channels range from 12 to 20 inches, with a few approaching the 10-pound mark. Chicken livers or night crawlers fished in the morning or evening are productive. There are a few shovelheads in the lake, and some weighing 10 to 12 pounds are taken every summer on bluegills or chubs.

Saugeyes have been introduced, and fishers near the spillway and around the beach catch the lion's share of them. Fish the two rock and gravel points from the beach to the dam with night crawler harnesses, small crank baits, and jigs and minnows. Fishing is good in late fall and early spring. Ice fishing produces saugeyes at the lower end near the two bridges. Saugeyes can also be caught off the rock fishing pier and off the rocks at the lower parking area. Saugeyes up to 21 inches are caught by those who target them.

Bluegills are in plentiful numbers and run 7 to 8 inches. Fish red worms or wax worms off any bank, and you'll catch your fill.

Crappies are plentiful but run only 6 to 8 inches. Catch them in early spring around any shoreline brush on minnows or jigs.

Trout are stocked in early April, and fishing for them is popular. Most trout are caught by the second week on Rooster Tails, corn, cheese, and Power Bait.

Special regulations: The lake is restricted to electric motors only. Bass between 12 and 15 inches must be released.

Facilities/camping: Groceries, ice, and gas can be found at the intersection of Highway 149 and Interstate 70 northwest of the lake. The state park has 125 camping sites and 2 cabins.

Additional information: Be sure to visit the pioneer cabins and the old barn located in the state park.

Directions: Belmont Lake is located approximately 7 miles west of St. Clairsville, south of the I-70 and Highway 149 intersection.

98 Burr Oak Lake

Key species: Largemouth bass, bluegill, sunfish, channel catfish, some saugeye (stocking was discontinued).

General description: This lake has a well-deserved reputation as one of Ohio's best bass lakes, but it's tough to fish. There are horsepower and size restrictions.

Overview: Located in the heart of the hill country of southeastern Ohio, Burr Oak was impounded by the U.S. Army Corps of Engineers in 1950 for the purpose of flood control on the east branch of Sunday Creek. The lake, which covers 628 acres, is surrounded by hillsides of mixed hardwood forest consisting of oak, hickory, poplar, ash, and pine.

Burr Oak State Park and Wayne National Forest surround the lake and provide various facilities. The state park has a lodge, cabins, campgrounds, a beach, five boat ramps, docks, a marina with boat rental and fuel, and numerous picnic areas, hiking trails, backpacking trails, and bridle trails. Park headquarters is located at Dock 4. There is wheelchair-accessible fishing at the marina, but all parking areas near the water also accommodate accessible fishing. Wayne National Forest offers hiking trails and camping.

Burr Oak Lake averages 15 to 20 feet in depth, is long and narrow, and characterized by steep, sloping hillside banks. The water is generally very clear; the fact that the Corps of Engineers restricts scuba diving near the spillway should tell you something. Bank access is limited; a boat is the only way to fish Burr Oak.

The fishing: Burr Oak has always maintained a reputation as one of the state's best big bass lakes. It could arguably be among the top 10 inland bass fisheries in Ohio. It can be a tough lake to fish, but those who know its secrets are rewarded with fine, heavy catches.

Fishing starts out early at the shallow north end and in shallow bays with lizards, spinner baits, and jig-and-pig combos. Work shoreline cover, of which there is plenty in the form of bank slips, fallen trees, old logs, and snags. The coves near the dam are good, but any "bass-looking" structure could hold a whopper. Later in the summer buzz baits fished in the evening over vegetation produces. Night fishing picks up considerably in the summer, with top-water baits. Lately "finesse fishing" has been catching on, using light lines, a long cast, and small plastics. Local bass tournaments typically do well in Burr Oak, with several 3- to 5-pound bass finding temporary residence in anglers' live wells. Fishers still manage to catch a lot of smaller bass, but a heavy one is usually waiting for somebody.

Channel catfish do well in this reservoir, and natural reproduction keeps the fishery well supplied. Cats can be found about anywhere, but the north end, near

Burr Oak Lake is surrounded by Wayne National Forest and has campgrounds, a marina, and a lodge.

Dock 3, gets the nod. Chicken livers, chubs, and night crawlers fished at night in summer will probably place a few 2- to 3-pounders on your stringer.

Crappies are abundant, but few reach over 12 inches. Fish the shoreline brush and around boat docks with jigs and minnows or a bobber and minnows.

Bluegills are also everywhere, perhaps overly abundant, but few obtain any size.

Saugeyes have done fairly well in Burr Oak, but the Division of Wildlife has discontinued stocking them. There is no natural reproduction of saugeye, therefore the fishery will slowly die out. What are left are nice ones. You can probably find them by fishing the rocks and cliffs around the spillway with small chartreuse crank baits and a jig and curly tail.

Special regulations: Burr Oak is limited to 10 hp. Bass between 12 and 15 inches must be released.

Facilities/camping: The state park has several campgrounds for group camping; however, the main campground has 90 camping units and is located off Highway 13. Wayne National Forest maintains a primitive campground with 19 sites, also located off Highway 13. Burr Oak State Park has a 60-room lodge and dining hall, plus 30 cabins located off Highway 78 on the east side of the lake.

Additional information: Almost every first-time visitor has to make a stop at the Rocky Boots Outlet Store in nearby Nelsonville.

Directions: Getting to Burr Oak and to its various facilities involves the most complex, curvy road system ever devised in Ohio. From Nelsonville take Highway 78 north. At the junction of Highway 13 and Highway 78, go either left or right, depending where on the lake you want to get. Signs are well marked. Best advice: Get a map.

99 Cambridge City Reservoir

Cambridge City Reservoir, located just southeast of Cambridge, is a beautiful small lake of 16 acres. It contains largemouth bass, bluegills, some crappies, and channel catfish. It would be quite place to fish if not for all the traffic noise from the nearby interstate. The shoreline is shaded with an abundance of cover, including overhanging trees, fallen timbers, and brush. There are only a few places where the lake can be fished from shore. Although there is no boat ramp, a small boat could be launched near the dam. I assume the lake is limited to electric motors only; there are no signs posting any restrictions.

Bass are taken by casting to the heavy shoreline cover along both banks. Unless fished to death, the lake appears to have the potential to produce some heavy bass. One local fisherman told me that the reservoir once produced some 20-inch bass, but mostly small bass are caught now.

Bluegills are plentiful but small, as are the crappies, which only reach 6 to 8 inches. You can catch them in early spring around the shoreline brush with minnows.

The Division of Wildlife stocks some brood-stock channel catfish every so often as needed. Mostly small channels are caught, but some 18- to 20-inchers have been taken on chicken livers near the pulloff along the dam.

Shoreline access, though limited, is along Reservoir Road on the north side of the lake and at the dam.

To get to Cambridge Reservoir, take U.S. Highway 40 east, turn south on Sigman Road, then west on Reservoir Road.

100 Clear Creek, Hocking County

Clear Creek Metro Park in Hocking County is owned and managed by the Columbus Metro Parks. The preserve is nearly 5,000 acres of mostly forested hills, cliffs, ravines, and rock outcroppings. Hemlocks and sycamores line the stream banks, while the drier ridges support a variety of oaks and hickory.

Public fishing is allowed on Clear Creek and Lake Ramona. Lake Ramona is 5 acres and has fishing for bass, bluegill, and channel catfish. Clear Creek, a tributary of the Hocking River, is stocked with brown trout, and smallmouth bass are available in spring.

Clear Creek is an absolutely beautiful stream that runs through the bottom of this preserve. Unlike most Ohio trout streams, this looks like one. Deep pools, riffle water, and gravel runs make this about as likely a candidate for a trout fishery as there is in southeast Ohio. The creek is small but sufficient and is cooled by a constant, even waterflow. In summer a heavy forest canopy shades the stream and the water stays at temperatures just within the acceptable range for trout to survive. Brown trout are stocked into the creek every fall.

Clear Creek has 5 miles of stream open to public fishing. Parking areas are well marked, and fishing access is excellent and well spaced to give an angler enough elbow room to fish. Easy to wade, the water begs for a wispy fly rod and a quiet approach. Minimum size for trout is 12 inches. There are good holes at several locations, but I won't tell you about them—half the fun is finding them yourself.

In mid-April and May, smallmouth bass moving upstream to spawn from the Hocking River are frequently caught from Clear Creek.

There is no camping within the preserve. Outside the preserve, Hocking Hills State Park has 172 campsites.

Clear Creek Metro Park is located 8 miles northwest of Logan, off U.S. Highway 33 on County Road 116.

101 Clouse Lake Wildlife Area

Key species: Bass, bluegill, sunfish, channel catfish; trout in spring.

General description: Best fished in spring because of extensive weed growth in summer.

Overview: Clouse Lake covers 49 acres. It has a rough, old blacktop boat ramp, a parking area, and several boat tie-ups along the shore near the ramp. Weed growth is so heavy that by summer fishing from shore is impossible. The only open water consists of small pockets between the moss beds that cover virtually the entire lake. The lake could benefit from several truckloads of weed-eating carp (white amurs). I am told this used to be a good bass lake, but siltation and agricultural runoff have made this lake resemble a marsh more than a lake.

The fishing: There are still a few bass hiding under the moss beds, but most run small, 12 to 14 inches. A few 3- to 4-pounders are caught each spring along the spillway with spinner baits and lizards. In summer, fish pockets in the weeds along the edges of the weed beds with plastic worms and buzz baits. In the late evening and early morning, fish activity is easily observed along the weed edges near the dam.

Bluegills are plentiful but small, seldom exceeding 5 inches.

The Division of Wildlife stocks channel cats on a semiregular basis. Catfish in the 15-inch range are caught before the weed growth renders shoreline fishing impossible.

Trout are stocked each spring before the weed growth covers the lake. Anglers have success with chartreuse Power Bait.

Special regulations: Boats are restricted to 10 hp.

Facilities/camping: No facilities or camping areas.

Additional information: The lake has excellent wildlife-viewing opportunities for various waterfowl and furbearers.

Directions: Take Highway 668 approximately 3 miles south of Somerset.

102 Conesville Coal Lands

The Conesville Coal Lands are roughly 11 miles long by 6 miles wide with 64 old strip-mine ponds. Nearly all require a small boat or float tube to fish. Some can be driven to on rough old 4x4 roads; most require a hike of some distance to reach. The area is owned by American Electric Power and requires a free permit to access. That permit can be obtained online at www.aep.com/environmental/recreation/recland/requestpermit.htm, or from the Division of Wildlife District Four Office in Athens.

The ponds are stocked with largemouth bass, bluegills, and channel cats. They are clear and deep with some weed growth in the shallows, and many have old snags and fallen trees that have slipped off the sandstone cliffs. Ponds range in size from 1 to 10 acres. Township and hull roads intersect the area. A good map is available online, but a compass and some good common sense are also needed.

Some of these ponds harbor bass close to the 10-pound mark and bluegills over a pound. Six-, 7-, and 8-pound bass are not unheard of, and bluegills much bigger than a man's hand are regularly caught. If you want the proof, visit the small country store at Wills Creek and see the photos for yourself. The ponds are located north and south of Wills Creek Lake. The bass are taken on a variety of baits, but chartreuse spinner baits, buzz baits, and plastics see the most action.

There are no camping areas, but there is an equine trailhead at Fallon Park at the intersection of County Road 429 and Highway 83. The park has restrooms, and camping by trail riders is permitted.

To get to the Conesville Coal Lands, take Highway 83 approximately 4 miles south of Coshocton. There is a small carryout bait store in the small village of Wills Creek, located just west of the coal lands.

103 Copper Hollow Wildlife Area

Key species: Largemouth bass, bluegill, sunfish, channel catfish.

General description: Cooper Hollow Wildlife Area offers some limited fishing in small ponds.

Overview: Fish are stocked in all the ponds here, but most are small, shallow ponds, normally covered with moss in summer.

The fishing: In all there are about a dozen ponds scattered throughout the wildlife area that offer fishing for small bass, bluegills, and some channel catfish. Some of the larger ponds can be accessed from a gravel hull road that follows the western boundary of the wildlife area. One pond on the southwest corner is estimated to be 6 to 8 acres. There is also some fishing for panfish in Symmes Creek from parking areas along CH&D Road. The Wildlife Area Headquarters are located off CH&D Road. Maps of the wildlife area are available there.

Additional information: One of the best examples of an early iron furnace is located at the entry to the Wildlife Area Headquarters.

Directions: Take Highway 233, or CH&D Road, for 3.5 miles north from Highway 279, east of Oak Hill.

104 Crown City Wildlife Area

Crown City Wildlife Area offers a half-dozen small ponds that contain some minor fishing for small largemouth bass, bluegills, and small channel cats. The area is rugged hill country and reclaimed mining land. Ponds can be found along Rocky Fork Road and along both sides of Rhappsburg Road.

Crown City Wildlife Area is located northwest of the small river town of Crown City, between Highway 790 to the north and Highway 775 to the south.

105 Cutler Lake

Key species: Largemouth bass, bluegill, channel catfish; trout stocked in early spring.

General description: A small, weedy lake, popular when the trout are stocked.

Overview: Cutler Lake, also known as Blue Rock Lake, is a small lake of only 15 acres surrounded by Blue Rock State Park. The lake is a local swimming hole more than a fishing lake, but some nice 2- to 3-pound bass are taken every season, and the lake is popular when trout are stocked in spring. The lower end and north arm of the lake are totally covered with lily pads by summer, leaving only a narrow channel to the open water near the dam.

The state park has a campground, hiking trails, a beach, a beach concession stand that serves as the park headquarters, and a primitive boat ramp. There is good shoreline access on the lake's north and west sides, but a small boat is helpful.

The fishing: In summer the bass hide in the lily pads that cover half the lake. Bass weighing up to 3 pounds are caught using plastic night crawlers and snag-proof Moss Frogs over and around the lily pads. Some explosive strikes will occur if you have the patience to stick with it. Fish the north arm and pads on the opposite shore across from the boat ramp. Some nice-size open pockets exist, which should be fished with buzz baits. In spring fish the east and north branches and the old snags and beaver hut across from the boat ramp.

Channel cats are present but small; 12- to 14-inchers are all you'll catch. Most fishing for cats is done near the dam, as it's the only open water to fish from shore. Most success comes from night crawlers fished on the bottom.

Bluegills are plentiful but small; you can catch them close to shore across from the beach on wax worms.

The Division of Wildlife stocks rainbow trout every spring, and naturally, this is a popular lake when that occurs. Use cheese or chartreuse Power Bait.

Special regulations: Only electric motors are permitted. The minimum length limit on bass is 15 inches.

Facilities/camping: Few facilities are at this lake. The nearest town is Duncan Falls. Primitive camping is available at the state park with 94 sites.

Additional information: A nice side trip is to visit the historic lock and dam on the Muskingum River at Duncan Falls.

Directions: At Duncan Falls, take Cutler Lake Road 6 miles south to Blue Rock State Park and Cutler Lake.

106 Dillon Lake

Key species: Flathead, channel catfish, largemouth bass, crappie, bluegill, saugeye.

General description: Dillon is well-known as a top catfish lake.

Overview: Impounded in 1961 by the U.S. Army Corps of Engineers for the purpose of flood control, Dillon Lake covers 1,400 acres. Normal pool level is 737 feet above sea level, and the lake has a total watershed of 750 square miles. Average depth on the lake is between 6 and 15 feet.

Three government entities administer Dillon Lake and the surrounding area, providing various access points. The Division of Wildlife administers the 3,612-acre Dillon Wildlife Area and provides access to the headwaters. The Corps of Engineers provides access to the tailwaters area, which has two gravel parking areas, picnic areas, and a wheelchair-accessible fishing pier.

Dillon State Park, on the southwest side of the lake, has a campground, cabins, a beach, picnic areas, shelter houses, two usable boat ramps, docks, and a makeshift marina.

The flood of 2005, which was within 6 inches of going over the spillway, devastated the state park. The flood damaged the beach house and marina to such an extent that both had to be taken down. The fuel tank that supplies the marina was flooded and destroyed, and a section of Highway 146 leading to the park also was flooded and damaged. The marina is now run from a camping trailer parked at the boat ramp, which can be moved on a half-hour's notice. Fuel is no longer available at the marina.

Siltation at the north end of the lake has rendered the Nashport and Pleasant Knob ramps virtually unusable, leaving only the two ramps near the dam available for launching. With the siltation also comes the fact the lake can become turbid overnight due to heavy rains upstream.

Shoreline access is fair and limited to the lake's north and east shores only. Some access is available from the wildlife area on the lake's west side near the Pleasant Knob boat ramp.

The fishing: Despite its troubles, the Dillon Lake area does provide a number of angling opportunities from tailwater fishing, to stream fishing, to fishing below Dillon Falls.

Dillon is a top catfish lake that offers some reasonable bass angling and crappie fishing. Saugeyes also are present in the lake, but fishing for them is reserved for the tailwaters in late winter and early spring.

Cat fishing is popular at Dillon, and rightly so. Anglers can expect good catches of channels and heavy flatheads on summer nights. From the shoreline, fish the beach area, around the dam, and along the east shore near the headwaters from the wildlife area access road R-7. A number of pulloffs at the water's edge are on that road, which follows the east shoreline for more than 2 miles. Two- to 5-pound channels and flatheads up to 20 pounds are caught using shad, chicken livers, night crawlers, and cut bait.

Bass fishing is good on Dillon, with most bass in the 13- to 14-inch range; a few up to 5 pounds have been reported. Anglers pound the shoreline cover, bank slips, downed trees, and brush near the dam with spinner baits, plastics, and crank baits. Good places are the slips across from the marina, the shoreline cover along the east shore below the cabins, the west shore near the dam, and in the creek channel just upstream from the Pleasant Knob boat ramp. In early spring spend time at the backs of bays, if lake conditions allow it. Siltation is a major problem at Dillon; caution is advised when fishing above the Pleasant Knob boat ramp.

There is no secret to crappies at Dillon: In early spring start fishing shoreline brush with jigs and minnows or a bobber and minnows. Concentrate south of the beach, as both shorelines are good. Some good crappies are taken, but like most flood control reservoirs, they have good years and bad years. Because of flood conditions the lake may be unfishable for long periods in spring.

Dillon Lake has an interesting relationship with saugeyes. Having been stocked with saugeyes since 1989, few get caught from the lake. Once a high-water event occurs in spring, anglers pick up saugeyes by the bucket loads below the spillway. The stocking in the lake provides saugeye fishing at the tailwater, at Dillon Falls, into the Muskingum River at the Zanesville Lock and Dam, and upstream at the Ellis Lock and Dam. Saugeyes are caught on the usual curly tail grub and jig combos.

At the old silted-in Nashport boat ramp off the wildlife area access road R-7, bow fishing for carp is excellent. I hope you get them all.

The tailwater fishing at Dillon is excellent for channels and flatheads in summer and for saugeyes in late winter and after high-water discharges. Anglers will fish right up into the "chute" for catfish, using shad and chicken livers, then use throw nets to haul their catch up the concrete walls. Smallmouth bass can be taken farther downstream. Saugeyes can be caught anywhere from just below the discharge all the way to Dillon Falls, a mile downstream. Some 30- to 40-pound flatheads have been taken from the spillway area, but channel catfish are usually the main target.

Sheepshead are also abundant and pesky. Large schools of shad can be observed in side eddies just off the current. Below the spillway is a small pool that is off the main stream with a wheelchair-accessible pier.

Downstream, access to the falls is across the bridge at a city park in the small town of Dillon Falls. A Division of Wildlife parking area near the city park provides access above the falls. In spring and summer, in addition to catfish and saugeyes, the falls area provides good smallmouth fishing.

At the other end of the lake, Pleasant Valley Road crosses over Licking River, and access to the river is at a pulloff on the north side of the bridge. Channel catfish, smallmouth, rock bass, and sunfish can be caught here.

Special regulations: A 12-inch minimum length limit on bass is in effect.

Facilities/camping: Dillon State Park has 195 campsites and 29 cabins. Canoes and pontoon boats are available for rent at the marina, but no fuel is available. There is a camp store at the campground entrance. Nearby Zanesville has all the amenities.

Additional information: The Blackhand Gorge State Nature Preserve is located approximately 8 miles west of Dillon State Park on the Upper Licking River.

Directions: Follow Highway 146 6 miles north from Zanesville.

107 Dow Lake (Strouds Run)

Key species: Largemouth bass, bluegill, sunfish, channel catfish, trout.

General description: Best known for its annual stocking of trout in spring.

Overview: Dow Lake covers 160 acres and was impounded in 1960. It is surrounded by the 2,445-acre Strouds Run State Park. The park offers hiking trails, a beach, boat rental, a crude boat ramp, docking, and a campground. Located just outside of Athens, the lake is frequented by a lot of college-age kids. Canoes and kayaks are common sights on the lake. Shoreline access is limited, but lengthy bridle and hiking trails do circle the lake. Parking is limited to the boat ramp–beach area and the spillway parking area off U.S. Highway 50. The west end where the ramp is located is weed choked, as are many of the coves. Lake depths can range anywhere from a few feet to 25 feet near the dam. Most serious fishing is done near the spillway. By the time you read this, Strouds Run State Park may be administered by the city of Athens or the Ohio Division of Wildlife, as Ohio State Parks is trying to shift the burden for maintaining the park to another government entity.

The fishing: Dow Lake has always been a constant producer of quality bass fishing. I recall back in the 1970s catching numerous small bass from the lake and even a few in the 3- to 4-pound range. Not much has changed. Work the shoreline cover, the weed edges at the southeastern end, and the beaver huts; you'll find bass. The steep banks on the lake's south side and near the dam were always top producers. Work the shoreline cover with spinner baits and lizards; use top-water baits in the evening. Bass up to 7 pounds have been caught from Dow Lake.

Channel cats are in good supply here, but the fish bite best on rising water. Use chicken livers and night crawlers. Some respectable cats up to 5 to 6 pounds are caught regularly. Try channel fishing at night at the end of the main park road, past the beach, and also around the dam.

Bluegills are common, but they're nothing to write home about.

Trout fishing is the big event at Dow Lake, when in early April the Division of Wildlife stocks 3,000 rainbow trout. Mealworms, Power Bait, cheese, and small Rooster Tails catch most of the trout. There are some who believe that a few trout survive all year long in the lake's deeper water near the dam.

Special regulations: Outboards are limited to 10 hp. Bass between 12 and 15 inches must be released.

Facilities/camping: The state park has 80 campsites. Amenities can be found at nearby Athens.

Additional information: Athens is a vibrant, historic college town; go enjoy it.

Directions: Dow Lake is located 7 miles east of Athens on Strouds Run Road. Take US 33 north from Athens and follow the signs. Access is also off US 50 east of Athens.

108 Egypt Valley Wildlife Area

Egypt Valley Wildlife Area is a big 17,500 acres and surrounds much of the north and south shore of Piedmont Lake. The area is a mixture of reclaimed strip-mine land and forested tracts. Much of the area has grazing cattle and fencing, so it looks more like the open range in Idaho than Ohio. There are an estimated 100 strip-mine and beaver ponds in the wildlife area that range from 0.25 to 5 acres. Bass, bluegills, and channel cats are in most of the ponds. A few ponds can be reached by road, but most are in the backcounty and require a good topographical map to find. Some of the ponds are in open reclaimed strip-mine land and have good shoreline access; others require a small boat or float tube to fish. Most of the area can be reached from the small towns of Hendryburg, Sewellsville, or Holloway, located about 22 miles east of Cambridge, just north of I-70.

109 Forked Run Lake

Key species: Largemouth and spotted bass, crappie, bluegill, channel catfish; trout in the spring.

General description: A small, locally fished, out-of-the-way lake with little boat traffic.

Overview: Lying less than a mile from the banks of the Ohio River, Forked Run Lake was impounded in 1952 and covers 102 acres. It's a beautiful lake with good water clarity that is overlooked by most anglers on their way to the Ohio River. It has a great deal of shoreline cover in the way of old stumps and timber, which is where you will find most of the fish. Forked Run is a long narrow lake, with depths averaging a deep 15 to 20 feet right off the banks. Forked Run State Park surrounds the lake and has a campground, a beach, hiking trails, picnic and shelter houses, boat rental, two boat ramps on the lake, and another boat ramp on the Ohio River.

There is little shoreline to bank fish from, with most access at the dam and toward the beach and again at the Curtiss Hollow boat ramp. The lake is best fished from a boat.

The fishing: Forked Run is an inviting lake, with water visibility approaching 5 to 6 feet in the late summer. Its banks are lined with old fallen timber and ancient stumps still showing their roots. The hillside terrain in which the lake is located is reflected in the steep shoreline banks.

Bass fishing begins early on Forked Run. Fish the coves and shoreline cover, stumps, and timber north of the Curtiss Hollow boat ramp and the Curtiss Hollow cove itself with jigs and pigs and spinner baits. Later in spring and early summer, concentrate on the longer main lake coves on both sides of the lake south of the Curtiss Hollow boat ramp. Work shoreline cover, beaver huts, the rocky outcroppings, and cliffs with plastic lizards and worms. Fishing slows down in summer but picks up again in mid-September. Spotted bass are found in the lake, which is not unusual considering the lake's proximity to the Ohio River. Most bass will average 12 inches, but a few 5- or 6-pound bass are caught every spring.

Nice crappies in the 10- to 12-inch range can be caught beginning in April and through early summer around standing timber, deep shoreline cover, and old beaver huts. Use minnows and a bobber and small Rebel minnows in summer. The beaver huts are good all summer long; fish them at the deep outer edges of the huts for summer crappies.

Bluegills are of a nice size, with some 7- to 8-inch 'gills caught in 4 to 5 feet of water at the tops of fallen trees in summer. Use wax worms, small jigs, sponge spiders, and a pinch Berkley Gulp to get the fish.

Channels are caught from the shoreline north of the dam and at pulloffs along Curtiss Hollow Road with chicken livers and night crawlers. Most channels average 15 to 18 inches.

Trout are stocked in early spring, and anglers use Power Bait, small Rooster Tails, cheese, and corn to catch them. The trout fishing usually lasts a couple of months, with most fish concentrating near the dam.

The fishing is also good at the tailwaters below the dam in spring, when fish from the Ohio River move up Forked Run Creek to spawn. Saugers, a few walleyes, largemouth, smallmouth, spotted bass, white bass, hybrid stripers, and channel and flathead catfish can all be caught in the creek below the spillway when the time is right. A park officer took a walleye of nearly 10 pounds from the waters below the spillway a number of years back.

The Ohio River boat ramp at Forked Run State Park is located a mile west of the park entrance. From that ramp you can easily access the excellent tailwater fishery of the Belleview Lock and Dam, which can only be reached by boat from the Ohio side of the river.

Special regulations: Forked Run Lake is limited to 10 hp.

Facilities/camping: The nearest town is the little village of Reedsville, located 3 miles east of the park entrance. Camping is available at the state park, which has 151 camping sites located at the top of the hill.

Additional information: Belleville Lock and Dam is 2 miles east of the state park and is well worth a visit.

Directions: Forked Run is not an easy place to find. Take Highway 7 from either Pomeroy or Coolville, then turn east on Highway 248 or Highway 681. Both are long winding roads that will test your patience.

110 Fox Lake

Key species: Largemouth bass, bluegill, sunfish, channel catfish.

General description: A quiet little lake that has quality fishing with horsepower and size restrictions.

Overview: Fox Lake was impounded in 1966 as part of the Margaret Creek Watershed Project for flood control. Fox Lake covers only 46 acres; it has a boat ramp and a wheelchair-accessible fishing pier. Additional access can be gained at the spillway via a long walk from the parking area. The lake lies in the rolling countryside of eastern Athens County, and getting there is half the fun. To find the lake, consider getting a good map that shows all the county roads. The lake is a bit turbid, but that doesn't seem to bother the fishing. At the spillway parking area, you will find walnut, crab apple, locust, and maple trees providing shade for the long walk to the lake. The area is clean with nicely mowed paths. An old fishers' trail follows the lake a considerable distance from the boat ramp and spillway. Access is at the lower east end at the boat ramp and at the spillway. Shoreline access is limited; the lake is best fished by a boat.

The fishing: Fox Lake is an impounded hollow, with steep banks lining both shores. You will find the bass along the shoreline. Old fallen timber, ancient stumps, shoreline slips, and overhanging trees provide the cover for a robust population. Surveys by the Division of Wildlife turned up several 22-inch bass. Fish both banks with chartreuse spinner baits, buzz baits in the evening, and plastics including lizards and tubes. Also fish the riprap along the dam. Weed growth is prevalent along the shallow shoreline and at the headwaters on the lake's east side. Some white amurs have been introduced to control the weed growth.

Good populations of channel cats are also present, with most averaging between 15 and 20 inches. Fishing for cats is done at the boat ramp, but the old path from the boat ramp leads to many fishing locations along the lake's south shore.

Bluegill and redear sunfish are also in good numbers, with nice hand-size fish readily available around any shoreline brush.

At the wheelchair-accessible fishing pier, anglers will find fish structures have been placed on the right side.

Special regulations: The lake is limited to 10 hp. Bass between 12 and 15 inches must be released.

Facilities/camping: There are no facilities or camping.

Additional information: A unique geological feature called Cradle in the Rock is located on the lake's north side.

Directions: There is no easy way to get to Fox Lake. Approximately 6 miles west of Athens on Highway 32, take Enlow Road north to Fox Lake Road, which eventually leads to the lake.

111 Hammertown Lake (Jackson City Reservoir)

Key species: Largemouth bass, channel catfish, saugeye, bluegill, redear sunfish, trout.

General description: An excellent spring trophy bass lake for electric motors only.

Overview: Hammertown Lake is the water supply reservoir for the town of Jackson, also known as Jackson City Reservoir. The lake covers 190 acres and is deep, averaging 20 to 40 feet with some 50- to 60-foot-deep water at the dam.

Hammertown is a clear lake with as much as 6 feet of visibility. A stunning lake, it is almost completely surrounded by forest and lies almost entirely within the boundaries of the Jackson City Park, except for the dam area, which is controlled by the Jackson City Water Company. The city park offers picnic areas, hiking trails, a shelter house, restrooms, and two boat ramps.

The boat ramp at the park off Jisco West Road is a rough, primitive gravel and concrete ramp that has seen better days. It is still possible to launch a small boat from there. The ramp at the west end, off Beaver Pike, is a much better gravel ramp. Due to the electric-motors-only restriction and the large size of the reservoir, it's much better to launch near where you are going to fish than to spend a couple of hours trying to get there the slow way.

Shoreline access is good around the park and west ramp, but there is a lot of lake that can be reached only by boat. Shoreline access can be found off Circle Drive on the lake's east shore, at the city park, and along the road that leads to the west boat ramp. The area around the dam is restricted and clearly marked. In summer the lake can fluctuate as much as 6 feet with water usage.

The fishing: Hammertown Lake is the lake every fisher in southern Ohio talks about. There are bass in these waters that are said to be of state record size. The best fishing for these lunkers is in early March and April. Because of the lake's depth, it does not warm up nearly as quickly as Tycoon Lake or nearby Jackson Lake. Bass are especially attracted to shallow gravel points and bars on the lake's north and northwest shoreline that receive the bulk of sunlight in early spring. But don't spend all your time there; the edges of any shallow point, the backs of bays, or the shallow ends could easily harbor an 8-pounder at that time of year. There is not an abundance of cover in Hammertown; most of it is limited to fish attractors placed at various locations, some fallen trees and logs, sandstone bluffs on the west arm, a few underwater boulders, and some weed growth on the north shore. Most anglers throw plastic crawdads, tubes, and lizards in watermelon seed, smoke, or pumpkin-seed to shoreline cover, points, and gravel shorelines. In summer you can see bass chasing minnows up on the shoreline; at other times bass take minnows or small bluegills off the surface. Fishing is tough during the summer, as most bass just go deep. Work the bluffs and deep edges with small plastics on light line in the early morning and evening hours. You will see a lot of smaller 10- to 14-inch bass cruising the shallow bars and shorelines in summer. In order to enhance the bass fishery, the Division of Wildlife has implemented a protective slot-length limit; all bass between 12 and 15 inches must be released.

Saugeye fishing is good at Hammertown, with most of the action happening in spring and fall. Again, concentrate on the deeper gravel bars and points, along the edges of gravel shorelines, and the shallow flats on the north shore. You could cast, but most success comes from slow trolling worms, small crank baits, and minnows. Saugeyes up to 20 inches have been caught. Fishing is good from March through May and picks up again in fall.

Channel fishing is very good at Hammertown; use chicken livers, chubs, or night crawlers on or near the bottom. Fish the deep-edge off points, off steep shorelines, and around sandstone bluffs. Some big channels have been taken this way; most are caught at night.

Trout fishing is a big event at Hammertown, where approximately 3,000 trout are turned loose in mid-April at the annual trout derby. Marshmallows, corn, Velveeta cheese, Power Bait, and mealworms always get the trout.

There are some nice hand-size bluegills at Hammertown; most will be caught near the shoreline and off the spawning beds in early June on red worms and mealworms.

Special regulations: Boats are restricted to electric motors only. All bass between 12 and 15 inches must be released. The area around the dam is off-limits to anglers. State game and fish laws apply.

Facilities/camping: No overnight camping is permitted.

Additional information: Just north of Hammertown Lake is the Katharine Lake State Nature Preserve.

Directions: To get to the Jackson City Park, take South Street west of Jackson, turn south onto Jisco West Road, and follow it to Hammertown Lake Road, which leads to the park. To get to the Circle Road access, continue on South Street to Circle

Road. To get to the west boat ramp, go west on Beaver Pike and turn south on Hammertown Lake Road. The road ends at the ramp.

112 Jackson Lake

Key species: Largemouth, bluegill, channel catfish, crappie.

General description: A good early spring bass lake with horsepower restrictions.

Overview: Impounded in 1938, Jackson Lake covers 242 acres and averages 3 to 6 feet deep. The shoreline of Jackson Lake is for the most part occupied by private property and lakeside homes; Jackson Lake State Park accounts for only a small percentage of the total real estate surrounding the lake. The state park, despite its small 107 acres, manages to offer excellent shoreline access along the lake's west bank and at the picnic and spillway areas south of Highway 279. The park has picnic areas, shelter houses, several parking areas, a beach, one boat ramp, and a small campground. Park headquarters are located at the campground on the west side of the lake. Wheelchair-accessible fishing is available at the spillway and the boat ramp located east of the bridge.

The lake can be divided into two halves, the north end and the south end, by the Highway 279 Bridge. If you like lily pads and weedy shorelines as I do, you'll love this lake. At the far north end, lily pad fields cover entire portions of the lake, and boat passage is possible only by narrow channels through the pads. The water color is a light tea stain, but Jackson is a relatively clear lake for such an older impoundment, with visibility as much as 2 to 3 feet in summer.

The fishing: I found some pretty good bass fishing at Jackson Lake, especially at dusk in summer, when bass would move into the banks and feed. While most of the bass average 12 to 14 inches, some whoppers do show up in spring. Because the lake is shallow, bass fishing can begin as early as late February if conditions are right. Fish tight against the shoreline cover, weeds, and fallen timber north of the Highway 279 Bridge with chartreuse spinner baits, plastics, tubes, and jigs. In the hot summer, fish evenings with buzz, spinner baits, and Rapalas around pads and against the weedy shoreline. This type of fishing will bring some excitement to your night. There are good populations of bass at Jackson, and most are hiding under the shade of lily pads.

There are plenty of channel cats, but they run small and fishing pressure is heavy. Fishing anywhere along the west shore seems to produce a few, as does fishing along the access road near the spillway.

Crappies are plentiful but small, with most averaging 8 to 10 inches. A minnow and a bobber is all you need. Look for crappies in early spring around old wooden boat docks, stickups, brush, and the spillway south of the Highway 279 Bridge.

Bluegills are everywhere, especially on any of the shallow, sloping west banks in late May to early June, when they seek spawning ground.

Special regulations: None; state game and fish laws apply. Outboards on Jackson Lake are limited to 10 hp.

Facilities/camping: Nearby, the town of Oak Hill has all the amenities. A small tackle shop and carryout is located just east of the boat ramp. The state park has 34 campsites, including sites close to the beach.

Additional information: Be sure to visit the remains of the old Jefferson iron furnace located on the hill east of the spillway.

Directions: Take Highway 279 west from Oak Hill approximately 3 miles.

113 Katharine Lake State Nature Preserve

Key species: Largemouth bass, bluegill, sunfish, channel catfish.

General description: Fishing in a wilderness setting.

Overview: Katharine Lake State Nature Preserve lies north of Jackson, encompassing 1,998 acres, and is open seven days a week from sunrise to sunset. The preserve boasts some of the largest and healthiest populations of the rare and endangered big leaf and umbrella magnolia trees in the state. At the center of the preserve is the pristine 60-acre Katharine Lake. Towered by sandstone cliffs, and lying at the bottom of a gorge, the lake was created by impounding Rock Run Creek. The lake has only a single, narrow entry point on its north shore. Access to the lake is limited and restricted to five boats per day on Friday, Saturday, Sunday, and Monday from April through October. A permit is required to access the lake, and reservations must be made in advance on the last Friday of each month between 8:00 a.m. and 4:00 p.m., by calling the preserve office at (740) 286-2487.

The lake is restricted to rowboats, canoes, and kayaks; no motors of any kind are permitted on the lake. Each boat must be carried down and back up a flight of steps 110 yards long from the parking area to the put-in/takeout point.

The fishing: Fishing is permitted on the lake, and anglers can expect good catches of largemouth bass and bluegills. The fish can be kept but cannot be cleaned on preserve property. A valid fishing license is required, and anglers must be in compliance with state game and fish laws. Bank fishing, picnicking, and swimming are not permitted.

Before entry to the lake, you must fill out a Lake Use Permit with your name, fishing license number if you are fishing, arrival and departure times, the purpose of your visit, and your watercraft registration number and type of boat. When you have finished fishing, you must list the total number of fish caught and kept and their species.

There are a number of other restrictions at Katharine Lake; all are intended to preserve the pristine condition of the lake and to leave it in such a condition that the next visitor will experience the same wilderness fishing as the previous visitor.

Katharine Lake offers the not-so-common experience of fishing in a wilderness setting, on a pristine lake in Ohio.

Special regulations: The following are prohibited: motorized watercraft, including electric motors; fishing with minnows; bank fishing; and cleaning fish on preserve

Katharine Lake is in a wilderness setting on a state nature preserve that permits fishing but requires anglers to make reservations.

property. Any violation of lake rules will result in suspension of lake use for one year. Notify the preserve manager of cancellations at least 24 hours in advance.

Facilities/camping: Katharine Lake has no facilities. Camping is not permitted in the preserve area. The nearby town of Jackson has all the amenities.

Additional information: The preserve has three nature trails at the south entrance. Part of the preserve is set aside as a scientific nature preserve.

Directions: Take U.S. 35 Highway north of Jackson, then head west on Rock Run Road. To access the south side and the nature trails, take Beaver Pike west of Jackson, then go north on Katharine Lake Road.

114 Lake Alma

Key species: Bass, bluegill, redear sunfish, channel catfish, trout.

General description: Small, weedy lake with excellent bass angling. Electric motors only.

Overview: Lake Alma is a beautiful little lake of only 60 acres that was originally built in 1903 as an amusement park, then later used as a water supply reservoir by the town of Wellston. Shaped like a donut with an island in the center, Lake Alma State Park has a beach, campgrounds, picnic areas, shelters, weekend boat rental, a small boat ramp, and a wheelchair-accessible fishing pier. The park road completely surrounds the lake, offering good shoreline access. There is a walking bridge to the island, which I estimate to be 5 acres and from which you can fish. The lake is weedy along the edges, making it difficult to fish from shoreline. White amur have been introduced to help control the weed growth. Lake Alma is very clear, with a slight tea stain.

The fishing: Bass angling is pretty good at Lake Alma for those who know its secrets. Averaging only 8 to 10 feet at its deepest, Alma is surrounded by lily pads. The plants may be a nuisance to some, but not to the bass angler because during summer that is where the fish hide. Lizards, worms, Rapalas, and spinner baits fished along and into the weed edges are how some pretty good bass are taken. Also fish around the island and off the west roadway and the steep bank on the south shore. The footbridge that connects the island is also good for bluegill and bass. Fishing surveys conducted by the Division of Wildlife have indicated good numbers of 1- to 4-pound bass in Lake Alma.

Bluegill and redear fishing are pretty good, with hand-size fish fairly common. For panfish, fish off the edge of the lily pads west of the beach and around the boat ramp and the footbridge. Also fish Little Raccoon Creek at the small picnic area west of the park, below Highway 349.

Channel cat fishing is only fair here, but the Division of Wildlife does keep the lake well stocked with channels, at 25 fish per acre.

Trout are stocked each October. The lake receives 750 10- to 12-inch rainbows.

Special regulations: Electric motors only.

Facilities/camping: There are full facilities at the nearby town of Wellston. Camping is available at the state park, with 83 campsites and 1 cabin.

Additional information: Nearby Lake Rupert is a top fishing spot.

Directions: Take Highway 349 east out of Wellston.

115 Lake Hope

Key species: Largemouth bass, bluegill, channel catfish, saugeye.

General description: An excellent small lake that receives little fishing pressure. Electric motors only.

Overview: Lake Hope, located in the heart of Zaleski State Forest, was at one time a dead lake due to runoff from iron mines located in the forest and throughout the southeastern Ohio hill country. In the mid- to late 1800s, mining iron ore from the sandstone bedrock was one of the nation's leading industries in high-grade iron. Iron furnaces burned 24 hours a day, stripping the hills of timber and leaving a lasting

Lake Hope is a small, remote lake tucked away in the hills of southeastern Ohio.

impression on the landscape. Seepage from the local mines caused many of the area streams to become fishless well into the 1970s. Efforts to stop the seeps and leaks have paid off, and fish began returning to the streams in the 1980s, resulting in an excellent fishery at Lake Hope today.

Lake Hope State Park was created in 1949, and many of the old park structures are still in use and well maintained, including the beach house, boat rental, and shelter. Sadly, in 2006 the old lodge built in 1949 from timber harvested from the forest caught fire and burned to the ground. The original building plans were recovered in the basement after the fire, still intact, and plans are under way to reconstruct the lodge the way it was. It should be completed by 2010. Lake Hope State Park has cabins, campgrounds, hiking trails, a beach, boat rental, a boat ramp, and a small lodge.

The fishing: Lake Hope and the surrounding Zaleski State Forest is one of my favorite places in Ohio. The remoteness and surrounding forest give the lake the feel of a place a thousand miles from nowhere. Lake Hope is an excellent little lake, covering only 120 acres. But it is perhaps the most beautiful 120 acres in all of Ohio. The bass don't grow large here, but 3- to 4-pounders are fairly numerous and a bunch of bass from 12 to 14 inches inhabit nearly inch of the lake. Because of the electric motor restriction, and its out-of-the-way location, Lake

Hope is seldom fished seriously. Most fishing is done by shoreline tourists and campers, whose primary reason for being here is to relax and enjoy the scenery.

There is no secret to catching bass at Lake Hope. Fish buzz baits and spinner baits along and into the lily pads. Use plastics and crank baits against shoreline structure and around the creek channel at the lake's northeast arm. Lake Hope is a good early spring lake, but good bass fishing is had all year long. In spring concentrate in the shallower north end. The water is clear, with a slight tint of green. You can see bass chasing minnows any time of day in summer. The lake averages about 10 feet, with some 20-foot water at the south end.

There are some good bluegills here, too, and they get as big as they can get in a lake this size. If you want to see some of them, feed the fish at the boat rental dock.

There are plenty of channel cats at Lake Hope, with most running from 12 to 15 inches.

Saugeyes are also present. The Division of Wildlife began stocking saugeyes in 2001. They don't seem to get a lot of attention, but again, most fishers who fish Lake Hope are shoreline anglers fishing for anything that bites.

There is not an abundance of shoreline access; most is limited to the lake's east side from Highway 278, at the south end where the beach and shelter house are located, and at the very tip of the northeastern arm. The best way to fish Lake Hope is by boat.

Lake Hope is a wonderful place to visit and fish when you are contemplating some of life's big decisions. It is also an excellent place to combine a cast-and-blast outing, as the hills in Zaleski Forest offer some of Ohio's best deer and turkey hunting.

Special regulations: Electric motors only.

Facilities/camping: Lake Hope State Park offers 67 cabins and 192 campsites. Facilities are far and few, so bring it with you. The closest town is McArthur, with all the small town amenities.

Additional information: Be sure to visit the Hope Furnace and hike to the old Moonville Railroad Tunnel located in Zaleski State Forest on Hope-Moonville Road.

Directions: Take Highway 278 north out of the town of Zaleski. To get to the town of Zaleski, take Highway 677 north from US 50, east of McArthur.

116 Lake Logan

Key species: Channel and shovelhead catfish, largemouth bass, saugeye, bluegill, crappie.

General description: Logan has become a great catfish lake.

Overview: Impounded in 1955, Lake Logan covers 400 acres, with an average depth between 10 and 20 feet. Lake Logan State Park is only 318 acres, and most of the recreation facilities are located on the lake's northern shore. The park provides two boat ramps, shelter houses, dock space, a beach, a boat rental, and a wheelchair-accessible pier. Residential housing populates a large portion of the shoreline, and several small bed-and-breakfast and lodging establishments are located along the lake's shores. Popular with local residents from the nearby town of Logan, fishing pressure is heavy. There was a time when Logan was the bass, catfish, and saugeye capital of Ohio, holding several state record fish.

The fishing: Bass fishing on Logan starts out in early April and continues through to the end of May or early June. There have been some 8-pounders caught, but 3 to 4 pounds is considered a good one nowadays. Anglers pound shoreline cover on the lake's east side above the beach toward the dam with spinner baits, motor oil plastics, and Rapalas and use buzz baits around the weed beds in late summer. Most of the bass caught are small.

Saugeye fishing still continues at Logan, and some respectable catches start to show up in late November around the bridge at the boat rental. The beach area also produces some fine catches beginning in mid-February through March; anglers use jigs and twister tail grubs in green or brown with orange tails. In summer saugeyes are located over deep structure and along riprap at the dam and causeway. Saugeye will also wash over the dam during periods of high water, and there is a parking area below the dam where anglers access some minor tailwater fishing.

Cat fishing is impressive at Logan. In one fishing season, 30-, 40-, and 50-pound shovelheads will be caught. Most fishing is done at night, but daytime fishing is also productive. The serious cat fishing is done west of the beach, off the fishing piers near the headwaters. It's a marshy, shallow mudflats-type area, usually choked with weeds in late summer, but the cats seem to love it. Plenty of nice 6- to 7-pound channel cats turn up. For flatheads, use live shad; channels like night crawlers, chicken livers, and special dough-ball mixes.

Crappies can be caught in early spring around shoreline brush, stickups, and boat docks using minnows and a bobber.

Bluegills and sunfish are overly abundant, but small, and can be found everywhere.

Special regulations: There is a 10-hp limit.

Facilities/camping: There are a boat rental and bait shop at the main boat ramp. Amenities can be found in the nearby town of Logan. There is no public camping at the lake. There are numerous bed-and-breakfasts and cottages in the area.

Additional information: Hocking Hills State Park is located approximately 12 miles south of Lake Logan. It offers fishing for trout at Rose Lake. Hocking River is also nearby. The section between Logan and Rock Bridge has some of the state's best smallmouth fishing.

Directions: Lake Logan is located just west of the town of Logan on Highway 664.

117 Lake Rupert (Wellston City Reservoir)

Key species: Largemouth bass, crappie, bluegill, saugeye, walleye, channel catfish.

General description: A good lake for just about everything that swims.

Overview: Lake Rupert is the kind of lake you wish was in your neck of the woods. It has weedy shallows, steep banks, shoreline structure, fish attractors, and an excellent population of game fish, with some wall-hanger bass, too. Rupert is located out in the middle of nowhere; the only facility is a single portable restroom at the boat ramp. There are several parking areas, and some are a long walk to the shoreline. Lake Rupert, also called the Wellston City Reservoir, is 322 acres big. It offers a boat ramp and several gravel parking areas off Highway 683 on the lake's west side, from which shoreline access is good. Along the lake's east side, access is gained at the end of two township roads, both of which involve a moderate walk to the shoreline. Upon my visit, those areas were trashy with some vandalism on signs posting size restrictions. The lake is surrounded by the Wellston Wildlife Area, which offers public hunting. On the lake's west side and near the dam, the shoreline is shallow, offering wading anglers a crack at some of the lake's excellent bass fishing.

The fishing: Although many small bass are eager biters at Rupert, come spring and fall some of the bigger bass start to show up. There are some giants at Rupert, with a few bass reaching upwards of 8 pounds. Watermelon seed lizards, spinner baits, and plastics fished along the weed edges and grassy points near the dam, at the beaver huts, and along the slips and shoreline structure on the lake's deeper east side account for the bulk of the bass caught. The creek channel along the lake's upper east side hugs the shore for a considerable distance, and several Christmas tree attractors have been placed along that shoreline. There are a couple of large coves; fish the shoreline structure, brush, and trees in those coves. Also fish the many grassy points and riprap along the dam and roadway.

Crappies are especially good at Rupert. The crappie fishing begins in late March and lasts through April, with crappies ranging around 10 inches. Fish the beaver huts, deep brush, shoreline structure, and fish attractors with minnows and a bobber.

Channel cat fishing is excellent, with most anglers fishing from the parking areas at the boat ramp and at the end of Bay Road on the lake's east side, from which access to a long narrow cove can be had. Chicken livers are good, but one angler told me that if you can get them, creek chubs are best. Channels upwards of 10 pounds are caught from Rupert.

Bluegills can be had just about anywhere along the shoreline; good hand-size 'gills are abundant.

Saugeyes are in good numbers. Stocking began in 1991 to replace the walleyes that were previously stocked. If any walleyes still exist, they should be whoppers by now. Fish the riprap along the main road and the dam, on the old roadbeds, and at the rock and gravel points with small crank baits. Fishing for saugeyes is always better in late evening and at night.

Access to the dam is gained from a parking area located off Highway 93, where some minor tailwater fishing is available. Access to Little Raccoon Creek is at the bridge that crosses the creek at the lake's north end.

Special regulations: All bass between 12 and 15 inches must be released. The lake is limited to 10-hp motors.

Facilities/camping: No camping or facilities are available at Lake Rupert. A gas and convenience store is located at the intersection of Highway 93 and Highway 683, south of the lake. Nearby Wellston has all the amenities. Camping is available at nearby Lake Alma State Park, which has 83 campsites.

Additional information: Lake Alma State Park is located approximately 3 miles south on Highway 349

Directions: Take Highway 93 north 5 miles from Wellston, turn west on Highway 683.

118 Lake Snowden

Key species: Largemouth bass, bluegill, redear sunfish, crappie, saugeye, yellow perch, channel catfish, flathead catfish.

General description: Primarily known as a bass lake, a reputation that is well deserved.

Overview: Lake Snowden is a public lake managed by Hocking College, which is located in Nelsonville. The lake covers 136 acres and was constructed in 1963. As part of the wildlife-related curriculum that Hocking offers, the college maintains a small fish hatchery below the dam, primarily raising largemouth bass from brood stock taken from the lake. The college maintains a very spacious campground, camp store, beach, boat rental, and boat ramp. The lake has limited shoreline access, restricted to the south end at the main entry and campground. Snowden is best fished from a boat.

The fishing: Bass fishing begins in early April at Snowden. It continues well into June and picks up again in September and October. Fish the points, coves, and shoreline cover with white buzz baits, spinner baits, lizards, and plastics. There are fish attractors and treetops at various locations along the shore; there is also heavy weed growth in most coves. The majority of bass are picked up by fishing the shoreline and off the weed edges in summer. Snowden has a shallow, sloping shoreline, with an average lake depth of 13 feet. Near the dam the water will reach 35 feet. Good bass will average 3 to 4 pounds, with a few reaching into the 6-pound-plus range. Sampling by the college has shown Snowden to contain a high density of 4-pound bass and bass within the protective slot-length limit of 12 to 15 inches.

Channel catfish are popular at Snowden; numerous catfish tournaments are held at the lake in summer. Channel cats up to 24 inches are caught, with an occasional large flathead taken. Most anglers fish off the shoreline near the main entry with cut bait, chicken livers, chubs, and night crawlers.

Saugeyes are also present, originally stocked in 1994 and again in 2004. Only a few anglers target the saugeyes, but some respectable saugeyes have turned up. Most saugeye fishing is done near the dam in the deeper water, along the riprap, and in the deep holes and creek channels. Yellow perch also turn up at these same locations.

Bluegill and sunfish can be caught just about anywhere along the shoreline; a lot of smaller fish turn up. Try the downed trees and fish structures south of the boat ramp.

Some good crappies up to 12 inches also come from the lake in spring. Fish the deeper shoreline brush along the creek channels across from the spillway with jigs and minnows.

Special regulations: Unlimited horsepower, idle speed only. Bass between 12 and 15 inches must be released.

Facilities/camping: There is a campground with 137 sites. The campground may or may not be open in the future depending on circumstances surrounding the possible sale of the property. A camp store is at the main entry. Various facilities, gas, beverages, food, and so on can be obtained along Highway 32.

Additional information: A private concern has expressed interest in purchasing the property surrounding Lake Snowden from Hocking College. If the college approves the purchase, access to the lake may be restricted in the future.

Directions: Take Highway 50/32 west from Athens approximately 7 miles. Lake Snowden is on the north side of the road.

119 Lake White

Key species: Largemouth, spotted, and smallmouth bass; rock bass; crappie; bluegill; channel catfish; saugeye; occasionally muskie.

General description: One of the best lakes in Ohio to catch feisty spotted bass.

Overview: Lake White was created during the Depression years by the Works Progress Administration (WPA). Once completed in August of 1935, it took only one night of a drenching thunderstorm to fill the 337-acre lake. Most of the property surrounding the lake at the time of construction was privately owned, thus the lakeshore today is populated with red and white houses and numerous private boat docks.

Lake White is a public resort lake. The original intent of the first property owners, Lake White, Inc., was to have all lakeside homes resemble houses along the Italian Riviera. Stipulations were placed on property deeds that required all homes built on the lake or surrounding hillsides to be white with a red roof, and they are.

Lake White was name after Ohio Governor George White and was one of the original state parks created in 1949 with the creation of the Division of Parks and

Recreation. Although Lake White State Park occupies only 92 acres on the lake's southeast corner, it has the only public boat ramp on the lake, two shelter houses, picnic areas, a small beach, and a small camping area. Thanks to a recent additional land purchase by the Division of Wildlife, the park now includes the tailwaters area below the dam.

Because private property surrounds the lake, little shoreline access is available to anglers; Lake White is best fished from a boat.

The fishing: Lake White has some pretty fair bass fishing, with a mixture of both largemouth and spotted bass and every so often some smallmouth bass. The bass are widely distributed, with no one place any better than another. Fish the shoreline cover, boat docks, willows, and lily pad edges at the west end with white spinner baits, plastics, and buzz baits. The lake has many points; most are rock or covered with riprap. The two northernmost points in the bend of the lake are top producers. The "swage" between the points is where most of the lake's smallmouth come from. Most largemouth average 12 to 14 inches; a 5-pounder is considered a very good catch. Some 2- to 3-pound smallies have been taken, but expect much smaller. Spotted bass averaging 11 to 13 inches are caught from the riprap along the dam and any shoreline cover in the lake's east end with small crank baits and plastics. A state record spotted bass of 5.25 pounds was taken from Lake White in 1976.

Saugeye fishing is good at the lake, with most averaging 16 to 20 inches. Some very nice ones up to 26 inches have been caught on small crank baits, jigs and minnows, and jigs and curly tail grubs. Cast, drift, or slow troll all the main lake points, most of which consist of rock or gravel. Work the flats in front of the Lake White Club restaurant and the flats and points along Valley Drive. Fishing is productive all year long, but the better months are February, March, April, October, and November. Fishing below the dam right after high-water releases in early spring will also supply a nice stringer of saugeyes.

Crappies are plentiful but run small; occasionally a crappie fisher will run into a school of 11- to 12-inch fish. Use minnows and small minnow-tipped jigs and vary your depth until you find fish. Most fishing is done in early spring, but crappies can be found in summer as well. Fish the shoreline brush, boat docks, and willows at the far-west end of the lake from mid-April through May.

Lake White has plenty of bluegills, but they run small. They can be caught with the usual wax worms and red worms from shore.

Channel fishing is popular here and they range from 12 to 24 inches. In fact, channels up to 24 inches are frequently caught. Most fishing is done at night along the old creek channel on the west end of the lake using chicken livers and night crawlers. If possible, fish for catfish during periods of rising water. There is very little shoreline access due to private property, but anglers can fish from pulloffs near the dam off Highway 552, just east of the junction of Highway 220 and Highway 552, and from the state park.

Muskies are an interesting study at Lake White. Stocked during the 1960s and 1970s, Lake White is perhaps one of the few impoundments in Ohio where muskies may actually reproduce. Locals tell me that muskies do indeed reproduce here. Credible eyewitness accounts have seen pairs of muskies in early spring in the headwaters at Pee Pee Creek. This is entirely possible, since it lies within the same lower Scioto River drainage as Scioto Brush Creek and Sunfish Creek, two of the state's best natural muskie streams. Pee Pee Creek is geographically the next watershed east of Sunfish Creek. This does not translate in a viable muskie fishery at Lake White, but the fact that every couple of years someone catches a 30- to 36-inch muskie from the lake 30 years after it was last stocked does raise some interesting questions.

Special regulations: None; state game and fish laws apply. Lake White is unlimited horsepower.

Facilities/camping: The town of Waverly is approximately 2 miles north and has all the amenities. Fuel can be purchased on the water at Bill's Bait House at the east end of the lake. Camping is available at the state park, which has 10 campsites.

Additional information: The old Lake White Club, established in 1938, is still serving dinner.

Directions: Take Highway 104 2 miles south of Waverly.

120 Little Muskingum River

The Little Muskingum River is an Ohio River tributary that makes its confluence with the Ohio River just north of the little town of Reno, east of Marietta. The Little Muskingum starts in central Monroe County, south of the town of Woodsfield, but doesn't become much of a stream until its junction with Clear Fork at the Knowlton Bridge Park. The Little Muskingum has five covered bridges on it. Highway 26, which follows along the Little Muskingum for most of its course, is known as the Covered Bridge National Scenic Highway.

The Little Muskingum and its tributaries have six public access sites, each with a small campground and restrooms, primarily intended as canoe access points for floating the stream. However, the Little Muskingum offers fishing for smallmouth bass, channel catfish, and sunfish and is one of only a handful of natural muskie streams in the state.

The Muskingum is a naturally turbid stream, but it does offer spectacular scenery and is one of the few streams that can be canoed and fished for any length in southeastern Ohio. Most of the stream is located within the boundaries of the Wayne National Forest, Athens Ranger District.

Smallmouth, though not in big numbers, can be taken on small crawdad-colored crank baits, foxtail Mepps spinners, and pumpkinseed tubes. Fish current areas at the head and tail of each pool, especially around any rocks or gravel formations.

Channel cats are pretty common and nice ones reach from 12 to 18 inches. Night crawlers, minnows, and sometimes spinners will get them. You can find channels at just about at any location in the stream, including the shallow pools and riffles.

Sunfish are common as well. You will find them under any tree, rock, or logjam.

Perhaps the most interesting fishing on the Little Muskingum is a chance encounter with a muskie. Muskies don't get overly large in streams; if you caught a 34-inch fish, you'd have a good one. Muskies will take large silver and gold foil crank baits; chartreuse spinner baits and brightly colored bucktails will also encourage a few muskies into following the bait back to the boat. Look for muskies in the largest, deepest pools on the stream. Most of the time big logs and logjams along deep banks will hold muskies, but don't discount boulders, mud cliffs, shallows, and current areas. Muskies can be anywhere.

River otters were introduced into the Little Muskingum in the early 1990s. Those who quietly float the river can on occasion catch a glimpse of this elusive furbearer.

The Wayne National Forest has stream access and camping at the following recreation sites: Ring Mill; Lamping Homestead, which has a 4-acre pond; Haught Run; Hune Bridge; and Lane Farm. The Lane Farm canoe access is the last downstream takeout location on the Little Muskingum that is still within Wayne National Forest. Access is also at the Knowlton Covered Bridge roadside park.

121 Monroe Lake

Monroe Lake is an absolutely beautiful and secluded small lake of only 39 acres. Cattails and old overhanging trees scream, "Fish me!" A single boat ramp, a dock, and a small footbridge located at the end of Township Road T-1001, out of the small town of Miltonsburg, are all there is here.

Monroe Lake was drained in 2001. Improvements were made to the boat ramp, and fish structures were added to the lake. The lake was then restocked in 2003.

Primitive camping is permitted at the lake. There is some limited shoreline access at the ramp in the way of old fishers' trails that lead around the lake.

Monroe is a fishy-looking body of water with good visibility. It contains largemouth bass, sunfish, and channel catfish. There have been some limited trout stocking in the past; check the updated trout-stocking report posted by the Division of Wildlife to see if Monroe Lake is currently on the list (www.ohiodnr.com/wildlife).

Heavy vegetation by way of lily pads and coontail is present at the boat ramp and in the creek arms. The shoreline cover consists of old fallen trees, snags, and brush. The Division of Wildlife has anchored a small number of fish attractors, called cribs, on the north side of the lake.

Bass up to 3 pounds have been taken off the shoreline cover with plastic night crawlers and chartreuse spinner baits. Fish both banks and the weed edges for bass. Sunfish are caught from the shoreline brush and along the edges of the lily pads. The only open water available for channel cat fishing from shore is at the dam. Channels reach 15 to 18 inches.

Monroe Lake is limited to 10 hp, and a special 15-inch minimum size limit on bass has been implemented.

Monroe Lake is located approximately 11 miles south of Barnesville off Highway 145 at Miltonsburg.

Robby Robinson caught this 40-pound flathead catfish while fishing at night on a Muskingum watershed lake. He used goldfish for bait. Photo by Robby Robinson

122 Muskingum River

The historic Muskingum River played a vital part in Ohio's early history. The Muskingum gets its start at the confluence of the Walhonding and Tuscarawas Rivers and stretches 112 miles. At one time, vast herds of elk and bison roamed its lower valleys. Old river towns, dating back to the late 1700s, were established along its banks. Zanesville was established in 1797, Marietta in 1788. In the late 1820s plans were made to create a system of locks and dams on the Muskingum. Later, during the late 1880s, the U.S. Army Corps of Engineers began making improvements on the old locks. Of the 11 dams that were constructed on the Muskingum, the old Ellis Lock and Dam is the farthest upstream. Constructed in 1904, it is 6 river miles upstream from Zanesville and is the only lock on the river that is not operational. Plans have been made to reconstruct the Ellis Lock, but as yet no financing has been approved for the reconstruction. If it were replaced, then it would be possible to take a boat from Coshocton, where the river begins, to Marietta. Most of the old locks were originally constructed between the 1830s and 1850s; the earliest was the McConnelsville Lock, constructed in 1830.

The Muskingum is fished in many ways. Anglers have a shot at smallmouth, largemouth, and spotted bass, sheepshead, hybrid stripers, stripers, white bass, rock bass, carp, bluegills, sunfish, crappies, longnose gar, saugeyes, sauger, walleye, muskie, channel cats, and some very large shovelhead (flathead) catfish. That said, most anglers contend that the quality fishing on the Muskingum is at the tailwaters of the old dams of which there are 10.

The old Ellis Lock and Dam offers anglers a shot at smallmouth and some heavy shovelhead catfish. Best fished from a boat, channel catfish, saugeyes, and sheepsheads are also abundant in the churning white water below the old dam. Ellis Lock and Dam, known as #11, is located 6 miles north of Zanesville, at the end of Ellis Dam Road. As part of the Ohio State Park System, it offers a boat ramp and 20 nonelectric campsites. It is one of the most remote of the lock and dams, thus perhaps the most beautiful too.

Good fishing is also below the Zanesville Lock and Dam, #10. Saugeyes from Dillon Lake wash into the river and provide an early spring and fall fishery. Big shovelhead catfish also haunt the waters below #10, and 40- to 50-pound shovelheads are caught there every year. Most anglers use shad for bait, but chicken livers, night crawlers, and bluegills work well too.

In the main river fish the rock bars and gravel islands for smallmouth; anywhere along the main river is good for catfish. Nice walleyes and sauger are taken from below the Lowell Dam and the Devola Lock and Dam, which is the first dam up the Muskingum from the Ohio River that is still intact. Root wads, logjams, and the tributaries are all places you shouldn't overlook; each can contain a variety of fish, from flathead to crappies. From the tailwaters at Lowell Dam, several muskies have been taken.

All dams can be accessed to some extent from nearby roads. To reach some of the tailwaters, however, is a rather risky venture across private property, down steep hillsides, and around dangerous waters. You have to assess the risk and see if it's

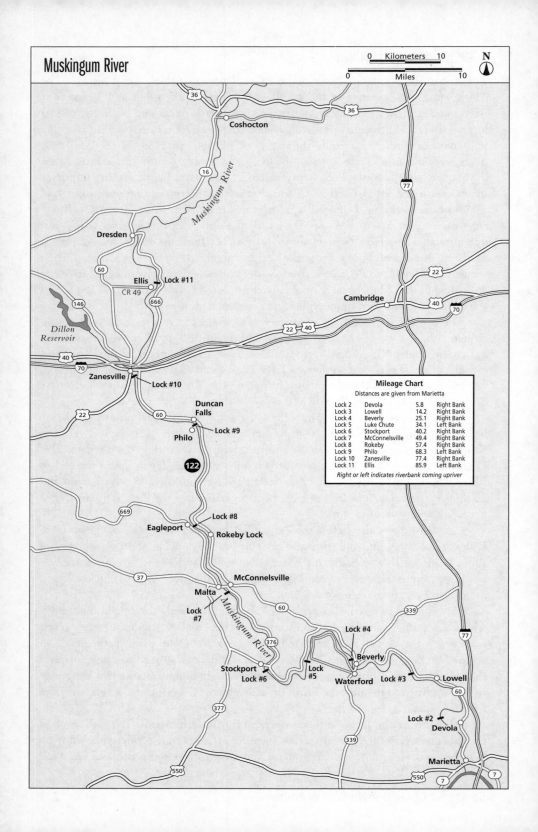

Muskingum River

0 Kilometers 10

0 Miles 10

N

36

Coshocton

36

16

Muskingum River

Dresden

60

Ellis — Lock #11
CR 49

666

146

Dillon Reservoir

Cambridge

22

22 40

40

70

40

70

Zanesville — Lock #10

22

Duncan Falls

60

Lock #9

Philo

122

669

Lock #8

Eagleport

Rokeby Lock

37

McConnelsville

Malta

Lock #7

60

Muskingum River

376

Lock #4

Beverly

Stockport

Lock #6

Lock #5

Waterford

Lock #3

Lowell

60

339

77

Lock #2

Devola

377

339

Marietta

7

550

550

7

Mileage Chart

Distances are given from Marietta

Lock	Location	Miles	Bank
Lock 2	Devola	5.8	Right Bank
Lock 3	Lowell	14.2	Right Bank
Lock 4	Beverly	25.1	Right Bank
Lock 5	Luke Chute	34.1	Left Bank
Lock 6	Stockport	40.2	Right Bank
Lock 7	McConnelsville	49.4	Right Bank
Lock 8	Rokeby	57.4	Right Bank
Lock 9	Philo	68.3	Left Bank
Lock 10	Zanesville	77.4	Right Bank
Lock 11	Ellis	85.9	Left Bank

Right or left indicates riverbank coming upriver

Anglers lock through the old dam to reach the productive tailwater below.

worth it. All tailwaters can be accessed safely by boat. The dams at Duncan Falls, Beverly, and Lowell can easily be accessed from the shoreline and provide great fishing for everything.

There are 11 campgrounds along the Muskingum; most are primitive campsites for through-boaters only. Five campgrounds are accessible by car; of those, only two are public: Ellis and Luke Chute Lock and Dam #5. Luke Chute is located south of Stockport, and there is no charge for camping there.

The Muskingum River is a designated water trail state park. There are 16 boat ramps from Coshocton to Marietta, plus an additional eight carry-in access points where you can a launch a canoe or kayak.

The boat ramps along the Muskingum River include the following: Indian Acres at Marietta, Beverly Lock and Dam, Luke Chute Lock and Dam (has public camping areas accessible by car), Stockport Lock and Dam, River's Edge Campground, McConnelsville boat ramp and Wharf Park, Malta ramp, Muskingum River Campgrounds, Green Acres Campground, Putnam Landing in south Zanesville, Riverside Park in Zanesville, Kirkbride Boating Company, Ellis Lock and Dam (has public camping areas accessible by car), Dresden Ramp, Coshocton City Access, and at the Baird Concrete access. Carry-in access is at every location except the Zanesville Lock and Dam.

123 New Lexington Reservoir

Key species: Largemouth bass, bluegill, channel catfish, trout.

General description: A small, clear lake with trout fishing in spring.

Overview: A small reservoir of only 26 acres, New Lexington Reservoir serves as the water supply for New Lexington. Just off Highway 13, north of town, turn north on Palmer Road to reach the small gravel boat ramp and shoreline access on the lake's west side. Just before Palmer Road there is a blue metal sign that reads NEW LEXINGTON WATER PLANT. Turning east at that sign will take you to the dam and spillway. The water is very clear with gentle-sloping clay and gravel shoreline; weed growth is present during the summer. Shoreline cover consists of downed trees, slips, and brush along the lake's east bank. The water level fluctuates due to demand.

The fishing: Small bass are present in good numbers, with a few individuals reaching 3 to 5 pounds caught each spring. Fish the east shore cover with tubes and spinner baits. Small bass are numerous, and you can catch a boatload of them. Channel cats are stocked every other year and provide some summer nighttime fishing for channels reaching 12 to 17 inches. Bluegills are plentiful, but small.

The Division of Wildlife stocks trout into New Lexington Reservoir each spring, as long as water levels are acceptable. Some trout left over from the spring stocking are caught during the summer at the spillway with green Power Bait.

Additional fishing can be had at the New Lexington Dam Reservoir, which resembles a large farm pond, located off Clayton Township Road 149. You can also fish the New Lexington Reservoir #2, located at the end of Township Road 150 off Clayton Township Road 149. Both provide angling for bass, catfish, and bluegill.

Special regulations: Electric motors only.

Facilities/camping: No facilities or camping. The town of New Lexington has everything.

Additional information: Take a look at the historic courthouse in New Lexington.

Directions: Take Highway 13 approximately 2 miles north of New Lexington and turn north onto Palmer Road.

124 Peabody Coal Lands

Peabody Coal Company has a few scattered tracts of old quarry ponds located in eastern Perry County. They range in size from 1 to 10 acres and are hard to find, but may be worth the search. I had to stop in a local gas station to inquire about directions. The ones I located were off an old hull road just past where James Town Road meets Highway 13, east of New Lexington. The ponds are deep, very deep, and extremely clear with a visibility approaching 8 feet. They cannot be easily fished from shore and require a canoe, kayak, or float tube. Most have some deep weed growth along the edges and a few scattered downed trees. One could readily observe small bass and bluegills around the old snags. While there are a number of ponds available for public fishing, several tracts appeared sold or leased. Heavy ATV use by locals is apparent, and some dumping is also evident. The ponds are stocked with bass and bluegills; channels or bullheads might also be present. The quarry ponds are located approximately 2 miles east of New Lexington on township and hull roads off Highways 13, 93, and 37.

125 Piedmont Lake

Key species: Muskie, saugeye, bluegill, rock bass, largemouth and smallmouth bass, crappie, channel and shovelhead catfish.

General description: Good bass and muskie fishing in one package, with horsepower restrictions.

Overview: The old Piedmont Lake was impounded in 1937 by the U.S. Army Corps of Engineers and is managed by the Muskingum Watershed Conservancy District. The lake covers 2,270 acres, is 9 miles long, and is almost 0.5 mile wide at its widest. It has only two boat ramps, both on the lake's south side; a full-service marina; a campground; and a motel. Shoreline access is poor; some limited access is available at the boat ramps and dam.

The lake is surrounded by forest, giving the appearance of being in the middle of nowhere. Because of a 10-hp limit, boating conflicts do not exist.

Piedmont reminds me of an old fish camp lake, the kind that used to be common in the northwoods during the 1950s and early 1960s and now can only be found at fly-in lakes in Canada. At the old marina, the dark pine and plywood walls support an array of mounted fish from the lake's glorious past, including the state record muskie that weighed over 55 pounds, caught by Joe Lykins in 1972. The marina serves as a fishers' headquarters of sorts, where they gather and tell their fish tales over hot cups of coffee. Places like this don't exist much anymore, but Piedmont is a lake that time has been kind to.

The fishing: Piedmont Lake is my favorite lake in southeastern Ohio. There is tranquility about the place; a slower pace of fishing and relaxation exist here. It is a quality lake as well; smallmouth, largemouth, catfish, crappies, saugeyes, and muskies are all in good supply and provide excellent angling for all who come and fish here. It is a rare lake of both quantity and quality.

Bass anglers here are as likely to catch a 4-pound smallmouth as they are a 4-pound largemouth; both inhabit basically the same cover and similar fishing techniques are applied in catching both.

Smallmouth fishing begins in late April, when the water temperature reaches 65°F to 66°F. Look for smallmouth around rocks, in the backs of coves, and in shoreline cover at the lower end of the lake between Jump Rock and a mile east of the Reynolds Road boat ramp. Also look for smallies off the riprap along the face of the dam. Fish the pockets and edges of emerging weeds with black, brown, or watermelon seed tubes, lizards, and worms. Jigs and pigs do well around the dam

The Ohio state record muskie is on display at the Piedmont Lake Marina. Caught in 1972, the fish weighed 55 pounds, 2 ounces.

area. Any cove with weeds in it holds bass. You should look for fresh water entering the lake from the head of the coves. Try to stay in 4 to 5 feet of water, working any wood and rock structures along the edges of the coves. Smallmouth fishing is good through May; many 2- to 3-pound smallmouth are caught, as are some in the 5-pound range. Later in summer, look for smallies at deeper big-rock shorelines in the middle portion of the lake along both shores. Estimates are that smallmouth make up 40 percent of the total bass population at Piedmont.

Largemouth are taken in basically the same way, by working the shoreline cover of downed tress, slips, and rocky shorelines with crank baits, spinner baits, tubes, plastic worms, and white buzz baits on summer evenings. Also work the deep outer weed edges and pockets in the coves. Always keep an eye out for big-rock and wood cover next to shore. Most bass fishing is done from Jump Rock to almost the headwaters. In summer there is some night fishing for bass with spinner baits. Bass fishing starts in late April and continues into September. Largemouth have been averaging 2 to 4 pounds, with a few approaching the 9-pound mark. Bass anglers are constantly encountering muskies while fishing, too.

Saugeyes have become routine catches at Piedmont, and anglers catch them in a variety of ways. Work shoreline rocks, points, gravel bars, and old roadbeds near the dam with small crank baits, Hot 'n Tots, worm harnesses, and jigs and minnows. Drift, cast, or slow troll the rocky shoreline. Most saugeye fishing is done from Smoke Hole Bay and north to the dam. Saugeye fishing is good all summer, but fish are on the bottom along the deeper rock shorelines and points. Many are picked up as incidental catches by anglers fishing for channel cats. Fishing for saugeyes picks up in September and continues all winter and through April. In March and April, anglers vertical jig for saugeyes with small silver spoons off the boat docks at the marina. From mid- to late April, a small run of saugeyes occurs up the headwaters into Stillwater Creek; fishing near the bridge where it crosses Stillwater, off County Road 100, with crank baits and jigs and minnows pays off.

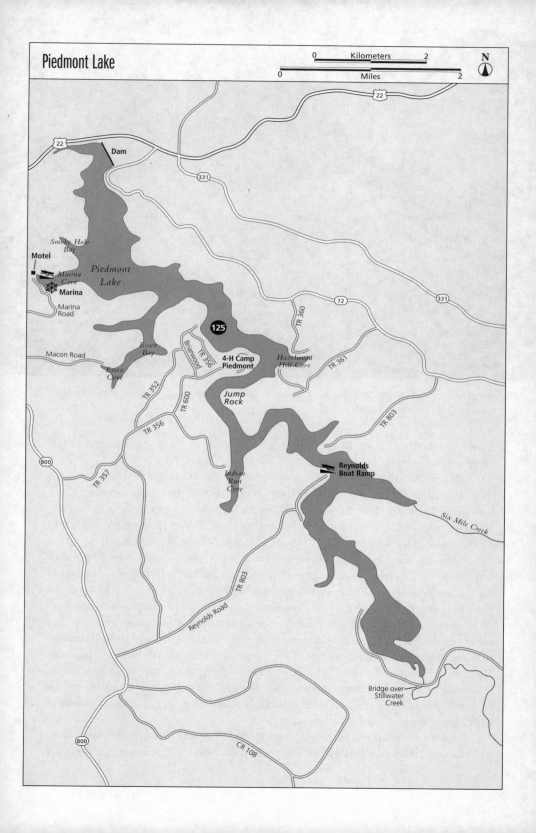

An elderly couple made this fine saugeye and catfish dinner for the author while he was working at Piedmont Lake.

Saugeyes usually average 16 to 22 inches, with a few in the 4- to 5-pound range; morning and evening are best.

Channel catfish are so common and widespread at Piedmont that you can catch them anywhere. That said, the best fishing is probably in the center, between Essex Bay and Jump Rock. Fish the bottom along the shoreline or any shallow coves, day or night, with chicken livers, shrimp, or night crawlers. The channels average 20 to 22 inches, with a few 6-pounders. Expect a saugeye or two with your catch.

There are some big shovelheads in Piedmont. Most average 25 to 30 pounds, but fish up to 50 pounds are caught occasionally. One such shovelhead was caught off the docks at the marina boat ramp a number of years ago. It was tied up at the dock for everyone to see for a few days, then turned loose. Nobody on the lake likes to keep those old shovelheads. They're set free more out of respect than for any other reason. The old shovelheads like the shallow water at night in these lakes, and those at Piedmont are no exception. Fish the areas north and south of the Reynolds Road boat ramp and toward the headwaters—along the shore or in the center, makes no difference. Sometimes those old shovelheads will get in water as shallow as 2 feet. Also fish Essex Bay for shovelheads. Use bluegills, goldfish, or shad and drift across the shallow flats at night.

Muskies are what put Piedmont on the map. The old state record muskie of 55 pounds and 2 ounces, caught from Indian Run Cove in 1972, still stands. There are those in Ohio muskie circles who think that record will never be broken. Muskie fishing starts early in Piedmont. In March muskie hunters are casting to the backs of coves and bays with bucktails, tandem spinners, and jerk baits. Old timber, logs, and rocks hold the fish during the spring. Fish muskies like you do bass; pound the shoreline cover in all the big coves from Six Mile Run to the dam. Some of the best early spring coves are the marina cove, Hazelwood Hill Cove, Essex Bay Run Cove, and Indian Run Cove. Casting for muskies is effective all season long. Cabbage, coontail, and pepper weed are prominent in all the coves, and muskies are either in the weeds or along the outer edge. June is when trolling takes off; again troll the weed edges where it drops off into deeper water. Most trolling in summer is done from Essex Bay and toward the dam, fishing for suspended muskies at 10 to 14 feet. Troll just off the shore on both sides and make a pass through the middle, repeatedly hitting all the lake points and old roadbeds. Another good place is off the point at the 4-H Camp Piedmont; work the point from the east side. Bagley's Shads in silver, chrome, chartreuse, and red and white are the best trolling bait. Bass-size crank baits worked against shoreline cover will also get a few muskies. In fall work Marina Cove and Smoke Hole Bay using Swim Whizz's and big tandem spinner baits.

Rock bass are in good numbers and quality at Piedmont and can be caught anywhere along the shore with anything. Rock bass up to 12 inches have been caught.

Bluegills are common, with the biggest ones caught during the spring spawn in late May and early June. Most are just good hand-size fish, but a few respectable bluegills over 12 inches are caught every spring along the shore. Wax worms are the preferred bait.

Special regulations: Piedmont Lake has a 10-hp limit. All black bass less than 12 inches must be released.

Facilities/camping: The Muskingum Watershed Conservancy District maintains a campground with 50 campsites. There is also a 6-room motel and 1 cabin available for rent. The marina has fuel, camping supplies, food, ice, marine supplies, and boat rental. It also serves as the campground and lodging headquarters (call 740-658-3735).

Additional information: The small town of Hendrysburg is south of Piedmont Lake. It is the birthplace of William Boyd, the motion picture and television actor who portrayed popular Western hero Hopalong Cassidy during the 1940s and 50s.

Directions: Take I-70 east of Cambridge 20 miles, then head north on Highway 800 for approximately 8 miles. The marina, campground, and boat ramp are at the end of Marina Road. The Reynolds Road boat ramp at the far-south end of the lake is located at the end of a rough township road, Township Road 803.

126 Pike Lake

Pike Lake is a small 13-acre lake located in Pike Lake State Park. The Civilian Conservation Corps (CCC) dug the lake by hand during the 1930s. Pike Lake State Park was created in 1949 when the Division of Parks and Recreation was formed. The park has swimming, hiking and bridle trails, small-boat rental, 12 cabins, and 80 campsites. There are bass, bluegill, and channel catfish in Pike Lake. Bass are small, averaging 12 inches, but some fish up to 16 inches are caught. Fish the weed edges around the small dock and dam and the steep east shoreline where there are fallen timbers and old logs along the shore. Small spinners and night crawlers catch the bass.

Bluegills are small, but a few hand-size ones do show up each year during the spawn in early June. To catch bluegills, try fishing red worms or Berkley Gulp beneath a bobber along the edge of the weeds.

Channel cats range in size from 12 to 15 inches; a few reach 4 to 5 pounds. To catch channels, fish off the shoreline along the dam in the evening with chicken livers or night crawlers.

The Kincaid State Fish Hatchery is approximately 6 miles southwest of Pike Lake State Park. This is where most of Ohio's muskies are raised in summer.

Pike Lake can best be reached by taking Pike Lake Road 6 miles south of Bainbridge. Signs are posted.

127 Pine Lake—Tar Hollow State Park

Pine Lake is located in Tar Hollow State Park and serves multifunctional recreational purposes. It has a fishing pond, swimming hole, and paddleboat dock. This small 15-acre pond was built in the 1930s by the Works Progress Administration (WPA) and eventually became a state park in 1949 with the creation of the Division of Parks and Recreation. The park has 99 campsites; hiking, biking, and bridle trails; picnic areas; shelter houses; small-boat rental; and a boat ramp. However, you don't need a boat to fish; the lake is easily fished from shore.

Every spring the lake holds a catfish outing for local schoolkids as part of an annual fishing program. A section of the lake is netted off, and 500 channel cats are released for the school-age children to try to catch. The catfish that don't get caught are set free to take their chances in the lake.

Channel catfish up to 4 pounds are caught from Pine Lake, but most are 15- to 16-inch fish. Just fish from the shore anywhere with night crawlers, and you'll catch a few.

Bluegills are of good size, with a few reaching hand size, 7 to 8 inches. A bobber and red worms or crickets will catch them.

There are some crappies, but they are small in numbers and size. They are usually seen in spring and are incidental catches by bluegill fishers.

You can catch bass from along the edge of the shoreline weeds with plastic night crawlers, small spinners, and small buzz baits at dusk. Most are only 12 inches long, but in 2005 a 5-pound lake record largemouth was caught. There's always hope.

About 500 rainbow trout are stocked into Pine Lake every fall; that is always popular.

Boats are permitted but limited to electric motors only. There is a 15-inch minimum size limit on bass.

Tar Hollow State Park is located far away from anywhere. The easiest way to get there is to take Highway 327 north off US 50, 10 miles east of Chillicothe.

128 Powelson Wildlife Area Lakes

Powelson Wildlife Area, located about 7 miles north of Zanesville off Highway 60, has about 15 old quarry ponds, most of which contain bass, bluegills, and channel cats. Several of the old ponds are shallow and covered with duckweed, while a few are deep and clear with some weed growth. Some of the ponds are a hike to get into. It's rough country here, so a good map is almost required, unless you know the area well. One pond that is easy to get to is on the east side of the area, off Highway 60 just before Powelson Road if you're coming in from Zanesville. Another 3-acre pond that is easy to access is located at the intersection of Ellis Dam Road and Beech Run. Several old ponds are located off Powelson Road; most are located down in hollows that require some effort to reach. Fishing quality varies with each pond; whether a pond is worth the effort or not is for you to determine. Be aware that Powelson Wildlife Area is full of deer and turkey and is heavily hunted during the deer gun season.

129 Raccoon Creek County Park (Gallia County)

Key species: Smallmouth, sunfish, channel catfish, rock bass.

General description: An 800-acre county park with stream fishing and camping.

Overview: Raccoon Creek County Park, located west of Gallipolis, offers some pleasant, quiet, small-stream fishing on a shady, remote creek in central Gallia County. The county park has numerous ball fields, picnic areas, several shelter houses, restrooms, hiking trails, and a small primitive campground right on the stream.

The fishing: Though fishing is not the primary use for this park, it does offer public access to a couple of miles of Upper Raccoon Creek. Fishing in the main park itself is difficult due to streamside brush, but a number of picnic areas in the main park are on the stream's banks. The best stream access is gained by following County Road 28 north of the main park. Park property exists along most of the stream, except where the stream veers away from the road—this is private property. Access is at a couple of roadside pulloffs, at trailhead parking areas along the county road, at the campground, and at the parking area at the bridge where the county road meets Highway 141 at the end of park property. The stream north of the park has a couple of inviting shallow riffles and deep pools where a smallmouth could be waiting. The stream, for the most part, is open, but there are some old snags and washed-out stumps along the stream's course. Perhaps the best way to fish it is to drop a canoe or kayak in at the bridge on Highway 141 and drift down to the main park, or beyond to the bridge on Highway 775, which is still on park property. It is an approximately 3- to 4-mile float from bridge to bridge.

Special regulations: None; state fish and game laws apply.

Facilities/camping: A small primitive park campground is located along the stream off County Road 28, north of the main park. Ice and beverages are available at the main park office.

Additional information: There are several natural areas and scenic hiking trails on the park property.

Directions: Take Highway 141 approximately 9 miles west of Gallipolis to Dan Jones Road (CR 28).

130 Rose Lake—Hocking Hills State Park

The 2 million visitors a year at Hocking Hills State Park do not come to fish 17-acre Rose Lake; they come to view the magnificent sandstone cliffs, scenic waterfalls, and caves that make this place one of Ohio's crown jewels. Rose Lake was originally intended as and serves as the park's water source. But like so may other beautiful things around here, so too is Rose Lake. A deep, cool, and clear lake, it is as inviting to fish as it is to view. Looking as close to a wilderness lake as we have in Ohio, Rose Lake sits among the forest with not a residence or building in sight. Fallen trees provide shoreline cover; pine, beech, and hemlock provide the shade.

To reach the lake requires a 0.5-mile downhill hike through the forest from a parking area set aside for fishers. Campers in the park also have to hike a considerable distance to reach the lake. But the walk is nice, and I can think of no place I'd rather be after viewing the wonderful Hocking County countryside than on Rose Lake with a spinning rod. The lake has bass, channel catfish, bluegills, and trout.

Bass are plentiful at Rose Lake, but they average only 12 to 13 inches. Some nice ones are available, but the lack of any boat access limits an angler to those near the shore. Still, the shoreline is manageable. You will have to do some rough hiking along the banks, as there are a number of old fallen trees and snags to fish around. Fish spinner baits and plastic lizards around the old sticks and logs that populate the shoreline. The water is very clear, so take that into consideration. Buzz baits do well in the evening around those same logs. If you want a nice bass, try to stay away from the "used" shoreline and strike off away from where the crowd fishes.

Channel catfish are stocked annually, and some good catches are made. You can legally fish at night on Rose Lake, but I get the impression that park rangers would rather have folks off the lake at dusk when the park officially closes, as it is a long hike back.

Bluegills are common here, and anglers using wax worms and a bobber regularly catch some nice, better-than-hand-size ones.

Trout fishing is the big event at Rose Lake and is well advertised in advance. Trout are stocked into Rose Lake in early spring, and at times a fall stocking takes place, too. Close to 200 anglers take advantage of the stocking, and within 2 to 3 weeks, most of the trout are caught—but enough survive to provide some trout fishing through June. Trout anglers use small brightly colored spinners and Power Bait to catch their five-fish limit.

Boats may be carried in, but motors are not allowed on Rose Lake. Personally, I can't imagine dragging or carrying a canoe or kayak 0.5 mile downhill and back up again. Perhaps a float tube would be a better choice if you cannot stand to fish from the shore.

Hocking Hills State Park has 24 miles of hiking trails, 40 cabins, a dining lodge, 172 campsites, and a campground pool.

To reach Hocking Hills State Park, take Highway 664 9 miles southwest of Logan. The fishers' access parking area is east of the park office on Highway 374.

131 Ross Lake

Key species: Largemouth bass, channel catfish, bluegill, crappie.

General description: A medium-size lake fished mostly by locals for catfish.

Overview: Ross Lake is a Division of Wildlife lake of 125 acres that was impounded strictly for fishing purposes in 1967, leaving a great deal of standing timber and old structures in place. The lake was named for the county in which it is located. Shoreline access is limited to the two entry roads that come in from the east and west. A boat ramp is located on West Hydell Road, as are two rock fishing piers, one of which is wheelchair accessible. A third stone pier is located at the end of East Hydell Road, on the opposite side of the lake.

Ross Lake averages 10 to 20 feet deep and has typical shoreline structure of fallen treetops, old stumps, and roadbeds. Over the years the Division of Wildlife has placed over 500 Christmas trees in the lake and has felled over 50 shoreline trees to provide fish habitat. It has been said that fish caught from Ross Lake have stocked over 100 local farm ponds.

The fishing: Bass fishing can be tough at Ross Lake, but occasionally it's worth it. Every spring a 5- or 6-pound bass is taken by a local angler. Bass fishing starts in March at Ross Lake, with anglers concentrating on the lake's north half. Most anglers simply fish the shallow shoreline structure on both banks with spinner baits and plastic night crawlers. Later, fishing moves to the stump fields scattered at the north end and along the old roadbed and old fence lines along that roadbed. In May and June fish the entire lake in the evening, working the shoreline cover, shallow stumps, rocks, and underwater timber with spinner baits, pumpkinseed lizards, and buzz baits. Most bass caught are small, around 12 inches, but 15- to 16-inch bass are common enough. According to the owner of a local bait shop, back in the mid-1970s a 9-pound bass was caught and is believed to be the lake record.

Crappies are plenty in numbers but small in size. Fish shoreline brush and around treetops from April through May with jigs and minnows. There have been some nice crappies in the 15- to 16-inch range caught, but they are hard to locate. Most crappies will average 7 to 9 inches.

Bluegills are common, but they are small and hardly worth the effort.

Channel cat fishing is popular in the morning and evening, and anglers usually catch their fill. Most fishing is done from the banks and off the three piers. Chicken livers and shrimp are the local favorites. Channels do not get large; most average 12 to 16 inches, but some 3- to 5-pounders are caught often enough to make the local cat fishers return for more.

Special regulations: A minimum size limit of 15 inches for bass is in effect. The lake is restricted to electric motors only. White amurs have been stocked to control weed growth; if caught they are to be immediately released.

Facilities/camping: No facilities or camping at the lake. There is a grocery store at the junction of Black Smith Hill and Charleston Pike west of the lake, and a local bait and tackle shop that has been in operation for over 25 years is at the west entrance to the lake.

Additional information: Three miles north of the lake is Great Seal State Park.

Directions: Take Charleston Pike east of Chillicothe, then Black Smith Hill to West Hydell Road. The lake is at the end of the road.

132 Salt Fork Lake

Key species: Largemouth bass, smallmouth bass, muskie, channel and shovelhead (flathead) catfish, saugeye, walleye, crappie, bluegill, white bass.

General description: The best bet in Ohio to land a 50-inch muskie.

Overview: Originally intended to be a reservoir for the city of Cambridge, Salt Fork Lake evolved into a strictly recreational impoundment that was completed in 1967 by the Ohio Department of Natural Resources. The lake is among the largest in Ohio, covering 2,952 acres. It is the largest state park in Ohio, at 20,542 acres. In addition to fishing, the Salt Fork Wildlife Area that borders the state park offers excellent deer and turkey hunting.

The state park facilities include a lodge, cabins, campground, two beaches, two marinas, hiking and bridle trails, dock rental, an 18-hole golf course, numerous picnic areas, and six launching ramps. Wheelchair-accessible fishing is available at either marina. At the Salt Fork Marina, on the lake's east branch, only fuel is available. At the newer Sugartree Fork Marina, located on the lake's west arm, fuel and boat rental are available.

The lake is not used for flood control or as a water source, resulting in stable water levels throughout the seasons. Conditions of prolonged drought or rain may raise or lower the lake by only 2 to 3 feet.

Salt Fork would have to be considered one of the crown jewels in the state park system. Ditto that for the achievements of the Division of Wildlife, considering among other things that Salt Fork is arguably the state's best muskie lake. Several 50-inch-plus muskies are taken from the lake every summer, and it is well on its way to becoming a top saugeye lake.

Salt Fork Lake in southeast Ohio usually leads the state in 50-inch muskies caught.

Salt Fork averages 20 feet, with lake visibility approaching 2 feet under optimum conditions. One look at the map shows a lake with a variety of fishing areas, from shallow wooded creek arms to countless bay and inlets, points, flats, slips, boulders, and spawning cavities to provide every species of game fish found in the lake the right conditions to thrive. Although there are a hundred places you can fish from shore, a lake this large requires a boat to fish effectively.

The Division of Wildlife District Four maintains a satellite office on the east side of the lake off U.S. Highway 22. The state park's headquarters are also located on the east side of the lake at the main park entrance off US 22.

Over the years the Division of Wildlife has been placing fish structures, called cribs, into Salt Fork Lake. To find out where the cribs are located, visit the Division of Wildlife Salt Fork office, where you will find maps posted on the bulletin board outside.

The fishing: Salt Fork may be reputed as a top muskie lake, but the shovelhead fishing here is incredible. Shovelheads over 60 pounds are caught nearly every summer, and the local bait store walls are filled with photos of 30-, 40-, and 50-pound shovelheads caught from Salt Fork Lake. The big shovelheads are caught on summer nights using shad, goldfish, and bluegills 4 to 5 inches long. The prime fishing for these big cats is in the east arm of the lake in the area of the "old" Salt Fork marina, from just south of the main entry road to the start of the ski zone. Fish the lake shelves and flats in 10 feet of water or less on both banks, as the big cats like to come up at night from the main lake channel to feed on the shallower lake shelves. Fishing either tight line on the bottom or with floaters to suspend the bait doesn't seem to make any difference, as they are caught both ways.

Channel cat fishing is also good on the lake, and cats are caught everywhere in summer, with sizes ranging from 12-inch "squealers" to 10-pounders, but most averaging 15 to 16 inches. Use shad, night crawlers, or chicken livers for bait. All the upper shallow ends are good areas. The backwaters in the east arm of the west branch at the end of Park Road 28 is excellent, as is the area just south of the boat ramp at the end of County Road 831 (which may also be shown on maps as road R-11). Across from the water treatment plant is another good area to try for channels. They are so common throughout the lake that any place is nearly as good as any other place.

Bass fishing is also good on Salt Fork Lake, but it is not regarded as a big bass lake by any standard. Most anglers catch numbers, not quality. There is a 15-inch minimum size limit on bass, and anglers catch high numbers of 14- to 14.5-inch bass. Ten- to 20-bass days are common; a good bass might weigh 3 to 5 pounds tops. Bass fishers frequently complain that there are too many muskies and encounter the toothy critters all too often when casting shoreline structure. The lake receives a lot of bass fishing pressure, and conflicts with pleasure boaters restrict most bass fishing to morning and evening hours in summer. Mid-April through May and September are the prime times to bass fish at Salt Fork. Fish the shoreline structure of weeds, timber, and slips and along the deeper rocky shorelines with watermelon seed tubes, plastic worms, and lizards. Buzz baits, any color, work well in the evening. Bass tournaments are held regularly, and nearly 90 percent of the bass fishing is tournament fishing. Good bass fishing can be had around the rocks and timber across from the cabins, on the shoreline south of the water treatment plant, and along both banks of the northwest arm of the lake. Any wood, in the way of fallen trees, or bank slips are good bets for bass.

Smallmouth are also present, and most fishing for them is confined to the rocky shoreline near the dam and the rocky shoreline between the cabins and the lodge. Tubes and crawdad-colored crank baits get the lion's share. Look for large rock, boulder, with some timber in the deeper waters near the dam, and you have found smallmouth.

White bass are present here, but in small numbers. They make a minor run up the tributaries beginning in mid-April. Few anglers fish for them, and most are incidental catches.

Crappies are in good supply at Salt Fork Lake; fishing for them takes place in April and May. Any shoreline brush or timber in 4 to 10 feet of water is a good bet. They are well distributed throughout the lake. Suspending minnows below a bobber is as good a way to take them as any. Crappies reach a respectable 10 to 11 inches.

Saugeye fishing is becoming popular, as more and more anglers target them. Saugeyes replaced walleye stockings in 2001, and they are found in the same general

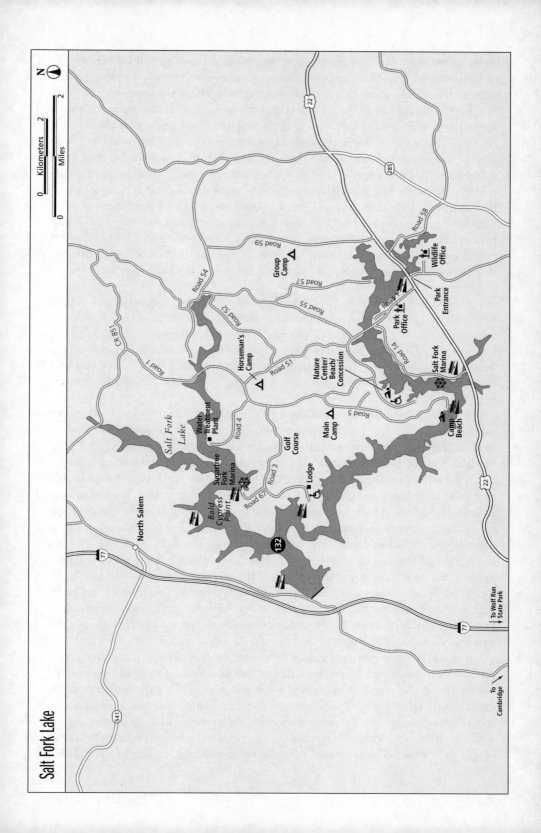

Salt Fork Lake

areas, as catches of both species are common. What walleyes are left are big, with 7-to 10-pound fish being caught. The number of walleyes will slowly decrease, but the potential for catching some very large walleyes will exist in the lake for some time. Saugeyes are caught in all the classic ways, with jigs and curly tail grubs and worm harnesses. Locally made Hot Dogs, Whizler, and Red Hook jigs with night crawlers are Salt Fork favorites. Another method in winter is to vertical jig ⅜-ounce chrome Vib"E"s over rocks and schools of shad. Drift or slow troll over the beaches, main lake points, flats, and edges in late fall, winter, and early spring. The two long points south of the water treatment plant on the west bank are as good an area as any to find saugeyes, as is Bald Cypress Point located just north of the Sugartree Fork Marina. Any long-sloping rock or gravel shoreline or point has saugeyes. Night fishing has not yet caught on here, which has proven effective in other lakes for catching the largest saugeyes. Most saugeyes average 20 to 24 inches, with a few 6-to 7-pound fish being caught. The potential for some very large state record–class saugeyes exist at Salt Fork.

Bluegills are common at Salt Fork, with a good one averaging about the size of a man's hand. Find them close to the shore around rocks in 3 to 4 feet of water. A state record bluegill, weighing 3.28 pounds, is reported to have come from Salt Fork Lake, but there is some doubt that it actually came from the lake, as it does not produce bluegills anywhere near that size. It has been suggested by a fishery biologist that the record bluegill came from a nearby strip-mine pond, of which there are many in the area.

It has been reported that Salt Fork produces more 50-inch muskies than any other lake in the state. The Division of Wildlife continues to stock 9- to 10-inch muskie fingerlings to ensure a bright future for Salt Fork muskies. Fishing for muskies starts in mid-April up in the tributaries at both ends of the lake and in the feeder streams of the bigger coves and bays. Early muskie anglers cast bucktails, big tandem spinner baits, and glider jerk baits, working them over logs, big timber, and shoreline boulders. As the weather warms, shoreline casting continues to produce, but muskies move to the deeper water closer to the dam. The same shoreline-cover pattern produces all summer. Look for muskies along the rocky shoreline between the cabins and the lodge, along the rocky shoreline south of Sugartree Fork Marina, in the weed beds back in the bays north of the cabin and lodge beach, and in the weed beds south of the water treatment plant. A fishery biologist told me that every fifth boulder has a muskie hiding around it, so look for large rocks and boulder structures near deep water. Bass techniques work well for muskies. In summer, the evening is a good time to pick up fish casting.

Trolling is the most popular way to fish for muskies and produces the largest catches. The best month is July, with August not far behind. Fish are suspended off the rocky shorelines in 10 to 12 feet of water and in the middle of the lake near the dam. Troll Bagley's Shads, Tuff Shads, and Crain Baits along the west and east shorelines north of the dam and across from the cabins. The hot summer spot is where the two creek channels meet at the junction of the two main branches north of the dam. Old hellbenders and waterdogs still produce, especially for follows.

Slow trolling long lines is the way most trolling is done. Muskies primarily feed on the suckers and carp in the headwaters, and shad in the main lake. Good fall muskies can be found in the backs of the deeper coves south of the boat ramp at the end of CR 831. Blue and silver Bagley's B-Flats work well in fall. Pretend you're bass fishing, and you'll catch muskies.

Special regulations: Bass less than 15 inches must be released.

Facilities/camping: Salt Fork has a huge campground with 212 sites, a 148-room lodge, and 54 cabins. A camp store is located at the campground entrance. Fuel is available at both marinas. Sugertree Fork Marina has boat rental. Several small convenience and bait and tackle stores are located outside of park grounds. Nearby, the town of Cambridge has everything.

Additional information: Visit the historic Kennedy Stone House, built in 1837, which has been fully restored. Listed on the National Register of Historic Places, the old stone two-story house was constructed from large stone blocks quarried from the property. It can be reached by vehicle from the main park road or by boat 1 mile north of Sugartree Fork Marina.

Directions: Salt Fork Lake is east of Interstate 77, just north of Cambridge. Take Highway 22 east from Cambridge to reach the main park entrance.

133 Scioto Brush Creek and Sunfish Creek

In Ohio you can count all the native muskie streams on one hand. Scioto Brush Creek and Sunfish Creek are arguably the top two in the state. Both are tributaries of the Lower Scioto River and have healthy, natural-occurring native muskie populations. They are most likely the only streams in the state where an angler has a reasonable chance of catching a wild, native, stream-born muskellunge.

The original native muskies that began the Ohio muskie program in the mid-1950s came from Sunfish Creek behind Kincaid Fish Hatchery in Pike County. In April 1954, Division of Wildlife fishery personnel set out nets on Sunfish Creek to capture native muskies, and they did. Eggs and milt from those few captured muskies gave birth to the muskie program. Fry hatched from those eggs went into Ohio's first muskie lake, Rocky Fork in Highland County. Rocky Fork Lake, 12 miles from the hatchery, was completed in 1954 and was just beginning to fill when it was stocked. It was the perfect beginning for Ohio's highly successful muskie program.

Sunfish Creek remains much the same today as it was in 1954. It lies in a mountainous, rural area in southern Pike County that has largely escaped development and change. It consists of many small to medium-size deep pools, with short riffle areas. The stream remains clear most of the time and has a tendency to clear up quickly after periods of heavy rain. Most of the larger, deeper pools have some wooded cover of logjams and old snags. This is where you'll find the muskies.

Muskies are found throughout Sunfish, beginning upstream at the Kincaid Hatchery and continuing to its confluence with the Scioto River at Riverdale.

Access is at most bridges, at roadside pulloffs along Highway 124, and along Sunfish Road, west of Riverdale. These are not public fishing areas, and if in doubt ask the landowner about fishing privileges. However, that said, most of these places have been used for years by local anglers. Muskies in Sunfish Creek are not large like their lake counterparts; most caught will be 30 to 34 inches. Occasionally muskies 36 inches and over are caught. Anglers use large bass-size (not muskie-size) crank baits, Rapalas, and spinner baits and work the wood, deep pockets, logjams, and lily pads. Muskie are notorious followers; watch behind your bait. Sometimes you can catch three muskies a day; sometimes you might catch three muskies a year. It's not productive fishing, but it's exciting fishing. You can catch muskies all summer long, but the best months are April, May, September, and October.

Much of what is said of Sunfish Creek can also be said of Scioto Brush Creek, located in Scioto County. Scioto Brush Creek is roughly 12 miles long from Otway to the Scioto River. At Otway, both forks of Scioto Brush Creek join to form the main branch. Although some muskies have been caught upstream of Otway, particularly in the south branch where locals call them "pickerels," the primary fishing for muskies begins at Otway and continues to its confluence with the Scioto River at Rushtown.

Scioto Brush is a larger stream than Sunfish; the pools are longer and deeper and have more lily pads and woody cover. Muskies caught from Scioto Brush aren't necessarily any bigger—you will still catch muskies averaging 30 to 34 inches—but more 40-inch-plus muskies come from Scioto Brush than from Sunfish. The largest I am aware of is a 47-inch, 27-pound muskie caught in April 2002 from Scioto Brush Creek near Otway.

Local muskie anglers do all their fishing by floating the stream using crank baits and spinners. Fish the wood, pools, lily pads, and everything in between.

Access is at Otway, Henley, Arion, McDermont, and the mouth at Rushtown.

134 Scioto Trail State Park

Scioto Trail State Park is located 6 miles north of Waverly or 7 miles south of Chillicothe, off Highway 23.

The park has two small lakes of approximately 15 acres each. Caldwell and Stewart Lakes both contain largemouth bass, bluegills, and channel catfish. A 15-inch minimum length limit on bass is in effect for both lakes. Boats are permitted but restricted to electric motors only.

Of the two, Stewart is the more interesting lake. It is definitely well worth spending a couple of hours on. It requires a short hike from the parking area, and shoreline access is possible via the Stewart Lake Trail that encircles the lake. Stewart resembles a large farm pond and is very inviting to fish, with cattails and some fallen timber along the banks. When Caldwell Lake was drained in 2001, the remaining fish population was transferred to Stewart, including some 3- and 4-pound bass and catfish. Use spinner baits and buzz baits along the edge of the cattails and around any treetop in the morning and evening. Bluegills are small but eager biters, so it is a nice place to take the kids fishing. Channels run small, but some 14- to 15-inch fish are entirely possible.

Caldwell was drained in 2001 and restocked in spring 2002. Bass up to 14 inches are caught with small yellow spinner baits around the island and along the edge of the water willows on both banks. Channels are doing well, with cats up to 17 inches being caught on night crawlers. Bluegills are small but plentiful. Occasionally trout are stocked into Caldwell in fall. During the drawdown, several fish structures in the form of submerged trees and cribs were added. Fishing around these increases your chances of catching fish; the structures can be located by bank markings. Caldwell is an easy little lake to fish from shore and an easy walk from the camping area. No need for a boat here.

Scioto Trail State Park has 76 campsites, a small beach, a boat ramp, and a camp store. Be sure to visit the old fire tower, which you'll pass on your way in.

135 Seneca Lake

Key species: Largemouth bass, saugeye and some walleye, striped bass, white bass, channel and flathead catfish, bluegill, crappie.

General description: The only striped bass fishery in the state.

Overview: Seneca is a large impoundment of 3,550 acres. It is almost 8 miles long if you were to stretch it out, and at some points it is over a mile wide. The lake averages anywhere from 10 to 20 feet deep, has three islands, and is covered on the western shoreline with cottages and camps, resembling a resort lake.

The lake was impounded in 1938 by the U.S. Army Corps of Engineers and is managed by the Muskingum Watershed Conservancy District (MWCD). If I had a complaint with MWCD lakes, it is that they are sorely lacking in boat ramps. Only three boat ramps serve this lake; only one is actually for free public use. To use the ramp at the campground, a fee is charged, which is higher on weekends. The marina boat ramp is reserved for rental dock users, leaving fishers with only the ramp at the dam.

There are two MWCD campgrounds on the lake. One is located at Seneca Lake Park on the lake's south shore. The other is at Marina Point, across from the dam. A full-service marina is located at the entrance to Marina Point Campground.

Shoreline access is at the dam at Secrest Park. Some limited shoreline access is at the headwaters end on the east side of the lake off Highway 147 and Highway 313.

The fishing: Striped bass at Seneca are caught from numerous locations around the spillway area. Stripers are taken off the riprap at the dam and off the rocks, points, islands, and open water on the lake's northwest shore around the boat ramp and Secrest Park. Chrome and gold crank baits, plastic Sassy Shads with white jig heads, and spinners are widely used. In the evening and early morning, fish can be seen chasing shad in the open water and are ready to hammer almost anything thrown their way if you can get to them in time. In summer, stripers are caught by trolling the deeper waters off of the two islands located near the spillway and along the entire northwest shoreline. Troll at 3 to 4 mph at depths of 10 to 15 feet using Bagley's Shads or big plastic shads in chartreuse, silver, or white, with heavy ¾-ounce jig heads. Shoreline anglers often pick up a few stripers along the spillway and at Seacrest Park. Striper fishing begins in April and continues through June and picks up again in September. Most good stripers run anywhere from 30 to 38 inches, weighing 15 to 20 pounds. Minimum size for stripers is 26 inches.

Eggs from striped bass netted from Seneca Lake are used in the production of hybrid stripers, which are a cross between striped bass and white bass.

Saugeyes instead of walleyes are now stocked into Seneca, but anglers still pick up few nice leftover walleyes while fishing for saugeyes. Saugeyes are widespread and can be found around the islands, near the points and rocky shoreline along the north shore, along the old roadbeds, and along the south shore to the high wall at Seneca Lake Park. Troll or drift using small crank baits, jigs and worms, night crawler harnesses, or jigs and minnows. Some of the prime areas include the three islands, the submerged island located on the east-north shore across from the spillway, picnic point and the high wall at Seneca Lake Park, and the points across from the park. Shoreline anglers pick up saugeyes in the evenings from the riprap at the dam and off the main point at Secrest Park. Fishing is best from late February through May and again late September through November. During periods of high water and during the months of January and February, saugeyes can be picked up from the tailwaters accessed from Hatchery Road, just south of the dam.

Largemouth bass are well distributed throughout the lake. Bass fishers wanting a little color in their water will find it at the lake's east end. Those who like it clear will find that toward the dam. Fish shoreline cover, weeds, and rocks along the lake's northeast shore; at the far north end, work the downed timber, around the docks and old shoreline snags. The bass in Seneca are not large, and you'll catch your share of small ones, but 3- to 5-pounders are common enough to make it interesting. Most anglers throw spinner baits and plastic night crawlers and work the rocks with crank baits. A few smallmouth are found in Seneca, which is always a bonus catch.

Channel cats are common and widespread at Seneca Lake; just fish anywhere and you will catch them. Chicken livers, shrimp, chubs, and cut bait will catch channels from 10 inches to 10 pounds. Some monster channel cats were found in Seneca Lake back in the 1980s, some approaching the 20-pound mark. Whether they're still there or not is questionable. Some of the better cat fishing is located in the backwaters at pulloffs located along Highway 147.

A few flatheads are also found in the lake, with some reaching 30 pounds. You can catch them at night using bluegills, creek chubs, or big shiners in the shallow headwaters between Highway 313 and Highway 147.

White bass are common in the lake, and they make a spring spawning run up into the headwater creeks and tributaries beginning in mid-April and continuing through mid-May. You can catch them on white Rooster Tails along Highway 147 at Beaver Creek, and from the Seneca Fork of Wills Creek off County Road C 16. After the run they start chasing schools of shad all over the lake, and you can still catch them with white Rooster Tails in the jumps.

Crappies are also widespread. Some years they are small, and some years they are just nice. Most average 9 to 10 inches, but during a good spring crappies between 11 and 14 inches are common. Fish any shoreline brush or around the boat docks with the old standard, minnows and a bobber.

Hand-size bluegills are everywhere; just wet a line using wax worms and a bobber. You will catch your fill.

Special regulations: There is a horsepower limit on Seneca Lake of 299 hp. Minimum length limit for bass is 15 inches, for crappies it is 9 inches, and for stripers it is 26 inches.

Facilities/camping: Seneca Lake Park has 50 available campsites. The Marina Point Campground has 140 sites. The marina has a restaurant, fuel, and boat rental. Gas, ice, and food are rare, but available at some local carryouts.

Additional information: Senecaville State Fish Hatchery is located below the Seneca Lake Dam and open to the public weekdays from 8:00 a.m. to 3:00 p.m.

Directions: Seneca Lake is located southeast of the Intersection of I-70 and I-77. Take Highway 313 east off I-77.

136 Somerset Reservoir

Somerset Reservoir is a small body of water, estimated at around 30 acres. It lies about 2 miles south of the town of Somerset on Big Inch Road between Highways 668 and 383. At the parking area a large sign has all the rules posted on it. There is no boat ramp, but carry-in boats with electric motors are permitted. Shoreline access is limited to the area just below the gravel parking lot and along the face of the spillway. Bass, bluegills, and some channel cats are present, but they run small. In the past the old reservoir gave up a few nice bass, but now only small bass seem to reside within its waters. Bluegills are also plentiful but run small as well; only a few bigger ones show up in early June when they spawn. Channel cats are present, but a 15-incher is considered a good catch. What fishing structure there is on the lake's southeast side consists of a few old snags and stickups. Water level in the reservoir can fluctuate due to demand.

137 Tri-Valley Wildlife Area

Tri-Valley Wildlife Area, located east of the town of Dresden off Highway 208, is a reclaimed strip-mine area that is supposed to have 10 ponds stocked with bass and bluegill, but I could locate only one. A good map, if there is one, would be helpful in locating the other ponds. A number of confusing township and gravel-hull roads intersect the area; signage was poor or absent. I did locate one nice-looking pond that I estimate at about 8 acres on the east side of Keyes Road near the intersection of Highway 208, approximately 5 miles east of Dresden. Access to the pond requires a hike of a couple hundred yards from a parking area near some storage tanks.

138 Turkey Creek Lake

Key species: Largemouth bass, channel catfish, bluegill; trout stocked in spring.

General description: The trout derby held at Turkey Creek Lake is the first and oldest trout derby in Ohio.

Overview: Situated in the hills of Shawnee State Forest, Turkey Creek Lake is a breathtaking beauty among Ohio lakes. Located in Shawnee State Park, the 51-acre lake was impounded during late 1960s, making it a rather young lake. Shawnee State Forest is Ohio's largest forest at 63,000 acres; within it is the 1,095-acre Shawnee State Park established in 1949 with the creation of the Ohio State Park system. Just downstream from Turkey Creek Lake is the old 28-acre Roosevelt Lake built by the Civilian Conservation Corps (CCC) in 1935. Several old forest ponds are also located within the state forest that were also built by the CCC.

The Shawnee State Park has a lodge, cabins, and a campground; an 18-hole golf course; numerous picnic areas; a beach on each lake; numerous hiking and bridle trails; boat ramps at both lakes; and boat rental at Turkey Creek Lake. There is also a state park boat ramp on the Ohio River that has a marina and dock rental.

Turkey Creek Lake is almost 30 feet deep at the dam, making it one of the few Ohio lakes that have holdover trout all year long.

The fishing: Largemouth bass are in good supply in this mountain lake. There are no lunkers, but there are plenty of 12- to 14-inch fish. Occasionally some 2- to 3-pound bass are caught. Most are taken by casting to shoreline cover on the lake's south side and west of the dam. The long, deep cove on the lake's south side has been known to have a nice bass or two taken from it. It has a narrow, deep channel that is lined with old stumps. Fish plastics and spinner baits tight to shoreline cover; old stumps and fallen timber are the best bets for bass. Bass seem to hit all summer long; the best month is May.

Channels are present, but they don't receive much attention. Fish the north shore off Highway 125 and at the mouth of the south cove. Chicken livers are a local favorite.

After trout, bluegills are probably the second most sought-after fish. Good hand-size catches are made by adults and youngsters all summer long. Fish anywhere, and you'll catch them. Use red worms or wax worms suspended 2 feet beneath a small bobber.

Trout put Shawnee on the map. When the first Ohio trout derby was held in the spring of 1966, Governor James Rhoads and U.S. Congressman William Harsha attended. The original derby was held in Turkey Creek stream below the Roosevelt Lake spillway, three years before Turkey Creek Lake was impounded. The stream had trout in it for 2 miles. According to the *Portsmouth-Times* newspaper, as many as 10,000 to 12,000 visitors attended the trout derby. Today the old derby is still alive and still well attended, but its location has since been moved to Turkey Creek Lake.

Trout continue to be caught for a month after the late-April stocking by the Division of Wildlife. Cheese, chartreuse and yellow Rooster Tails, corn, and wax worms take the lion's share. Later, slow-trolled Rooster Tails pick up plenty of post-derby trout around the dam. Because the fish are stocked from the boat ramp at the dam, most fishing takes place there as well.

Fishing at Roosevelt Lake is mostly limited to small bass, bluegills, and some small catfish. Occasionally an escaped trout from Turkey Creek makes its way into the lake and gets caught. Fish the dam and north bank; the south feeder stream is also a good place to pick up some lively bluegills and small bass.

There are five nice forest ponds that were built by the CCC in the late 1930s that still provide some scenic and quality fishing. All are stocked with largemouth, bluegills, and channel catfish. The two best are Pond Lick, located by the old CCC camp on Pond Run Road, and Bear Lake, located at the horse camp on Forest Road 4. Wolfden Lake and McBride also have some fish but are subject to overfishing by locals. Churn Creek Lake is also fished hard by locals.

The Shawnee boat ramp on the Ohio River will get you into the mouth of Kinniconick Creek on the Kentucky side of the river.

Special regulations: A special slot-length limit on bass has been imposed; bass between 12 and 15 inches must be released. Turkey Creek and Roosevelt Lake are limited to electric motors only.

Facilities/camping: Shawnee Lodge has 50 rooms and 25 cabins to rent; the state park campground located on Roosevelt Lake has 107 sites. Outside the park, facilities are few and far away. Portsmouth is the closest town, and it has everything.

Additional information: The flood-wall murals at Portsmouth are highly regarded and a must-see attraction.

Directions: Take Highway 125 east from West Union 20 miles, or take Highway 125 west from U.S. Highway 52, west of Portsmouth.

139 Tycoon Lake

Key species: Largemouth bass, bluegill, redear sunfish, crappie, channel catfish.

General description: One of the better big bass lakes of southeast Ohio, with size and motor restrictions.

Overview: Covering 204 acres, Tycoon Lake is on the short list of select lakes that the Division of Wildlife is trying to turn into a trophy bass lake. And by all reports, it's working. Located in central Gallia County, Tycoon is surrounded by the Tycoon Lake Wildlife Area. The lake has numerous parking areas, excellent shoreline access, one boat ramp, primitive camping, and a wheelchair-accessible pier. The lake is weedy along the bank, and several coves are covered with thick growths of lily pads. White amurs have been introduced to control weed growth. If they are caught, they are to be immediately released. Visibility is normally 4 to 5 feet. The average depth is 6 to 9 feet at the deepest. The lake contains endless stump fields, and fishing at night can be hazardous to your electric motor. Impounded by damming a lowland swamp, all timber was left in the lake.

The fishing: In many parts of the lake, the gentle sloping, shallow shoreline allows wading along the edges, but a boat is the most practical way to fish Tycoon. The lake is not used for flood control, and because it is a shallow lake with a stable water level, it is an excellent early spring bass lake. There are some big bass that come from Tycoon, and to keep it that way the Division of Wildlife has implemented an 18-inch minimum size limit. Starting in late February and early March, the bass move into shoreline cover and pitching jig-and-pig combos and Carolina rigs to shallow cover has resulted in the boating of some 7- to 8-pound bass. Later in the summer, as the bass move deeper, fishing chartreuse-colored crank baits and watermelon seed plastics in 7- to 8-foot-deep stump beds produces. Fall is another excellent time to catch good bass at Tycoon; in October bass begin hitting topwater and buzz baits fished over shallow stumps and shoreline. Some fishers have reported 50-fish days at Tycoon.

Nice black crappies are also noted at Tycoon. In early spring fish timber and around the emerging lily pads with minnows and bobbers. Crappies will average 10 to 12 inches, but 14- to 15-inch crappies are not hard to find.

Channel cats are also in excellent supply here, and plenty of 3- to 4-pound channels await night anglers.

Good hand-size bluegills can be caught during May and early June along shallow stumps and close to shore.

Additional fishing opportunities can be found at the Rio Grande City reservoir just west of town. Only bank fishing is permitted, but the small, 7-acre lake does provide an abundance of small bluegills. There are bass, though most are small, and some channel cats. Trout are stocked each spring.

Special regulations: Minimum size for bass is 18 inches. Only electric motors are permitted on Tycoon. All grass carp (white amurs) must be released.

Facilities/camping: No facilities other than a restroom at the boat dock. The nearby town of Rio Grande has all the amenities. Camping is permitted; seven primitive campsites are located at the south boat ramp.

Additional information: The original Bob Evans Farm is located in Rio Grande. You can't call yourself a Buckeye until you've eaten breakfast at Bob Evans.

Directions: Tycoon Lake is located on Eagle Road approximately 3 miles north of Rio Grande, off Highway 325.

140 Veto Lake

Key species: Largemouth bass, spotted bass, channel and flathead catfish, bluegill, redear sunfish, crappie.

General description: Little pressure on a lake that is well off the beaten path.

Overview: Veto Lake is a nice-looking body of water that appears larger than the stated 160 acres it is supposed to be. A boat ramp, a dock, and wheelchair access are located off Veto Road, east of the small town of Veto. The lake also has a small picnic area and shelter house across from the spillway. Just east of the boat ramp is Lake Road, which turns north and follows the lake's north shore for approximately 2 miles. The lake averages 6 to 10 feet deep and is turbid or stained most of the time. The edges are lined with weeds and water willows, and a number of lily-pad fields are located in the lake's headwaters. Shoreline access is good all along Lake Road, but to reach deep water on the lake's south shore, you need a boat. The lake apparently floods repeatedly in spring, which is why the Division of Wildlife gave up stocking saugeyes in the late 1990s.

The fishing: A few good bass have come from Veto in the past, and I suspect a few more are still lurking beneath its murky water. Fish the stumps, shoreline cover, and emerging weeds in the headwaters of the north and west arms in spring. Also fish the shoreline flats and weeds on the lake's north shore, which have been traditionally good areas to pick up an April bass. Use spinner baits and plastics around the shoreline wood and along the weed edges. In summer, work the deep shoreline cover, steep bluffs, and old creek channel as it swings in close to the south bank. There is an abundance of shore cover of old snags and fallen and overhanging trees. On summer evenings work the weedy points off the main lake with buzz baits. Most bass are small, but some 3- to 4-pound fish do turn up. Spotted bass are also present, and may be mistaken for largemouth by the untrained eye.

There are some good bluegills and redear sunfish here, most of which are caught during the spawn along the shallow bars on the north shore. In summer stay close to shade on the south bank using wax worms or red worms.

The channel catfish in Veto Lake are good; most average 12 to 16 inches, with a few bruiser flatheads surprising some anglers. Most cat fishing is done from pulloffs along Lake Road. The upper ends of both the north and west arms are best, but you'll need a boat to reach them.

In spring you can pick up crappies from 8 to 10 inches along the shoreline brush and downed tree tops. Minnows suspended under a bobber work best.

Some tailwater fishing is also available in spring and can be accessed by parking at the gate at the spillway.

Special regulations: Veto Lake has a 10-hp limit.

Facilities/camping: There are no facilities or camping at the lake; the nearest town is Belpre, which has everything.

Additional information: Blennerhassett Island Historic Park is located on the Ohio River just west of the town of Belpre.

Directions: Take Highway 339 5 miles north of US 50, west of Belpre.

141 Waterloo Wildlife Area (Penrod Lake)

Still officially known as the Waterloo Wildlife Research Station, Waterloo used to have some of the best public turkey hunting in the state. Before the Division of Wildlife District Four office moved to their new larger facility in Athens, Waterloo was a busy research center for all forest woodland game management projects in the state. The research center at Waterloo is no longer used, but the building still exists and from there you can pick up a wildlife area map from a map box attached to the building.

If you continue to drive the gravel lane past the old facility, you will notice one pond on your right. The road eventually ends up at Penrod Lake, after a scenic pass around some sandstone cliffs. Penrod is a small lake of approximately 3 acres and offers fishing for small bass, bluegills, sunfish, and bullheads. The lake also has an abundance of turtles. It can be readily fished from shore, and if you're turkey hunting, you could easily pass the idle hours between hunts fishing in the tranquility of this little lake.

142 Waterloo/Big Rock Lake at Liberty Wildlife Area

Key species: Largemouth bass, bluegill, crappie, channel catfish.

General description: A seemingly forgotten or abandoned lake.

Overview: On the Pike-Jackson County line there is a large lake off the beaten path. I estimate it at close to 50 acres. Public fishing is evident, and it appears that attempts to limit damage by off-road vehicles have been in vain. There are several rough parking areas on the lake's north side. There are two primitive boat ramps, but only one is usable. All parking areas and ramps have become a deposit for old tires, broken bottles, pop cans, and trash.

The lake is just south of the little-known and equally remote 145-acre Liberty Wildlife Area, on Wick Line Road in Jackson County. Outside from the garbage and old tires, the lake is beautiful. I observed wood duck boxes placed at the shallow west end. The far-south bank was heavily wooded, with a steep hillside terrain. Access to the lake is along Big Rock Road at several pulloffs and gravel and sand parking areas. There is a brick structure located on a narrow peninsula out in the lake that reminds me of structures used in water supply reservoirs. Outside that abandoned structure, nothing else has been built anywhere on or near the lake, and there are no signs indicating such.

The lake is shown in the current *DeLorme Ohio Atlas & Gazetteer* as Jackson Lake, and can be found on page 85. The lake may also be named Beaver–Big Rock Lake/Reservoir. The Division of Wildlife has it listed as Waterloo Lake, named after the Waterloo Coal Company that once operated in the area. Waterloo is listed under public lakes' fishing prospects published by the Ohio Division of Wildlife, but a lake map is not available. It is said to be an old coal-mining pond.

The fishing: This lake is best fished from a boat, and there is a very usable gravel ramp located along Big Rock Road. I spoke to a few local boys who had just wrapped up a late afternoon fishing and had a few 12- to 14-inch bass to prove it. They said the bass fishing was pretty good, with a few nice ones caught in spring. They had been throwing top water in the shallows at the west end that day. They indicated that some crappies were caught in spring from around the shore and that a few local cat fishers did have some luck on channels, but other than that they didn't know anything about the lake either, or its name.

Directions: Take Highway 335 5 miles north of Beaver, go east on Big Rock Road. The lake is on the right.

143 Wayne National Forest Lakes and Ponds

Key species: Bass, bluegill, sunfish, channel catfish, and trout. Trout are stocked in Lake Vesuvius and Timbre Ridge Lake in spring.

General description: The Wayne National Forest offers a variety of fishing opportunities ranging from strip-mine ponds to stream fishing.

Overview: Wayne National Forest is divided into two districts, Ironton and Athens. In the Ironton District, located north of the town of Ironton, anglers have two lakes and number of old strip-mine and quarry ponds from which to choose. The lakes and ponds are stocked with bass, bluegill, channel catfish, and trout. The Ironton District office is located 7 miles north of Ironton on Highway 93.

There is some quality fishing to be found in some of the old quarry ponds, and exploring the area for possible 6-pound-plus bass is half the fun, although I would advise a good map and compass, and possibly a snake bite kit. Lake Vesuvius is bouncing back after being completely drained in 2001. It has been restocked, and fishing structures and cribs were anchored to the bottom to enhance the fishery. On my last visit there, the bass appeared numerous and sizable. Boat rental is also available at the lake. Probably one of the nicest places to fish in the national forest is Timbre Ridge Lake; it's tough to find but rewarding to fish, and above all peaceful and quiet—and isn't that what we're all really looking for anyway?

The fishing: In the Hanging Rock Recreation Area, there are 51 strip-mine ponds, 27 of which have been stocked with bass, catfish, and bluegills. A pamphlet, "Hanging Rock Area Fishing Guide," is available from the Ironton District Office. In it, it lists each lake by numbers that have been stocked and contain fish. These old strip-mine ponds are best fished with a small pontoon boat, float tube, canoe, or kayak, as a single, rough downhill path is all that leads to most. There are no paths around the ponds, and bushwhacking your way around the edge is not advisable because of thick growth, copperheads, ticks, and cobwebs. At a few ponds it is possible to portage from one pond to another.

The ponds in Hanging Rock are so clear that visibility is easily 6 to 8 feet. Ponds vary in size from a couple of acres to 10 acres or more. The Division of Wildlife has stocked white amurs in selected ponds to control the weed growth. The main road through the area has several pulloffs and gravel lanes leading to some of

Timbre Ridge Lake is just one of the many fishing lakes and ponds available to anglers in the Wayne National Forest.

the larger ponds. Other ponds require a hike via the off-road vehicle trails. If you have an off-road vehicle, you could ride to nearly all the ponds, as the Hanging Rock Recreation Area is set aside for off-road use. Some nice 5- to 6-pound bass have come from these ponds; it's remote, rugged, and beautiful. Camping is permitted, and several campsites are located along the main entry road next to some lakes; there also are restrooms at various locations.

Another area where strip-mine ponds are located is 0.5 mile north of the small village of Arabia on Highway 141 on Coffee and Tea Creek Road. You need a stout four-wheel drive to reach them.

Lake Vesuvius is a small lake of 143 acres, originally constructed in 1939 by the Civilian Conservation Corps. The lake has a boat ramp, boat rental, a beach, three campgrounds, a nature center, and a boardwalk along its western shoreline with wheelchair-accessible fishing. Of note are the 1,000 trout stocked in Vesuvius for a Wheeling Sportsmen event held each spring. Anglers will find bluegills, sunfish, catfish, and bass. Vesuvius was drained in 2001 for dam renovation. Most bass, which average 10 to 15 inches, are caught by pitching spinner baits and plastics to shoreline cover. In order to improve the bass fishery here, the Division of Wildlife has implemented a 15-inch minimum length limit. Fishing should improve as time goes on; it's a beautiful lake and well worth a visit, but best fished from a small boat, as shoreline access is limited to the boardwalk, dam, and beach area. A hiking trail encircles Vesuvius, and some access can be had from that trail. Of note is the old iron furnace located near the dam and a nature center operated by Ohio University. To reach Vesuvius take Highway 93 north from Ironton 6 miles, and watch for signs.

Timbre Ridge Lake is the crown jewel of the Ironton District lakes. The 100-acre lake was purchased from a land management company that went broke trying to develop a lakeside community. It's an absolutely stunning lake, with water visibility 5 to 6 feet. The only access, which is nearly impossible to find, is at the dam at the end of a lane off Scottown-Lecta Road, south of the town of Lecta on the winding Highway 775. At the dam there is a boat launch, restroom, and the lake's only shoreline access. The lake is best fished from a boat, but small bass can be picked up off the face of the dam at dusk and dawn.

Timbre Ridge is also a local swimming hole, and the favorite "beach" is the boat ramp. The lake has good numbers of small bass between 10 and 14 inches, bluegill, sunfish, and channel catfish. The channel cat fishing is also good, and nearly every night locals fish for channels up to 24 inches off the earthen dam. Night crawlers, chicken livers, and chubs are their bait of choice. To catch bass, fish the backs of coves and on the southern shoreline with lizards, tubes, and chartreuse spinner baits.

I was told that when the Timbre Ridge Lake was first opened up to public use in 1991, many 6- to 7-pound bass were caught. To improve the bass fishing, the Division of Wildlife has imposed a special slot-length limit on bass; all bass between 12 and 15 inches must be released. Good numbers of bluegills exist everywhere on the lake, and at spawning time in early June some 10-inch ones are caught. There is submerged weed growth along the edges, but it's not excessive. Every spring the Division of Wildlife stocks over 1,000 trout into the lake.

Special regulations: Only electric motors are permitted on Lake Vesuvius and Timbre Ridge Lake. A 15-inch minimum size limit on bass is in effect on Lake Vesuvius. Bass caught between 12 and 15 inches must be released at Timbre Ridge Lake. All white amurs caught must be immediately released back into the water.

Facilities/camping: Camping at Lake Vesuvius is at the Iron Ridge campground with 41 sites, at Oak Hill campground with 32 sites, and the Two Points group campground. Primitive camping is also permitted at the Hanging Rock Recreation Area. Facilities are few and far between in the Wayne National Forest; a small carryout shop with ice, food, and beverages is located on Highway 93, just before you enter the Lake Vesuvius region. Another is located on Highway 650 on the east side of Hanging Rock Recreation Area. The town of Ironton has all the amenities.

Additional information: The river town of Ironton has many old historical buildings and several quaint eateries throughout town.

Directions: Hanging Rock is located north of Ironton off Highway 650. Wayne National Forest Ironton District Headquarters and Lake Vesuvius are north of Ironton on Highway 93. Timbre Ridge Lake is located north of Ironton off Highway 790, south at Lecta.

144 Wills Creek Reservoir

Key species: Flathead and channel catfish, bass, bluegill, crappie, and saugeye.

General description: An excellent flathead fishery in the tailwaters below the dam.

Overview: Wills Creek is an old reservoir impounded in the 1940s by the U.S. Army Corps of Engineers. It is a long, narrow lake covering only 421 acres and appears more like a slow-moving river than a lake. Siltation appears to have reduced the lake to roughly half the size of what it was when it was first impounded. There is one boat ramp located just south of the intersection of Highway 83 and County Road 410. Shoreline access is adequate, with a number of access sites on Wills Creek Road on the lake's south shore. Other access is along County Road 410 and Township Road 145 at the headwaters end of the lake. Access to the tailwaters is at the dam off County Road 497; a wheelchair-accessible pier is also located there.

The fishing: Catfish are the primary target at Wills Creek, as channel and shovelhead catfish like the reservoir's slow-moving, shallow, turbid water. Night crawlers and chicken livers are the baits of choice. Most of the cat fishing is done off Wills Creek Road at the various numbered access points. Upstream are a few access points off CR 410, but they are back along muddy lanes, perhaps requiring a four-wheel-drive vehicle. Channels range in size 1 to 10 pounds, and shovelheads up to 20 pounds are in the lake.

There are a few nice bass that occasionally come from the lake, but 3 pounds is about tops. Numerous small bass inhabit the mouths of the clear feeder streams on the lake's south side. Little shoreline cover exists, except for some ancient shoreline stumps and a few old flood-delivered snags.

Crappies are also present, but not in any outstanding numbers. A few 12-inchers are caught in early spring by locals fishing with minnows around the old snags and near the dam.

Saugeyes are stocked but in reduced numbers, because this is a flood control lake and so is prone to frequent flooding. There are some small gravel bars near the dam and sandstone cliffs, which have produced saugeyes on jig and grubs in the past.

Perhaps the best fishing on Wills Creek is in the tailwaters. Big shovelhead catfish make their way up to Wills Creek Dam from the Muskingum River. Thirty- and 40-pound shovelhead are frequently taken from the concrete chute below the dam. Plenty of channels cats are caught too, but the giant shovelheads are what everybody is after. And they catch the cats in the most unusual way, by jigging chartreuse grubs and curly tails in the white water and along the concrete wall. One individual told me it took him over an hour to land a 37-pound shovelhead that he had caught this way.

Saugeyes are caught from the Wills Creek tailwaters beginning in early February on chartreuse grubs and jigs. An old state record saugeye weighing 10.25 pounds came from these tailwaters in 1989. In late winter and after high-water releases, they still catch some respectable saugeyes in the 24-inch range here.

Smallmouth bass are also in good numbers at the tailwaters, as every April through May spawning fish make their way upstream from the Muskingum River as water conditions permit.

Special regulations: Outboards are limited to 10 hp.

Facilities/camping: No facilities or camping at the lake. The nearby village of Wills Creek has a small country store and bait shop.

Additional information: Take a look at the catfish photos at the carryout located in the small village of Wills Creek.

Directions: Take Highway 83 south of Coshocton approximately 8 miles.

145 Wolf Run Lake

Key species: Largemouth bass, bluegill, sunfish, channel and flathead catfish, crappie, yellow perch; trout in spring.

General description: One of the clearest lakes in southeast Ohio with visibility over 6 feet.

Overview: Impounded in 1966 as part of the West Fork Duck Creek Watershed Project, Wolf Run covers 220 acres. It is named after the Wolf family, the first settlers in the area, and not from wolves who roamed the area in packs during the 1700s.

Dedicated as a state park in 1968, Wolf Run State Park has hiking trails, a beach, picnic areas and a shelter, one launch ramp, and a campground. It is the only state park to have an airfield with a fly-in camping area. The town of Caldwell occasionally uses the lake as a water source, and scuba diving takes place here.

The lake is over 60 feet deep at the dam, with water as clear as an alpine lake. Trout stocked in spring are able to survive all summer long near the dam.

Shoreline access is very good, as the Buckeye Trail follows the north branch shoreline and the Lakeview Trail follows the shoreline on the east branch.

The fishing: Several bass in the 7- to 8-pound range have been caught from Wolf Run Lake, but the lake record of 10.1 pounds, caught on May 14, 1983, will not be easily eclipsed. Years back a magazine article described the great bass fishing at Wolf Run, and that brought in hordes of anglers to this small lake that had to suddenly bear an intense amount of fishing pressure. The crowds of weekend fishers are gone now; some say the added press and resulting bass tournaments caused the lake to be overfished during spawning season, which left the spawning beds to the bluegills, resulting in a decline in bass fishing. The Division of Wildlife has implemented a slot-length limit to enhance and protect the bass fishery. Bass now average 2 to 5 pounds.

Bass fishing starts early on Wolf Creek. Anglers begin pounding shoreline cover and emerging weeds with spinner baits and plastic night crawlers soon after ice-out. On summer evenings white buzz baits worked along the deep weed edges do well. Bass are picked up all season long from shoreline cover, weeds, and rocks.

April, May, June, and September are the best months. Work the backs of coves in both creek arms; most bass are taken from weeds, which consist of coontail and pepper weed.

Channel cats are good in both size and numbers. Cats up to 10 pounds are caught at night by using chicken livers fished off the shore west of the boat ramp along Lakeview Trail and on the north arm of the lake off the Buckeye Trail. Some big flatheads up to 40 pounds are caught by fishing bluegills and shiners from these same areas. The old creek channel swings close to the boat ramp, and a lot of cat fishing is done in that channel.

Saugeyes are just getting started in Wolf Run. They are small, averaging 14 to 16 inches long. They are fished from the campground toward the dam. Anglers work off the rocky points on both sides and along the face of the dam using jig and worms. Most saugeyes caught, however, are incidental catches from anglers fishing for bluegills or bass.

Anglers catch a lot of nice crappies from Wolf Run; some reach 16 inches, but most average a respectable 12 to 14 inches. Fish the shoreline brush with minnows and a bobber 2 to 3 inches off the bottom.

Some nice bluegills and sunfish come from the lake; they are often bigger than hand size. Fish the weed pockets, especially during the spawn in early June. While fishing for bluegills, it is common to catch small 3- to 4-inch yellow perch.

This is a nice trout lake, but it is very popular with local anglers. Fishers are shoulder-to-shoulder when the trout truck arrives to deliver the load of rainbows at the boat ramp. Within a week the trout disburse and fishing picks up near the dam. Trout can still be caught four to five months after the initial stocking in April. Later, trout will be caught by anglers fishing at night near the dam with minnows and glow sticks taped to their bobbers. Occasionally a 2- to 3-pound holdover trout, stocked from previous years, is caught.

Special regulations: Outboard motors are limited to 10 hp. A special slot-length limit requires all bass between 12 and 15 inches be released.

Facilities/camping: The state park campground has 138 campsites and 1 cabin. Facilities are at the small town of Belle Valley, just off I-77.

Additional information: On September 3, 1925, the 680-foot-long navy dirigible, the USS *Shenandoah*, crashed near the town of Ava, killing 14 of the 43 seamen aboard. A monument to those who lost their lives is located at the small town of Ava, 5 miles north of Wolf Creek Lake on Highway 821.

Directions: Wolf Run Lake is north of Caldwell, on the east side of I-77, at the junction with Highway 821.

146 Woodbury Wildlife Area

Woodbury Wildlife Area is a vast area of over 19,000 acres located approximately 5 miles west of the town of Coshocton. It consists of a mixture of forest, reclaimed strip-mine land, brush, some marsh, and more than 100 small to medium-size coal-mine ponds. They are typical strip-mine ponds, very clear with some weed growth and plenty of old timber and woody structure. Most ponds are stocked with large-mouth bass, bluegill, and channel catfish, and are best fished from a float tube, kayak, or canoe. Many of the ponds require a hike to fish and are difficult to get into. Only a few ponds are accessible by car from parking areas and roads. Several of the wildlife area ponds were originally stocked by helicopter.

Several county and township roads intersect the wildlife area. You need a good map and a conversation with the wildlife area manager to be sure which ponds are fishable before hiking off to some distant pond. Camping is permitted at a primitive camping area 1 mile south of headquarters.

The Woodbury Wildlife Area headquarters is located on Highway 60, about 3 miles south of Warsaw. The easiest way to get to Woodbury Wildlife Area is to take Highway 541 west of Coshocton.

Southwest Ohio—Wildlife District Five

Southwest Ohio is not a bad place to live if you're a fisher, particularly a stream fisher. It has some outstanding smallmouth fishing, plus it even has a little trout fishing in the southern reaches of the Mad River. The entire Great Miami and Little Miami Watersheds are good smallmouth streams as any found anywhere in the state.

The Ohio River pools of Markland and Meldahl offer the only fisheries in the state for the big blue catfish that can weigh up to 100 pounds. The Ohio River tributaries in the Meldahl pool are among the most popular and productive bass tournament locations, with clubs from Cincinnati, Dayton, and Springfield.

There are also several good lakes here where any fisher would gladly spend a day. Rocky Fork is perhaps the best bass and catfish lake in southwest Ohio. Acton Lake and Cowan Lake are a couple of excellent bass fishing lakes. Caesar Creek Lake is an up-and-coming muskie lake, plus it has some of the most productive tailwater fishing of any lake in southern Ohio. Paint Creek Lake has a top tailwater fishery for saugeye. When it's on, one of the better crappie lakes in Ohio is at Grand Lake St. Marys. Nearby, Lake Loramie is a pretty good saugeye lake in its own right. Great pond fishing also awaits anglers in some of the wildlife area ponds and lakes.

If I had to pick a crown jewel in southwest Ohio it would have to be Ohio Brush Creek. As a fisherman, I sometimes enjoy a measure of solitude and the beauty of my surroundings in addition to catching fish. Ohio Brush Creek has all of this and more.

147 Acton Lake

Key species: Largemouth bass, bluegill, channel catfish, crappie, saugeye.

General description: Acton Lake has as a reputation as a quality bass lake.

Overview: Created by impounding the beautiful Four Mile Creek in 1957, Acton Lake covers approximately 600 acres and is surrounded by 2,936-acre Hueston Woods State Park. The park has a campground; a beach; a boat ramp; a marina and snack bar; boat rental; docks; hiking, biking, and bridle trails; several picnic and parking areas; and a wheelchair-accessible pier, all of which can be accessed by Main Loop Road, which circles the lake. The state park also has cabins and a 94-room lodge on the lake's southeast side and a state nature preserve. The lake is generally clear, with 3 to 4 feet of visibility near the dam, and is popular with sailboaters and college students from the nearby Miami University in Oxford. The lake has a 10-hp limit with varying depths from 6 to 20 feet. Acton Lake starts out shallow and marshy at its lower north end, but ends up 30 feet deep at the spillway.

The fishing: One fisherman described the Acton Lake as the best bass fishing in Butler County. Three- to 5-pound bass are not uncommon; 14- to 16-inch bass are

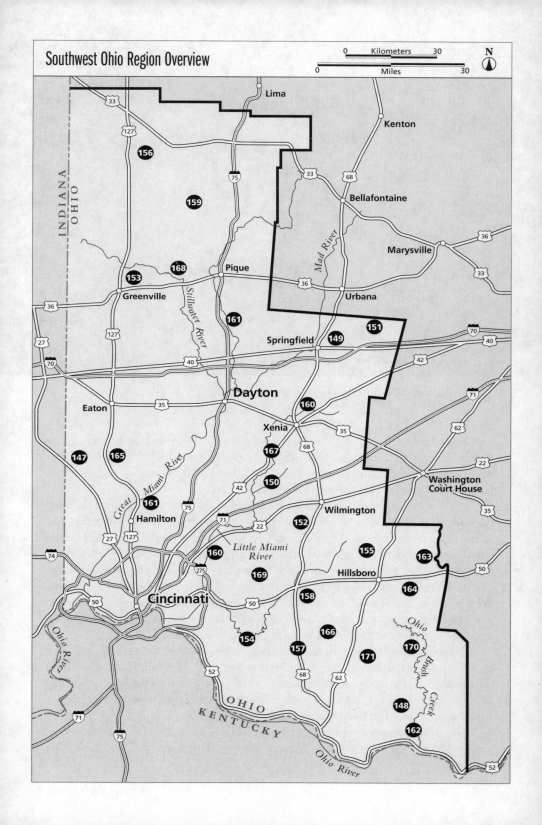

Tina Welch with a bluegill she caught from Acton Lake.

regularly caught. There is a 15-inch minimum size limit on bass, and it appears to have helped. The limited horsepower discourages major bass tournaments, and water skiers and jet boaters are not found here. The only interference anglers might face is a few scantily clad college students in canoes.

The best bass fishing occurs at the south end of the lake, especially on the deep east-side shoreline below the state park lodge near the location where the old streambed brushes against the shoreline. Fish the shoreline cover, bank slips, fallen trees, brush, and old snags with chartreuse spinner baits, black plastic night crawlers, lizards, and watermelon tubes. Summer evenings are good for top-water action; white buzz baits and fly rod poppers do well around the south island and off the riprap pier and around the shoreline weeds on the southwest shore and near the dam. Bass fishing starts in early April and is at its best in May and June, picking up again in September and October.

Crappie fishing is good; most fish average a good 9 to 12 inches and are found around the docks, old snags, and fallen trees in 5 to 8 feet of water. Fish the east-side shoreline cover and any snags lodged on the old streambed near the boat ramp. The best crappie fishing is from late March through early May; minnows and a bobber fished about 3 to 4 feet deep will get a bucketful.

Bluegills are in good supply, with most averaging a respectable hand size or bigger. Find them near the west shore from parking areas off the Main Loop Road. The north side of the riprap pier is an excellent place and a good area for big spawning bluegills during late May and June. Red worms, wax worms, or a pinch of night crawler is all you need.

Channel cats are plentiful, and when the water rises you can catch them by the stringerful from the creek at the north end of the lake, where Main Loop Road crosses Four Mile Creek. Some channels up to 10 pounds are caught here when the conditions are right. Any pulloff along the west side is also excellent, including the fishing pier. Chicken livers and night crawlers fished on summer nights are your best bets. The best fishing is from the middle of the lake, north toward the headwaters.

Saugeye were first stocked in 2004, and anglers were finding them off the flats north and south of the wheelchair-accessible pier at Sugar Camp and near the beach at night. Most fish were averaging 12 to 15 inches, but in time 18-inch and better saugeyes will be caught. Try slow trolling small crank baits, or casting jigs and grubs along the west shoreline, off the few lake points in the center of the lake, and along the flats on the shoreline just west and east of the dam. In spring and summer most saugeye are incidental catches by bass fishers throwing crank baits into shallow shoreline cover. During early spring and periods of high water, saugeyes can be taken below the dam.

There is wheelchair access at the riprap fishing pier at the Sugar Camp parking area on the lake's west side. From the nonelectric campsites at the north end of the park, you can access the upper branch of Four Mile Creek for some wading and small-stream fishing. Below the spillway, access to Four Mile Creek is at the parking area at the bridge. Four Mile Creek, which flows southeast joining the Great Miami River at the town of New Miami, has a reputation as a quality smallmouth stream.

Special regulations: A 15-inch minimum size limit is in effect for largemouth bass, with a five-fish limit. There is a 10-hp limit on Acton Lake.

Facilities/camping: The state park campground has 488 sites, the lodge has 94 rooms, and 25 cabins are available. Nearby Oxford has all the amenities and is well worth a visit.

Additional information: The Hueston Woods State Nature Preserve includes a 200-acre old-growth forest.

Directions: Acton Lake is located east of Cincinnati and north of Oxford, off Highway 732.

148 Adams Lake

Key species: Largemouth bass, channel catfish, bluegill; rainbow trout in March.

General description: One of the first lakes in Ohio to be stocked with trout in early spring.

Overview: Adams Lake is a beautiful lake of 47 acres situated in the center of Adams County, just northeast of West Union on Highway 41. It is surrounded by

Adams Lake State Park, with restrooms, picnic tables, grills, and shelters. The park is used by local residents and fishers, and has been a popular spot for family reunions as far back as I can remember.

The lake is fairly shallow and marshy at the west end, but does have a deep, narrow channel that runs up to and under a small bridge on Logans Lane. At the east end, the lake broadens out considerably, and some 15- to 20-foot-deep water is found near the spillway. Below the spillway is a small pool that's popular with anglers.

A single boat ramp with parking is located across from the park maintenance building near the main entrance.

The fishing: Each spring Adams Lake usually has the distinction of being the first lake in Ohio stocked with trout by the Ohio Division of Wildlife. The stocking of 2,500 rainbow trout usually takes place the first week of March and is popular with local anglers. You would think they had been waiting all winter long for the hatchery truck to arrive. Within days the trout scatter and can be caught from one end of the lake to the other. Most anglers, however, concentrate near the dam and the boat ramp, and at times the small pool below the spillway offers better fishing than the lake. Hundreds of trout have washed over the dam only to be caught in the spillway pool and in the creek below the dam that eventually leads into Ohio Brush Creek. The trout are taken on wax worms, cheese, Power Bait, and small lime green Rooster Tails.

Come late spring, the trout are gone and so are most anglers. In summer bluegills, small bass, and just-the-right-eating-size channel cats are the main catch. Adams Lake is weedy along the edges, with lily pads, a few sticks and stumps, and riprap boulders along the dam. One can walk the south bank and do all the fishing he or she desires. Fishing is not great, but it's not bad either. Occasionally a 5-pound bass gets caught along the south shore near the sunken cedars on plastic night crawlers, spinner baits, or buzz baits.

Channel cats and small bluegills are fairly plentiful, and most fishing for them is done from the south shore and near the dam using night crawlers and red worms. The lake is a popular spot for local kids' fishing events and various school and church activities.

Years ago Adams Lake was a fairly good bass lake. In the not too distant past, the dam developed some troubles that necessitated the drawing down of the lake and the creation of another spillway. The lake was cleansed of all fish for the purpose of removing the undesirable species and restocked with bass, bluegills, and channel cats. A special regulation on bass was put into effect, and it appears to have helped.

Special regulations: Bass less than 15 inches must be released, and the lake is limited to electric motors only.

Facilities/camping: No camping permitted; the closest state park campground is Shawnee State Park, with 107 sites. Nearby, the small village of West Union has all the amenities.

Additional information: Anglers should enjoy a home-cooked meal at the Olde Wayside Inn in West Union. Built in 1804, the old inn and restaurant is a registered historical landmark with the Ohio Historical Society.

Directions: Adams Lake is located on Highway 41, 1 mile northeast of West Union.

149 C. J. Brown Reservoir

Key species: Walleye, white bass, crappie, largemouth and smallmouth bass, channel and shovelhead catfish, bluegill, sunfish.

General description: One of the few places to fish for walleye in southwest Ohio.

Overview: Located northeast of Springfield, Clarence J. Brown Reservoir was impounded in 1974 by the U.S. Army Corps of Engineers as a flood control lake. The lake covers 2,120 acres, with 11 miles of shoreline, and has depths ranging from 10 to 30 feet. The surrounding 1,900-acre Buck Creek State Park, named after the stream that was impounded, has hiking and bridle trails and a paved bike trail that connects to the Little Miami Scenic Bike Trail. The park also boasts a swimming beach that is nearly a mile long. The Buck Creek ramp, located at the main park entrance, is the lake's only public ramp. There is another single launch ramp located at the marina for dock users. At the marina there is a snack bar and gas, but no boat rental as of this writing.

Both the state park headquarters and an Ohio Department of Natural Resources watercraft office are located at the main entry. Opposite of the lake is the U.S. Army Corps of Engineers office and visitor center. In winter the lake is drawn down 3 feet from a summer pool of 1,012 feet above sea level.

The lake is a summer playground for all sorts of watercraft, including skiers, tubers, jet boaters, pleasure boaters, and you name it. In summer, fish mornings, evenings, or weekdays, or be content to fish in the no-wake zones on weekends.

The fishing: C. J. Brown is primarily a managed walleye lake. The Division of Wildlife sets nets each spring to capture female walleyes for eggs and to survey populations. Every year Wildlife District Five in Xenia publishes the results of those nettings. Those test-net results show 80 percent of the walleyes are between 15 to 20 inches in length, with 16 percent over the 20-inch mark.

Good walleye fishing can be had at C. J. Brown, with most fishers concentrating on the old stream channel, roadbeds, and flats. Walleyes in the 7- to 8-pound range are occasionally caught, with most being in the 15- to 18-inch range. On a good day local anglers who know the water can regularly catch the six-walleye limit. Fish the humps west of the campground, the flats off that point, the old stream channel, the old roadbeds between the campground and the boat ramp, and north of the campground point. A few also are picked up in front of the beach and off the face of the dam at night and in early spring. Night crawler harnesses, crank baits, and jigs and minnows take most fish. Slow trolling and vertical jigging work well. Find a hump or roadbed and start fishing. Expect to catch a few channel cats, too, as they are plentiful in this lake. The best months for walleye are late April, May, and June.

Of late the smallmouth fishing has been coming on strong at C. J., and a few in the 5-pound range have been showing up at local bait and tackle shops to prove the point. However, largemouth fishing is not so great, with most fish running small, averaging only 12 to 14 inches. Work the shoreline cover, the riprap and rock, and around the bays from the boat ramp past the marina. The riprap around the dam gives up some good smallmouth. The best bass fishing is found at the south end of the lake, along both shores, but in summer heavy recreational use restricts fishing to morning and evening. Spinner baits, tubes, and plastics will cover about 90 percent of the bass fishing in C. J. Brown.

The white bass in the reservoir can be counted on for a run up into the head-waters at Buck Creek every April. Jigs with white Sassy Shads and white Mepps get the lion's share. Most white bass run small, 8 to 10 inches, but there are enough respectable 14- to 16-inch fish to make the effort fun and worthwhile.

As in all Ohio lakes, crappies can be counted on to hit when nothing else will in spring. Come April through May, find crappies under boat docks at the marina, pilings, and any old timber or brush in 5 to 10 feet of water. Although not large, crappies in the 9- to 10-inch range are not uncommon, with most being caught on minnows and crappies jigs.

Channel cats are here in good supply, with most of the quality cat fishing at the shallow headwaters just south of the islands. There is an old rough-and-tumble gravel lane off Grant Road, about a mile south of Moorefield Road, that leads to the east side of the lake, which is popular with cat fishers. A small boat could also be launched from there. Other upper lake access points are at the Buck Creek Bridge at Moorefield Road and off Temple Street at New Moorefield. Channel cats are so common here they can be caught from any shoreline, and the area around the marina is as good as any. The old streambed north of the campground and the old roadbed are good bets, too. Most channels will average 1 to 3 pounds, with more than a few reaching between 5 and 10 pounds. Chicken livers or cut shad fished deadline at night seems to be the way to catch a stringer full. I am told a few nice flatheads are caught every summer as well, using small bluegills and chubs in the old channel between the north islands and the campground.

Bluegills are common, with most running between 4 and 7 inches—nothing to write home about, but easy to catch. They can be found anywhere and caught using red worms, wax worms, or crickets anywhere off the shore and from the marina and fishing platforms.

There is a decent tailwater fishery below the spillway for small bass, channel catfish, and walleye in early spring and after high-water discharges.

Wheelchair-accessible fishing platforms are located at the dam and at the marina. Wheelchair access is available nearly everywhere at the marina, which is a popular and productive fishing area as well.

There are some old fish structures located east of the Buck Creek boat ramp and on the east shore north of the campground. Other fishing opportunities can be had across the road from the dam at the Old Reid City Park, which has several ponds available for fishing.

Special regulations: Walleyes must be a minimum of 15 inches, with a limit of six. Largemouth and smallmouth must be a minimum of 12 inches, with a limit of five.

Facilities/camping: The Buck Creek State Park campground has 111 campsites. The town of Springfield is just southwest of the lake and has everything you need. The state park marina has gas, ice, and food and is open all summer.

Additional information: Southeast of the lake, at the intersection of I-70 and U.S. Highway 40, is some great antiques shopping at the Heart of America Antique Mall.

Directions: C. J. Brown is located just northeast of Springfield.

150 Caesar Creek Lake

Key species: Largemouth and smallmouth bass, white bass, saugeye, muskie, crappie, channel and shovelhead catfish, bluegill, sunfish.

General description: An up-and-coming muskie lake with a great tailwater fishery.

Overview: Caesar Creek Lake is a mammoth reservoir of 2,835 acres, with over 40 miles of shoreline. Completed in 1977 by the U.S. Army Corps of Engineers, this flood control lake is deep by Ohio standards, with depths averaging anywhere from 40 to 90 feet, and contains a number of islands. Standing trees are in nearly all the coves, and most of the shoreline is fairly steep and rocky and unusually clear for an impounded lake in the Buckeye State. Visibility is easily 2 to 3 feet on any given summer day.

There are two fishing platforms. One is located at the Flat Fork Ridge Picnic Area near the spillway, and the other is a wheelchair-accessible platform near the youth fishing pond east of park headquarters.

Like most Ohio reservoirs impounded during 1970s, Caesar Creek Lake was not stocked upon completion, leaving it to the two feeder streams, Caesar Creek and Anderson Fork, to supply the brood stock for the new lake. The Ohio Division of Wildlife later added saugeyes and more recently muskies to offer anglers a mixed bag of fishing opportunities. The 7,940-acre Caesar Creek State Park offers hiking, biking, and bridle trails, a campground, a horseman's campground, a public beach, and numerous picnic and parking areas. There is also a marina in the works and canoe access on the Little Miami River.

The adjoining 2,959-acre Caesar Creek Wildlife Area offers access to Upper Caesar Creek. Below the dam is the 483-acre Caesar Creek Gorge State Nature Preserve.

Caesar Creek Lake has five boat ramps, including the campground ramp, and a carry-on launch next to the North Pool boat ramp. It is also possible to launch a canoe at the Upper Caesar Creek headwaters from a parking area located on the east side of the Spring Valley–Paintersville Road Bridge. The Caesar Creek Wildlife Area has a few small ponds available for fishing that also double as wildlife-viewing areas.

Caesar Creek Lake tailwater is typical of the good access and facilities the Army Corps of Engineers provides for fishermen below the dams of many large reservoirs.

Park headquarters are located off Highway 73, just west of the bridge that crosses the lake. The U.S. Army Corps of Engineers headquarters and visitor center is located off Clarksville Road, just west of the dam.

Four government agencies administer Caesar Creek Lake and the surrounding area: Ohio Division of Parks, Division of Wildlife, U.S. Army Corps of Engineers, and Division of Natural Areas and Preserves.

Summer pool on Caesar Creek Lake is 849 feet above sea level. In fall the lake is only lowered 3 feet, to a winter pool of 846 feet.

The fishing: I receive a lot of mixed signals about the fishing at Caesar Creek Lake. One angler referred to as the Dead Sea, while others were exuberant about its fishing. That tells me that sometimes the fishing is good and at other times it's bad.

The Division of Wildlife began stocking muskies in Caesar Creek Lake in 1998, creating Ohio's newest muskie lake. In the early years, muskie stocking was fairly heavy, but it has now settled to approximately one fish per acre, which means roughly 3,000 6- to 9-inch muskies are stocked annually.

Muskie fishing has typically gotten off to a slow start, but lately bass and crappie anglers have started complaining about muskie bite-offs causing poor fishing, a sure sign that muskies are becoming more entrenched in the lake. Another positive sign is that muskie fishers who used to prowl other lakes are beginning to fish here. The Division of Wildlife has great hope that Caesar Creek Lake will develop into one of Ohio's premier muskie lakes, and in time it just might happen.

Casting and trolling seem equally effective for Caesar Creek Lake muskies. Work all the deep timber coves on the south and east sides of the lake with chartreuse tandem spinner baits, Bulldogs, jerk baits, and Bagley's Shads. The timbered coves west of the Highway 73 Bridge are the most productive; Flat Rock Creek is the number one choice. Troll around the islands and points at the west end, along the old stream channel and any drops or flats off that channel, in front of the coves, and along the old roadbeds. Suspended main-lake muskies feed primarily on gizzard shad. Chrome, silver foil, shad, and chartreuse Bagley's Super Shads slow trolled 10 to 15 feet deep 30 to 45 feet behind the boat get the fish. The best trolling is from June through August, with the backs of coves turning on for the casters as early as April. Muskie will average anywhere from 30 to 40 inches, but bigger fish are just around the corner.

Saugeye fishing has been very good at Caesar Creek Lake, with some 25-inch fish coming to net. In a lake as deep as Caesar Creek, saugeye fishers are looking for shallow bars, flats, and submerged lake points. Slow troll the old roadbeds east of the bridge and the many points off Fifty Springs Picnic Area. Also slow troll the shallow flats surrounding the islands. Look for saugeye in 6 to 12 feet of water, concentrating on flats and points from Fifty Springs to the campground. Jigs with minnows, small crank baits, and night crawlers produce best.

Of course crappies are everybody's favorite, and the fishing seems to cycle here as it does everywhere, with good years and bad years. On good years, however, 12- to 15-inch crappies can be had, with most averaging 10 inches. Look for crappies in the timbered coves and on shoreline slips and downed trees anywhere on the lake. Any wood will hold fish, and brush and docks near shore will have a share of them, too. Jigs and minnows fished 6 to 15 feet deep beginning in early April and continuing through May will produce some nice catches during a good year.

White bass are common in the lake, with spring runs up into the headwaters of Caesar Creek and Anderson Fork in April and early May. Most white bass are only 8 to 10 inches long; occasionally a few larger ones are caught. White bass can also be caught chasing shad off the surface on the main lake in summer. White Mepps and Rooster Tails work as good as anything.

Bass fishing is pretty good at Caesar Creek Lake. High numbers of undersize juvenile bass are caught regularly by tournament fishers, with an occasional 3- or 4-pound fish being taken. A popular bass tournament lake, open bass tournaments are held every Tuesday evening at the Wellman Meadows boat ramp located off Oregonia Road. A club tournament is held most weekends somewhere on the lake. Fish the shoreline cover, downed timber, rock and riprap, and brush from one end of the lake to the other. Work the back ends of timber coves in spring. Bass are numerous but tend to run small—most will average only 10 to 12 inches with a few in the 14-inch range. White, yellow, or chartreuse spinner baits, small crank baits, Rapalas, and plastic lizards are what most bass fall for.

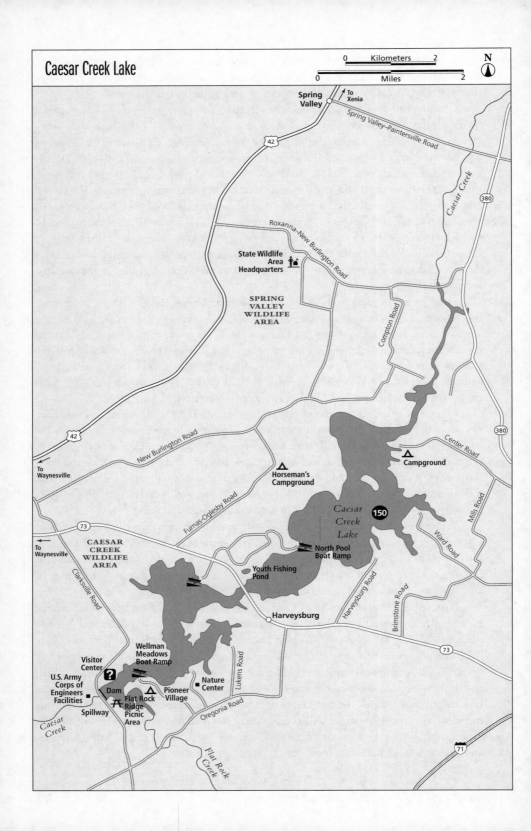

Caesar Creek Lake

Cat fishers do fairly well; channels average 2 to 4 pounds and every so often a fisher will land a 15-pound flathead. Try fishing at night under the Highway 73 Bridge, along the old roadbeds east of the bridge, on the flats, and in the old stream channel in front of the campground. Chicken livers, night crawlers, shad, bluegills, and homemade stink bait work well.

Bluegill fishing is good at Caesar Creek Lake, with nice hand-size fish. The best bluegills are caught during the spawn in late May and early June from shallow flats and brush and timber close to shore. Any picnic area or boat ramp will have bluegills. In spring red worms or wax worms fished under a bobber 2 to 5 feet deep will get plenty of fish; sometimes in the hot summer, bluegills may be as deep as 15 feet.

The tailwater fishing at Caesar Creek is something special to fish, as all manner of game fish call this creek home—even the occasional paddlefish has been seen here. Smallmouth and largemouth are here in good numbers, saugeye and muskies make it through the chute from the lake, white bass run up this creek from the Little Miami, and the tailwaters are full of sunfish, rock bass, and bluegills.

The Corps of Engineers has a small recreation area below the spillway. There are hiking trails, restrooms and picnic areas, a bridge over the stream, and a wheelchair-accessible fishing pier. The recreation area adjoins the Caesar Creek Gorge State Nature Preserve, opening the creek to well over 2 miles of public fishing. The water is as clear as a trout stream, and it is possible to float and fish the entire stream from the dam to its junction with the Little Miami River. Fishers' foot trails follow the creek downstream to some excellent fishing holes.

There is a small youth fishing pond located just past the park headquarters. It is stocked heavily with bass, catfish, and bluegills and is open to anyone under the age of 15.

Special regulations: A 15-inch minimum size limit on bass; 9-inch minimum size limit on crappies.

Facilities/camping: Gas, bait, food, ice, and groceries can be found at Harveysburg or at Waynesville, 3 miles west. Caesar Creek State Park, located on Center Road off Highway 380, has a 287-site campground with a boat ramp and beach.

Additional information: If you're a history buff, take time to visit the historic pioneer village located next to the nature center off Oregonia Road. The hike from Flat Fork to Wellman Meadows will take you past some very scenic waterfalls. Nearby Waynesville has become renowned for its antiques shops. The Spring Valley Wildlife Area, northwest of Caesar Creek Lake, offers additional fishing, waterfowl viewing, and hunting.

Directions: To get to Caesar Creek Lake, take I-71 from Columbus or Cincinnati to Highway 73 west; follow the signs.

151 Clark Lake

Key species: Largemouth bass, bluegill bullhead, crappie; trout stocked in March.

General description: A popular lake in spring, when the rainbows are stocked.

Overview: Located approximately 8 miles east of Springfield, Clark Lake is a small body of water of only 98 acres that sits in the quiet countryside of east-central Clark County in the Clark Lake Wildlife Area. It offers a boat ramp and eight parking areas and has easy bank access with mowed paths that lead to various shoreline locations. It's an older lake, thus very shallow with an average depth from 2 to 5 feet. The lake was dedicated in 1957 by the Clark County Game and Fish Association.

The fishing: Clark Lake is a quiet little lake when you're ready to get away from the crowds at C. J. Brown. It offers both pleasant scenery and some quality fishing.

Bluegills are bountiful here, although they generally run small—usually less than 6 inches. An angler can catch a bucketful with wax worms fished from anywhere along the shore. May and June are the best times; try fishing the brush close to shore.

The lake also contains a healthy population of bullheads, which are easily fooled with half of a night crawler fished near the bottom off any of the earthen piers. A few good channels also inhabit the lake.

Small bass, 8 to 12 inches, are present, although not in any great numbers. An occasional lunker weighing 4 to 5 pounds is caught every spring. Most of the bass are picked up from the shoreline around the overhanging trees and weed edges and from any old log, snags, or brush along the shore, in the bays, and off the edges of the piers. Spinner baits, jigs, plastics, and small buzz baits will usually trigger an aggressive strike.

Crappies are also present. In a good year they may average 9 inches, sometimes bigger. Look for them around the shoreline brush and snags near the dam. Minnows and a bobber are all an angler needs.

The real draw on Clark Lake is its trout fishing in spring. The Division of Wildlife stocks between 2,000 and 3,000 rainbow trout each March, and fishing for them can be had until late May. Corn, cheese, Power Bait, wax worms, and maggots fished on the bottom, and occasionally a yellow Rooster Tail, will catch trout. Try fishing for them off the three earthen piers at the south end of the lake, around the boat ramp, and near the dam. After a good rain and some high water, a few trout can be found below the spillway.

Sinking Creek, below the spillway, offers some limited fishing for bass, bluegill, and catfish.

Carry-in boat launching is possible from the parking areas located on the eastern side of the lake.

Special regulations: 10-hp limit.

Facilities/camping: The only facility is a portable restroom at the boat ramp. Camping is at nearby Buck Creek State Park, with 111 campsites.

Additional information: North of Clark Lake on Highway 54, there is the small crossroads village of Catawba, which has an old-time general store that sells pop, sandwiches, and pizza.

Directions: Take Highway 54 north where it intersects with I-70, east of Springfield, to Old Columbus Road. Follow Old Columbus Road west to Vernon Road, and then go north. Clark Lake Wildlife Area is on the east side of Vernon Road.

152 Cowan Lake

Key species: Muskie, saugeye, largemouth bass, crappie, bluegill, channel catfish.

General description: Quality fishing in the company of sailboats.

Overview: A wonderful 692-acre lake located in southern Clinton County, south of Wilmington. Completed in 1950, the lake was dedicated as a state park in 1968. Cowan Lake State Park has four boat ramps, a camping area, a full-service marina with boat rental, docks, a beach, picnic areas, and shelters houses. Cowan was one of Ohio's original muskie lakes and still receives an annual stocking of one muskie per acre. Popular with the sailing crowd, on any given weekend you can watch literally dozens of sailboats glide across the waves and around the island in a mesmerizing chase to capture the wind.

Cowan's depth averages anywhere from 10 to 25 feet, and the lake is approximately 2.5 miles long and 0.5 mile wide. The visibility is at best 12 to 14 inches, and its headwaters at the east end are covered with lily pads.

The fishing: Fishing for all species is very good at Cowan. Largemouth bass do very well here. As one park ranger put it, "You fish long enough, you'll catch a 5-pounder." Cowan is under a 15-inch minimum length limit for bass. Fish the shoreline slips and downed trees in the coves, around the old docks, around any stumps at the east end, and in some cases the edges of the lily pads. The north shoreline across from the east boat ramp is a good place to start, as is the north shore and coves across from the marina. Spinner baits, purple plastic night crawlers, crayfish, and buzz baits will awaken a sleepy bass. Fishing starts in mid-April and stays fairly steady throughout the summer. A lot of bass caught are in the 12- to 14-inch size range, but plenty of 16- to 18-inch bass are taken, too.

Muskie catches aren't common catches, if only because the number of muskie anglers has fallen off recently. But fish averaging 30 to 36 inches are caught by those who target them. Occasionally a rare 42-inch muskie is caught, and at least Cowan has been a consistent producer of muskies. Most muskie fishing is concentrated near the deeper west end of the lake. Troll Muskie Point, the long point across from the marina boat ramp, with a Bagley's chrome or silver foil Super Shad. Also troll the points and creek channel along the north shore across from the marina toward the dam. Gizzard shad are present in the lake and are considered the main forage for muskies. Ninety percent of the muskies caught from Cowan come from between Muskie Point and the dam.

White crappies are plentiful, averaging 6 to 10 inches, and bucketfuls are taken every spring. Fish any downed trees along the north shore and in the campground cove and around the old wooden boat docks and houseboats on the southeast shore. From the marina toward the dam on the south shore is also productive. Minnows and crappie jigs fished 4 to 6 feet deep will put fish in your bucket. Anglers on this lake fish more for crappies than for any other species.

Since its introduction, saugeye have come on well, and some 24-inch fish have been caught. Ohio Department of Natural Resources holds out great hope for the saugeye, and all indicators are good. Try the sandbar at the end of Muskie Point, around the riprap on Austin Island, in front of both beaches, and the points across from the marina and around the dam. Slow troll shad-colored Shad Raps and jigs with either night crawlers or minnows.

Channel catfish also are doing well, and any look at the bait store photos proves it. Some nice 10-pound channels come from Cowan. Channels are found throughout the lake; however, most local cat fishers will fish the south shore off the riprap pier, from the shoreline, and from the boat ramp and docks east of the public beach with chicken livers or night crawlers on summer nights.

Bluegills up to 9 inches have been reported, with most averaging 6 to 7 inches. Anywhere near the shore, around the campground cove, and near the south shore between the marina and the beach will have plenty of bluegills. Wax worms or a pinch of night crawler will catch them. The best fishing is in late May and June when the spawn is on.

Another fishing opportunity exists below the spillway, which is quite popular. Park at the parking area at the spillway and follow the path downhill. Muskies, saugeyes, bass, and crappies are all taken from the spillway pool.

Special regulations: There is a 10-hp limit on outboards; a 15-inch minimum size limit on bass.

Facilities/camping: Nearby Wilmington and Blanchester have all the amenities. Cowan Lake State Park has a total of 254 campsites, with some overlooking the lake. The park also has 27 cabins. The campground has a camp store and restaurant, beach, and boat ramp. Park headquarters are located at the campground entrance. There is a full-service marina, bait and tackle shop, and boat rental at South Shore Marina, located at the west end of the lake.

Additional information: A very fine restaurant called the Spillway Lodge is located on Cowan Creek Road just west of the dam.

Directions: To get to Cowan Lake, take Highway 730 for 6 miles southwest of Wilmington.

153 Darke Wildlife Area

Key species: Largemouth bass, channel catfish, bluegill.

General description: A small wildlife area with some limited pond fishing.

Overview: Darke Wildlife Area covers only 316 acres but has six or seven fishable ponds, depending on the aquatic weed growth. Located east of Greenville on U.S. Highway 36, Darke Wildlife Area is actually divided into three different tracts with fishable ponds on each. Most ponds are very clear. One pond was stocked with the grass-eating white amurs by the Division of Wildlife to control weed growth.

The fishing: Good populations of bass, small bluegill, and some channel catfish can be found. I encountered some ponds so heavy with weed growth as to make fishing almost impossible. A small canoe or float tube would be helpful. Ponds range from 1 to 5 acres, with most only a short walk from the parking areas.

Special regulations: All grass carp (white amur) must be immediately returned to the water unharmed.

Facilities/camping: None, but nearby Greenville has everything.

Additional information: Most Wildlife Area ponds are stocked with bass, bluegills, and channel catfish on a two- to three-year basis.

Directions: Take Highway 36 4.5 miles east from Greenville.

154 East Fork Lake

Key species: Largemouth, smallmouth, and spotted bass; hybrid striper; channel and flathead catfish; white and black crappie; bluegill; sunfish.

General description: One of only a handful of Ohio lakes stocked with hybrid stripers.

Overview: Located east of Cincinnati, East Fork has the distinction of being the last lake in Ohio impounded in the name of flood control by the U.S. Army Corps of Engineers in 1978. That impounding created one of southwest Ohio's largest lakes at 2,160 acres, with over 35 miles of shoreline. The lake is over 7 miles long and a mile wide in some places.

Standing timber was left in most coves, and stumps line a good portion of its steep banks. It is a deep lake, with 60- to 80-foot water depths quite common. The lake extends far back into the headwater stream with numerous arms and fingers. The Division of Wildlife did not stock East Fork Lake at the time of its impoundment, allowing the native stream fish to populate the lake. Hybrid stripers were later released in East Fork in 1983.

It was a controversial lake at the time of its impoundment, drowning out what many considered to be one of Ohio's finest smallmouth streams, the East Fork of the Little Miami. With its close proximity to one of the state's fastest-growing regional areas, East Fork Lake is among the state's most-visited state parks. The Corps of Engineers' official name for the lake is William H. Harsha Lake, named after a popular congressman, William H. Harsha of the sixth district.

The lake and area around the lake are administered by three agencies: the Corps of Engineers, Division of Parks, and the Division of Wildlife, which oversees the

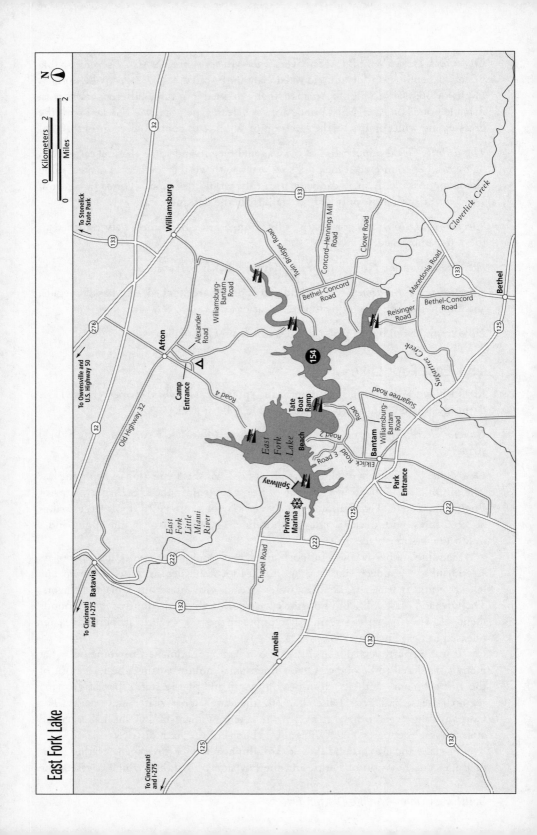

East Fork Lake

2,705-acre East Fork Wildlife Area. The state park headquarters is located at the south park entrance off Highway 125, at Elklick Road. In fall the lake is lowered 4 feet to a winter pool of 729 feet above sea level.

The East Fork State Park is one of Ohio's largest at 4,870 acres. The lake has six boat ramps; a campground; numerous hiking, biking, and bridle trails; a public beach; and picnic areas and shelter houses. There is no lakeside marina, but a private marina does exist on Slade Road as you enter the park from the west. Horsepower is unlimited.

The fishing: As expected on any lake this size next to a major metropolitan area, it does receive its fair share of usage, but that's not to say it's crowded. East Fork is such a large impoundment there seems to be plenty of room to roam. The lake does see its share of tournaments, however. Every Tuesday evening in summer, an open bass tournament is held at the Tate boat ramp located on the south shore. Crappie and catfish tournaments are held regularly, and all manner of fishing contests, various outings, and activities occur on any given weekend.

The bass fishing is good, but most catches reach only in the 13- to 14-inch class; rarely do bass over 4 pounds appear. Early spring beginning in April and again in October and November are when the bass fishing is at its peak. Fish the standing timber and shoreline trees, rock, stumps, and slips in the headwater coves of East Fork, Cloverlick Creek, and Sugartree Creek. Bass fishing is about as good in one creek as the other. Look for bank slips on creek bends and brushy steep banks where the old stream channel swings close to the shore. Most bass are caught back in the coves. Main-lake coves on the north shoreline are also good. Look for downed timber, brush, and bank slips; occasionally bass will be found on the deep points. The riprap along the dam and spillway also give up a few bass and some smallmouth. Fish spinner baits, plastic crawls and lizards rigged Texas- or Carolina-style, buzz baits, and crank baits. East Fork is a busy lake; the timbered coves offer the only refuge a bass fisher can find on this lake in summer.

Smallmouth, which used to be common in the lake after it was impounded in the late 1970s, is a rare catch now. No doubt those native fish from the stream, with a few growing to generous size in the new fertile lake, are all but gone now. Spotted bass are fairly common in the main lake and headwaters, but only reach 10 to 12 inches, and I suspect most anglers who catch them can't tell them from a largemouth. The more aggressive spotted bass will readily hit small crank baits and 4-inch plastic night crawlers.

As with most Ohio lakes, crappies seem to be the primary species that most anglers want to catch. Good catches of a respectable average size of 10 to 12 inches can be made from late March until early June from the wooded coves, around standing timber, and among any treetop that happens to be resting in 10 to 20 feet of water. There is no secret to finding crappies on East Fork. Minnows and a slip bobber fished 6 to 10 feet deep will usually find fish. Sometimes bigger but fewer crappies can be found under a school of small fish. Adjust the depth of your bobber to find the fish.

First stocked in 1983, the hybrid stripers are highly prized by anglers. The sizes range from 2 to 4 pounds, and every once in while a 6-pound fish will entitle some angler to bragging rights. Slow trolling chrome, silver, and shad-colored deep-diving crank baits and Shad Raps is the primary method to catch hybrids at East Fork. Chicken livers fished around the beaches catch a few, and every now and then in summer you can catch hybrids in the jumps, chasing shad in the middle of the lake. Trolling for hybrids is best in front of the two beaches—the public beach and the campground beach. The deep, 60- to 80-foot open water in the north end of the lake also produces stripers for trolling fishers. Fish deep when trolling in summer; some anglers use downriggers to get crank baits down 15 to 20 feet. Each year more than 1 million hybrid striper fry are placed in East Fork Lake.

Good catches of catfish are occasionally made, but cats don't seem to get a lot of attention from anglers. Fish the headwater coves and the creeks at night with chicken livers or night crawlers. The east-end boat ramps on Reisinger Road and Twin Bridges Road are good areas, as are the coves and points west of the public beach on the main lake. Most channels run anywhere from 1 to 3 pounds; 5- to 6-pound fish are not uncommon.

There are several ponds in the wildlife area that are worth a visit if an angler is so inclined to explore. Most require a hike. Before the lake was impounded, some of those ponds held 5- and 6-pound bass. I know, because I fished them.

Additional fishing opportunities exist in the tailwater section of East Fork. Take Spillway Road off Slade Road, go down the hill, and park at the first parking area on the left. Follow the short path down to the stream, at which you'll come to a beautiful little section of stream that begs to be fished with a fly rod. That little stretch is sometimes full of 10- to 12-inch feisty smallmouth eager to jump on a well-placed olive Woolly Bugger. Try fishing it in May.

At the end of Spillway Road are picnic areas, shelter house, restrooms, and access to the tailwater immediately below the spillway. Smallmouth, sunfish, and some nice channel cats populate the tailwaters below the dam.

Special regulations: A 15-inch minimum size limit is in effect for stripers, with a daily limit of four.

Facilities/camping: Nearby, the villages of Bethel, Williamsburg, and Batavia have all the amenities. East Fork State campground is one of the largest in the state, with 384 sites and 4 cabins. The campground is located south of Old Highway 32, near Half Acre Road.

Additional information: Just outside the park on Highway 125 is one of the few and one of the best drive-in theaters left in Ohio, the Starlite Drive-In Theatre.

Directions: To reach East Fork Lake, take Highway 32 (Appalachian Highway) to the Half Acre Road exit near Batavia, turn south, and follow the signs.

155 Fallsville Wildlife Area

Key species: Largemouth bass, bluegill, channel catfish.

General description: A little hidden gem of quality pond fishing.

Overview: Located in the farming belt of northeastern Highland County, Fallsville Wildlife Area consists of 1,761 acres and is a mixture of crop fields, restored prairies, dove fields, and weedy meadows. It offers quality fishing with several nice ponds that range in size from 1 to 8 acres.

The ponds are maintained with regular stockings on two- to three-year cycles. A total of seven fishable ponds are part of the wildlife area, two of which are catch and release. Several more ponds exist as shallow, weedy frog ponds that are subject to low-water levels during dry spells. Several of the ponds require a hike of 0.5 mile or more to reach.

Fallsville Wildlife Area is unique in the respect that it is actually two different wildlife areas, with an additional southern unit that consists of 379 acres that were purchased in 2003. Located within that tract is a high-quality 8-acre lake.

The fishing: Fallsville Wildlife Area has two very nice ponds, well worth the hike required to get to them. The other ponds are near parking areas and receive a fair amount of fishing pressure.

From Hillsboro, take Highway 73 northwest approximately 6 miles to Powell Road. Turn east and go less than 0.5 mile to two parking areas. On the right is one small pond. At the other parking area, back a long lane on your left, is another barely fishable pond that requires a quarter-mile hike to reach.

Continue east on Powell Road to just past Carey Road, and pull into the parking area. From here, hike 0.5 mile south on the tractor trail to a remote, but extremely clear pond that is called Land-Lock Pond. Some weed growth is present, but fishing is good and worth the modest hike.

Head east another 0.5 mile on Powell Road, and you'll find a parking lot on the right at the dog-training area. The large pond located here was renovated in 2006 and should offer quality fishing.

Powell Road ends at Careytown Road South. Turn right (south) to the area headquarters, where maps are available. Behind headquarters is a small catch-and-release pond full of bluegills and small bass. Just past headquarters and back a lane is another parking area, from which a path leads to a very deep, fishable quarry pond where an old mill once stood. Continue downhill on the path to a very scenic waterfall, hence the name Fallsville.

Continue down Careytown Road approximately 2 miles, until you come to the South Unit, with signs clearly marking its location. Park here and hike the tractor trail east almost 0.75 mile to a very fine 8-acre lake. This is a quality catch-and-release fishing lake and is worth every step it takes to get here. The lake is absolutely breathtaking, located on a rise with a cluster of mature white pines on the hill above overlooking it. It is quite a sight to behold. The water is very clear, the bass are well educated, and the bluegills are big. A small float tube would be nice to fish from, but it's very easy to fish from shore or to wade.

The purchase of the South Unit came about because the lake was so popular with trespassing fishers that the Division of Wildlife decided to approach the owner about selling the property so as to open it up to the public.

Special regulations: There are two catch-and-release ponds, both clearly marked with signs. State game and fish regulations apply.

Facilities/camping: There are no facilities at the wildlife area. There is camping at nearby Rocky Fork State Park, which has 210 campsites. The closest town is Hillsboro, which has all the amenities.

Additional information: In September, sportspeople may choose to hunt doves in the morning and fish for bass in the afternoon.

Directions: Fallsville Wildlife Area is located approximately 6 miles northwest of Hillsboro off Highway 73.

156 Grand Lake St. Marys

Key species: Walleye, white and black crappie, largemouth bass, yellow perch, flathead (shovelhead) catfish, channel catfish, bullhead catfish, bluegill.

General description: Once a grand lake that now suffers from heavy algae bloom and unabated nutrient loading.

Overview: Grand Lake St. Marys is one of Ohio's canal lakes, and its largest, built in the late 1830s and 1840s by the hands of German and Irish immigrants using shovels, picks, mules, and oxen. It is the state's largest man-made lake at 14,362 acres, with roughly 56 miles of shoreline. Average depth of the lake is 8 to 9 feet.

The lake is approximately 9 miles long and 3 miles wide. Built on the divide between the Lake Erie Watershed and the Ohio River drainage, feeder streams at the south of the lake flow north into the reservoir. At the outlet at the spillway at Celina, Beaver Creek flows into the Wabash River, eventually draining into the Ohio River at Mount Vernon, Indiana.

Grand Lake St. Marys suffers from algae bloom, and the lake is green with it. Visibility is a poor 1 inch in summer. This condition is caused by nutrient loading from agriculture runoff and the growing housing developments on the lake's south side. The fishing so far seems to hold up despite this, but according to some anglers, fish have changed their habits. Some fishers have given up and are leaving.

There are miles of canals, scattered islands, an old oil-well site, 10 boat ramps and a new ramp on the way, and three scenic lighthouses. There are also eight marinas at last count, numerous lakeside restaurants, bait and tackle shops, and a seemingly endless number of rock jetties, piers, and wharfs to fish from. Fishing access is very good, and the Ohio Division of Parks and Recreation, the Division of Wildlife, and the Mercer County sportsmen's clubs have worked to create these fishing opportunities.

Grand Lake St. Marys State Park covers 591 acres and offers a campground, five beaches, numerous shelters, picnic areas, and parking areas. It is unlimited horsepower, but some hazardous stumps do exist. Weed growth is limited to the shoreline and in the backs of some canals.

Fishing for flatheads on the still waters of Grand Lake St. Marys is a great way to spend a summer day.

The fishing: Fishing at Grand Lake St. Marys is a tale of two lakes, depending on whom you talk to. Some are optimistic and others are resigned to the fact that St. Marys is a dying lake. Sheepshead are beginning to establish themselves, and the sheer numbers of carp are signs of a desperate lake. The water is beyond pea green—it's lime green with algae bloom—and canal and shoreline development continue unabated. The crappie fishing is not what it used to be, and the yellow perch have declined or crashed. Still, fishing continues, and the health of the lake will hopefully be monitored by all parties who have a stake in its long-term well-being.

Walleyes are relativity new to Grand Lake St. Marys, stocked since 1999. Walleyes don't grow as fast as saugeyes, which is what the Division of Wildlife would like to place in the lake. But because of existing regulations concerning drainage into the Lake Erie Watershed, walleyes were it. Fishing for walleyes hasn't caught on yet, but some anglers are trolling and drifting for them in the open lake, searching for fish around hard bottom areas, points, and islands with worm harnesses, Shad Raps, and jigs and minnows. Windy Point, Safety Island, and around the old oil-well site are good places to start. There are some walleye catches reported, and a few in the 24- to 25-inch range have been caught. Each year the Division of Wildlife stocks approximately 600,000 to 700,000 fingerling walleyes into the lake. In some earlier years, they stocked much more than that.

Crappies are what Grand Lake St. Marys is known for, and several major crappie tournaments are held here every year. But like crappies everywhere in the state, they have their good years and bad years. There was a crappie crash in 2001 and 2002 that resulted from low-lake levels caused by dry weather conditions. Crappies are making a slight rebound, but catches are not what they used to be. The fishing is still there, however, and anglers with the know-how still score a few nice ones weighing as much as 2 pounds. Fishing is around and under the thousands of boat docks, under pontoon boats, and deep in the shady cover and brush located in the countless coves, canals, and channels around the lake. Special rods called Sharp Shooters, developed for this kind of fishing, are designed to throw under pontoon boats and docks. Fishing is good in spring from April through May, but after Memorial Day it slows down considerably. Minnows, crappie jigs and tubes, and small spinners all produce well.

Cat fishing at Grand Lake St. Marys is something to write home about, and the lake is well-known for its flathead fishing. Cats weighing close to 50 pounds are often caught. One fishery biologist reports seeing a flathead he estimates was 5 feet long. Channel cat fishing is good, too; most average 1 to 3 pounds but every so often a 6- to 8–pounder is caught. Some nice bullheads are taken also.

Fishing is done from the many jetties and rock piers located around the lake. A fishery biologist tells me that most catfish stay within 30 feet of the rocks. For flatheads use chubs, small carp, shad, or bluegills for bait. A stout line, a strong reel, and a heavy rod is also required. Channels are also found throughout the lake and can be caught on cut shad, chicken livers, and night crawlers.

Perch fishing is hot and cold. There have been a few spectacular years in the past, but things have slowed down considerably. When the perch are on, the ice fishers take advantage of it. When the perch are off, few ice fishers are seen. Perch are schooling fish and can be found almost anywhere on the main lake. Look for channels and deep pockets. Most perch are caught fishing minnows near the bottom. Slow drifting minnows over the lake bottom will often find a school.

There is some good largemouth fishing at Grand Lake St. Marys, with a lot of fish in the 12- to 14-inch range. Tournament results show steady and productive bass fishing, with 4- to 5-pound bass not uncommon. Fish for them along the shoreline riprap, main lake structures, rock piers, old pilings, and the coves and canals with spinner baits, crank baits, and plastics. The brushy coves, points, and canals on the lake's south shore are the most productive. Fish tight to cover; visibility is poor on Grand Lake St. Marys. Bass will be found in the many canals and creeks in spring, moving out to points, rocks, and coves come summer.

Bluegill fishing is pretty good here, especially in spring. Around the many docks and brush in the backs of canals is where anglers find them. A simple bobber and wax worm is all that is required. Although a lot of bluegills caught are decent hand-size fish, they are not the jumbo 'gills that come from its neighbor, Indian Lake. The best bluegill fishing takes place in spring and early summer.

Ninety percent of the fishing at Grand Lake St. Marys is done in the old channels and canals. The lake's primary forage base is gizzard shad. Good fishing exists

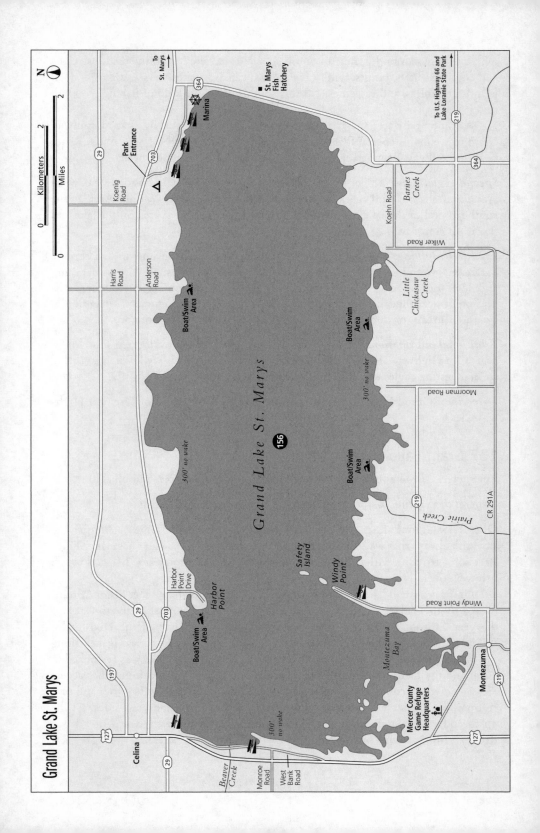

Grand Lake St. Marys

wherever you can find it, but the south shore of the lake has all the feeder streams and countless bays, points, wildly overgrown canals, snakes, cuts and coves, small islands and inlets, and eagle nests. If this sounds like your kind of fishing, you will find it here.

A minor tailwater fishery also exists below the unusual U-shaped spillway south of Celina. A special Fisherman's Parking Lot is located off West Bank Road, near the spillway. Fishing for channel cats is reported to be good here.

Special regulations: None, but for boaters, there are special ski zones, no-wake areas, and channel and marker buoys. The Mercer County Wildlife Area at the southeast end of the lake has a special waterfowl management area on the lake and this is off-limits to boaters.

Facilities/camping: Nearby St. Marys and Celina have all the amenities. The state park campground located just east of St. Marys has 204 campsites, with a boat ramp and dock for campers. There are numerous private campgrounds and lodging facilities on or near the lake. Contact the Auglaize and Mercer Counties Convention & Visitors Bureau for information at (800) 860-4726 or www.seemore.org.

Additional information: The St. Marys Fish Hatchery is nearby, located south of St. Marys on Highway 364. The Mercer County Wildlife Area is well worth a visit; in spring, nesting eagles can be seen from the observation tower.

Directions: Grand Lake St. Marys is about 20 miles southwest of Lima off Highway 29.

157 Grant Lake

Key species: Largemouth bass, channel cat, shovelhead, crappie, and bluegill.

General description: Good spring crappie fishing for nice-size fish.

Overview: Grant Lake is an old lake but still seems to provide some quality fishing. It wasn't always that way. Back in the 1960s, Grant was an excellent bass lake. Then, after some troubles with the dam, Grant lost a great deal of its game fish and rough fish took over.

Grant is a small lake at only 181 acres, averaging less than 7 feet deep. Administered by the Village of Mount Orab, it tends to be dingy most of the time. Over the years, through Nature Works and some effort on behalf of the Division of Wildlife, the dam and spillway at Grant Lake were repaired, riprap was placed along the face of the dam, and other improvements were made. The lake was restocked in 2004, and the fishing has improved. There is one boat ramp and four other access areas where you could also launch a small craft. Shoreline access is good, and several parking areas are located on the south end, at the east and west sides. At the north end, access is questionable, but an angler can fish off the Carpenter Road Bridge. Fishing from a boat would be beneficial but is not necessary.

The fishing: Fishing for crappies is very good at Grant Lake, with some as big as 16 inches showing up in anglers' creels from early spring through early June. Most are taken with a simple slip bobber and minnow fished 3 to 5 feet deep. Crappies are caught from all over the lake, including the spooky old creek channel that runs under the bridge at Carpenter Road. Any stickup, brush, or old snags near 5-foot-plus water is likely to contain a few nice crappies.

Channel catfish have also taken hold in Grant Lake, with a few in the 8-pound category being caught. Most average 15 to 18 inches, but expect a few larger ones to start showing up as the channels stocked in 2004 start to put on some weight. Chicken livers fished near the dam and at the parking area off Lake Grant Road should yield a few squealers for the skillet. Shovelheads close to 20 pounds have been caught, but like 8-pound channel catfish, fish this size are the exception rather than the rule. There is some effort afoot to turn the lake into a catfish lake.

A few largemouth bass have been caught, but most run a small 8 to 12 inches, and there are some unconfirmed reports of increasing smallmouth. Fish the riprap at the dam and old snags and slips along the deep east bank with chartreuse or yellow spinner baits and with white buzz baits in the evening.

The lake is very shallow and marshy at its upper north end. If bow fishing is your thing, then this is your place, as carp are still very numerous in the lake.

To find the boat ramp, drive 1 mile south on U.S. Highway 68 from Mt. Orab. Turn right (west) on Lake Grant Boulevard, drive to the end of the road, and the ramp is on the left. Other access can be found off US 68. To find the access, drive south on US 68 from Mt. Orab about 2 miles. Turn west onto Highway 774 and drive 0.5 mile to Highway 142 (also known as Lake Grant Road). Turn north on Highway 142 and immediately look for a public parking area on the east side of the road.

Special regulations: There is a 10-hp limit.

Facilities/camping: None, but close by the village of Mount Orab has everything you need.

Additional information: There are a couple of nice cozy pizza eateries in Mount Orab.

Directions: To get to Grant Lake, take Highway 32 east from Cincinnati to Mount Orab, turn south on US 68. Grant Lake lies just at the corporation limits, south of town.

158 Indian Creek Wildlife Area

Key species: Largemouth bass, bluegill, channel catfish.

General description: The area has a small reputation for some quality pond fishing.

Overview: Indian Creek Wildlife Area consists of 1,800 acres of flat, patchy hardwood stands and weedy, marshy fields dotted with numerous ponds and potholes.

A popular place for bird-dog trials and dove and pheasant hunters, the area also has a reputation for fishing. Most of the larger ponds are easy to drive to, a few require a hike, but all are worth some effort. For the most part, these are weedy ponds that vary in size from 1 to 10 acres, with large cattail stands, duckweed, moss, and lily pads providing cover for fish and home for waterfowl.

The fishing: Fishing is best in spring and early summer, because as summer drags on, the weed growth just increases. Occasionally some nice bass are taken from the larger ponds, but judging from the well-worn paths to some of the better ponds, they do receive some light to moderate fishing pressure. A few ponds are so shallow and weedy that they are better suited for frog gigging than fishing, but a few are deep enough to hold some respectable bass and a decent channel cat or two. For bass use spinner baits, plastic snag-proof frogs, and buzz baits, as they work best in the weeds and moss. Most ponds are shallow and turn on as early as March. The larger bass from Indian Creek are usually caught in spring.

From Fayetteville take U.S. Highway 50 east; just outside the village limits is the Indian Creek Wildlife Area sign. Turn south on Snowhill Road, follow it to Murray Corner Road, and then, after the stop, continue past Campbell Road to the first parking lot on the right. There are two good lakes separated by a dike; both lakes can be fished from the bank, but are better fished from a tube or canoe, especially the more southern lake of the two. It is possible to fish the one closest to the parking lot; pull your canoe over the dike that separates the two and fish. If you're daring, you could drag your canoe across yet another dike and fish the biggest pond in the wildlife area, the Greentree Marsh Pond.

Another lake worthy of a cast is at the second parking lot on Campbell Road, just past the point where it joins Township Road D4. This small pond is catch and release only and seems to get considerable pressure.

Continue west on Campbell Road, and just past the Sportsmen Service Center, take the south spur, which ends at another very fishable pond. Another pond of note is located on Turner Road. Take Turner Road south from Murray Corner Road to the first parking lot on the right; from there walk east across the field to a couple of very nice fishable ponds. There are many other ponds that can be explored and fished under the right conditions, but most are weed choked and intended for waterfowl use.

Special regulations: There is one catch-and-release pond, at the junction of Campbell Road and Road D4.

Facilities/camping: There are no facilities at the wildlife area, but the little village of Fayetteville is close by and has gas stations, sandwich shops, and refreshments.

Additional information: Indian Creek Wildlife Area has a first-class public archery range.

Directions: Take US 50 from Milford, or Hillsboro, to Fayetteville, and then take US 50 east or US 68 south to Indian Creek Wildlife Area. Watch for signs.

159 Lake Loramie

Key species: Saugeye, crappie, channel catfish, largemouth bass, bluegill.

General description: An old shallow canal lake that still provides quality fishing.

Overview: Another one of Ohio's historic canal lakes, Loramie covers 1,665 acres and is over 6 miles long. The Lake Loramie State Park offers camping, canoe rental, picnic areas, shelter houses, six boat ramps, two beaches, and numerous access points and plenty of parking areas on the lake. Loramie does have some limited development along its banks. The lake was originally constructed in 1824 to supply water to the Miami-Erie Canals. Loramie has an average depth that varies between 4 and 6 feet. The water is stained, with a visibility of 6 inches at best.

The old canals, bays, and fingers off the main lake offer good fish habitat in the way of overhanging trees, shoreline brush, stumps, and timber. Some minor weed growth is present along the edges, and lily pads grow in the backs of the shallow canals and inlets. There are also a number of islands connected by bridges at the west end.

As with all canal lakes, stumps are present along the edges and can be potential hazards, especially at low lake levels.

The state park headquarters is located at the junction of Fort Loramie–Swanders Road and Highway 362. Good shoreline access is available from any of the 407 acres of state park lands located at the west and east ends of the lake and at the ramps and picnic areas.

The fishing: Lake Loramie is one of those quality lakes I received a lot of good vibes from. Anglers I talked with are content with the fishing, and the lake seems to produce well for all species. Fishing pressure has increased here in part due to the relatively poor fishing conditions at nearby Grand Lake St. Marys.

Crappie fishing is very good in spring, with a few 16-inch fish showing up. Most anglers will encounter good numbers of nice crappies from 11 to 14 inches. April and May are the best months for Loramie's crappies. Anglers will find plenty of crappies under the docks and houseboats anchored in the bays and inlets on both sides of the lake, from Filburn's Island to Miller's Slew. As expected, crappies are also found in the downed timber, stumps, and brush scattered along the shoreline in the main lake and in the old canals. Most crappies fall for minnows or bright crappie jigs fished 2 to 4 feet deep.

Bluegills are nice and plentiful—no monsters, but healthy, thick, hand-size 'gills are the rule. Most spawning occurs the first week of June, and that is when anglers can catch their fill. Fish the brush close to the banks in any of the slews, canals, or inlets with maggots or wax worms.

Largemouth bass fishing is also very good; most bass average about 12-plus inches, with several in the 4- to 5-pound range making an occasional appearance. The lake is popular with the bass tournament circuit. Largemouth are typically found holding tight against the shoreline cover in the slews and canals and along the rock and riprap shorelines and lily pads found around the dam and islands at the

Fred Nickol fishes for bluegills at Lake Loramie during July.

west end. Plastic tubes, lizards, and buzz and spinner baits are the primary baits tied to most bass rods at Loramie.

Channel cats are abundant in Loramie, and fishers complain of catching too many while fishing for crappies. Most channels caught are anywhere from 1 to 2 pounds, with a few nice 4-pound and up channels taken as well. There are some shovelheads in Loramie, too. The catfish are well dispersed among some of the more popular fishing locations at Miller's Slew and Luthman Road and from the many picnic areas and boat ramps at the west end of the lake. Chicken livers, night crawlers, shad, and minnows all work well.

Next to crappies, saugeyes are perhaps the most beloved fish on this lake; some believe that the stocking of saugeyes has actually improved the overall fishing by having an impact on the once-overabundant small fish. Saugeyes in the 5- to 7-pound range are not unheard of, and a few anglers will tell stories of much larger fish. Find saugeyes on the deeper north bank in the no-wake zone between Hegemanns Landing and the Luthman Road access. Casters can also pick up saugeyes from the riprap and rocks at the islands and dam at the west end of the lake. Ice fishing for saugeyes is phenomenal as well, with most winter catches taking place at Siegle's Bridge located east, at the headwaters end of the lake. Night crawler harnesses, jigs with minnows, Shad Raps, and crank baits fool most of the lake's saugeyes.

The boat ramps are located throughout the lake with two carry-in sites: one at Miller's Slew and the other at the Siegle's Bridge parking area. The spillway is located on Highway 362, and good tailwater fishing exists there for saugeye, channel cats, and crappies. Parking areas are at the spillway.

Special regulations: Largemouth bass minimum size is 12 inches, with a five-fish limit. The lake has a combination of no-wake zones at the east end, 25 mph travel zones in the middle, and an open speed zone near the west end. Thankfully no water skiing is permitted on the lake.

Facilities/camping: The state park campground has 174 campsites with a boat ramp, canoe rental, and docking at some shoreline camping sites.

Additional information: Nearby Fort Laramie is a historic small town worthy of a visit. The Buckeye Trail skirts the west end of the lake at the state park campground. At the spillway is the Lake Loramie Artists Co-Op with local artwork on display.

Directions: Lake Loramie is located south of Minster, just east of Highway 66.

160 Little Miami River

Key species: Smallmouth bass, sunfish, rock bass, channel catfish, white bass.

General description: A very popular canoe stream with excellent fishing throughout.

Overview: The Little Miami River is Ohio's only designated State and National Scenic River. It was Ohio's first designated State Scenic River, earning that distinction in 1969. The river gets its start in Clark County, at the junction of Lisbon Forks and Gilroy Creek, and flows in a southeasterly direction for approximately 100 miles through five counties until reaching its conclusion at the Ohio River, east of Cincinnati.

Unlike its bigger sister, the Great Miami, the Little Miami does not flow through any major metropolitan areas until it reaches Hamilton County. It skirts several small towns and villages, which have done a good job of keeping the river protected and providing numerous public access points by way of county and municipal parks.

Popular with the canoe and kayak crowds, there are over 86 miles of river that can be floated, beginning at John Bryan State Park, and 25 access points from which to fish or launch a small boat. Admittedly some of these access points are no more than gravel pulloffs next to bridges, but most are state, county, or village access points.

The Little Miami is a limestone-based stream and has a large assemblage of fish species, mussels, and aquatic invertebrates. It consists of long and short pools, some of which are deep; wide bends; numerous riffles; a rock and gravel bottom with little siltation; and a wooded stream corridor for most of its route.

The Little Miami has three low-head dams: one is above Grinnel Road downstream of John Bryan State Park; a small dam is located near the US 68 Bridge; and

The Little Miami River has excellent smallmouth fishing and is popular with canoeists.

the third is just upstream of the Corwin-Waynesville area. The Little Miami Scenic Bike Trail follows the river for 50 miles.

The fishing: The Little Miami is one of the best smallmouth streams in southwestern Ohio; its fertile, oxygenated waters provide a nursery for minnows, darters, crayfish, and hellgrammites. Good spawning habitat exists in the way of stone and gravel bars located throughout the stream. Like all streams, it does become high and turbid after prolonged rains, but throughout most of the summer the stream is relativity clear with over 2 feet of visibility.

The Little Miami has three noted tributaries that are large enough to provide excellent fishing: Caesar Creek, Todds Fork, and the East Fork. All three provide world-class smallmouth fishing.

At the headwaters, the first fishing location on the Little Miami is at a small millpond in the town of Clifton on the Green-Clark County line, at Clifton Reserve Park on South River Road. The small pond was impounded by the Clifton gristmill in 1869, which is still in operation. The Clifton Gorge State Nature Preserve begins below the mill, but no fishing is permitted here. The next downstream fishing can be done at the John Bryan State Park, just east of Yellow Springs. Here the stream is still small but roomy enough to fly cast for small bass, rock bass, and sunfish.

Downstream, the Little Miami increases in size and access can be found at Jacoby Road and at US 68. Other access points include the following: U.S. Highway

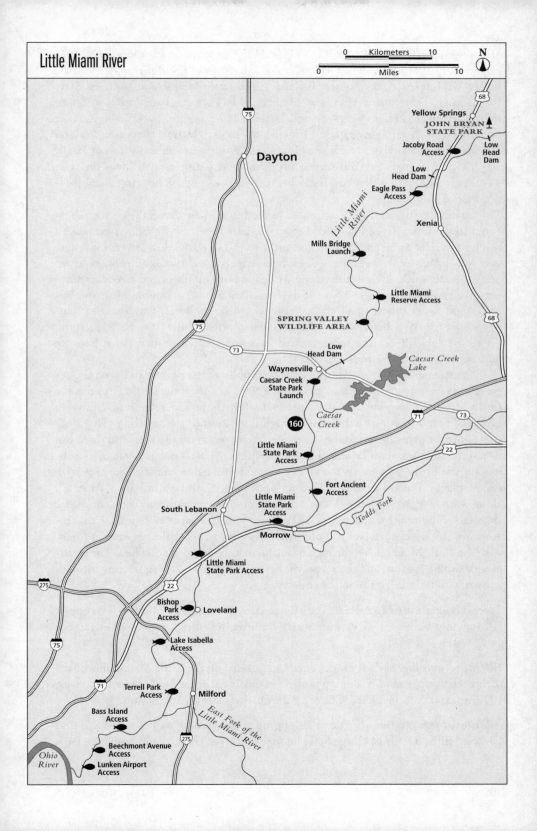

Little Miami River

Kilometers 0—10

Miles 0—10

N

I-75

Dayton

Yellow Springs
JOHN BRYAN STATE PARK
Jacoby Road Access
Low Head Dam
Low Head Dam
Eagle Pass Access
Xenia
68

Little Miami River

Mills Bridge Launch

Little Miami Reserve Access

SPRING VALLEY WILDLIFE AREA

Low Head Dam
Waynesville
Caesar Creek State Park Launch
Caesar Creek Lake
Caesar Creek

160

71   73
22

Little Miami State Park Access

Fort Ancient Access

Little Miami State Park Access
South Lebanon
Morrow
Todds Fork

Little Miami State Park Access

I-275

I-75

22

Bishop Park Access   Loveland

Lake Isabella Access

71

Terrell Park Access   Milford

Bass Island Access

East Fork of the Little Miami River

275

Beechmont Avenue Access

Lunken Airport Access

Ohio River

35 Bridge; Indian Ripple Road; Washington Mill; Constitution Park located off U.S. Highway 42 at Spring Valley. Other access can be found behind the pond at Spring Valley Wildlife Area; at Waynesville; and at the Little Miami Caesar Creek State Park access. There also is access at Mathers Mill; Fort Ancient; Morrow; South Lebanon; the U.S. Highway 22 Bridge; Loveland Community Park; Lake Isabella; Miamiville; Milford; Terrace Park; Plainville; the soon to be open Armleder Park on Wooster Pike; Highway 32 near the Highway 125 intersection; and south of Highway 125, across from Lunken Airport. A paved bike path closely follows the river 40 miles from Spring Valley to Miamiville, as fishers can opt to bike to fishing locations along the stream.

Channel catfish are well distributed in the Little Miami, with the better fishing closer to the Ohio River. Flatheads begin to appear here as well. White bass make a run up the river as far as Caesar Creek, but from Loveland, downstream is where you will encounter greater numbers. Hybrid stripers are also caught from the lower pools. Smallmouth reach healthy proportions in both numbers and size from Caesar Creek and downstream; 12- to 15-inch smallmouth are common. Most smallies are caught using tubes, small cranks, spinners, hellgrammites, crayfish, and minnows, and for fly fishers, Woolly Buggers and crayfish imitations. The closer you get to the Ohio River, the more spotted bass you will encounter. Rock bass are numerous, as are the various sunfish.

The stream is easy to wade at any of the public access points, and several offer good bank-fishing opportunities. But fishing from a canoe is the best way to fish the Little Miami. Numerous access points make launching and retrieving a canoe a breeze. The water is gentle but has enough flow to keep you moving. That does come with a downside as far as fishing goes, however, as on the weekend there can be a sometimes-constant flotilla of canoes and tubes. This is not as much of a problem on the lower portion of the river, as the stream gains considerable size with room aplenty. But from Warren County upstream, it can be a nuisance. After all, along with a party of canoes can come swimmers, tippers, smokers, drinkers, splashers, loudmouths, and partyers. I'm sure you've seen it all before. As recreational water users ourselves, we unfortunately have to share the resource at times.

The Little Miami flows through beautiful mature wooded corridors. The smallmouth fishing is great, and the scenery is better. Even when you're floating through a town, you'll think you're in the country.

Special regulations: No special regulations; current state game and fish laws apply. If canoeing, be aware of various water hazards, low-head dams, strainers, and swift water.

Facilities/camping: Several canoe rentals are located on the Little Miami; most have their own campground. Camping is also at available at John Bryan State Park, with 100 sites, and at some Green County Park Districts stream access sites.

Additional information: If you're fishing upstream, you'll want to visit the Old Clifton Mill and Clifton Gorge State Nature Preserve. The Little Miami State Park

Bike Trail follows the Little Miami River for most of its route; you can access the stream via the bike path. The Little Miami flows through Clark, Green, Warren, Clermont, and Hamilton Counties.

Directions: Access to the Little Miami can be gained from US 68, US 42, and US 50 and from various county and state roads that follow or cross the river from Cincinnati to Yellow Springs.

161 Great Miami River

Key species: Smallmouth bass, some largemouth and spotted bass, white bass, rock bass, sunfish, channel catfish, flathead catfish; hybrid stripers closer to the Ohio River.

General description: The Great Miami River and its tributaries make up one of the greatest smallmouth fisheries south of Lake Erie.

Overview: The Great Miami River gets its start at the spillway of Indian Lake in Logan County and flows 170 miles southeast to the Ohio River, west of Cincinnati. There are 56 access sites, 13 boat ramps, and 15 low-head dams on the river. It has 10 major tributaries; the Stillwater, the Mad, and the Whitewater are the largest.

   The Great Miami has broad riffles and long pools over boulder, gravel, or sand bottoms, and flows past or through 10 major metropolitan areas. The Miami is almost two different rivers, the river that flows into Dayton and the river that flows out of Dayton. In downtown Dayton, the Miami picks up the additional flow of two tributaries—the Mad and the Stillwater, which greatly increase its volume. The Great Miami has watershed drainage of 5,385 square miles. Aquifers below the streambed provide ground water and maintain good summer flows.

   The banks of the Great Miami are lined with industry—most of it gravel extraction—and housing, highways, and industrial parks, with some forested corridors. From Indian Lake to Sidney, the Miami is a rural stream that flows through the farming belt of western Ohio. As it moves south, it visits more populated and industrialized areas and becomes a full urban river by the time it reaches Dayton, and it continues that way with only a mild respite where it enters Hamilton County. It is perhaps at its final last best just before it reaches the Ohio River, where the surrounding flood plain has become locally known as the Oxbow, a wetlands area preserve.

The fishing: Fishing is generally good on the Great Miami. As with all streams it is subject to high water and frequently muddies from upstream rains. Upstream of Dayton, excellent smallmouth fishing exists throughout, and I would gladly spend any day there fishing the tail ends of pools and riffles for the bronze acrobats. Fishing actually begins at the foot of the Indian Lake spillway for channel cats, crappies, and saugeye.

   It is a popular stream for canoes, rowboats, and all manner of small watercraft, but the river is large enough to allow for those intrusions and still pursue quality fishing. Perhaps the best way to fish it is by canoe, beaching at every riffle and pool

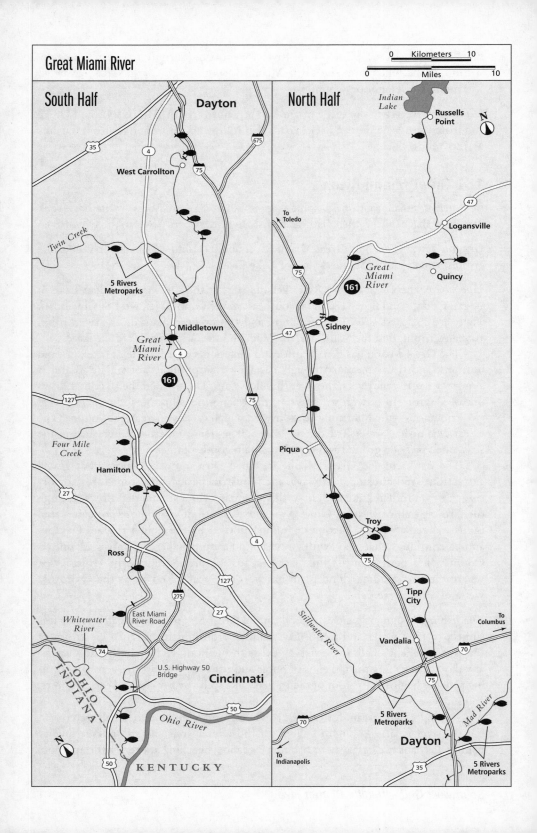

to fully fish it out before proceeding. The tailwaters below the low-head dams, of which there are several, are fishing hot spots worthy of your time. The highly oxygenated water below these spillways just seems to draw fish in.

Saugeye were stocked in the Miami from 1988 through 1997 in the Troy and Sidney areas but was halted because of concerns that it would affect the genetics of native sauger should they reach the Ohio River. Saugeyes washed over the spillways from Indian Lake and Lake Loramie are also in the river, producing the occasional saugeye catch.

Cat fishing is as popular here as it is anywhere. Two- to 3-pound channels are common, with some big shovelheads appearing more likely below the city of Hamilton. Most cat fishers use bluegills, chubs, gizzard shad, or chicken livers for bait. Bank access is not hard to find on the Miami, but you sometimes have to look for it near the deep holes you want to fish. It's a big river that begs to be fished and explored.

Nearly all the tributaries are in themselves excellent smallmouth streams. Watermelon seed or pumpkinseed tubes, small crawdad-colored crank baits, and jigs with curly tail grubs, soft crawls, and Woolly Buggers all work well for stream smallmouth. The Mad, known better as a trout stream in Clark County, held the state record smallmouth for over 50 years. The Stillwater is a renowned smallmouth stream, too. Five Rivers Metroparks in Montgomery County have accesses on the Mad, the Stillwater, and Twin Creek in Dayton. Good smallmouth fishing extends all the way down the river; dams at West Carrollton and Hamilton are local hot spots. One of the nicer sections of river is between Interstate 74 and U.S. Highway 27 along the East Miami River Road. There are two access sites along that stretch. Four Mile Creek and the Whitewater River are highly regarded tributaries by local anglers. There is one unmarked access site at the mouth of the Whitewater by a couple of gravel pulloffs at the US 50 Bridge.

For a complete map of access points, visit the Miami Conservancy District Web site at www.miamiconservancy.org and download a map from that site. Other access information can be found at the following park districts: Shelby County Park District, www.shelbycopark.org; Miami County Park District, www.miamicountyparks.com; Five Rivers Metro Parks, www.metroparks.org; Warren County Park District, www.co.warren.oh.us/parks; Metro Parks of Butler County, www.butlercountyohio.org/countyparks; and Hamilton County Park District, www.greatparks.org.

Special regulations: Be aware that various park districts have their own set of regulations. The Great Miami flows through six counties and numerous towns and villages, each with their own set of park rules. Numerous low-head dams exist. Be careful fishing next to low-head dams, especially after heavy rains, as swiftly rising water can catch you by surprise. Strong currents during periods of high water and unseen stream obstructions always exist.

Facilities/camping: No state parks exist on the Great Miami. Camping is done haphazardly along the banks and sandbars by overnight floaters. Private campgrounds are few, and canoe rentals are spotty. Every town along the Great Miami has all the amenities.

Additional information: The Great Miami is designated as a Class II river.

Directions: The Great Miami flows from Indian Lake to Cincinnati. You can gain access at numerous places, from gravel country roads to points where I-75 runs alongside or crosses the river.

162 Ohio Brush Creek

Key species: Smallmouth, largemouth, and spotted bass; channel and flathead catfish; white bass; sunfish; rock bass; gar; sheepshead; sauger; hybrid striper; carp.

General description: Float or wade for some scenic fishing on one of southern Ohio's best smallmouth streams.

Overview: Ohio Brush Creek begins modestly in southern Highland County, winding for some 57 miles through the center of Adams County before its confluence with the Ohio River east of Manchester. Ohio Brush Creek is a limestone-based stream, designated by the Ohio EPA as exceptional warm-water habitat. The stream contains over 62 different species of fish and serves as the dividing line between the western till plains and the Allegheny Plateau.

Over 125 rare and endangered plants, animals, and mussels share the 278,000-acre watershed. Such an assemblage of rare and endangered species sparked the creation of the Edge of Appalachia Preserve in 1960, which has grown into a collection of eleven preserves located in eastern Adams County along the lower Ohio Brush Creek Watershed. The total preserve system is 12 miles long and consists of 13,000 acres of rocky hollows, forested mountains, small prairies, riffles, waterfalls, and miles of stream.

In the historical context, the internationally known Serpent Mound effigy is located high on the banks overlooking the upper portion of Ohio Brush Creek.

Such is the treasure of Ohio Brush Creek that its value has finally been recognized locally, resulting in a committee being formed by the Adams County Tourism Office, which led to the creation of four public access sites on the stream where anglers can launch a canoe or kayak.

Ohio Brush is an excellent smallmouth stream, but it also attracts those who just want to float a canoe in a stream with the utmost serenity. There is little housing and no industry along its banks, which instead consist mostly of rural farmland and forested hills. The stream is a chain of long rocky pools punctuated with a series of riffles and fast runs. In spring the visibility in the stream can be as much as 3 feet. This is an easy river to float from April through June, but then the stream becomes too low, and wading is the best option. From time to time, various local canoe outfitters have tried to operate on the stream, only to fold up shop. So it's best to bring a boat and explore the stream on your own terms.

Young Michael Ferrell with a nice smallmouth caught from Ohio Brush Creek during a summer float trip. Photo by Mike Ferrell Sr.

The fishing: Ohio Brush is a highly regarded smallmouth stream among that select circle of stream fishers who would rather wade a creek fishing than do practically anything else. Good smallmouth fishing can be found throughout the entire stream. Most smallies average 10 to 12 inches, but every year a couple of 20-inch smallmouth are the talk of the town. Catching 14- to 16-inch fish is not uncommon. Plastic tubes in watermelon seed or pumpkinseed, red squirrel tail Mepps spinners, and small crawdad-colored cranks do very well in the stream. Olive or black Woolly Buggers and crayfish imitations are all a fly angler needs. If a fisher wants to cheat, hellgrammites or small crayfish fished with a small split shot about 6 inches up from the hook will catch so many smallies that it should be outlawed. Smallmouth can be found at the head of pools, at the tail of pools, and at times in the middle of pools—they're everywhere. Smallmouth spawn from the last week of April through mid-May; the best fishing is from May through the July Fourth weekend. After July fishing is tough, but it picks up again in late September. For the floating angler, May is probably the best month to be on the stream. Water levels are high enough to allow a good float, and the water is usually clear.

Longear, pumpkinseed, and warmouth sunfish and rock bass are also plentiful in the stream and can be caught with wax worms, red worms, and small spinners and flies.

Channels are common and best fished from May through September. Upstream of the Highway 125 Bridge, anglers can catch channels in the pools below the riffles with minnows, night crawlers, and hellgrammites. In the lower portion, chicken livers, shrimp, and night crawlers are what they use. Some nice flathead weighing 10 to 15 pounds come from the stream as far up as the Highway 41 Bridge. The best fishing for them, though, is in the lower river pool below the Beasley Fork Bridge. There, flatheads can reach 40 pounds. The mouth of Brush Creek is also another good place to try for big flatheads.

White bass make an annual spring run up Ohio Brush from the river. This run usually occurs the third week in April. Some years are better than others, but a good year is usually spectacular. Whites will average anywhere from 10 to 16 inches. The best fishing is from the Highway 125 Bridge downstream to the Beasley Fork Bridge. Use white Mepps spinners and small jigs with white twister tails for the best luck.

Spotted bass are well distributed throughout the stream, too. While most are found in the lower riffles and pools below the Highway 125 Bridge, several of the larger pools upstream contain small resident populations. These fish hardly reach over 12 inches, but are full of spit and vinegar.

The West Branch of Ohio Brush Creek near Seaman is worth fishing, too. While the stream is too small to float, wading anglers like its smaller confines. The smallmouth fishing from April through June is excellent. After that the fishing gets tough. This branch appears to contain more longear and pumpkinseed sunfish than the main stem of Brush Creek.

In spring a few sauger are in the stream as far up as the Highway 348 Bridge. Some saugers as big as 16 inches have come out of Brush Creek.

Longnose gar, carp, and sheepshead are plentiful in the stream. Hybrid stripers are found from the Ohio River upstream to the Beasely Fork Bridge. Some weighing as much as 5 pounds are caught in the spring on chicken livers and spinners.

The public canoe launches are at the Highway 73 Bridge at Serpent Mound, the Highway 41 Bridge, the Highway 348 Bridge, and the Highway 125 Bridge. All public access sites are clearly marked. There are some pulloffs on Waggoner Riffle Road along the stream. Access on the West Branch is at the bridges. Boat ramps are on Waggoner Riffle Road at Brush Creek campground and off U.S. Highway 52 at the mouth of Brush Creek.

Special regulations: None; state game and fish laws apply.

Facilities/camping: Camping is at the private Brush Creek campground on Waggoner Riffle Road, and at the mouth of Brush Creek at Yates Landing. Facilities can be found at nearby West Union, Seaman, and Peebles.

Additional information: Serpent Mound, operated by the Ohio Historical Society, is open Wednesday through Sunday. For more information about the preserve, contact the Edge of Appalachia Preserve office located on Waggoner Riffle Road.

Directions: To get to Ohio Brush Creek, take Highway 32 45 miles east of Cincinnati. The villages of West Union, Seaman, Peebles, and Manchester can all serve as jumping-off points to fish Ohio Brush Creek.

163 Paint Creek Lake

Key species: Largemouth, smallmouth, saugeye, bluegill, channel and flathead catfish, white bass, crappie.

General description: The hottest tailwater fishery in southwest Ohio.

Overview: Paint Creek Lake is among the last few lakes impounded in Ohio by the U.S. Army Corps of Engineers, reaching its pool level in 1974. It covers 1,190 acres, is well over 5 miles in length, and has over 30 miles of shoreline. Plenty of standing timber and structures were left in the lake prior to flooding, which provided fast fishing for both largemouth and smallmouth in its early years. The Division of Wildlife did not originally stock the lake when it was first impounded, allowing the two main feeder streams, Paint Creek and Rattlesnake Creek, to supply the brood stock for the new reservoir.

The main lake averages 15 to 25 feet deep. It is pretty shallow in the headwaters, as siltation has deposited a good amount of sediment at the stream mouths. There are three public ramps on the lake and a couple of canoe drop-offs located in the Paint Creek Wildlife Area on Rattlesnake Creek.

Paint Creek has three government entities that administer various portions of the lake and the surrounding area. The U.S. Army Corps of Engineers administers the dam and tailwaters area. Ohio State Parks administers the 5,652 acres of park land surrounding the main lake. In the headwater streams of Upper Paint and Rattlesnake Creeks, the Division of Wildlife administers the 5,090-acre Paint Creek Wildlife Area.

Within the state park there is a marina with boat rental, fuel, and dock rental; a beach; hiking, biking, and bridle trails; a campground; numerous picnic areas; and shelter houses. Park headquarters is located off US 50, 12 miles east of Hillsboro.

Below the dam in the tailwaters area, the Corps of Engineers provides ample parking, picnic areas, and restrooms. Summer pool levels at Paint Creek Lake are maintained at 798 feet above sea level. Starting October 1, the lake is dropped 9.5 feet to a winter pool of 787.5; by April the lake is again at summer pool.

The fishing: Fishing is good at Paint Creek Lake. While largemouth is dominant in the lake, the upper headwater streams of Rattlesnake and Paint Creeks have robust smallmouth populations. Upper Rattlesnake Creek has produced some nice 5-pound smallmouth.

To find smallmouth in Rattlesnake, launch at the ramp located off Highway 753 and motor upstream to the first riffle. Another option is to launch a canoe at the Centerfield Bridge and float and fish your way downstream. On Paint Creek an angler can launch at the Taylor Road ramp at the north end of the lake and motor upstream until the boat bottoms out, then fish up to Paint Creek Falls. Not only is the fishing good, but the scenery is nice.

For a few years after the lake was first impounded, smallmouth and spots were common catches, now largemouth is the predominant bass. While the majority of bass will run less than 13 inches, plenty of 15- to 17-inch largemouth are caught from Paint Creek. In April, after the water has reached pool level, start working the timber and wood in the backs of the creeks and coves with spinner baits and black jigs with pork or plastic trailers. As it warms up, begin fishing the main lake cover of rocks and wood with cranks and plastics. In summer, shorelines close to where the old creek brushes up against the bank will hold bass. The deep point at the state park campground is a good bet, as is anywhere the channel swings close to shore; use a depth finder or map to locate these places. Another good bank close to the old streambed is the south shore of Rattlesnake Creek, a mile east of the Highway 753 ramp. Bass hold shallow in Paint Creek and will be found no deeper than 6 or 7 feet. Work crank baits, plastic tubes, lizards, and worms in any rocks, bank slips, or old stumps found along these channel-edge shores. At night in summer, use big plastic night crawlers or jigs with trailers in the same places; some nice 3- and 4-pound bass have come from the lake at night.

Good cat fishing can also be had, and a few big ones do show up, especially on rising water. Channels are well distributed and most run 2 to 4 pounds, with a few over the 10-pound mark. The lake's best is a 17-pound channel. Chicken livers, shrimp, and night crawlers are local favorites. Good areas to catch channels from shore are the Rattlesnake Creek ramp and north of the public beach.

Big shovelheads have found a home in the lake, and 10- to 20-pound fish are not uncommon, with a few approaching 40 pounds. Shovelheads are taken on live bait from Paint Creek by anglers using 3-inch bluegills, big chubs, and shiners and fishing in the old stream channels in Rattlesnake and Paint Creeks at night.

Crappies do well at Paint Creek, and it's a noted crappie lake. Starting in April, find crappies in the timber and stumps upstream in the two creek arms and in the stumps and slips on the shore just south of the point where the two main channels meet. The tree line just upstream of the Highway 753 Bridge is a good place to find spring crappie, too. In the lake, any timber, bank slips, or stumpy cove will hold crappies in spring. Come fall, crappies will stage off the campground point and at other locations where the old stream channel brushes up close to the bank on the main lake. Crappie fishing holds up well through Memorial Day and then picks up again in fall. To catch crappie from Paint Creek, fish about 6 feet deep over cover with minnows and crappie jigs.

What put Paint Creek on the map was its saugeye fishery. It was one of the original lakes that Ohio begin stocking with the walleye/sauger hybrid in 1982. Because Paint Creek is a flood control lake with fluctuating lake levels, saugeye fishing is not considered good. The majority of saugeye caught from Paint Creek Lake are caught below the dam.

What saugeye are caught from the lake are taken from the shallows around the hazard zone buoys by drifting or casting night crawlers, jigs with curly tail grubs or minnows, and small crank baits. Look for saugeyes on the shallow flats 6 to 10 feet deep. The flats in front of the Taylor Road boat ramp are good, as is the saddle between the islands and the shoreline near the public beach. Most catches of saugeye are incidental, usually caught by bass fishers working crank baits around the rocks. The best saugeye fishing on the lake takes place in fall.

The saugeye fishing for which Paint Creek Lake is famous is its tailwater fishery. Few anglers actually fish for saugeyes in the lake, but when the Corps of Engineers is releasing water, it can be elbow-to-elbow below the dam. Hundreds of saugeyes, anywhere from 8 to 18 inches, will be caught from the stream below the dam during periods of high-water releases. Plenty of small fish will be caught, but several nice 15- to 16-inch saugeye will be caught as well. Saugeye don't get large in Paint Creek; 20 inches is about tops. But what they lack in size, they make up for in numbers. Small $\frac{1}{16}$- to $\frac{1}{8}$-ounce yellow, pink, or chartreuse jigs with orange or chartreuse curly tail grubs catch most of the saugeyes from the tailwaters. If the bite is a little slow, tip the jig with a minnow instead. The best fishing is anytime during a high-water release and during late fall, winter, and early spring.

The Corps of Engineers has created a picnic and parking area below the dam, which can be reached by going across the dam and taking the first road downhill. There is over a mile of stream that can be fished below Paint Creek Dam. Not only do anglers catch saugeye by the bucket, but smallmouth, sunfish, rock bass, and channel cats are almost as plentiful. An Ohio state record longear sunfish was caught from these tailwaters.

Upper Rattlesnake and Paint Creeks receive a white bass run in April. From the Paint Creek Wildlife Area that extends nearly 6 miles upstream, Rattlesnake can be accessed from any of the well-marked parking areas off Cope Road. Rattlesnake is a good-quality stream, worth the effort to fish its upper reaches. The same can be said of Paint Creek, from which the Paint Creek Wildlife Area extends to the corporation limits of Greenfield. Access to Upper Paint Creek requires a hike from the parking areas, but it can also be reached off Highway 753, south of Greenfield, at Crosley Road and Old Paint Creek Road.

White bass are also caught off the lake flats from the jumps when they're chasing shad in summer. Most white bass average 10 to 14 inches and can be caught using white Mepps spinners or $\frac{1}{4}$-ounce rattletraps.

Special regulations: Minimum size limit on all bass is 15 inches, with a five-fish limit.

Facilities/camping: Outside of park property, there are not many facilities. The town of Greenfield is 20 minutes away and has all the amenities. The state park campground has 195 campsites. Park headquarters is located on US 50, about 12 miles east of Hillsboro.

Additional information: The Seven Caves and the Highlands Nature Sanctuary located near the park entrance on US 50 are well worth a visit.

Directions: To get to Paint Creek Lake, take US 50 to the Highland-Ross County line from either Chillicothe or Hillsboro and follow the signs.

164 Rocky Fork Lake

Key species: Largemouth and smallmouth bass, crappie, channel and flathead catfish, bluegill, saugeye.

General description: One of the top bass and catfish lakes in southwest Ohio.

Overview: Rocky Fork Lake in Highland County was impounded in 1953 and is one of the original muskie lakes in Ohio. Shortly after its impoundment, muskie fry were stocked into Rocky Fork Lake from the Kincaid fish hatchery with eggs taken from native stream muskies captured in Sunfish Creek.

Rocky Fork covers 1,992 acres, has 31 miles of shoreline, and averages 15 to 25 feet in depth. Rocky Fork State Park surrounds the lake with 1,384 acres and offers an abundance of shoreline fishing opportunities. The park also has camping, two public beaches, hiking trails, picnic areas, docks, and pontoon boat rental at North Beach Marina, where fuel is also available.

The lake has six boat ramps—one at the campground, one at North Beach, two near the spillway, one at South Beach, and another at Fisherman's Wharf. Wheelchair accessibility is available at all locations. The lake is nearly 6 miles long and 0.5 mile wide at its widest. It has no horsepower restrictions, with an open zone in the middle and no-wake zones at both ends of the lake. Park headquarters is located at the campground.

Rocky Fork is without a doubt my favorite lake in Ohio. It's where I caught my first muskie and took my wife fishing on our first date. In its early years it was a premier muskie lake, but a bad case of the bacterial infection red spot during the 1980s finished off the fishery, and a decision was made to halt the stocking efforts.

During the 1960s and 1970s, the land around Rocky Fork saw a tremendous growth in residences. A fishery biologist with the Division of Wildlife, who lived near the lake, always believed the generally poor sewage systems from the residences were to blame for the bacteria. About that same time, siltation was building up at the upper end, and dredging began. Some in the know blamed the dredging as a possible cause for the infection. Whatever the reason, the bacteria seemed only to affect muskies, and during those days it wasn't unusual to see a floating 36-inch muskie. Although dredging continues, a new sewage plant was recently built to accommodate the residences and businesses around the lake, doing away with the old inefficient septic tanks. Since that time, water visibility has increased, and most will point out that fishing has improved remarkably.

The fishing: Rocky Fork has become somewhat of a local favorite with bass clubs; bass tournaments are held here frequently and with excellent results. The lake also has a reputation for quality cat fishing; several flatheads in the 30- to 40-pound range are caught every year. Crappies are always a big attraction, especially in spring. Although not overly large, they make up for it in abundance. Bluegills are everywhere, and smallmouth are nearly as common as the largemouth. Saugeyes are a promising recent introduction into the lake, replacing the walleyes that were once stocked.

Rocky Fork Lake

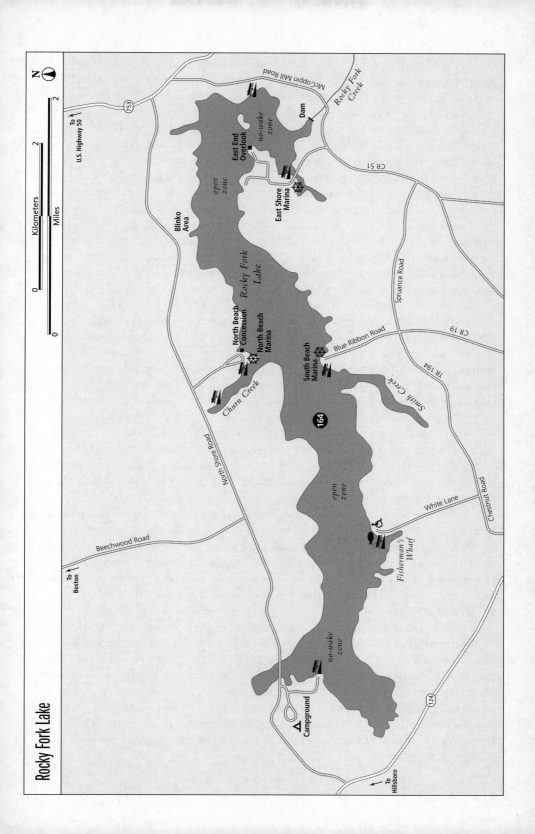

In the past walleye fishing in Rocky Fork was fairly good, with some occasional whoppers approaching 8 pounds being caught by trolling muskie fishers on Hellbenders and Waterdogs. Saugeye fishing is new, but I'm sure as time rolls on, catches will improve and double-digit saugeyes will replace those few double-digit walleyes that were once caught. Look for saugeye on the gravel point and rock points just west of North Beach. At South Beach slow troll in front of the beach and in the flats just west of the beach. Fish the point at Smith Creek and the flats to the west of the point. Any of the rocky points from the Blinko Area toward the dam will hold saugeye, and the flats around the islands are always hot. Troll or cast night crawlers, jigs with minnows, and Shad Raps. Fishing is good in spring and fall, and at night in summer.

Come winter, saugeyes are found under the Lucas Lane Bridge, and jigging Rapalas or jigs with minnows will catch them. With most lakes, saugeyes do well in the tailwaters, and Rocky Fork is no exception. At one time the tailwaters below Rocky Fork dam were open to public fishing but they are now closed. It is a shame, too, because Rocky Fork Creek below the spillway is an excellent fishery in itself.

Bass fishing is excellent throughout the lake, from the stumps and logs at Fisherman's Wharf to the rocky banks near the spillway. Rocky Fork is probably one of the better bass lakes in southwest Ohio, with many good-size largemouth and smallmouth between 14 and 20 inches. Fish the shoreline cover, the rocks, old stumps, logs, and the few fallen trees with spinner baits, plastic night crawlers, and cranks. The shoreline across the lake from Fisherman's Wharf to North Beach is good, as is the west bank of Churn Creek across from the North Beach boat launch. From the Blinko Area east and along the south shore, fish the rocky points and any wood with cranks, spinner baits, and tubes. This is the best smallmouth water in the lake, and a 4-pound smallie is not out of the question. At the west end near Fisherman's Wharf fish the old stumps and timber with buzz baits in the evening and jitterbugs at night. Fishing starts in April, is probably at its peak in May and June, then picks up again after Labor Day.

Nighttime cat fishing is popular with anglers spread out all over the lake in summer, and a look at the photos in any bait shop will tell why. Channels can be caught from any location on the lake and get a nice 3 to 5 pounds, with 10-pound channels not uncommon. Even channels over 20 pounds have been reported. Most channels are caught using chicken livers or night crawlers and various homemade catfish concoctions. The most popular spot on the lake for channels is off the bank at Fisherman's Wharf. South Beach is popular, and the rock pier at the Blinko Area is another hot spot for channels. Summer nights are the best times to channel fish.

Flathead fishing is also excellent at Rocky Fork, with good numbers of 20- to 30-pound cats. Every year it seems some angler breaks the 50-pound mark. The big cats are caught on live bait of every description from goldfish to gizzard shad. Most flatheads are caught off the flats along the old stream channel from South Beach to Fisherman's Wharf on the lake's south side. The area between the Wharf and the campground is also good. Try fishing at night from the shore at Fisherman's Wharf. If fishing from a boat, then anchor and fish deadline or use floats with glow sticks attached.

Perhaps the most popular fishing is for crappies from late April through early June. Buckets full of crappies are caught by practically anybody who fishes for them; whether from boat or shore, anglers' success seems to fall about equal on all. Fish the brush, timber, and old treetops and snags around Fisherman's Wharf and the south shore toward the beach. The docks and bank cover around the North Beach boat launch is also excellent. From shore, fish off the stone pier at the Blinko Area and around the old docks at the East End Overlook. Crappies are widespread and plentiful. A simple crappie minnow fished 6 feet deep will catch 30 to 40 crappies in half a day of fishing, averaging 9 to 10 inches in length.

Bluegill is the first fish for every youngster, and youngsters won't be disappointed here. Find all the 'gills anyone would want to catch off any of the docks and around the shore using a simple float with a red worm. Most bluegills average 6 to 7 inches, and the best time to catch them is during the spawn in early June.

As with any Ohio lake, Rocky Fork has its rough fish. There are some carp here that look like pigs. Bow fishing is great sport at Rocky Fork, and my only hope is that you get them all.

Special regulations: None; all state fish and game laws apply. Speed and no-wake zones are clearly marked.

Facilities/camping: Rocky Fork State Park has 210 campsites, including 50 lakeshore sites. Full amenities, gas stations, bait and tackle shops are all found on North Shore Road. Lake maps are widely available at all facilities.

Additional information: Hillsboro has restaurants for every taste, and some very fine fishing can be had at the old Hillsboro city reservoir located on U.S. Highway 62 north of town.

Directions: Take Highway 124 east of Hillsboro 4 miles out of town, then turn left (north) on North Shore Road.

165 Rush Run Lake

Key species: Largemouth bass, bluegill, crappie, channel catfish; rainbow trout stocked in spring and fall.

General description: Great bass lake with good shoreline access, but the clear water makes fishing challenging.

Overview: Rush Run Lake is located within the hilly terrain of the 1,174-acre Rush Run Wildlife Area in southern Preble County. The lake was constructed in 1970, covers 58 acres, and averages 10 to 15 feet deep, with a few deeper pockets near the dam. Much of the timber was left during the time of its construction and it still stands today in the lake's coves and inlets. Visibility on the lake is exceptional, easily 4 to 6 feet in summer. There is a concrete boat ramp, a spacious parking lot, and walkways that lead to the three wheelchair-accessible fishing platforms. Shoreline access is very easy, with fishers' paths following the edge of the lake.

Anglers fishing for bass on Rush Run Lake.

The fishing: Rush Run is a high-quality fishing lake that every fisher in southwest Ohio should visit at least once. There is a 15-inch minimum length limit on bass, and judging from what I observed, there's plenty of bass over and above that. Locals tell me that several 4- to 5-pound bass are caught every spring from the lake, but the fish are smart and not easily fooled. It is the only lake I visited that bass actually appeared to outnumber the bluegills. While most bass average 12 to 14 inches, from what I observed around the rocks at the dam, good numbers of 15- to 16-inch bass were plainly visible.

Rush Run is a reputed early season bass lake. Fish the backs of coves in the south arm for the best early season action; also good is the south shoreline just east of the dam. Once bass become more active, work the shoreline cover and brush in all the coves with spinner baits, lizards, and jigs and pigs. The rock and riprap along the face of the dam attract bass all season long. Buzz baits also work well in late spring and in summer. More than a few bass have been caught using buzz baits and plastic jerks around the standing timber in the evening. If fishing from the shoreline, fish the rocks along the face of the dam for the best shot at a heavy bass. The water is clear, the bass are educated, and long casts with light line are necessary if you want to catch something worth bragging about.

I am told some good crappies are caught in spring around the timber, stumps, treetops, and bank slips, with some approaching 15 inches. Most are taken with a simple slip bobber and a minnow fished 6 feet deep or more.

Some nice channel cats, weighing up to 5 pounds, are caught with night crawlers, chicken livers, and minnows. Most fishing for them is done from the shore near the boat ramp.

There are plenty of bluegills—a few better than hand size. Just walk the banks, fishing the shoreline brush and shallows with wax worms or red worms. During early June, anglers can sight fish from the shoreline for big spawning bluegills. Come summer, fish are deep in the timber.

Approximately 2,500 trout are stocked in Rush Run Lake in spring and 1,000 in late October to the fanfare of local fishers. Fish the waters around the boat ramp and off the dam with cheese, corn, Power Bait, and small spinners. A few trout survive until May from the spring stocking; in fall trout can be caught all winter long.

White amurs were introduced into the lake to control weed growth. If caught, they must be immediately released unharmed.

Special regulations: There is a 15-inch minimum size limit on bass, with a daily limit of five bass. The lake is limited to 10-hp outboards. Rush Run Lake is open to fishing from 6:00 a.m. to 10:00 p.m.

Facilities/camping: There is a boat ramp, and the lake is wheelchair accessible. Outside of that, there are no other facilities at the lake. Camping is possible at nearby Hueston Woods State Park, which has 488 sites.

Additional information: There is another small pond located behind the wildlife area headquarters located on Northern Road that offers fishing for bass and bluegills.

Directions: There is no easy way to get to Rush Run Lake, which is located about 9 miles northwest of Oxford off U.S. Highway 127 and 3 miles north of Somerville on Northern Road.

166 Sardinia Village Reservoir

Just north of the small village of Sardinia, across from Highway 32, is the old village reservoir. I am told it contains bass, bluegill, channel catfish, and crappie. Fishing is from the bank only, as no boats are permitted on the reservoir. Shoreline access is good on the south end at the dam, but the rest of the shoreline is overgrown with trees and brush, making any attempt to fish along the banks an interesting adventure at best. The reservoir is a nice-looking small reservoir I estimate at 10 acres. Occasionally a 3-pound bass is caught; many years ago the old reservoir was known to produce a few 5-pound bass. Bluegills are small, but a few hand-size bluegills are caught in spring. The channel cat fishing is popular with local residents, and channels 12 to 15 inches are taken on chicken livers and night crawlers. A few small crappies are caught in spring on minnows and spinners.

Parking is at the gravel parking area off Mowrystown Road off Highway 32. Parking is also permitted at the old waterworks building. A picnic table and trash cans are the only facilities at the reservoir, but the area around the dam is kept nicely mowed and well maintained.

The village of Sardinia is located approximately 30 miles east of Cincinnati off Highway 32.

167 Spring Valley Wildlife Area

Key species: Largemouth bass, bluegill, some bullhead catfish.

General description: Primarily intended for waterfowl, Spring Valley does have some limited fishing.

Overview: Spring Valley Wildlife Area covers 842 acres located on the county line between Greene and Warren Counties. It has a 150-acre weedy pond and marsh with a waterfowl- and wildlife-viewing platform, and adjoins the Little Miami River on its west side.

The fishing: Not a primary fishing destination, but the large weed-filled pond has been known to give up a decent bass or two. It is loaded with bluegill and is, for whatever reason, popular with anglers. The lake is constantly being drawn down to encourage weed growth for waterfowl and only averages 2 to 3 feet in depth. The best fishing is on the deeper dike side next to the Little Miami River. Several large sycamore trees provide shade, and a few lunkers have come from here. Additional fishing can be found in the Little Miami River adjoining the wildlife area.

Special regulations: None; state game and fish laws apply.

Facilities/camping: No facilities are at the lake. Camping can be found at the Frontier Campground adjoining the wildlife area.

Additional information: Nearby is Waynesville, renowned for its antiques shops. Caesar Creek Lake is only a few miles away, and a visit to the Caesar Creek Gorge State Nature Preserve is well worth the time.

Directions: Take Roxana–New Burlington Road east off US 42, north of Waynesville, then head south on Pence Jones Road past the wildlife area headquarters. Parking is at the lake, off Collett Road on the wildlife area's west side.

168 Stillwater River

Key species: Smallmouth bass, rock bass, sunfish, channel catfish.

General description: The Stillwater is a quality smallmouth stream.

Overview: Designated an Ohio State Scenic River in 1975, the Stillwater gets its start in central Darke County and then flows south along Highway 48 to meet its conclusion with the Great Miami River in Dayton. It doesn't become much of a fishing stream until it crosses under Highway 185 south of Versailles, just inside the Darke County line. That location is listed as an access site, but I couldn't find access until I reached the Bradford-Bloomer Bridge a few miles downstream. Access there is plainly marked; parking is on the west side of the bridge. These reasons cause me to suspect various stream access maps and whether they are updated regularly. I always said access is wherever you find it, even if you have to look for it.

The fishing: Stillwater is a typical southwest Ohio smallmouth stream, with long, deep pools. It is punctuated by a series of riffles and small potholes, with sand, gravel, and rock bottoms. There is an abundance of crayfish, hellgrammites, and sunfish here. Fishing on the Stillwater is reputed to be good; I just like the scenery and the water is clear.

Downstream from the Bradford-Bloomer access, there is fishing for 36 miles before the Stillwater joins with the Miami. The next access is the Stillwater Prairie Reserve at the parking area near the ranger station. A short walk south and you are at the stream's edge. This is wonderful fly-fishing water, and it can be waded downstream to the Range Line Road access or upstream to Highway 185. You could make arrangements to be picked up there, or turn around and fish it again all the way back to where you started. After the Range Line Road access, there are 15 more access sites before reaching the big Miami. Following Highway 48 south, access can be gained at the parking areas at bridges off US 48. Community parks like Covington Community Park, West Milton Community Park, and Englewood Metro Park are also access areas. The Stillwater is an excellent canoe stream, but be aware of low-head dams, the first of which is just beyond the point where Greenville Creek meets the Stillwater. There are some nice sections of river downstream toward Englewood, before it becomes civilized, that make the area well deserving of its scenic designation. The Stillwater starts out country but ends up city; I'll take the north half.

Special regulations: The Stillwater River has a one-fish, 15-inch minimum size limit on smallmouth bass from the Highway 718 Bridge downstream to the Frederick-Garland Bridge near the Miami-Montgomery County line.

Facilities/camping: The small villages of Covington and West Milton have all the amenities. The only campground on the Stillwater River is the Stillwater Beach campground, located on Versailles-Southeastern Road near the Darke-Miami County line.

Additional information: Greenville Creek, a tributary of the Stillwater and another State Scenic River, is well worth fishing. Access is at most bridge crossings off US 36. For a map of the public access sites on the Stillwater River and Greenville Creek, visit the Miami Conservancy District Web site at www.miamiconservancy.org.

169 Stonelick Lake

Key species: Largemouth bass, crappie, catfish, bluegill, trout.

General description: A popular lake when trout are stocked in spring and fall.

Overview: Stonelick is a small lake of 171 acres located in northeast Clermont County. It is an old lake, built in 1949 to create a wildlife area for sportspeople. The lake is surrounded by the 1,058-acre Stonelick State Park, which has camping, hiking trails, a public beach, picnic areas, a shelter house, boat rental, and a boat ramp on the north shore off Highway 727. The park also has a wheelchair-accessible pier at the dam. The Ohio Division of Parks purchased additional property below the spillway, where some small stream fishing can be had in spring. Park headquarters is at the campground.

The fishing: I remember my uncle taking me on my first fishing trip to Stonelick Lake; we fished Bell's Point all day. I also recall the late, great Billy Beecraft, of Cincinnati, catching from Stonelick what I thought was the largest stringer of bass ever caught in a tournament, where the old submerged roadbed crosses the channel east of the beach. At one time this was one hot bass lake; now most of the attention is on the trout fishing. There is still plenty of bass fishing to be had at Stonelick, and several good bass weighing between 3 and 4 pounds come from the lake each spring. To find them, fish the shoreline cover and weed edges across from the beach and toward the dam. Nowadays the bass seek cover under overhanging trees, brush, old stumps, deadfalls, and weeds from the camping area to the dam on the lake's north shore, and they hang close to the shoreline. Fish spinner baits and plastics tight against cover and pitch buzz baits to the weed edges. Also fish Bell's Point at the end of the old headquarters road near the dam and the shoreline east of it. The best fishing is in April and May.

Crappies are taken off the brush and snags in the west end of the lake from both shorelines. Minnows and jigs will catch crappies that average 6 to 8 inches.

There are good numbers of channel cats in Stonelick, with a few reaching up to 10 pounds. A 65-pound shovelhead is rumored to have come out of this lake. For channels, fish the shoreline anywhere from the campground to the beach on the south side of the lake and off the dam. The picnic area across from the public beach is a top spot, too. Shoreline access is excellent all around the lake, and channels can be found everywhere. In summer use chicken livers, shrimp, and cut shad at night.

Most of the angling attention nowadays is placed on the trout. To say they are popular would be an understatement. Over 3,000 trout are stocked in March, and another 2,500 are stocked again in October. Most anglers fish around the dam with Power Bait, maggots, wax worms, corn, cheese, and small Rooster Tail spinners. Angling pressure is intense, and most of the trout are gone in a few weeks. After periods of heavy rain in spring, some trout wash over the dam and into the small creek below.

Special regulations: Electric motors only. The limit on trout is five fish.

Facilities/camping: Camping is at Stonelick State Park, with 115 sites and 1 cabin. At the campground office, boat rental and loaner fishing tackle are also available.

Additional information: On the north shore of the lake is a landmark indicating the first settlement in Wayne Township in Clermont County.

Directions: To get to Stonelick take Highway 133 north from US 50 near Owensville, head west at Highway 727, and then follow the signs.

170 Tranquility Wildlife Area

Key species: Largemouth bass, channel catfish, bluegill, crappie.

General description: Good pond fishing with no crowds at a nice secluded place.

Overview: Tranquility Wildlife Area, established in 1956, covers 4,260 acres and is located in north central Adams County. It is well-known for its quality deer and turkey hunting and less known for its fishing, except by the locals.

Tranquility has 12 ponds listed, but a few more exist as watering holes and frog ponds that are not on the maps. Many of these ponds offer good fishing and are stocked every third year by the Division of Wildlife. Some of the ponds are easy to access with parking lots close by, while others require a hike of varying distances. Township roads intersect the area, and a map is helpful to find most of the ponds. The ponds vary in size from a few acres on down, with most located within the weedy fields that make up a good portion of the wildlife area's habitat.

Tranquility is a mixture of hardwoods, thick red cedars, and vast weedy fields, located in a valley between Highway 770 to the west, Old Highway 32 to the south, and Louisville Road to the north. The wildlife area boundary is clearly marked with yellow signs. Tranquility is popular in the hunting seasons, but in summer you'll have most of the fishing to yourself.

The fishing: Largemouth bass and channel cats are what most anglers go for here. Bluegills are plentiful, as in most ponds, and occasionally a few nice ones show up. There are crappies in the pond by parking lot D-12, and several years ago a fisherman caught one from there that was near state record size. But the crappies are mostly incidental catches.

The five larger ponds next to the parking areas get the most attention from anglers, and they are easy to access, but that's not to say that the other ponds aren't hiding a 5-pound bass under the moss. Every pond is worth a cast. Moss beds, cattails, and lily pads, with an occasional fallen tree, make up the bulk of the cover in these ponds. All can be fished from shore, and fishers' paths surround most ponds, but a float tube would be of benefit. A fisher could spend the day pond hopping and be in good fishing most of the time.

You can make a loop of sorts by taking Fairview Road north, just east of the little town of Tranquility, from which you can access seven ponds from parking lots. When you reach the end of Fairview at Louisville Road, turn left (west). Follow Louisville Road to May Hill, go south on Highway 770 a quarter of a mile to a bad curve, and then take Wildlife Road right down the hill, past the shooting range; you can access three ponds from that road. Once you come out on Highway 770 again, go 0.5 mile and turn left (east) onto O'Banion, which dead-ends at a parking lot and a short hike south to another pond. Back out on Highway 770, go south and end up again at Tranquility. A few ponds can be accessed off Old Highway 32 between Peebles and Tranquility.

Special regulations: None; state game and fish laws apply.

Facilities/camping: You're out in the middle of nowhere; just to get a pop you'll have to drive 10 miles. The closest town would be Peebles, which is filled with small diners and pizza places. Same goes for Seaman, which has a nice, clean, small-town Tasty Freeze located on Old Highway 32. There is no camping at Tranquility, but there is a hotel on Highway 32 in Seaman.

Additional information: Tranquility Wildlife Area has a rifle and handgun range that is popular, and wildlife is abundant, so bring your binoculars.

Directions: To get to Tranquility Wildlife Area, take Old Highway 32 out of either Seaman or Peebles; signs mark the wildlife area boundaries.

171 Winchester Reservoir

Key species: Largemouth, channel catfish, bluegill, sunfish, crappie; one undocumented muskie stocking in the 1970s.

General description: A small reservoir that still gives up a respectable bass for those who earn it.

Overview: The old village reservoir used to be Winchester's drinking supply. Located about a mile west of Winchester on Tri-County Road (Old Highway 32), the lake covers approximately 25 acres. It's a beautiful lake. The water is usually a dark olive clear, weedy, and mossy. Beavers reside in its headwaters and waterfowl are abundant in fall. The water is deep enough at the dam to harbor some good fish, but the banks on both sides are steep enough to make walking the shoreline impossible. In addition, the reservoir is becoming considerably shallower at it headwaters. The reservoir is best fished from a boat launched from the concrete ramp located at the parking lot.

The fishing: Back in the 1960s some huge bass used to prowl the steep west bank and the water was clear enough to see some of those hawgs from time to time. I like to think there are still a few old bass hanging around those steep banks. The bank is full of overhanging trees and enough old snags have fallen in to hide a good bass. Moss covers the shoreline in summer, and where there are no trees, cattails line the bank.

In spring, fish the shallow south end for early bass. Nesting bluegills and spawning bass like the supply of fresh water that continually flows in from the small headwater stream. Spinner baits fished slowly around the cover and snags will usually draw a strike.

In summer try to throw spinner baits against the deep west bank cover. Admittedly, though, sometimes plastics are the only thing that will get under those overhanging trees and across the fallen treetops. There are a couple of small, but deep inlets that are also worth a try. I wouldn't be afraid to use a buzz bait anywhere on the lake, along the moss edge or around the old waterworks structure. This is primarily a bass lake, so fish it like one.

The crappie bite is good in April and May, with crappies reaching 8 to 9 inches. Most are caught using minnows around the old snags on the west bank.

The bluegills are small but can easily be caught from around the moss edges with red worms, crickets, or grasshoppers. In spring, during spawn, a few nice hand-size 'gills can be caught from the south end.

Channel cats are present but seldom fished for. Moss, weeds, and snags make bottom fishing difficult, if not impossible. Shoreline access is so limited that it restricts any kind of bank fishing.

The fishing is not easy at the old reservoir; the big bass are secretive and hard to find. And the muskies, well, who knows.

Special regulations: Electric motors only.

Facilities/camping: There is a parking lot and boat ramp, but no camping or facilities at the reservoir. There is a diner in Winchester and a Budget Host Inn at the intersection of Highway 136 and Highway 32.

Directions: From Winchester take Old Highway 32, now called Tri-County Road, approximately 1 mile west of town.

Lake Erie

Lake Erie is the only place in Ohio a person can make a living fishing. With an estimated 400,000 Ohio anglers who fish the lake every year, and approximately 800 charter boats operating out of the lake's harbors, the fishing industry on Lake Erie is estimated to generate $680 million dollars annually for the state's economy.

The walleye fishing is so vast that fishery biologists estimate 20 to 40 million walleye inhabit the lake in any given year. As a result of the highly successful class of 2003 spawn, and to a lesser degree the 2001 class, an estimated 42 million walleye were available to anglers in 2006. According to biologists, the 2003 class will provide quality walleye fishing until the year 2012, and will produce trophy walleye fishing until the year 2021. Walleye live long, and the 2003 class will be available to fishers for up to 18 to 20 years. On an average, approximately 600,000 walleyes are taken by Ohio anglers each year from Lake Erie. A nickname coined by Ohio Governor James Rhodes in 1980, "the Walleye Capital of the World," still holds true.

In a 2005 study on Ohio's Lake Erie fisheries, it found that 84 percent of the charter boat industry targeted walleye, followed by yellow perch at 15 percent. According to the study, charter boats were only responsible for 8 percent of the total sport harvest, while private boat anglers accounted for 92 percent of the catch and 88 percent of the angling effort. The primary game fish targeted by private boat anglers was split between yellow perch at 48 percent and walleyes at 41 percent. The study also showed that in some years that number can switch, with walleyes being targeted more by private boat anglers.

The total harvest of yellow perch by Ohio sport fishers is estimated to be around 5.8 million fish. Biologists estimate smallmouth bass accounted for 7,400 of the fish caught from Lake Erie, and the number of steelhead caught from the lake in 2005 is thought to be 10,500.

If 89 percent of the private fishers target walleyes and yellow perch, that leaves a measly 11 percent to pursue smallmouth and steelhead, the lake's other primary game fish species. A few anglers also catch white bass, but seldom target them. White perch, sheepshead (freshwater drum), carp, and channel catfish are also taken from the Great Lake but are incidental catches and usually disdained. The channel catfish, a desirable sport fish found in inland lakes and in the Ohio River, is under a health advisory in Lake Erie.

Fishing from shore on Lake Erie is at the break walls, piers, beaches, lighthouses, seawalls, and harbor mouths. In the harbors, anglers can fish from boat slips, ramps, docks, harbor walls, and parks. There are over 70 listed public access areas from which anglers can fish from the shoreline, but in reality there are literally hundreds of places on Lake Erie to fish from shore. Several of the public fishing areas include piers that may charge a nominal fee to fish off of them. Bradstreet Landing Pier, located just west of Rocky River, is one such pier that has parking and picnic areas and is of historical significance. There are fishing piers at Port Clinton, Sandusky, Huron, Avon Lake, Rocky River, and Fairport Harbor. From piers, anglers catch walleye, perch, smallmouth, and sheepshead, and from central basin piers, they catch steelhead. Break walls are common around any harbor, boat ramp, industry, or town and represent some of the best shoreline fishing opportunities on the lake. Most, if not all, are smallmouth magnets, and big walleyes are attracted to them at night. From the breakwalls in the central basin, steelhead are caught in the fall as they stage near the harbor and creek mouths awaiting to make a spawning run up the Lake Erie tributaries. From the seawalls, anglers catch perch, white bass, sheepshead, catfish, occasionally walleye, and steelhead. If an angler fishes from the beach, he can expect to catch catfish, sheepshead, carp, and at night some walleyes.

The Division of Watercraft lists 81 boat launches along the Lake Erie shore from Toledo to Conneaut; 29 are public ramps. Some public ramps charge a launch fee, while others do not. The majority of boat ramps are located at commercial marinas or private clubs, where an angler must be a member to dock there. Others are private or commercial ramps that permit public launching for a fee.

There are 11 state parks on Lake Erie and the islands. Boat ramps are at Maumee Bay, Catawba Island, East Harbor, South Bass, Kelleys Island, Cleveland Lakefront, and Geneva State Park. Nearly all the state parks offer swimming beaches, hiking trails, and fishing from piers or break walls. Camping is offered at six state parks, and marinas are located at East Harbor, Geneva, and Maumee Bay. There are two marinas at Cleveland Lakefront.

Lake Erie is divided into three basins. The western and central basin fall within Ohio's boundaries.

The following information applies to all Lake Erie sites:

Special regulations: On Lake Erie the daily bag limit on walleye is 6 fish, with a minimum size limit of 15 inches. The daily bag limit on yellow perch is 30 fish. The daily bag limit on bass is 5, with a 14-inch minimum size limit. The daily limit on steelhead is 2, with a minimum size limit of 12 inches. At certain times in summer, within the boundaries of the reef complex, the area will be closed during live fire exercises at Camp Perry. Always be sure to check current regulations.

Facilities/camping: On the western basin, camping is at Maumee Bay State Park with 252 campsites, 24 cabins, and 120 rooms available at the lodge. Kelleys Island State Park has 127 campsites. South Bass Island State Park has 135 campsites and 5 cabins. Middle Bass Island State Park has 21 primitive campsites. East Harbor State Park has 365 electric and 205 nonelectric campsites.

On the central basin, Geneva State Park has 88 campsites, 12 cabins, and 109 rooms at the lodge.

Additional information: The Lake Erie Circle Tour follows the lake from Toledo to Conneaut.

Directions: Lake Erie can be accessed at all locations from Interstate 90 and Interstate 80.

CAPT. KEITH UNKEFER
HOME: 888-698-2381
BOAT: 419-341-2506

Pooh Bear
CHARTERS & CRUISES

WALLEYE • PERCH
• SM. MOUTH BASS •
• STEELHEAD •

Anglers on the charter boat Pooh Bear *out of Vermilion Harbor caught these walleyes during September.*

Artificial Reef GPS Coordinates

Edgewater artificial reef "A"	Latitude 41 30 .148 N	Longitude 81 45 .575 W
Edgewater artificial reef "B"	Latitude 41 29 .970 N	Longitude 81 45 .416 W
Euclid artificial reef "C"	Latitude 41 35 .933 N	Longitude 81 33 .804 W
Cuyahoga County Reef	Latitude 41 30 .175 N	Longitude 81 47 .266 W
Experimental Reef A	Latitude 41 30 .271 N	Longitude 81 47 .533 W
Experimental Reef B	Latitude 41 30 .256 N	Longitude 81 47 .041 W
Lorain Mountain Reef	Latitude 41 28 .150 N	Longitude 82 12 .750 W
Lorain Fishermen's Reef	Latitude 41 28 .076 N	Longitude 82 12 .758 W

172 Western Basin

Key species: Walleye, smallmouth bass, yellow perch, channel catfish, white bass, and sheephead.

General description: The western basin of Lake Erie has no equal when it comes to spring and early summer walleye fishing.

Overview: The western basin is notorious for its walleye and smallmouth fishing and contains the bulk of Lake Erie's reefs, shoals, and islands. The western basin is the shallowest end of the most-shallow lake in the Great Lakes. Depths at the west end average 20 to 30 feet, and it is considerably shallower around the reef complex, at depths ranging from 3 to 12 feet. In Maumee Bay anglers will find water only 6 to 8 feet deep. If an angler moves 10 miles eastward of the islands, depths will increase to 40-plus feet. Although those depths are not favorable for steelhead, for walleyes and smallmouth it is a spawning nursery and feeding grounds of immense magnitude.

Division of Wildlife fishery biologists believe there are three distinct groups, or spawning populations, of walleye in the western basin of Lake Erie. That distinction is drawn by spawning locations: the Maumee group, the Sandusky group, and the open lake group, which spawn on the open lake's reefs and shoals.

Smallmouth also spawn on the reefs and shoals on the open lake reef complex and around the islands. Smallmouth spawn at water temperatures between 55°F and 65°F. These usually occur from mid-May through mid-June on Lake Erie. To protect the spawning bass fry from invasive predators like the round goby, the Division of Wildlife has restricted the possession of bass on Lake Erie from May 1 through June 23, but still permits catch-and-release fishing during that time. Some anglers believe this doesn't go far enough and would like to see the season closed to fishing during this critical time in the life cycle of the smallmouth. Because gobies are bottom-dwelling fish, smallmouth nests are particularly vulnerable to predation once the male bass has been removed, even if only briefly.

Yellow perch fishing ranks right along with the walleye as the most sought after game fish. It is the only viable commercial fishery still in business on the Ohio side,

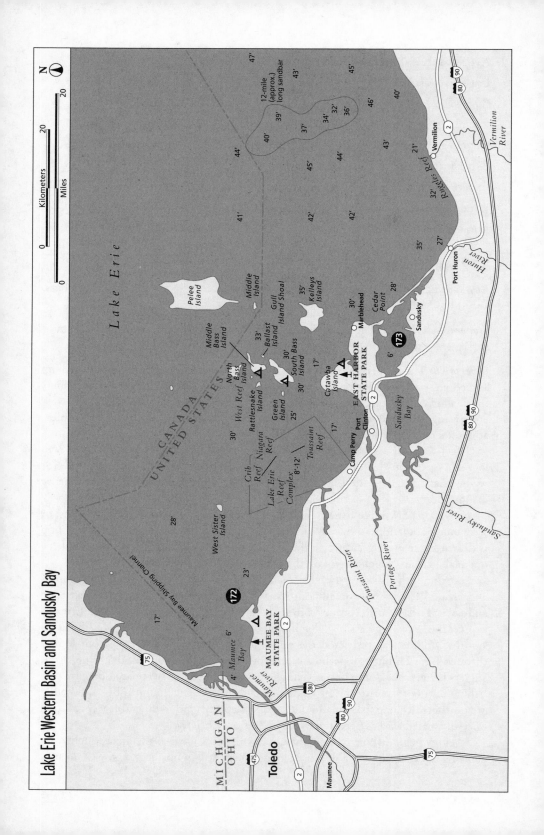

Lake Erie Western Basin and Sandusky Bay

even though legislative attempts have been made to close the industry down. Nothing tastes better than a perch sandwich, and if you want to invite me up to a perch fry sometime, please do. Perch spawn in the open lake flats, laying large egg sacs that drift in the currents or sometimes collect on the bottom before hatching. Perch are most commonly found in large schools within the deeper waters of the open lake, but can also be caught just as readily off piers, break walls, and seawalls. A sometimes-eager biter, perch primarily feed on emerald shiners. They are the most sought-after fish when the lake freezes over. The best perch fishing is in fall from September through October.

White bass can usually be found in the open water, chasing shiners in the summer. In late April, after the walleye have finished their spawning run, white bass make a run up the tributaries of Maumee, Portage, and Sandusky. By late May, they're usually back in the lake and can be found feeding beneath boiling schools of shiners or shad. They are common in the open water on the western basin and around the break walls near shore. In 2005, biologists estimated that more than 78,000 white bass were caught from the western basin.

Walleye: The spring walleye run up the Maumee and Sandusky Rivers is legendary and usually begins in mid-March, and is finished by mid-April. Charter captains start showing up in the shallow Maumee Bay area on April 1, finding fish around small bottom irregularities and looking for structures, and fish in the deeper water and on sediment edges along the Maumee Shipping Channel. Use small spoons, hair jigs, weight-forward spinners, and small cranks slow trolled or drifted along the bottom. The big females usually rest for a few days after spawning, but once recovered, look out. Some of the biggest walleyes of the year can come from Maumee Bay during the brief window between spawning and moving day. Once the water temperature reaches into the 50s, around May or later, the fish start to move east.

The same can be said of the open reef complex north of Camp Perry and around the islands in spring. In March and April, fish over top reefs and shoals with ½- to 1-ounce purple or green bucktail jigs, sometimes tipped with a minnow, or use weight-forward spinners tipped with half a night crawler. Anglers find success casting, drifting, or vertical jigging over the reef and reef edges. The males usually stay longer on the reef after spawning is completed, but by mid-April the females move off the reef and into deeper water. After a few days to recover, the big females can be picked up by slow trolling large cranks and deep divers like Husky Jerks, Smithwick Rattlin' Rouge, and night crawler harnesses, about 1 mph, 10 to 12 feet deep.

Come May walleyes start to move north and east of the reef complex into 25 to 30 feet of water. Casting and trolling cranks, weight-forward spinners, small spoons, and night crawler harnesses still pick up fish. In May, June, and July, the harbors around Port Clinton, Catawba Island, and East Harbor are abuzz with charter boats and fishers fishing off Marblehead and the waters east and west of the islands.

Throughout late spring and summer, fish swim in the cooler 30- to 40-foot water, and schools are located by using depth finders and graphs. Dipsy and Jet Divers are used to get lures down 15 to 30 feet or more. At times walleyes will be very near the bottom, at other times the fish will suspend, so varying trolling depths helps locate fish. Planer boards are also used to carry the line away from the center of the boat and off to the edge. As a boat passes over walleyes, the school splits, leaving a fishless zone directly behind the boat. Planer boards keep lures away from the disturbance of the boat and off to the side, thus keeping the bait within the school of fish. Small, thin Michigan Stinger spoons are tied on a 6-foot leader behind a diver and trolled from 50 to 150 feet behind the boat. Downriggers are also used to get spoons down to deep walleyes.

Good areas to look for summer walleyes are along the flats north of the Camp Perry reef complex, between North Bass and West Sister Islands. Also look along the south passage between Catawba and South Bass Islands, in the deep water of the middle passage northwest of Kelleys Island, and in the deep water east of Marblehead.

Come late summer, August through early fall, walleye continue to migrate east into still deeper, cooler water, and the ports of Huron and Vermilion become the temporary headquarters to the fleet of walleye charters. Approximately 5 miles offshore and slightly northeast of Vermilion is a 12-mile-long sandbar that extends to the Canadian border. The bar is irregular in shape and averages about 0.5 mile wide, with depths varying from 32 to 38 feet deep. The area is a traditional late-summer and early fall walleye spot. Troll Stinger spoons, Wally Divers, or Reef Runners behind divers and off planer boards about 100 feet behind the boat over the top of the bar, fishing the water from the bottom to halfway up. Locate walleye using a depth finder or graph; some walleye schools can be more than a mile long.

Come fall, sometimes late fall, when the water temperatures begin dropping under 55°F, big walleye will stage just offshore of Ruggles Reef, between the ports of Huron and Vermilion. Troll the deep edge of the Ruggles Reef complex, which extends out anywhere from 0.5 mile to a mile offshore from Ruggles Beach to east Vermilion. In late fall, shoreline anglers have a good chance to tangle with some big walleyes off the break walls and piers at Huron and Vermilion. Night fishing can also pay off in late fall and early winter if you slowly retrieve big cranks off those same break walls and piers. The first couple of hours after dark seem the most productive for night fishing. After the spring spawn, late fall is the best opportunity to pick up a trophy walleye.

Smallmouth bass: Some of the best smallmouth fishing in North America is on Ohio's northern border. A smallmouth from Lake Erie doesn't look like a smallmouth from anywhere else in the state. While stream smallmouth seldom exceed 15 inches and are more normally proportioned, the Lake Erie giant is fat from a rich diet of gobies and crayfish and averages almost 17 inches in length and over 2.5 pounds. It is shaped like an over-inflated football, and it almost appears to be an entirely different subspecies of bass. The minimum length for smallmouth entry into the Fish Ohio Awards is 20 inches, which is a gross injustice to anybody fishing for smallies south of the big lake; they just don't get that big anywhere else but in Lake Erie.

If there is an upside to the zebra mussel invasion, it is its effect on water clarity in Lake Erie. In some areas visibility is as much as 10 feet. This in turn has improved the smallmouth fishery. But of late a few charter captains have begun to notice a decline in the bass fishery on the Ohio side, and many charters are now taking smallmouth anglers into Canadian waters off Pelee Island. The heavy tournament pressure on smallmouth, resulting in the relocation at weigh-ins; the exotic introduction of round gobies that prey on smallmouth nests and fry; and the continued fishing for smallmouth during spawning season are a few of the reasons charter captains give for the decline. The captains are also quick to point out that the introduction of gobies has had a positive effect as well, in that the goby has become the primary forage for smallmouth, contributing to the overall weight of the bass.

All the charter captains I talked to in preparing this book are now actively encouraging catch-and-release smallmouth fishing. Allow the prolific, abundant, and tasty walleye and ring perch to supply the table fare; the smallmouth's real value lies in its fighting ability.

The best smallmouth fishing on Lake Erie is generally perceived to be around the reefs and islands from Camp Perry to Marblehead, and stretching north to North Bass Island. Those in the central basin may argue that the vast shoreline reef from Fairport Harbor to Conneaut is equally as productive and nearly as large.

It takes a smallmouth three to four years to reach 14 to 15 inches in Lake Erie, which has some of the highest growth rates for smallmouth in the Great Lakes. May and early June are when smallmouth spawn in Lake Erie. Spawning takes place in the western basin near rocky shore areas, near the reefs and shoals around the islands, and on the reef complex north of Camp Perry.

Good areas to search for bass are off the western shore of Catawaba Island and the shoreline north and east of Marblehead. Farther east, the Ruggles Reef complex that stretches from Ruggles Beach to east of Vermilion is another good producer.

The Camp Perry reef complex, Toussaint Reef, Crib Reef, and Niagara are but a few of the reefs on the complex that hold good numbers of smallmouth. On the islands, the rocks and reefs southeast and north of South Bass to Ballast Island are excellent. On Middle Bass Island, fish around the entire island and west at Rattlesnake Island. North Bass Island is the same; fish the rock and reefs around the island and to the west at West Reef. The Gull Island Shoal is good, and anywhere off Kelleys Island and the Kelleys Island Shoal is excellent smallmouth fishing. From shore, any break wall or stone pier will harbor plenty of smallmouth bass.

For a realistic shot at big fish, fish prespawn bass in April, before the season closes, around the island's rocks and reefs in less than 6 feet of water with tubes and jigs. Bass do not migrate from their home range, they only move from shallow to deeper water as the summer progresses. Most bass will average between 1.5 and 2 pounds; a 5-pound smallie is a big fish. Fish the rocks, reefs, shoals, or any weeds in 15 feet or less water with tubes, jigs, small cranks, shiners, or crayfish.

Watermelon seed and pumpkinseed tubes probably catch more smallmouth than anything else thrown on Lake Erie. Lizards, plastic crawls, and double-tailed grubs produce almost as well. Small cranks like crawdad-colored Shad Raps, and Fat Raps, Hot 'n Tots, and Balsa B's pick up plenty of bass and can be worked quickly around the rocks and break walls. Skirted and bucktail jigs with a double twister tail grub or craw attached are effective. A lot of anglers use drop shot rigs on Lake Erie, with plastic night crawlers, lizards, shads, and craws. Spinner baits and buzz baits are good at times too, as bass can be found from the surface on down.

The best smallmouth fishing is late June through early July, then again from September through early November. From the shore, anglers should fish the harbor break walls—especially at the end of a wall. The harbor break wall at Port Clinton is good, as are any break walls that extend for a considerable distance into the lake.

Yellow perch: Yellow perch are right on top when it comes to the total number of angling hours spent on Lake Erie, rivaling walleye as the top fish most anglers go for. The popularity of yellow perch does not lie in its fighting ability, but its sheer numbers and delicacy make it a desirable and easy catch.

Perch are widespread throughout Lake Erie, but do not migrate across great distances like walleye do. They instead spend their lives in the relativity deeper waters of the western basin near the soft, flat, mud bottoms in depths varying from 20 to 45 feet. Perch forage primarily on emerald shiners, although small crayfish, night crawlers, and wax worms have been successfully used to catch them. Perch in the western basin average 8 to 10 inches. As an angler travels eastward, the average perch size increases to between 9 and 11 inches; east of Cleveland, yellow perch average 10 to 12 inches.

The standard perch rig is a spreader with a couple of Eagle Claw snells baited with emerald shiners. If you're in fish, catching two at time is fairly common. Fish the rig just off the bottom, allowing the natural swaying of the boat to give the spreader just enough movement to attract perch.

The easiest way to locate perch is to look for groups of boats and join in. Perch can also be found by watching the sonar or graph for schools of fish. Perch gather in large schools, so finding them shouldn't be a problem. Once fish are located, drop the spreaders overboard and give it 20 minutes. If no luck, move on and find another school with perhaps more active fish. If the bite is on, you can catch as many as you like up to the limit. Keep in mind that every fish you catch has to be cleaned. But if you like fish, and who doesn't, it's a labor of love. If you promise your neighbor a few, he or she might be willing to help out with the cleaning.

Look for perch in deep, 30- to 40-foot water. Good spots are north of the Camp Perry reef complex, the deep water west of Rattlesnake Island, and the area between South Bass and Kelleys Islands. The deep waters east of Kelleys Island and the waters between Marblehead and Kelleys are good. The deep waters east of Marblehead are excellent, as is about a mile offshore at the mouth of the Sandusky Bay. River mouths are good areas to find perch, too. A couple of miles offshore of Huron, Vermilion, and Lorain are all excellent places.

Perch fishing is best from September through November, and that is when 12- to 15-inch perch are caught. When the lake freezes over, look for ice shanties and you'll find perch. Finding and catching perch is not complicated; deciding what friends to invite over to a fish fry—that could get dicey.

Many of the small towns along Lake Erie offer public piers for anglers to enjoy.

173 Sandusky Bay

Key species: Crappie, walleye, panfish, largemouth and smallmouth bass, channel catfish, and white bass.

General description: Sandusky Bay is known for great early spring crappie fishing.

Overview: An intimidating body of water at 38,000 acres, Sandusky Bay offers some fishing relief when the winds kick up on the big lake. It is different from Lake Erie in that it is primarily a largemouth, crappie, catfish, and bluegill fishery. Beginning in mid-March the upper river gets a massive spring run of walleye and then white bass in late April. After spawning walleyes move out of the bay quickly, but white bass can be caught all summer long.

Sandusky Bay warms up quicker than the big lake, and usually by mid-April anglers start picking up catches of crappies. By May crappie fishing is in full swing. Look for crappies around pilings, docks, the bridges and marinas, and various industrial structures. Good-size crappies are typical in Sandusky, with most reaching into the teens. Minnows and crappie jigs fished 4 to 6 feet deep is about the norm.

Largemouth are much more common than smallmouth in the bay, which is typical for the tributaries of Lake Erie. Sandusky is generally cloudy, so stick with white, yellow, or chartreuse spinner baits. Jigs with crawls and tubes work well, as do cranks worked along the riprap and pilings. Work the riprap at the bridges, the weed edges, docks, and pilings. Largemouth do well in Sandusky, with most fish averaging 12 to 15 inches. The best fishing is May and June, followed by the fall months. Smallmouth are found near the mouth of the bay on the backside of Cedar Point, and around the break walls and riprap near town.

Bluegills are fairly common around the bays, inlets, and bridges. Channel cats can reach a respectable 12 to 15 pounds in Sandusky, and anglers can find them in summer around the bridges. Yellow perch can be taken from the mouth of Sandusky at the end of the Cedar Point break wall. In winter, ice fishing produces good catches of bluegills and yellow perch; just look for the shanties when trying to find perch.

Anglers can launch at the Dempsey Wildlife Area boat ramp on the north shore of the bay or at the Sandusky Municipal Ramp. Some shore fishing is available from city parks.

174 Central Basin

Key species: Walleye, smallmouth bass, steelhead, white bass, yellow perch.

General description: The central basin of Lake Erie is the home of Ohio's steelhead fishery.

Overview: Moving eastward, the central basin gains depth but loses the islands' and reefs' complexes that make the western basin such fertile spawning and feeding grounds. Depths in the central basin average 50 to 70 feet, with a relatively featureless, flat mud-and-rock bottom. To improve the fisheries close to shore, a number of artificial reefs have been constructed just offshore of Lorain and Cleveland. One of the more famous artificial reefs is the old Cleveland Browns stadium that was demolished during the late 1990s and deposited in three places off Cleveland Lakefront. These reefs have been especially attractive to smallmouth in the summer.

Steelhead, lake trout, coho, chinook, and pink salmon have been, to varying degrees, part of the fisheries in the central basin for a long time. During the 1960s, 1970s, and 1980s they were part of an ongoing effort by the Division of Wildlife to establish a salmonoid fishery for Ohio anglers. Meeting only with limited success, all attempts by Ohio to establish salmon in the central basin have been discontinued. However, the stocking of rainbow trout into the lake continued, and when the Division of Wildlife began releasing Little Manistee River steelhead from Michigan, it was like a bolt of lightning to the Lake Erie fisheries. Today this steelhead-stocking program rivals in scale the highly successful reintroduction of wild turkey by the Division of Wildlife in the 1960s.

Between 400,000 and 500,000 6- to 8-inch yearling steelhead are stocked into Vermilion, Rocky, Chagrin, the Grand, and Conneaut Creek every fall. Not only

A cooler of walleyes is the reward for a successful outing on Lake Erie.

does this provide an excellent stream fishery in fall, winter, and spring, but as the steelhead move into the cooler lake waters every summer, it provides an offshore fishery that rivals the walleye.

The fishing: The best shoreline fishing in the central basin is at the break walls, seawalls, beaches, power plants, and piers located at harbor mouths, marinas, parks, and towns along the coast. The break walls are top producers for smallmouth from late spring through early fall. In fall, break walls attract steelhead, walleyes, and perch; and in the early spring walleyes and perch. Fishing from the seawalls yield yellow perch in spring and occasionally walleye, smallmouth, white bass, and sheepshead in summer and fall. From the piers, anglers will encounter walleyes in spring and fall; smallmouth, white bass, and sheepshead in summer; and yellow perch in spring and fall. From the beaches at night, some good-size walleyes are taken. At the Eastlake and Cleveland power discharge, fishers find steelhead in fall and winter and white bass in summer. Beginning in October, steelhead migrate into the tributary streams in the central basin, returning to the lake by the end of April. The harbors contain largemouth, sheepshead, bluegills, rock bass, crappies, channel cats, and steelhead in fall and winter. In late December anglers will occasionally catch big burbot, a freshwater cod, from the end of the break wall at Fairport Harbor using big shiners or gizzard shad for bait.

On average, walleyes and ring perch tend to run bigger in the central basin than they do in the western basin. The Ohio state record walleye and ring perch both came from the central basin of Lake Erie. Technically, the central basin starts at Cedar Point and ends at Erie, Pennsylvania; however, for general descriptive purposes the waters east of Lorain to Conneaut will be used here.

Walleye: While the majority of Lake Erie walleyes spawn in the western basin, a small population does spawn in the Grand River. That population is not significant, and nearly all walleyes in the central basin are postspawn female fish moving eastward from the western basin reefs and the Sandusky River. While the walleyes move eastward, they encounter the rainbow smelt population and their diet, which consisted mostly of gizzard shad and emerald shiners, now consists primarily of smelt and shad. In fall shad become the primary forage.

In the central basin, walleye fishing starts in mid-May. Troll the shoreline 15 to 35 feet deep from Lorain to the Rocky River. Side scan sonar reveals a rocky shoreline, extending anywhere from 0.5 to 1 mile offshore from just east of Lorain to just west of the Rocky River. Also troll the artificial reefs and break walls off Cleveland riverfront. Use small cranks, weight-forward spinners, and night crawler harnesses. In summer most walleye move well offshore, but smaller fish can still be picked up from the shoreline. Later in the summer the rock shoreline from Fairport Harbor to Conneaut produces good numbers of fair-size walleyes; troll along the deep edge where the rock meets the mud bottom.

In summer, boats have to travel a considerable distance offshore to find walleyes in the central basin, going as far as 5 to 10 miles and sometimes all the way to the Canadian border. With a temperature preference between 55°F and 60°F, look

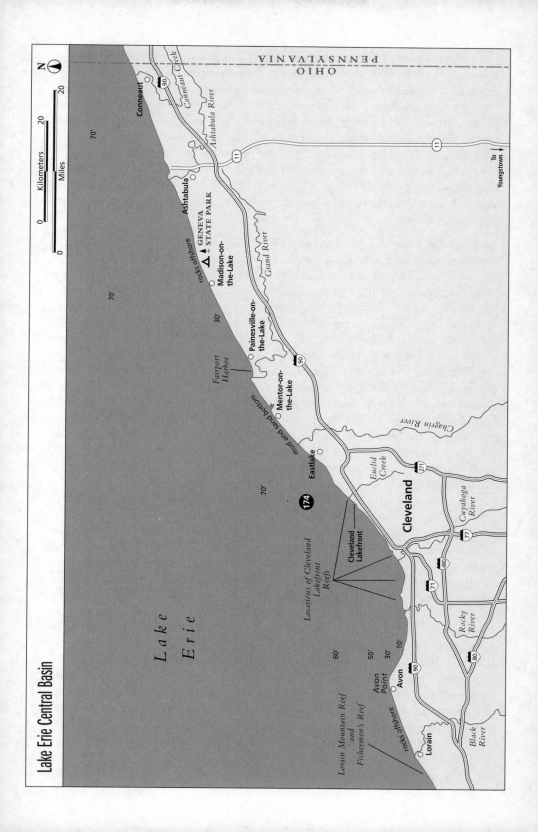

Lake Erie Central Basin

for walleyes over 40 to 60 feet of water in July and August. Fish will suspend anywhere within the range of 30 to 55 feet deep in summer. Locate walleyes using a depth finder or graph; look for clouds of smelt just above the thermocline. Walleyes during summer will stage at or just above the thermocline, as do the smelt. Oftentimes, steelhead will be among the schools of walleye and smelt. Wire line trolling gets bait deep, but most anglers utilize sinkers and divers or downriggers, trolling at 2 to 2.5 mph. In summer, Michigan Stinger spoons or Northern King spoons are almost exclusively used for walleyes. Colors vary from red gold to purple and are tied onto a leader approximately 6 feet back from the diver. By late October, fish start moving toward shore and begin returning west, and the waters north of Huron and Vermilion become the hot spots for Lake Erie walleyes.

Smallmouth bass: The piers, break walls, rock structures, and lighthouses from Lorain to Conneaut produce some great shoreline smallmouth fishing. Use tubes and small crawdad-colored cranks along the rock and riprap on both sides of the wall and directly off the end. Smallmouth fishing starts in April and continues through September and into early October. Most bass off the banks will average 15 to 18 inches, and they feed primarily on gobies and crayfish.

In the central basin, smallmouth are more shoreline oriented and are seldom found over a mile from shore. Starting in May and continuing through summer, smallmouth will be located in depths ranging from 10 to 25 feet. The rocky shoreline starting east of Lorain to just east of Avon Point is excellent. The rocks begin about an eighth of a mile from shore and extend out into the lake approximately 0.5 to 0.75 mile in most places. There is another narrow bank of rock bottom just east and west of the mouth of the Rocky River. Cleveland Lakefront is comprised mostly of a mud and sand bottom, but the break walls and artificial reefs provide some smallmouth action in summer. Studies done on the artificial reefs show they hold fair numbers of smallmouth from late summer through fall.

Outside of break walls and a small chunk of rock bottom about a quarter of a mile off the mouth of Euclid Creek, the shoreline from Cleveland to Fairport is made up of sand and mud and does not hold a lot of smallmouth. From Painsville-on-the-Lake to Ashtabula, the bottom is again comprised of rock and reaches about a mile offshore. Just beyond the Ashtabula River, the rocky bottom starts again and continues to the Pennsylvania state line. The rocky stretch of lake bottom from Painesville to Conneaut contains some of the best smallmouth habitat in the central basin, and the rocky bottom here is over a mile wide in most places. From Conneaut Harbor, fish the break walls and rocky bottom and shoreline on both sides of the harbor.

Not all rocky bottoms are created equal; look for humps, boulders, rock fingers, ledges, and bottom irregularities when searching for smallmouth. Where the rock ends and the mud bottom begins is generally 30 to 35 feet below the surface and a mile out. Fishing pressure for smallmouth in the central basin is almost nil, with most anglers concentrating on walleye and yellow perch.

For smallmouth use watermelon seed or pumpkinseed tubes, jigs with craws, deep Wee-R Rebels, and at times Hopkins spoons for vertical jigging. Drop-shot rigs with plastic worms work well too. Drifting crayfish and leeches 10 to 30 feet deep will produce some big smallmouth, and along where the rocky bottom meets the mud edge, an occasional walleye will be hooked as well. Bass taken offshore from the deep rocks will average 18 to 19 inches with a true shot at 5-pound-plus fish a real possibility.

Yellow perch: Although it's possible to catch a bucket of perch off the break walls in spring, September is when the action takes off in the central basin. Starting in early September anglers find perch about 2 to 5 miles offshore in the central basin located in 30 to 50 feet of water. As the water cools, perch will move closer to shore, and by mid-October anglers may have to travel only 0.5 mile to a mile out. A couple of miles north out of the harbor at Fairport is an excellent location for perch; Fairport is also host to the annual Lake Erie Perch Fest put on by Lake County.

To locate yellow perch watch for other boats—where boats are gathered, perch are below. Large schools of perch can also be located on a depth finder or graph. Once found, they don't move much. Once perch are located, anchor and drop a perch spreader baited with two emerald shiners overboard near the bottom. Most perch locate near or on the bottom, following schools of emerald or golden shiners. If the school is active, you'll start catching fish within 10 minutes. Perch are light biters, so it pays to be alert. If nothing happens for 15 to 20 minutes, then it's time to pack up and find a school of hungry fish. If an angler finds active fish, a limit is only two to three hours away. Perch in the central basin tend to be larger than perch in the western basin, averaging 10 to 12 inches, with a few that are 14 inches or better caught every fall.

Steelhead: Steelhead provide a double fishery for Ohio anglers. In fall, winter, and early spring, the central basin tributary streams and harbors host migratory runs of spawning steelhead that are available to shoreline and wading anglers. In summer the steelhead move offshore and provide an exciting, if not a trophy fishery for charters and private boat owners. Figures resulting from recent studies estimate that between 10,000 and 11,000 steelhead are taken from the central basin each year by Ohio anglers. The majority of steelhead charters go out of Fairport, Ashtabula, and Conneaut Harbors and travel over 8 to 10 miles to the prime fishing waters offshore from Cleveland to Conneaut.

Search out the deepest pools in the central basin; water from 50 to 60 feet is not too deep. Use a depth finder or graph to locate schools that forage at or near the thermocline. Schools of rainbow smelt often hold at the thermocline and make up a large percentage of the trout's diet. Past studies revealed that emerald shiners, zooplankton, and rainbow smelt make up the bulk of the trout's summer diet. Once the clouds of bait fish are located, steelhead won't be far away. Often pods of steelhead and schools of walleyes will mingle.

In summer, steelhead will hold at the edge of the thermocline, which may vary in depth but will generally average 40 to 50 feet deep throughout most of the summer. At the thermocline, water temperatures will hold between 50°F and 60°F; below the thermocline water temps dip to 45°F to 50°F.

Downriggers are the most effective way to get Little Cleo's, Flatfish, perch-colored or black and silver Rapalas, or black or chrome spoons down to the thermocline. Dipsy or Jet divers can be employed as well, as can wire line-trolling methods to get to the fish. Occasionally a chinook, pink salmon, lake trout, or brown trout is caught, too. The average size of most steelhead caught from the central basin is between 25 and 32 inches.

In fall, steelhead can be taken from the break walls and harbor mouths at Fairport and Conneaut, with Conneaut Harbor seemingly the better of the two. Fish start coming into the break walls as early as late August, with the best fishing from September through November. A few steelhead are picked up all winter long and through the ice. One-quarter-ounce Little Cleo spoons, Bluefox spinners, and jigs and maggots take steelhead off the break walls in fall. The best fishing is usually early in the morning. Steelhead can also be caught from the warm-water discharge at the Eastlake power plant during fall and winter.

By October, steelhead have moved inshore and start to enter the harbor mouths, rivers, and streams of the central basin from Huron to Conneaut to undertake the annual spawning run. Steelhead generally make the annual run two to three times during their lifespan. A fully mature female will weigh over 10 pounds and exceed 30 inches in length. Males will frequently reach 33 inches and weigh up to 13 pounds. However, most steelhead average 28 to 30 inches and will weigh 8 to 10 pounds.

When steelhead enter the rivers, look for pods of fish holding in the deepest pools, usually just below a series of riffles. When spawning occurs in late March, fish will be up on riffles and sight fishing is possible.

White bass: The best way to locate white bass is to look for seagulls working the water where schools of white bass are surface feeding on shiners or shad. Use small jigs with twister tails, spinners, or Rattle Traps and throw right into the disturbance. White bass are widespread and can be found offshore, near power discharges, and around harbors.

Ohio River

The Ohio River is second only in scope to the fisheries on Lake Erie. It is perhaps more diverse than any other fishery in the state. There are over 20 species of fish an angler might catch on a hook dangling in the water of the sometimes muddy Ohio River. It is a different fishery for sure, at times challenging because anglers here have to contend with an environment unlike that found anywhere else in Ohio. Still there are fish to be found—sometimes large ones—and those who fish the Ohio River regularly, like myself, love its power, its diversity, and above all, the mystery and lore of what's just below the surface.

175 Western Unit

Key species: Largemouth, smallmouth, and spotted bass (Kentucky bass); flathead (shovelhead), blue, and channel catfish; black crappie; white bass; striper; hybrid striper; sauger; walleye; bluegill; sunfish; paddlefish; longnose gar.

General description: The Meldahl Pool east of Cincinnati has some of the highest catch rates for bass of any pool in the Ohio River.

Overview: The Ohio River is a 450-mile-long fishery bordering the state's south and east sides. Approximately 170 miles are considered the western unit, stretching from the Indiana state line to just west of the town of South Point at the confluence of the Big Sandy River, forming the Kentucky-Ohio border. The Ohio River averages approximately a quarter of a mile wide and varies in depth from 20 to 50 feet, with a bottom comprised primarily of hard gravel and sand. The western unit of the Ohio River is defined by three pools: the Markland Dam pool, the Meldahl Dam pool, and the Greenup Dam pool. Of those three, only the Meldahl and Greenup Dams are located in the western unit.

The **Markland Locks and Dam** are located approximately 60 miles downriver of Cincinnati, at Markland, Indiana. Markland Dam backs up a 95-mile-long pool from the dam, past Cincinnati, to the foot of Meldahl Dam. The tailrace is located on the Indiana side and is a highly regarded striper and blue cat fishery, but it is outside the scope of this book.

The **Meldahl Locks and Dam** are located between the towns of Chilo and Neville on U.S. Highway 52. Meldahl Dam is 396 river miles from the Ohio-Pennsylvania state line and backs up a 95-mile-long pool to the foot of Greenup Dam. At Meldahl Dam the tailwater fishery is located on the Kentucky side and can be reached by road from Highway 8, near Foster, Kentucky, about 25 miles west of Maysville. The tailrace can also be reached by a 15-minute boat ride from the Neville boat ramp, located just off US 52, which is 2 miles downriver of the dam. Anglers have an excellent chance of hooking a pure striper from the tailwaters

Ben Cross unhooks one of 50 white bass he caught in late May from the Ohio River near Brush Creek Island.

below Meldahl due to the fact that Kentucky has continually stocked pure stripers into the Markland pool since 1975.

The **Greenup Locks and Dam** are located approximately 14 miles east of Portsmouth. Greenup Dam is 300 river miles downstream from the Pennsylvania state line and backs up a 62-mile-long pool. Greenup is one of the better tailwater fisheries on the river, is located on the Ohio side, and is easily reached off US 52 at the Highway 10 Greenup exit. It can also be reached by boat from Burks Point boat ramp, which is located at Allentown, just 3 miles downriver of the dam.

At both Meldahl and Greenup Dams, the tailwaters have various boating restrictions in place, and buoys mark the upstream limits at which boats are permitted.

Found in this section of river are marinas, floating restaurants, two ferries, various industries, numerous small towns, and two major metropolitan areas—Cincinnati and Portsmouth on the Ohio side. There are seven major Ohio tributaries located in the western unit: the Miami River, the Little Miami, Bullskin Creek, White Oak Creek, Straight Creek, Eagle Creek, Ohio Brush Creek, and the Scioto River.

In 2006 there were 23 boat ramps in the western unit of the Ohio River. The number changes every few years as villages and towns build new ramps to enhance recreational opportunities within their communities.

Visibility on the Ohio River varies from muddy to clear, averaging 12 to 18 inches during the summer to over 2 feet during prolonged periods of dry weather. When boating or fishing on the river, expect strong currents, muddy or rising water, barge traffic, pleasure boaters, floating debris and various boating hazards, and heavy boat traffic in congested areas. Give wide berth to barges and be careful of swells encountered behind them.

The fishing: Fishing is diverse but can basically be summed up by saying large-mouth, smallmouth, spotted bass, catfish, crappies, stripers, hybrid stripers, and sauger are the primary species targeted by most anglers. The river from Cincinnati to Meldahl Dam is perhaps the only viable fishery in Ohio for blue catfish. That species can achieve a weight of over 100 pounds and can be found in reasonably good supply in the Markland pool that stretches through Cincinnati, 70 miles to Meldahl Dam. Above Meldahl Dam, their numbers decrease significantly.

Channel catfish and shovelheads are plentiful, with 25-pound channels not out of the question, and 30- to 40-pound shovelheads fairly routine for those serious about the sport. Fishing for shovelheads on the Ohio River requires the use of stout "saltwater tackle," heavy sinkers, weighing from ½ to 2 ounces, to keep baits anchored in the current, and large 4/0 and up hooks. Skipjacks, gizzard shad, chubs, bluegills, small carp, chicken livers, night crawlers, goldfish, and about anything imaginable can be used for bait. The serious fishing is always done at night, and anglers might be surprised at the numbers of big catfish, including blues, that are caught after midnight from around the floating restaurants docked on the river in Cincinnati and Northern Kentucky. The tailwaters of the Meldahl are also an excellent location for big flathead and channels, as is the mouth of Three Mile Creek, Ohio Brush Creek, Big Indian Creek, and the tailwaters at Greenup Dam.

Bank fishing for catfish is probably at its best and easiest in southern Ohio, from the shoreline at Meldahl Dam. At Meldahl, anglers can fish downstream of the locks at the public access located off US 52, 70 miles east of Cincinnati. A pothole-filled gravel lane turns west off the main entrance road, and a fishers' parking lot is located at the end of that lane. Paths lead down to the riprap along the riverbank, and anglers have well over a mile of shoreline from which to fish. Big channel, flat-head, and blue catfish are taken from here, and sauger, white bass, hybrids, and largemouth and smallmouth bass are taken from along the riprap shoreline.

Back in the 1960s paddlefish, or spoonbills as they are called, were frequently hooked and landed below Meldahl Dam, and the bank at one time was littered with their big bony skulls and paddles. Paddlefish numbers have steadily declined as a result of the construction of the locks and dams on the Ohio River that took place during the late 1950s and early 1960s. However, a surge in sightings since 2000 and recent studies offer some evidence that paddlefish are making a slight comeback.

Boating anglers who know their way around the river at night and possess a little common sense and a steady hand at the helm can do well fishing from a boat for big shovelheads and blues. Look for the deepest holes in the river, tributary mouths, deep cuts around river structures, and warm-water discharges from power plants.

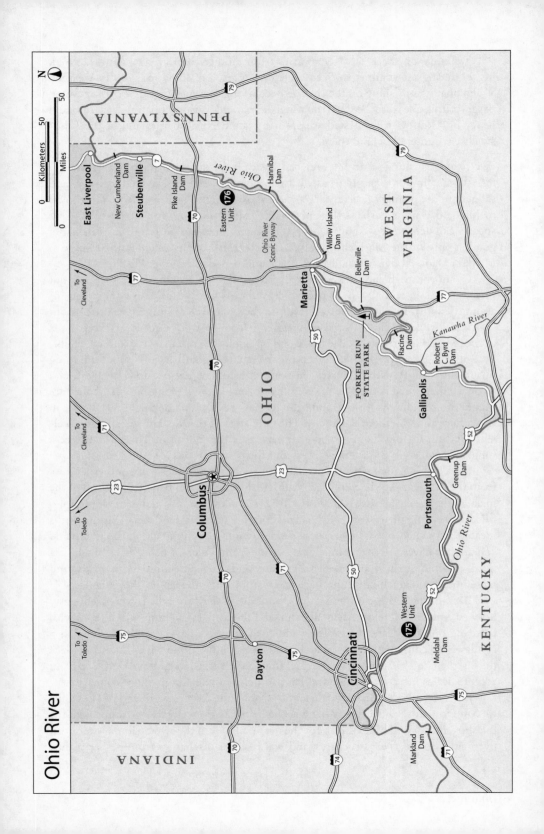

Ohio River

Fishing at night on the Ohio River can be worse than dangerous; it can be deadly and calls for extreme caution and attention. At night, barges can sneak up without warning, and every summer barge and boat collisions claim lives.

Tournament bass fishing is the number one sport on the river, and on summer weekends any number of clubs hold tournaments at one of several boat ramps. The most popular are White Oak Creek, Eagle Creek, and Aberdeen. Bass fishing starts in the tributaries in late March and as the Ohio warms and clears up; fishing shifts to the river by early June and stays fairly steady through October. Smallmouth are just as likely to be caught as largemouth, as their numbers have increased greatly over the past several years in the Meldahl pool. Spotted bass are smaller and abundant in the river and can be found throughout the river near any fish-holding structure. If conditions are stable, largemouth will usually spawn in the tributaries around Memorial Day weekend.

The Ohio River tributaries located on the Meldahl pool consistently produce some of the highest catch rates for bass of any pool on the river. The better Ohio side tributaries are Bullskin, White Oak, Straight Creek, Eagle Creek, and Ohio Brush Creek. White or chartreuse ¼- to ⅜-ounce spinner baits catch more bass from the river than anything, followed by ¼-ounce crawdad, gold, or silver foil crank baits and then watermelon seed, pumpkinseed, black, or purple plastic worms and tubes. Buzz baits and plastic jerk baits like flukes or Bass Assassins in chartreuse or silver glitter win plenty of tournaments also.

Look for bass in the river and tributaries around any fish-holding structure, such as rock banks, old stumps, overhanging trees, undercut banks, shoreline snags, old junk that was washed or dumped into the water, gravel, sand or rock points, various man-made structures, and small islands of vegetation.

In the Ohio River tributaries, throw to bank cover, downed shoreline timber and brush, old logs, snags, and old rubber tires. Any shoreline cover could hold bass, particularly if there is some deeper water close by. Anglers won't find bass on soft mud flats, but hard bottom sand or gravel bars or benches will attract plenty of bass. Stay in the channels, and at the edges of channels, work the steep banks and any bank slips. Bass in the tributaries are shoreline-cover orientated.

In the main river, look for bass on rocky banks, riprap, and rock outcroppings; the bigger the rock, the better. Most of the better rock and stone banks are on the Kentucky side of the river, but there are a few good stretches of rock on the Ohio side, too. Fat Raps and other deep-diving crank baits work well and can be fished quickly along the rock banks. There are also any number of submerged stump beds and root wads along the shoreline that hold bass; these are best fished with spinner baits, buzz baits, or plastics worms, lizards, or tubes, fishing slowly from one stump to the next.

Any shoreline trees, especially ones with heavy root growth, around undercut banks are like heaven to river bass. Although difficult to fish, bass will take cover in the shade beneath the undercut and forage and will seek security among the roots.

Grass beds are becoming more and more common on the river, and bass are taken off them. While admittedly I have had limited success from grass beds, some anglers do quite well using spinner and buzz baits and plastics around the weed edges.

Sandbars or gravel or sediment bars that build up at the mouth of tributaries, even small tributaries, will attract bass. Here, small crank baits really shine, and smallmouth seem to have a natural affinity toward the gravel bars. The same goes for the long gravel bars and sandbars at the heads of the islands. The gravel bars off Manchester and Brush Creek Islands extend quite far into the river and have deep water just off the channel side. Any cover on the bar greatly enhances the potential for attracting smallmouth and spotted bass.

White bass, hybrid stripers, and stripers all roam the river and are very different species, but all exhibit similar schooling traits. They are the open-water foragers of the river and can be frequently caught in the jumps as they drive their prey against the surface to feed.

White bass are in good numbers throughout the river, and come mid- to late April they make a spawning run upstream into the tributaries. Some excellent fishing can be had when the run is on, with some of the bigger females reaching 15 inches or more. If an angler hits the peak of the run, 25-fish days are not uncommon. Good white bass runs occur in all the tributaries, with the Great Miami, Little Miami, White Oak, Ohio Brush Creek, and Scioto all receiving notable runs. White Mepps, size #2 and #3, are the standard white bass spring-run bait, but small white or silver Sassy Shads and grubs on ⅛-ounce lead-head jigs do almost as well, as do white fuzzy jigs and white streamers on fly tackle.

Locate white bass in the jumps on the river in summer and you can catch fish from daylight until dark. Most schooling white bass will average 8 to 12 inches, with some weighing almost a pound. A few bigger white bass are occasionally taken, but any white bass over 15 inches from a school is a good fish. Look for schooling white bass at tributary mouths and barge, bridge, and power-plant structures on the river. The mouth of Three Mile Creek just east of Aberdeen is good for white bass, as is Ohio Brush Creek, the Scioto River, and the heads of the islands at Manchester. If the jumps are hot, then ⅛- to ¼-ounce tail spinners, white jigs and grubs, and small ¼-ounce chrome Rattle Traps will pick up white bass as fast as an angler can throw them.

Stripers and hybrid stripers are the glory fish of the river, with a few stripers reaching 15 to 20 pounds and most hybrids averaging 2 to 7 pounds. Hybrids are found throughout the river, near bridge and barge structures, rocky points and reefs, warm-water discharges during winter, and the Manchester Islands during summer.

Hybrids are also found at tributary mouths, notably the Great Miami and Scioto Rivers. As a side note, navigation up the Scioto River is extremely difficult and at times impossible due to heavy sediment deposits at the mouth of the river and in the lower Scioto River channel. Hybrids do run up the Scioto River, and pulloffs along Highway 104 between East Portsmouth and Highway 32 are the best way to reach them.

In January, February, and March, the warm-water discharge at Three Mile Creek, located east of Aberdeen at the Stuart Generating Plant, is a top spot for winter hybrids and the location from where a state record 16-pound hybrid striper was caught. Two parking areas are located off US 52 near the plant, and well-worn paths lead to the creek and the warm-water discharge.

If you want constantly big hybrids, then the tailwaters below the dams are undisputed. The U.S. Army Corps of Engineers allows boats only so close to the tailwaters, therefore long casts are the rule. Ten-foot surf poles are the norm for tailwater fishers who use jigging spoons, weighted Poppin' Bob floats, and blade lures that cast like a bullet to achieve the distance needed to reach the white water. Striped bass are also present in the tailwaters, as Kentucky Fish and Wildlife stocks pure stripers in the Markland, Meldahl, and Greenup pools. Stripers are stocked as 1.5-inch fingerlings, at three to five fish per acre, and grow to 30 inches in length by their sixth year. Striper fishing in the tailraces reaches its peak in June, July, and August, with stripers usually moving out of the tailwater by late September and October.

The hybrid striper is the dominate tailwater game-fish species and active throughout the fall and winter. Hybrids can be caught on a variety of baits, from live or cut shad, to white jigs with grubs, and chrome jigging spoons. What I consider the more successful baits are the weighty shad imitations like Rattle Traps, or blade lures like Heddon Sonars, Vib"E"s in chrome or gold, or weighted Poppin' Bob floats with a small jig and Zoom Fluke attached. Fishing for hybrids in the tailwaters below any Ohio River dam is good all year, with the fall months of October and November perhaps the best.

One of the hot spots on the river in southern Ohio is the Greenup Dam tailwaters, the only tailwater fishery on the Ohio-Kentucky border that is located on the Ohio side. To get there take the Greenup exit off US 52, 15 miles east of Portsmouth. Immediately after the exit take the next road west (right), which is the access road to the dam and will lead to a roadside rest and the fishing access parking area. Access the tailwaters by either going directly down the gravel path to a concrete fishing platform or follow the dirt roadway west to the riprap shoreline just downriver of the dam. Anglers fishing from the platform can cast directly into the tailwaters and the power-plant discharge. The Greenup Dam hydroelectric plant is a prefabricated unit that was constructed in France and shipped across the Atlantic to Baton Rouge, Louisiana, where it was unloaded and towed 1,594 miles up the Mississippi and Ohio Rivers to its present site. The discharges from its three turbines are well within casting range of the fishing platform.

The tailwaters at Greenup offer shoreline anglers some of the best opportunities on the river to tangle with big hybrid stripers, pure stripers, and sauger. Shovelheads, with some approaching 50 pounds, and heavy channels have also come from these tailwaters. Hybrid fishing begins in May and is good throughout summer and fall, with some of the best action occurring from September through early November. Stripers are taken from the tailwaters all summer long.

The extra leverage good graphite surf rods provide in distance casting makes them as popular here as they are in Cape Hatteras, North Carolina. Top Greenup tailwater lures include weighted Poppin' Bob floats with plastic flukes or strips of cut shad suspended 18 inches below on 12- to 14-pound-test mono; and 1- to 2-ounce fish-head jigs with white or silver Sassy Shads. Five- to 10-pound hybrid stripers are regulars at Greenup. A few are even bigger, often approaching state record size, and more than a few 30-inch stripers are caught every summer. Cast right into the turbulence, but also expect to catch a mixed bag of sheepshead, white bass, sauger, gar, catfish, and the occasional walleye.

Sauger fishing at Greenup is excellent from October through December, as long as the water doesn't dip below 40°F. Fishing picks up again in late February or early March, depending on weather, and continues until May. Small ⅛- to ¼-ounce jig heads with chartreuse or orange grubs fished along the riprap shoreline just west of the dam is a top spot for sauger; any sandbars or points along that riprap are sure to hold sauger during those months, too. The best sauger fishing is done at night. The sauger can range anywhere from cigar size to 24 inches in length.

Outside the tailwaters, sauger is plentiful but don't seem to get much attention in this western section of the river. Most are incidental catches by bass fishers as they fish the rocky or gravel shorelines. The sandbars at the head of Manchester and Brush Creek Islands hold sauger, as do the sediment bars at the larger tributary mouths. A few sauger are taken from the upper tributaries in early March and April, with some getting into the 20-inch range. For the best success, fish night crawlers, small spinners, crank baits, or jigs and grubs slowly along the rocky shorelines, gravel bars, and sandbars.

Black crappies are in good numbers in the Ohio River and are caught in the tributaries from early April through mid-May. Eagle Creek tributary is noted as one of the better crappie spots, and some nice crappie stringers can be caught if the timing is right. Twelve- to 15-inch crappies are not uncommon; most average around 10 inches. Minnows are the preferred bait; deep brush, snags, old docks, and bridge piers are good places to find them in Eagle Creek. Bullskin Creek, just upstream from Meldahl Dam, is another good crappie tributary. Fish the old snags along the main stream channel.

Muskies are few and far between, but occasionally one is caught from the river. The Licking River that empties into the Ohio across from Cincinnati is a natural muskie stream, upstream at Cave Run Lake near Morehead. Kinniconick Creek, a Kentucky stream that empties into the Ohio west of Portsmouth, is another natural muskie stream, as is Tygarts Creek, which empties into the river across from east Portsmouth. Two tributaries of the lower Scioto River have natural populations of muskies—Scioto Brush Creek and Sunfish Creek.

The public boat ramps on the Ohio, from Cincinnati east to Greenup Dam, are at Riverside, the Cincinnati Public Landing, Schmidt, Woodland Mound, New Richmond, Moscow, Neville, Bullskin Creek, White Oak Creek, Straight Creek, Eagle Creek, Aberdeen, Manchester, Manchester Islands, Ohio Brush Creek, Rome, Shawnee State Park, Portsmouth City ramp, and Burkes Point. The city of Ironton has a public ramp in town off Center Street. There is also a public launch near the mouth of the Great Miami River at Shawnee Lookout Park, but the ramp is so silted in that launching anything but a small carry-in boat is impossible.

Special regulations: A reciprocal license agreement between Ohio and Kentucky allows Ohio anglers to fish the main stem of the river with a valid Ohio fishing license and the Ohio River from the shore in Kentucky. There is a 12-inch minimum length on largemouth, smallmouth, and spotted bass, with a 6-bass limit. The sauger and walleye limit is 10 fish. There is a 30-fish limit on hybrid striped and white bass, and no more than 4 can be over 15 inches. The daily limit on crappies is 30 fish. Muskies must be 30 inches to keep, with a 2-fish limit.

Facilities/camping: There are 22 public and private boat ramps in the western unit, numerous marinas near Cincinnati, and several private campgrounds going east past New Richmond. White Oak boat ramp is a full-service ramp with gas, food, and camping, as is Shawnee. Camping is available at White Oak and at Ohio Brush Creek boat ramps. Camping is also available at Woodland Mound, but you must use a fully self-contained unit and stay a week or longer. There is public fishing access at all boat ramps and at Fernbank Park, located west of Cincinnati. Public access is also available at Point Pleasant on US 52, at the mouth of Big Indian Creek. Back in the 1960s Big Indian Creek was a noted spawning stream for spoonbill (paddlefish).

Additional information: The Ohio River tributaries of White Oak, Straight Creek, Eagle Creek, and Ohio Brush Creek offer excellent stream fishing for smallmouth bass, sunfish, rock bass, and channel catfish in their upper reaches. Most streams get a spring run of white bass during the last week in April, but the Little Miami River, White Oak Creek, and Ohio Brush Creek receive exceptionally good runs. Public access is available at four locations on Ohio Brush Creek, plus an additional boat ramp is located on Waggoner Riffle Road, east of West Union.

Directions: Take US 52 east of Cincinnati to access the Ohio River as far as Greenup Dam. Take US 50 west of Cincinnati to access the Ohio River and the mouth of the Great Miami River.

176 Eastern Unit

Key species: Largemouth, smallmouth, and spotted bass; sauger; walleye; white bass; hybrid striped bass; crappie; bluegill; sunfish; channel and flathead catfish; muskie; sheepshead; longnose gar.

General description: Great fishing for hybrids, white bass, sauger, and walleye in the tailraces below the dams.

Overview: The section of river from the confluence of the Big Sandy River in West Virginia, across from South Point, Ohio, to the Pennsylvania state line is 277 river miles long and contains seven locks and dams, 24 major tributaries, and 34 islands. If the width of the river is estimated at a quarter of a mile wide, fishers would have roughly 70 square miles of the Ohio River to fish from South Point to the Pennsylvania state line.

Ohio and West Virginia have a reciprocal fishing license agreement that allows anglers from either state to fish in the Ohio River and in any of its embayments and

Bob Pocki admires a nice walleye caught at the Pike Island Dam tailwaters on a jig and minnow.

tributaries to the first dam or riffle. It also permits anglers to fish the Ohio River from the shoreline of either state. That agreement enables Ohio anglers to fish the tailraces from the West Virginia side.

Although Ohio Department of Natural Resources lists 29 launch ramps, 20 are public ramps and the rest are private launches, normally owned by boating clubs or marinas that are either open to club members or allow launching for a small fee.

The fishing: In a survey conducted in 1992, it was found that 67 percent of the fish caught on the Ohio River came from the tailwaters below the dams. The most popular game fish were largemouth, smallmouth, and spotted bass, followed by hybrid stripers and white bass, sauger and walleye, and finally catfish.

Smallmouth and walleye numbers increase in the upper river pools due to two factors: the greater degree of drop and the resulting faster water, and the greater amount of stone shoreline and rock cover on the Ohio River from Pennsylvania downriver to Racine Dam. All of this provides more suitable habitat for smallmouth and walleyes than the normally slow-moving long pools backed up behind Markland and Meldahl Dams. I suspect water quality, visibility, and spawning habitat have improved to the point that smallmouth are fast becoming the dominant bass in the Ohio River, while the tributaries remain the primary domain of largemouth. The same theme occurs in the tributary rivers of Lake Erie, where largemouth dominate the harbors and river mouths, but smallmouths take over outside the harbors.

Walleye numbers increase above Belleville Dam, but this may be because the West Virginia Division of Natural Resources has been stocking the upper Ohio River with native-strain New River walleyes since 2004. The fingerlings are 2 inches in length when stocked and grow 10 to 12 inches during the first year, reaching the 18-inch minimum length for harvest by their third or fourth year. According to West Virginia fishery biologists, the Ohio River walleye being stocked could eventually reach 12 to 14 pounds.

There are eight pools along the Ohio–West Virginia border. Each could be considered a different lake in its own right, but similar fish-catching patterns are constant throughout the river.

Look for largemouth in the tributaries starting in late March. Work the bank structure, brush, logs, stumps, and root wads with spinner baits, plastics, and buzz baits. Largemouth usually spawn in the tributaries in late May through early June. After the spawn, largemouth numbers appear to increase in the river. Look for rocky shorelines, the steeper or deeper the better. Fish the rocky banks with deep-diving crank baits and hit every large boulder twice. The confluence of stream mouths is usually good, particularly if there is a sediment bar that forms on the upstream side of the river mouth. The best sediment bars may have some old lodged timber, stumps, or root wads, and if the bar has a hard bottom of gravel, you have found a hot spot. Old slews and backwater areas can be good if they have some depth, structure, and current, otherwise most are havens for rough fish, carp, and gar. Tree-lined banks are excellent, especially if the trees grow in long rows along the river banks and have root systems that extend well into or over the water, creating undercuts and root wads. Look for grass beds and stumps along the shoreline. Fish those close, as bass have a tendency to hold tight against cover in the river and often will be right in the tangle of roots. It takes a bull's-eye cast to trigger a strike. Old stumps, especially the sizable ones with extended roots, can be fished effectively with plastic lizards, night crawlers, and buzz baits.

Warm-water discharges are fairly good for bass, as they attract large amounts of baitfish. Look for structures around the discharge. If rocks or wood structures exist, then in all likelihood a bass will too.

Islands are among my favorite places to find smallmouth bass on the Ohio River. Spotted bass also often hang around the edges of islands, if wood or rock structures are present. Find bass on the structures at the heads of the islands. Long shallow gravel bars, or shoals, 1 to 5 feet deep, will often form at the head of an island; if old snags or drifting trees have lodged on the bar, then smallmouth will use those structures as current breaks. Crank baits work well, as do spinner baits fished over the top and plastics fished in the slack water created by the structure. Bass will also be located along the island banks where timber has lodged and stumps are present, but they seem to prefer a shoreline with a lesser current or off the main channel.

Look for sauger and walleye along the rocky shoreline, along gravel bars that form at tributary mouths, at the heads of islands, and at warm-water discharges; however, most sauger and walleye will be caught from the tailwaters below the dams. Small crank baits fished slowly along the rocks will generate strikes, as will jigs, grubs, and small Sassy Shads. The mouths of the Hocking River and the Muskingum River are good places to find sauger, and in lesser numbers, a few walleye too.

White bass and hybrid striped bass can be found at tributary mouths, around industrial structures, near warm-water discharges, offshore at the heads of islands, and at times in the middle of the river feeding off schooling shad. Anywhere shad are present in numbers, so too will white bass and hybrids. The number one spot for hybrids and white bass in the river is in the tailraces below dams. Year after year some of the largest hybrids in the state are caught in the tailwaters.

While most hybrids will average 2 to 6 pounds, several 8- to 12-pound fish are caught every season from the tailraces. Occasionally I hear rumors of state record size hybrids approaching 18 pounds coming from a few of the tailwaters. Hybrids are caught using lead jigging spoons that weigh from ½ to 2 ounces in silver, white, or chartreuse, and ¾-ounce blade lures like Vib"E"s or Heddon Sonars. Rattle Traps in silver or gold chrome also work, and white Sassy Shads attached to a ½-ounce fish-head jig are also good. Perhaps one of the most effective methods is a borrowed saltwater rig, straight from the shores of Cape Hatteras, North Carolina. Anglers use a weighted Poppin' Bob float and tie on an unweighted translucent silver Slug-Go or small white Sassy Shad about 24 inches behind the float. The Poppin' Bob float gets their attention, and wham, they hit the plastic shad behind the float.

Crappies can be found in nearly every Ohio River tributary beginning in March. Look for old snags, docks, and brush in at least 5 feet or deeper water; sometimes the closer to the channel the structure is the better. Bridge abutments are good, too, as are the various stone, wood pilings, and old concrete structures found in backwaters and tributaries throughout the river. Fishing usually lasts until late April or early May, then crappies seem to disappear from the scene only to reappear again the following spring.

Channel and flathead catfish can be caught off the shore from any location along the river. Channels can reach over 20 pounds, and flatheads can be upwards of 50 pounds or more. River and stream mouths are generally good places, as are warm-water discharges, bridge abutments, and old lock and dams. Big flatheads and channels are also taken from below the dams in the tailwaters and from the slower water below the locks. Use live bait such skipjacks, gizzard shad, small bluegills, chubs, or big shiners for flatheads; chicken livers, cut shad, or night crawlers for channel cats. The old U.S. Number 9 Lock and Dam, about 3 miles south of New Cumberland Dam, is a good area for flatheads, as is the mouth of the Muskingum River.

The **Robert C. Byrd Locks and Dam,** located 240 river miles from the Ohio-Pennsylvania state line, backs up a 42-mile-long pool. The dam is located about 9 miles south of the town of Gallipolis. The tailwaters are on the Ohio side, there is parking, and a newly constructed wheelchair-accessible fishing platform provides easy walking to the tailwaters. Hybrid stripers, white bass, sauger, a few walleyes, and occasionally a striper are the primary catches. Flathead and channel catfish are also taken. Smallmouth can be caught from the riprap above and below the tailwaters. The riprap areas around the shipping islands above the dam are also good for smallmouth. The K. H. Butler fishing access and boat ramp is located about 3 miles south of the dam off Highway 7, and from there the tailrace is but a short boat ride away.

The **Racine Locks and Dam,** located 198 miles from the Ohio-Pennsylvania state line, backs up a pool that is 34 miles long. The dam is located approximately 4 miles south of the small village of Racine off Highway 338. The tailrace is on the Ohio side; fishing access, parking, and a picnic area are located at the dam. A set of steps leads down to a walkway along the steep riprap bank from which anglers can reach the tailwaters. Hybrid stripers, white bass, sauger, some walleye, and channel and flathead catfish are the primary catches here. The tailwaters are noted for attracting big hybrids and sauger. A boat can be launched at the Syracuse village public ramp that is approximately 8 miles downriver from the dam.

The **Belleville Locks and Dam,** located 164 river miles from the Pennsylvania state line, backs up a 42-mile-long pool. The dam is located approximately 18 miles south of Belpre on Highway 124. Though the tailrace is on the West Virginia side, access to the river below the locks is achieved by a gravel access road plainly marked with a U.S. Army Corps of Engineers fishing access sign. From the road, anglers can hike down to the river's edge and fish for flathead, channels, and sauger. To reach the tailwaters by boat, anglers can launch at the Forked Run State Park boat ramp located a couple miles south of the dam. By vehicle, anglers must cross over to West Virginia by taking the U.S. Highway 33/Highway 824 Bridge 16 miles south of the dam, or the US 50 Bridge at Belpre and follow Highway 68 to the village of Belleville. The tailwaters below Belleville Dam in West Virginia are one of the most easily accessible tailwaters on the Ohio River. There is ample parking, restrooms, a fish-cleaning station, and lighting, steps, and a walkway down to the river's edge. It is easily the most impressive tailwater fishing facility on the river. Anglers catch hybrids, sauger, channel and flathead catfish, some walleye, and white bass. Belleville tailwaters are known for their excellent sauger fishing.

There are no camping facilities at Belleville, but Forked Run State Park is just a stone's throw from the dam and has 151 campsites.

The **Willow Island Locks and Dam** is located 122 river miles from the Pennsylvania state line. Willow Island Dam backs up a pool that is 35 miles long. The dam can be easily reached by driving 9 miles east of Marietta on Highway 7. Though the tailrace is on the West Virginia side, I could not locate any fishing access to the lock area on the Ohio side. Anglers will have to cross into West Virginia at the bridge in Newport, 6 miles east of the dam, and take Highway 2 6 miles west to Willow Island. Parking, restrooms, and walkways can be found at this access. To reach the tailwaters by boat, launch at the Marietta municipal ramp off Highway 60 just north of town on the Muskingum River; it's about an 11-mile boat ride to Willow Island Dam. The tailwaters are known producers of hybrids, sauger, and catfish.

The **Hannibal Locks and Dam** back up a pool that is 42 miles long. The dam sits 87 river miles from the Pennsylvania state line and is located at the small burg of Hannibal across from New Martinsville, West Virginia, on Highway 7. The pool above the Hannibal Dam is the primary smallmouth and walleye water on the Ohio River. The river has more flow, and with an abundance of rocky shoreline, the smallmouth and walleye thrive in this section of river.

Fishing access below the dam at the lock area on the Ohio side is limited. An angler's best bet is to launch at the Monroe Park and Marina ramp, just a couple of miles south of the dam off Highway 7. To access the tailwaters cross into West Virginia at the Highway 7 Bridge at New Martinsville, then take Highway 2 north 0.5 mile to the tailwater access. Hannibal Dam has one of better tailwater fishing accesses on the river, and anglers can cast into the boiling discharge of the generating plant from a circular concrete fishing platform. Good walkways, lighting, and restrooms make this a better than ideal fishing location. The shoreline riprap gives up smallmouth and sauger, and at night a few walleyes and some flathead catfish are caught. Hannibal is known to produce good-size hybrids and plenty of white bass.

The **Pike Island Locks and Dam,** just 44 river miles from the Pennsylvania state line, backs up a short 30-mile pool. The dam is located at the river town of Yorkville, off Highway 7. The tailwaters are easily accessed from the Ohio side by driving through Yorkville to the river's edge and then turning south toward the fishers' access area parking lot. Above the dam, quality smallmouth, walleye, and hybrid fishing await the angler. Below the dam, the tailwaters provide some of the best sauger and walleye fishing on the river.

From the parking area, anglers can walk the steps down to the long fishing pier that extends into the river. Anglers fishing off the pier catch hybrid stripers, white bass, sheepshead, sauger, walleye, and catfish. Several walleye in the 5- to 8-pound range have been caught off the pier, and a few 10-pounders have also been reported. Jigs and minnows, fished on the bottom, catch most of the sauger and walleye, followed by white and chartreuse grubs and then jigging spoons. Anglers fishing from the pier seem to catch about as many sauger as walleyes.

Big Sassy Shads and silver or white lead jigging spoons thrown into the swirling tailrace will pick up hybrids weighing anywhere from 7 to 10 pounds. Hybrid fishing is good all year long. White bass are also common and range from 12 to 16 inches.

For sauger and walleye, vertical jig grubs or minnows, or ½-ounce jigging spoons, off the pier near the bottom. Another method is to fish a simple floater and minnow near the bottom. Sauger will get up to 20 to 21 inches, while most walleye are 12 to 16 inches; 6- to 7-pound walleye are fairly common catches from the pier. The best times to catch sauger and walleye are early and late in the day in spring, fall, and winter.

A few black crappies are caught from the pier in early spring by anglers fishing with minnows and a bobber. Some crappies reach up to 15 inches.

The rocky shoreline south of the pier is an excellent place to pick up small-mouth from the shoreline that weigh up to 2.5 pounds. Smallmouth fishing is good from late April through early June using small crank baits, minnows, and spinner baits.

Some big flatheads have also been taken from the pier, with some weighing as much as 30 to 50 pounds. Most flathead are caught using small bluegills, shad, or chubs for bait, but a few have been taken using jigging spoons off the bottom. Channel cats are common catches too, but seldom get over 5 pounds, with most averaging 1 to 3 pounds.

Lead jigging spoons that weigh anywhere from ½ to 2 ounces and come in silver, white, chartreuse, and orange can be purchased for 60 cents each from Herman Miller, who manufactures the spoons and sells them from the back of his 1980 Ford pickup at the Pike Island Access parking lot. Fishing lure sales are not unheard of at other tailwater fisheries. At one time at Meldahl and Greenup Dams, jigs, spoons, and blade lures could be purchased from local manufacturers who parked near the popular fishing areas and sold their homemade baits out of the trunks of their cars.

The **New Cumberland Locks and Dam** is the first dam on the Ohio portion of the river. The New Cumberland Dam is only 14 miles from the Pennsylvania state line and backs up a 22-mile-long pool that extends into Industry, Pennsylvania. The dam is located approximately 11 miles south of East Liverpool on Highway 7. Anglers can access the river at the locks below the dam from a small community park across the highway from the village of Stratton. The tailrace below Cumberland Dam is on the West Virginia side, and the only shoreline access available is a rough-and-tumble quarter-mile hike from Highway 2 down to the riverbank. There are no facilities there, and anglers are on their own. There have been some reports of good catches of hybrids, walleyes, and nice smallmouth bass from the Cumberland tailwaters. A better way to reach the tailwaters is to launch at the New Cumberland public ramp in West Virginia, located off Highway 2. From the ramp, it is only a mile upstream to the dam. Anglers can get to New Cumberland by crossing a bridge over the river at either East Liverpool or Steubenville.

Special regulations: A reciprocal agreement between West Virginia and Ohio permits anglers to fish the Ohio River, its banks, embayments, and tributaries up to the first dam or riffle. Black bass are limited to 6, with no size limit. Saugers or saugeyes are limited to 10, with no size limit. Hybrid striped bass and white bass have no limit, but anglers can catch no more than 4 over 15 inches in length. Minimum length for walleye is 18 inches, with a 2-fish limit.

Facilities/camping: Forked Run State Park, with 151 campsites, is the only state park campground near the Ohio River. Camping is permitted at various boat ramps and at private campgrounds along the Ohio River. Only the most basic facilities such as restrooms and picnic tables are available at most locks and dams.

Additional information: The Ohio River Scenic Byway follows the river from East Liverpool to Cincinnati.

Directions: U.S. Highway 50 and US 52, Highway 7, and Highway 124 follow the Ohio River for its entire length. All dams, tributaries, and ramps are located off these roads.

For More Information

Below is a list of agencies that are of benefit to Ohio fishers. The Ohio Division of Water was included because of their comprehensive listing of low-head dams on streams and rivers throughout the state. The U.S. Army Corps of Engineers Web site lists information about lake levels and locks and dams on the Ohio River. The Muskingum Watershed Conservancy District (MWCD) Web site provides links to all MWCD lakes and parks. Metro Park Web sites list fishing access and maps to various streams and rivers. Also listed are various fishing-related Web sites that offer useful information.

Ohio Department of Natural Resources
2045 Morse Road
Columbus, OH 43229
(614) 265-6565
www.ohiodnr.com

Division of Parks and Recreation
2045 Morse Road, Building C-3
Columbus, OH 43229
(866) 644-6727
www.ohiodnr.com/parks

Ohio Department of Watercraft
2045 Morse Road, Building A
Columbus, OH 43229
(614) 265-6480 or (877) 426-2837
www.ohiodnr.com/watercaft

Ohio Division of Forestry
2045 Morse Road, Building H-1
Columbus, OH 43229-6693
(614) 265-6694 or (877) 247-9231
www.ohiodnr.com/forestry

Ohio Division of Natural Area &
   Preserves
2045 Morse Road, Building F-1
Columbus, OH 43229
(614) 265-6453
www.ohiodnr.com/dnap

Ohio Division of Water
2045 Morse Road, Building B
Columbus, OH 43229-6693
(614) 265-6717
www.ohiodnr.com/water

Ohio Office of Coastal Management
105 West Shoreline Drive
Sandusky, OH 44870
(419) 626-7980 or (888) 644-6267
www.ohiodnr.com/coastal

Ohio Division of Wildlife
2045 Morse Road, Building G
Columbus, OH 43229-6693
(800) 945-3543
www.ohiodnr.com/wildlife

Wildlife District One
1500 Dublin Road
Columbus, OH 43215
(614) 644-3925

Wildlife District Two
952 Lima Avenue
Findlay, OH 45840
(419) 424-5000

Wildlife District Three
912 Portage Lakes
Akron, OH 44319
(330) 644-2293

Wildlife District Four
360 East State Street
Athens, OH 45701
(740) 589-9930

Wildlife District Five
1076 Old Springfield Pike
Xenia, OH 45385
(937) 372-9261

Fairport Fisheries Unit
1190 High Street
Fairport Harbor, OH 44077
(440) 352-4199

Sandusky Fisheries and
 Enforcement Units
305 East Shoreline Drive
Sandusky, OH 44870
(419) 625-8062

Inland Fisheries Research Unit
10517 Canal Road SE
Hebron, OH 43025
(740) 928-7034

Muskingum Watershed Conservancy
 District
1319 Third Street NW
P.O. Box 349
New Philadelphia, OH 44663-0349
(330) 343-6647 or (877) 363-8500
www.mwcdlakes.com

U.S. Army Corps of Engineers Louisville
 District
600 Dr. Martin Luther King Place
Louisville, KY 40202
(502) 315-6766
www.lrl.usace.army.mil

U.S. Army Corps of Engineers
 Huntington District
502 8th Street
Huntington, WV 25701
(304) 399-5000
www.lrh.usace.army.mil

U.S. Army Corps of Engineers
 Pittsburgh District
2200 William S. Moorhead Federal
 Building
1000 Liberty Avenue
Pittsburgh, PA 15222-4186
(412) 395-7500
www.lrp.usace.army.mil

Wayne National Forest Athens District
13700 Highway 33
Nelsonville, OH 45764
(740) 753-0101
www.fs.fed.us/r9/wayne

Wayne National Forest Ironton District
6518 Highway 93
Pedro, OH 45659
(740) 534-6500
www.fs.fed.us/r9/wayne

Cuyahoga Valley National Park
15610 Vaughn Road
Brecksville, OH 44141-3018
(216) 524-1497
www.nps.gov/cuva

Maumee River Access and Information
Toledo Metro Parks
5100 West Central Avenue
Toledo, OH 43615-2100
(419) 407-9700
www.metroparkstoledo.com

Walleye Fishing Information (March through June)
(419) 407-9700; choose option 2

Sandusky River Information
Sandusky County Convention and Visitors Bureau
712 North Street
Freemont, OH 43420
(419) 332-4470 or (800) 255-8070
www.sanduskycounty.org

Lake Erie Islands–Port Clinton Information
Ottawa County Visitors Bureau
770 Southeast Catawba Road
Port Clinton, OH 43452-2654
(800) 441-1271
www.lake-erie.com

Lake Erie, Kelleys Island, Port Huron, Vermilion Information
Sandusky/Erie County Visitors Bureau
442 Milan Road, Suite A
Sandusky, OH 44870
(419) 625-2984 or (800) 225-3743
www.sanduskyohiocedarpoint.com

Vermilion River and Black River Access
Lorain County Metro Parks
12882 Diagonal Road
La Grange, OH 44050
(800) 526-7275
www.loraincountymetroparks.com

Rocky River, Euclid Creek, and Chagrin River Access
Cleveland Metro Parks
4101 Fulton Parkway
Cleveland, OH 44144-1923
(216) 635-3200
www.clemetparks.com

Grand River Access
Lake Metroparks
11211 Spear Road
Concord Township, OH 44077
(440) 639-7275
www.lakemetroparks.com

Lake Erie Central Basin
Lake County Visitors Bureau
35300 Vine Street, Suite A
East Lake, OH 44095
(800) 368-5253
www.lakevisit.com

Ashtabula River Access
Ashtabula Township Park Commission
Indian Trails Park
1700 East First Street
Ashtabula, OH 44004
(440) 964-3819
www.lakeshoreparkashtabula.org

Miami River, Mad River, Stillwater River, and Twin Creek Access
Five Rivers Metro Park
1375 East Siebenthaler Avenue
Dayton, OH 45414
(937) 275-7275
www.metroparks.org

Big and Little Darby Creeks and Clear Creek Access
Metro Parks
1069 West Main Street
Westerville, OH 43081-1181
(614) 891-0700
www.metroparks.net

Little Miami River Access
Hamilton County Park District
10245 Winton Road
Cincinnati, OH 45231
(513) 521-7275
www.greatparks.org

**Little Miami River Access and
  Camping**
Green County Parks
651 Dayton-Xenia Road
Xenia, OH 45385
(937) 526-7440
www.co.green.oh.us/parks

Ohio Department of Development
Division of Travel and Tourism
www.discoverohio.com

**AEP ReCreation Lands, Conesville
  Coal Lands, Avondale WLA, permits
  and maps**
www.aep.com/environmental/recreation/
  recland

**Public Access on Ohio Rivers and
  Streams**
www.ohiodnr.com/watercraft/boat/rivers

**Ohio River Boating and Marina
  Information**
http://boatingontheweb.com/ohio_
  river.asp

West Virginia Wildlife Fisheries
www.wvdnr.gov/fishing/fishing.shtm

Pennsylvania Fish and Boat Commission
http://sites.state.pa.us/PA_Exec/Fish_
  Boat/fishin1.htm

**Kentucky Department of Fish and
  Wildlife Resources**
www.kdfwr.state.ky.us

State Record Fish in Ohio Submissions
www.outdoorwritersofohio.org

Fish Ohio Awards Information
www.fishohio.org

**Freshwater Line Class Records
  Information**
National Freshwater Fishing Hall of Fame
www.freshwater-fishing.org

Ohio Huskie Muskie Club
http://web.tusco.net/ohiohuskiemuskiclub

Ohio Central Basin Steelheaders
www.ohiosteelheaders.com

Ohio Bass Federation
www.ohiobass.org

Lake Erie Fishing Information
www.ohiodnr.com/wildlife/fishing/
  fairport/gofish.htm

Lake Erie Fishing Forecast
(888) 466-5347

Lake Erie Charts
www.noaachartsonline.com

Index

About the Author

Tom Cross penned his first fishing column in 1972 for the *Clermont Sun* newspaper while still in high school. After moving to the family farm in Adams County, he began writing a locally syndicated outdoor column for the *Peoples Defender, The News Democrat,* and the *Times-Gazette.* In 2006 Tom was awarded a 25-year plaque of appreciation from the *Peoples Defender.* His writings and photos have appeared nationally in *Outdoor Life, Field & Stream,* and *North American Whitetail.*

The author with a steelhead taken from Paine Creek in March. Photo by Chip Gross

Throughout his years as a writer and photographer, Tom has garnered many awards, including the Outstanding Media Achievement Award and the prestigious Lou Klewer Award from the Outdoor Writers of Ohio. Three times he received the coveted Editorial Excellence Award from Brown Publishing. The Adams County Chamber of Commerce selected Tom to receive the Community Service Award for being an advocate for the county through his writings.

Tom has been an active member of the Outdoor Writers of Ohio for over 25 years, serving as its president and now as Chairman of the OWO State Record Fish Committee, which oversees Ohio's State Record Fish Program.

The author is more than a writer, he is a dyed-in-the-wool fisherman, having fished in 16 states besides Ohio and Ontario, and has won his share of angling awards. Tom was twice awarded the Kings Trophy by the Kentucky Silver Muskie Club for having released the largest muskie in commonwealth waters—both muskies were over 47 inches. He has caught everything from bonefish in the Florida Keys, to Guadalupe bass in the Texas Hill Country, to bull trout in Montana. While Tom is an avid muskie fisherman, he also enjoys fishing for hybrid stripers and wading Ohio streams for smallmouth, steelhead, and trout.

Above all, Tom is a family man, living on a farm that has been in his family since the 1850s with his wife, Judy. Together they have raised three children, who all love to fish. Tom is actively involved in the community, serving as a township officer and as the executive director for the Adams County Travel and Visitors Bureau.